Banking, Monetary Policy and the Political Economy of Financial Regulation

Banking, Monetary Policy and the Political Economy of Financial Regulation

Essays in the Tradition of Jane D'Arista

Edited by

Gerald A. Epstein

Professor of Economics and Co-Director, Political Economy Research Institute (PERI), University of Massachusetts, Amherst, USA

Tom Schlesinger

Financial Markets Center, USA

Matías Vernengo

Associate Professor, Bucknell University, USA

Edward Elgar

Cheltenham, UK • Northampton, MA, USA

Published by
Edward Elgar Publishing Limited
The Lypiatts
15 Lansdown Road
Cheltenham
Glos GL50 2JA
UK

Edward Elgar Publishing, Inc.
William Pratt House
9 Dewey Court
Northampton
Massachusetts 01060
USA

A catalogue record for this book
is available from the British Library

Library of Congress Control Number: 2013949789

This book is available electronically in the ElgarOnline.com
Economics Subject Collection, E-ISBN 978 1 78347 264 2

ISBN 978 1 84844 367 9

Printed on FSC approved paper

Printed and bound in Great Britain by
Marston Book Services Ltd, Oxfordshire

Contents

PART IV GLOBAL FINANCE

PART V THEORETICAL CONSIDERATIONS

Contributors

Robert A. Blecker is Professor of Economics at American University, a Research Associate at the Economic Policy Institute (Washington, DC), a Senior Research Fellow of the Center for Economic and Policy Research (Washington, DC), and a Research Scholar at the Political Economy Research Institute (University of Massachusetts, Amherst, MA). His articles have appeared in numerous refereed journals, and his books include: *Fundamentals of U.S. Foreign Trade Policy: Economics, Politics, Laws, and Issues* (2nd edition, Westview Press, 2003); *Taming Global Finance: A Better Architecture for Growth and Equity* (Economic Policy Institute, 1999), and *U.S. Trade Policy and Global Growth* (edited volume, M.E. Sharpe, Inc., 1996). Professor Blecker received his BA in economics from Yale University in 1978 and his MA and PhD in economics from Stanford University in 1983 and 1987, respectively.

Patrick Bond teaches at the University of KwaZulu-Natal School of Built Environment and Development Studies (Durban, South Africa) where since 2004 he has directed the Centre for Civil Society. His research focuses on political economy, environment (energy, water and climate change), social policy and geopolitics, with publications covering South Africa, Zimbabwe, the African continent and global-scale processes. His most recent books (including co-authored and edited books) are *Elite Transition* (3rd edition, 2014), *South Africa: The Present as History* (2014), *Politics of Climate Justice* (2012), *Durban's Climate Gamble* (2011), *Zuma's Own Goal* (2010), *Climate Change, Carbon Trading and Civil Society* (2009), *Enclavity in African Economies: The Work of Guy Mhone* (2007), *The Accumulation of Capital in Southern Africa: Rosa Luxemburg's Contemporary Relevance* (2007), and *Looting Africa: The Economics of Exploitation* (2006).

James Crotty (Professor, University of Massachusetts, Amherst) earned his PhD from Carnegie Mellon University. He is a macroeconomist with broad interests whose research in theory and policy attempts to integrate the complementary analytical strengths of the Marxian and Keynesian traditions. His writings have appeared in such diverse journals as *American Economic Review*, *Quarterly Journal of Economics*, *Cambridge Journal of*

Economics, *Review of Radical Economics*, *Monthly Review*, *Journal of Post Keynesian Economics*, and *Journal of Economic Issues*, as well as in many edited collections.

Gary A. Dymski (Professor, University of California, Riverside and University of Leeds) received his doctorate in economics from the University of Massachusetts, Amherst in 1987. He has been a fellow in economic studies at the Brookings Institution, and since 1991 has been a member of the Economics Department at the University of California, Riverside. Gary's most recent books are *Capture and Exclude*: *Developing Nations and the Poor in Global Finance* (co-edited with Amiya Bagchi, Tulika Books, 2007) and *Reimagining Growth*: *Toward a Renewal of the Idea of Development* (co-edited with Silvana DePaula, Zed Books, 2005). His current research interests include: money, space, and inequality; the social and economic aspects of banking and finance; financial regulation and economic policy; financial fragility and financial exclusion; and the subprime and other financial crises.

Gerald A. Epstein (Professor, University of Massachusetts, Amherst) received his PhD in economics from Princeton University. He has published widely on a variety of progressive economic policy issues, especially in the areas of central banking and international finance, and is the editor or co-editor of six volumes, most recently *Financialization and the World Economy* (Edward Elgar, 2004) and *Capital Flight and Capital Controls in Developing Countries* (Edward Elgar, 2004). Professor Epstein's current work focuses on developing macroeconomic policies to promote just and sustainable improvements in living standards.

Korkut Ertürk is a Professor of Economics at the University of Utah. He holds a bachelor's degree from New York University and a PhD from the New School for Social Research. He has been a consultant to various UN agencies over the years and is the author of numerous articles in academic journals.

James K. Galbraith is the Lloyd M. Bentsen Jr. Chair in Government/Business Relations and Professor of Government at the Lyndon B. Johnson School of Public Affairs (University of Texas, Austin). He holds degrees from Harvard and Yale (PhD in economics, 1981). He studied as a Marshall Scholar at King's College, Cambridge from 1974 to 1975, and then served in several positions on the staff of the U.S. Congress, including Executive Director of the Joint Economic Committee. He was a guest scholar at the Brookings Institution in 1985. He directed the LBJ School's PhD Program in Public Policy from 1995 to 1997. He currently directs the University of Texas Inequality Project, an informal research group based at the LBJ School. His latest book is *Inequality and Instability: A Study of the World Economy Just Before the Great Crisis* (Oxford University Press, 2012). He is a member of the Lincean Academy, the oldest honorary scientific society in the world, a Senior Scholar of the Levy Economics Institute, and Chair of the Board of Economists for Peace and Security.

Robert N. McCauley is a Senior Adviser at the Bank for International Settlements (BIS) (Basel, Switzerland) and previously served as Chief Representative for Asia and the Pacific at the BIS Asian Office. Before joining BIS in 1994, he worked for 13 years for the Federal Reserve Bank of New York, serving at times as chief economist for the interagency committee of bank supervisors that rates country risk. There he wrote on international comparisons of the cost of capital, foreign bank lending to U.S. corporations and the unprofitability of foreign direct investment in the U.S. In 1988, he worked for the Joint Economic Committee of the US Congress. In 1992 he taught international finance and the multinational firm at the University of Chicago's Graduate School of Business. He currently serves on the Council of Management of SUERF, the European Money and Finance Forum.

Perry Mehrling joined the faculty of Barnard College (New York) in 1987. He has also held visiting positions at the Sloan School of Management at MIT, and at Boston University. His research focuses on the foundations of monetary economics and the history and applications of monetary economics and finance. He is also the Director of Education Programs for the Institute for New Economic Thinking. Professor Mehrling is the author of *The New Lombard Street: How the Fed Became the Dealer of Last Resort* (Princeton University Press, 2011) and *Fischer Black and the Revolutionary Idea of Finance* (John Wiley & Sons, 2005; reissued in a revised paperback edition in 2012). He received a bachelor's degree from Harvard University, a master's degree from the London School of Economics, and a PhD from Harvard University.

Daniel H. Neilson (Institute for New Economic Thinking [INET] and Simon's Rock College) earned his BA from Bard College of Simon's Rock in 2001 and his PhD from Columbia University in 2009. In addition to his work for INET, he teaches economics at Simon's Rock.

Gökçer Özgür (Hacettepe University, Turkey) received his BA from Orta Doğu Teknik Üniversitesi in 1999 and his PhD from the University of Utah in 2007. His research interests are in monetary theory, political economy and history of economic thought.

Thomas Palley (New America Foundation) was formerly Chief Economist with the US/China Economic and Security Review Commission. Prior to joining the Commission he was Director of the Open Society Institute's Globalization Reform Project, and before that he was Assistant Director of Public Policy at the AFL-CIO. He holds a BA from Oxford University, and an MA in International Relations and PhD in economics, both from Yale University. His most recent books include *From Financial Crisis to Stagnation* (Cambridge University Press, 2012) and *The Economic Crisis: Notes from the Underground* (Createspace, 2012).

Esteban Pérez Caldentey (Economic Commission for Latin America and the Caribbean ECLAC, Santiago, Chile) obtained his PhD at the New School for Social Research and has worked at the United Nations Economic Commission for Latin America and the Caribbean since 1995, working in the Mexico and Trinidad and Tobago offices before moving to Santiago. He has published extensively in academic journals such as *Journal of Post Keynesian Economics*, *Review of Political Economy*, *Inestigación Económica* and others. His areas of research are macroeconomics, development and history of economic ideas.

Codrina Rada is an Assistant Professor at the University of Utah, and obtained her PhD in economics at New School for Social Research in 2007. In partnership with Jose Antonio Ocampo and Lance Taylor, she wrote *Growth and Policy in Developing Countries: A Structuralist Approach* (Columbia University Press, 2009). She has also published several peer review journal articles and book chapters. Recently she has received a grant from the Center on Aging at the University of Utah to conduct a survey on the impact of the migration of adult children on the well-being of older parents in Eastern Europe.

Ellen D. Russell is an Assistant Professor in Digital Media and Journalism and Society, Culture and Environment at Wilfrid Laurier University (Ontario). Her recent publications include *New Deal Banking Reform and Keynesian Welfare State Capitalism* (Routledge, 2008). She received her PhD in economics from the University of Massachusetts, Amherst, and has received degrees from Queens University and University of Toronto. She was formerly Senior Economist at the Canadian Centre for Policy Alternatives, and is an occasional columnist on economic affairs for rabble.ca.

Tom Schlesinger is the founder and executive director of the Financial Markets Center, a think tank that has followed the Federal Reserve policies since 1999. In 1988 he co-organized a meeting of several organizations working on banking issues in Washington, DC, to discuss developing a common agenda. Out of these discussions rose the Financial Democracy Campaign (FDC). Schlesinger was one of the co-coordinators of the FDC along with Steve Kest, the Executive Director of the national community group ACORN. Prior to that, Schlesinger directed the Southern Finance Project, a North Carolina-based research center that worked with a wide range of grassroots organizations, unions, journalists, and public officials interested in financial markets and policy issues.

Mario Seccareccia has been teaching at the University of Ottawa since 1978. He has authored/co-authored or co-edited some 12 books or monographs, and has published over one hundred articles or chapters of books. He is also editor of the New York-based *International Journal of Political Economy*. His principal research interests are in the areas of monetary economics, macroeconomics, history of economic thought and methodology, labor economics, and Canadian economic history. He has been appointed Visiting Professor of Economics at the University of Paris-Sud, the University of Bourgogne and the University of Grenoble in France, and has lectured at the Post Keynesian Summer School of the University of Missouri in Kansas City, the Minsky seminars at Bard College, and the graduate programme of the National Autonomous University of Mexico.

Lance Taylor is Schwartz Center for Economic Policy Analysis Faculty Fellow and Emeritus Professor of Economics at the New School University (New York). He received a BS degree with honors in mathematics from the California Institute of Technology in 1962 and a PhD in economics from Harvard University in 1968. He has been a professor in the economics departments of Harvard and the Massachusetts Institute of Technology, among other research institutions. He has published widely in the areas of macroeconomics, development economics, and economic theory. His most recent book is *Maynard's Revenge*: *The Collapse of Free Market Economics* (Harvard University Press, 2011).

Matías Vernengo (Bucknell University) obtained a BSc and MSc from the Universidade Federal do Rio de Janeiro and a PhD from the New School for Social Research in 1999. He has taught at Kalamazoo College, the University of Utah, the Universidade Federal do Rio de Janeiro, and was Senior Research Manager at the Central Bank of Argentina. He is also a co-editor of the *Review of Keynesian Economics* (*ROKE*).

Robert H. Wade (Professor, London School of Economics) was educated in Washington, New Zealand, and Sussex University and worked at the IDS, Sussex from 1972 to 1995. He has also worked at the World Bank (1984–88). He has undertaken fieldwork in a range of countries including Italy, India, Korea and Taiwan. In 2008, he was the recipient (jointly with José Antonio Ocampo) of the Leontief Prize in recognition of his outstanding contribution to economic theory that addresses contemporary realities and supports just and sustainable societies. His books include *Irrigation and Politics in South Korea* (Westview Press, 1982), *Village Republics: The Economic Conditions of Collective Action in India* (Cambridge University Press, 1988, 1994) and *Governing the Market: Economic Theory and the Role of Government in East Asia's Industrialization* (Princeton University Press, 1990, 2003). The latter won the American Political Science Association's 1992 Best Book in Political Economy award.

Martin H. Wolfson is Emeritus Professor of Economics at the University of Notre Dame. He taught economics at Notre Dame from 1989 to 2014. Before that, he was an economist at the Federal Reserve Board in Washington, DC. He is the author of *Financial Crises: Understanding the Postwar U.S. Experience* (Second Edition, M.E. Sharpe, 1994) and co-editor (with Gerald A. Epstein) of *The Handbook of the Political Economy of Financial Crises* (Oxford University Press, 2013). He received the Rev. Edmund P. Joyce, C.S.C., Award for Excellence in Undergraduate Teaching (2010) and the Grenville Clark Award for 'advancing service to the community with a concern for social justice' (2006) from the University of Notre Dame.

PART I

Appreciation and Introduction

1. Jane D'Arista: an appreciation

Tom Schlesinger

The papers in this book were originally presented at a conference in honor to Jane D'Arista in the spring of 2008 at the Political Economy Research Institute at the University of Massachusetts Amherst. Throughout her career as an author, analyst, congressional staff economist and teacher, Ms. D'Arista has brought together several strands of heterodox economics. While she may be characterized accurately as one of the last great institutionalists, her work also defies easy classification. Perhaps the clearest way to view Jane is as a tough-minded empiricist who has produced critical, original insights into the functioning of the financial system and economy – and done so with the uncompromising goal of improving human welfare.

Jane D'Arista followed a non-traditional and rather remarkable path to her place as a profound teacher, thinker and adviser on monetary and financial affairs. After graduating from Barnard College and beginning a family Jane took a position on the staff of the U.S. House Banking Committee in 1966. Under the chairmanship of Representatives Wright Patman and Henry Reuss (who replaced Patman in 1975) her responsibilities included the preparation of hearings, research and investigative projects. In this era, practitioners regarded the congressional research and oversight functions as serious obligations and the Banking Committee's staff work routinely displayed a depth and rigor that would become virtually extinct in the Capitol Hill culture of more recent years. From 1975 to 1976 Jane served as a staff member and consultant on international banking to the Financial Institutions and the Nation's Economy (FINE) Study, the first major examination of the financial system to assess the impact of American banks abroad and foreign banks in the U.S. (see "Foreign Bank Activities in the United States" and "U.S. Banks Abroad," 1976).

The most noteworthy venture Jane undertook during this period was an account of the Federal Reserve's first two decades of policymaking. Based on detailed archival records of the Fed's deliberations and actions, *Federal Reserve Structure and the Development of Monetary Policy: 1915–1935* was published by the Banking Committee in 1971 and painstakingly described the central bank's formative struggles over doctrine, policy goals and control of policy levers. Written in her "spare time" while juggling the demands of other staff work for the Committee and raising four young children, Jane's study blazed a trail for historical examination of the Fed through careful scrutiny of its internal records. Hailed by reviewers such as Anna Schwartz (*Journal of Economic Literature*, June 1995, 869–71) the study continues to be mined by scholars drawn to its insights into the external financial conditions, concealed in-house conflicts and competing modes of economic thought that helped shape the central bank's institutional development and policy innovations.

After serving on the Banking Committee staff for 12 years Jane moved to a senior position at the Congressional Budget Office where her analytical duties focused largely on international capital flows, foreign investment in the U.S., debt problems of developing countries and the recycling of OPEC (Organization of the Petroleum Exporting Countries) surpluses. In 1983 she was named chief finance economist for the House Energy and Commerce Committee's Subcommittee on Telecommunications, Consumer Protection and Finance. Three years later the subcommittee issued *Financial Restructuring: The Major Policy Issues*, Jane's comprehensive survey of changes in the U.S. and international financial markets. Her report presciently warned of the sector's growing instability and vulnerability to shocks. Subsequently, M.E. Sharpe republished the 1986 report and Jane's 1971 Federal Reserve history as a two-volume set, *The Evolution of U.S. Finance* (D'Arista, 1994a, 1994b)

After two decades on Capitol Hill, Jane D'Arista left Washington and co-founded the LL.M. Program in Banking and Financial Law at Boston University's Morin Center for Banking and Financial Law. Jane would remain at the Morin Center for 12 years following the untimely death of her husband, the painter Robert D'Arista. In addition to mentoring dozens of international students enrolled in the LL.M. program, Jane continued to engage in financial and monetary policy debates through her affiliation with the Economic Policy Institute and Political Economy Research Institute (PERI) as well as participation in an assortment of working groups and symposia.

In 1999, Jane became program director of the Financial Markets Center, a nonprofit research institute. Over the next seven years she authored quarterly assessments of domestic flow of funds data and international capital flows for the Center, identifying the unsustainable imbalances and the permissive, pro-cyclical policy regimes that led to successively larger and more disabling asset bubbles and crashes. Throughout this time Jane continued to find outlets for her love of teaching at the University of

Massachusetts Amherst, New School University and the University of Utah.

When the large-scale financial crisis Jane had long warned about erupted in 2008, the need for aggressive government action became unavoidable and the prospects for sweeping reform suddenly appeared to parallel the opportunities available to Franklin Roosevelt's New Deal. In this new circumstance Jane's insights provided a compass for policy change. In addition, Jane stepped forward to play a central role in organizing a broader set of intellectual resources to address the crisis and link those resources to reform-minded citizen groups. Early in 2009 she co-founded (with Gerald Epstein) a committee of economists and other analysts for Stable, Accountable, Fair and Efficient Financial Reform (SAFER). Along with Jennifer Taub, a law professor at the University of Vermont, SAFER worked closely with Americans for Financial Reform (AFR), a network of over 200 labor and community groups that struggled against the massively powerful financial lobby in an attempt to shape and support strong and effective financial regulation and reform in the wake of the Great Financial Crisis of 2008. Jane worked tirelessly to share her vast knowledge of the relevant financial issues, even as she never lost her critical perspectives on some of the weak and woefully inadequate rules that came out under the Dodd–Frank financial reform law. The period after the crisis of 2008 was a particularly rich period for Jane, as she wrote numerous papers, chapters for books, policy briefs for SAFER and other outlets, and gave a large number of radio and television, and video interviews, including on the Public Broadcasting System (PBS) and with the Real News Network. (See the abridged list of Jane D'Arista's "collected economics works" at the end of this chapter.)

During her decades of intellectual labor several overarching themes have distinguished Jane's research, writing and advocacy. These include her insistence on the primacy of the financial system's economic function, her perception that reckless market developments were undermining the sustainability of the U.S. and global financial systems (and with them the fate of the real economy), and her conviction that bold policy reforms were required to avert crisis, restore stability and systematically enhance equity.

By focusing on flow-of-funds trends, financial firms' balance sheets and other empirical observations – and by discounting the relevance of fashionably misleading creeds – Jane was able to see more clearly than most observers some of the central problems disfiguring the financial landscape over the past four decades (see *Flow of Funds Review and Analysis* and *Capital Flows Monitor, 1996–2006*). In her 1986 *Financial Restructuring* study she stressed that the channels for saving had changed radically since the Great Depression – when the regulatory framework that was dismantled in the 1980s and 1990s had been created – and that nonbank financial intermediaries had become far more important elements in the financial system. New instruments that may have been unimaginable in the 1930s were now commonplace. Household savings that previously nested in insured depository institutions were now dispersed broadly as the liabilities of insurance companies, pension funds and other intermediaries in what would eventually be termed the "shadow banking sector," carrying significantly more risk than would have been tolerated by the old regulatory regime. Indeed, in her seminal 1993 paper with Tom Schlesinger, Jane identified the dangers emanating from what they called the "parallel banking system," long before others coined the term "shadow banking system," which has now become so prominent in discussions of the great financial crisis of 2008 (see "The Parallel Banking System," 1993). And Jane correctly anticipated that these risks could only compound as debt levels for households, businesses and the financial sector itself rose to unprecedented heights.

Jane was also critical of the so-called Washington Consensus and export-led growth policies the International Monetary Fund (IMF) prescribed for all developing and emerging economies after the financial crises of the 1980s and 1990s. She cautioned that these policies would have significant consequences in strong-currency countries other than the United States, which might not be willing or able to carry the current account deficits needed to ensure their success. In addition she argued that strategies of the large private financial institutions that dominate the international payments system intensified emerging economies' vulnerability to financial crises. Financialization and liberalization increased exchange rate fluctuations and the exposure of developing countries to external shocks. Moreover, she noted, the risks inherent in the external accumulation of sovereign U.S. debt could have dire consequences for America, too, if a collapse in asset prices triggered the debt deflationary cycle of borrowers reducing their spending in order to deleverage and thereby further suppressing demand in a weakening economy. (See, for example, "Reforming the Privatized International Monetary and Financial Architecture," 1999; "Replacing the Failed Washington Consensus," 2009; "The Evolving International Monetary System," 2009)

Despite the thrust (not to mention the accuracy) of her assessments, Jane has never succumbed to pessimism. Indeed, like John Maynard Keynes her work has demonstrated a singular flair for practical-minded prescriptions that would make markets work better for most citizens. When the vast majority of the economics profession and policy community enthusiastically promoted deregulation as a panacea for the financial sector, Jane championed the idea of adapting the regulatory framework to evolving market practice by both enlarging and rationalizing the scope of government supervision and rulemaking (see "Rebuilding The Framework for Financial Regulation," 2009) Likewise she has advocated the introduction of asset-based reserve requirements in order to shore up the diminished leverage of domestic monetary policy instruments in a financial economy that is no longer dominated by bank deposits.

Employing a similar analysis Jane also proposed the modernization of household savings guarantees. As she noted, deposit insurance was originally established during the Great Depression in order to prevent runs on banks (see "No More Bank Bailouts; A Proposal for Deposit Insurance Reform," 1991). But as the financial system restructured during the final decades of the 20th century, the likelihood increased for equally destructive runs on insurance companies, mutual funds and other institutions that had become major administrators of families' financial assets. Asserting that a new federal guarantee system should protect the core savings of ordinary Americans rather than the franchise of individual financial institutions, Jane offered a farsighted plan to mitigate household risk without engaging in the open-ended bailout of miscreant financial firms that has become a hallmark of U.S. public policy since the 1980s.

In addition, Jane has argued that credit allocation is a potentially useful instrument for environmental policy, and proposed the establishment of a U.S. Environmental Finance Authority, modeled on existing institutions that support home mortgage lending and designed to promote capital flows into endeavors advancing environmental goals (see "Where Credit is Due: Allocating Credit to Advance Environmental Goals," 2002). At the same time she urged a fundamental redirection of international financial institution lending so as to support environmentally beneficial projects and policies in developing countries.

Jane's work has extended across the globe. For example, she has proposed changes in the international financial architecture that would redress the chronic instability and structural inequities embedded in emerging economies' dependence on exports for growth as well as the perversely recurring flow of capital from poor to rich countries. Jane's proposal envisions closed-end mutual funds for emerging market investment – pools of patient capital managed by the public sector that would finance development strategies geared toward increasing domestic demand and raising incomes more equitably (see "Replacing the Failed Washington Consensus," 2008). To deal with distortions perpetuated by the reigning privatized, dollar-based international monetary arrangements Jane also proposed the establishment of an International Clearing System. In the spirit of Keynes such a system would be coordinated by a global public agency and enable cross-border monetary exchanges to take place in each country's own currency, thus allowing governments and central banks to conduct robust economic policies at a national level. In addition, the monetary reform would permit all countries to service external debt with wealth generated in their domestic markets and thus curb the unsustainable imperative for export-led growth. (In addition to the references above, see "Financial Regulation in a Liberalized Global Environment," 2002.)

In brief, Jane D'Arista's analysis has been prophetic and her ideas bold. Over time, her work has helped persuade numerous scholars and policy makers that another world was possible. And as anyone who has interacted with her directly can attest, this process of persuasion has been reinforced by Jane's uncommon warmth and generosity as well as an abidingly collegial spirit and democratic sensibility. The essays in this book reflect the various ways in which Jane D'Arista's thought was and remains influential. Her work and teaching has been a profound inspiration for students, colleagues and activists, and will continue to serve as a stepping stone for new thinking about monetary and financial policies for a more equitable and civilized society in the years to come.

APPENDIX: SELECTED WORKS OF JANE D'ARISTA

1969, "Summary of Activities of the Reconstruction Finance Corporation," *Congressional Record*, U.S. House of Representatives, Washington, DC. August 4.

1971, *Federal Reserve Structure and the Development of Monetary Policy: 1915–1935*, Staff Report of the Subcommittee on Domestic Finance, Committee on Banking and Currency, U.S. House of Representatives, Washington, DC: Government Printing Office. December. (Reprinted in 1994a, see below).

1976, "Foreign Bank Activities in the United States" and "U.S. Banks Abroad," in *Financial Institutions and the Nation's Economy*, Compendium of Papers Prepared for the FINE Study, Book II, Committee on Banking, Currency and Housing, U.S. House of Representatives, Washington, DC: Government Printing Office, June.

1977, "The Foreign Bank Invasion," *The Banker's Magazine*, Autumn 1977.

1979a, "Private Overseas Lending: Too Far, Too Fast?" in Jonathon D. Aronson (ed.), *Debt and the Less Developed Countries*, Boulder, CO: Westview Press.

1979b, "United States Congressional Restraints: The Ties That Bind," in Lawrence G. Franko and Marilyn J. Seiber (eds), *Developing Country Debt*, New York: Pergamon Press.

1985, "The International Debt Problem in a Monetary Context," in Penelope Hartland-Thunberg and Charles K. Ebinger (eds), *Banks, Petrodollars and Sovereign Debtors: Blood From a Stone?* Lexington, MA: Lexington Books.

1986, *Financial Restructuring: The Major Policy Issues*, Report of the Subcommittee on Telecommunications, Consumer Protection and Finance, Committee on Energy and Commerce, U.S. House of Representatives, Washington, DC: Government Printing Office. July. (Revised version included in 1994b, see below).

1991, "No More Bank Bailouts: A Proposal for Deposit Insurance Reform," Briefing Paper, Economic Policy Institute. June 1.

1993, "The Parallel Banking System," in Gary A. Dymski, Gerald Epstein and Robert Pollin (eds), *Transforming the US Financial System; Equity and Efficiency for the 21st Century*, Armonk, NY: M.E. Sharpe.

1994a, *The Evolution of U.S. Finance, Volume 1: Federal Reserve Policy: 1915–1935*, Armonk, NY: M.E. Sharpe.

1994b, *The Evolution of U.S. Finance, Volume II: Restructuring Institutions and Markets*, Armonk, NY: M.E. Sharpe.

1999–2006, *Flow of Funds Review and Analysis* and *Capital Flows Monitor*. Quarterly reviews of developments in U.S. and international financial markets. Philomont, VA: Financial Markets Center.

1999, *Reforming the Privatized International Monetary and Financial Architecture*, Philomont, VA: Financial Markets Center. (Reprinted in *Challenge*, **43** (3), 44–82.)

2002a, "Rebuilding the Transmission System for Monetary Policy," *Financial Markets and Society*, November, 1–28.

2002b, "Financial Regulation in a Liberalized Global Environment," in John Eatwell and Lance Taylor (eds), *International Capital Markets: Systems in Transition*. New York: Oxford University Press.

2002c, "Where Credit is Due: Allocating Credit to Advance Environmental Goals," (with James Boyce), *Challenge*, May–June, **45** (3), 58–82.

2005, "The Role of the International Monetary System in Financialization," in Gerald A. Epstein (ed.), *Financialization and the World Economy*, Cheltenham, UK and Northampton, MA, USA: Edward Elgar.

2006, "The Dilemmas and Dangers of the Buildup of U.S. Debt: Proposals for Policy Responses," in J.J. Teunissen and A. Akkerman (eds), *Global Imbalances and the U.S. Debt Problem: Should Developing Countries Support the U.S. Dollar?* (with S. Griffith-Jones), The Hague: Forum on Debt and Development (FONDAD).

2007–08, "U.S. Debt and Global Imbalances," *International Journal of Political Economy*, **36** (4), Winter, 57–8.

2008, "Replacing the Failed Washington Consensus," *Journal of Post Keynesian Economics*, **30** (4), Summer, 215–35.

2009a, "The Evolving International Monetary System," *Cambridge Journal of Economics*, **33**, 633–52.

2009b, "Setting the Agenda for Monetary Reform," Working Paper 190. Political Economy Research Institute (PERI), University of Massachusetts Amherst.

2. Introduction

Gerald A. Epstein, Tom Schlesinger and Matías Vernengo

Most of the essays in this volume were first presented in May 2008 at a conference and celebration held in honor of Jane D'Arista at the Political Economy Research Institute (PERI) at the University of Massachusetts Amherst. The Great Financial Crisis had been emerging since at least the winter of 2007, but the full-blown global emergency that hit with the collapse of Lehman Brothers and AIG had not yet occurred. Still, those at the conference were acutely aware that the world was at an economic conjuncture of historic magnitude and that Jane D'Arista had for years been identifying, analyzing and warning against many of the forces that had led to that very moment.

We did not publish these papers earlier partly because so many of those assembled, including Jane herself, have been in high gear trying to understand and, equally importantly, trying to devise responses to the economic crisis, which has persisted since the May 2008 celebration as the responses of governments in the US and Europe grew ever more perverse. Austerity has become the dominant policy in Europe and to some extent in the US even as unemployment remains criminally high and is rising to emergency levels in parts of Europe. One slight sliver of hope has, ironically, come from the response of some key central banks – much too late and timid, but compared with the collapse of stimulative fiscal policy, very welcome nonetheless. The Federal Reserve, the Bank of England, and, reluctantly and inadequately, the European Central Bank launched more expansionary and experimental responses to the continuing crisis. But as Jane D'Arista repeatedly warned before the crisis, the traditional transmission belt of monetary policy has been highly damaged, if not completely broken, and so recovery-oriented monetary policies have not had nearly as much positive impact as needed, or as many officials expected.

Given the open-ended nature of this crisis and the destructive governmental responses, there is no point in waiting further for this chapter of the crisis to end as, it now seems, that may be a bit like waiting for Godot. So we here present slightly revised and in some cases, slightly updated versions of the papers presented in Jane's honor, most of them written in areas that Jane has made important contributions to during her long career (see Chapter 1).

We have divided the chapters in this volume into four sections (apart from the introductory material) each reflecting, broadly speaking, an area that Jane has been concerned with in her scholarly and policy endeavors. The first part is focused on "Federal Reserve Policy," which has long been a concern of Jane's. Early in her career she authored a path-breaking history, *Federal Reserve Monetary Policy: 1915–1935* (D'Arista, 1994a), and subsequently has written widely about flaws in the current approach to monetary policy-making as well as the need for institutional and structural changes to make it more effective.

FEDERAL RESERVE POLICY

In Chapter 3, James Galbraith critiques the macroeconomic doctrines of Milton Friedman and the so-called "New Consensus" view of central bank policy, showing how they have been wrong-headed, and in the latter case, totally irrelevant to an understanding of what caused the Great Financial Crisis or what should be done about it. Galbraith contrasts these irrelevant or dangerous views with macroeconomic and financial analyses that can be used to constructively diagnose the crisis and fashion genuine solutions: the work of John Maynard Keynes, John Kenneth Galbraith, Hyman Minsky and Jane D'Arista. Discussing the pathways to a restoration of economic stability and prosperity, Galbraith lays out what he calls the "D'Arista Doctrine":

> Elements of the D'Arista Doctrine include the reestablishment of effective quantity control over the extension of money and credit, through the application of reserve requirements to the entire universe of financial institutions and activities, based on assets rather than liabilities, and with repurchase agreements as the primary operating tool of monetary policy. The effective use of differential reserve requirements on assets of different types would give the central bank a powerful new regulatory tool against the concentration of financial investment that is the hallmark of bubbles, while the broad application of reserve requirements would equally extend the lender of last resort function, preventing the concentration of banking power that now characterizes financial crisis.

Galbraith's chapter raises several important questions about Federal Reserve policy that connect to Jane D'Arista's work on the Federal Reserve, especially her seminal research on Federal Reserve policy from 1915 to 1935 (D'Arista, 1994a): Why does the Federal Reserve adopt the policies that it does? How do these policies evolve over time? The other two chapters in

Part II address these two questions using the historical and institutional methodologies well employed by D'Arista in her own work.

Chapter 4 analyzes the development of Federal Reserve monetary policy during the post-World War II era. Martin Wolfson explains its evolution as the outcome of a political struggle among the key class forces – labor, finance capital and non-financial capital – contesting the direction of monetary policy. Wolfson argues that the result of this contest led to a policy of "leaning against the wind," which tried to keep inflation within limited bounds while also moderating interest rates in order to prevent significant slowdowns in growth. This represented a compromise between non-financial capital, which preferred somewhat higher inflation, and finance capital, which preferred to keep inflation lower. However, the factors shaping policy changed in the early 1980s with the growing prominence of Hyman Minsky's money-manager capitalists (such as pension funds and other institutional investors) and intensified international competition that constrained the ability of non-financial capitalists to readily raise prices. Under these new conditions financial and industrial capitalists coalesced around a desire for much lower inflation. With labor even less powerful in this period than earlier, an implicit low-inflation target was adopted by the Fed. This remained in place until the financial crisis of 2007 hit.

The key question moving forward is whether the Federal Reserve has now developed a new approach to monetary and financial policy, given its failure to prevent the massive financial crisis of 2007, and its struggles to overcome the destructive aftermath. As Matías Vernengo and Esteban Pérez Caldentey show in Chapter 5, at least some key central bankers made fundamental re-assessments of basic economic doctrine in the 1930s and radically transformed the policies they proposed in light of this reassessment. Following in Jane D'Arista's footsteps, Vernengo and Pérez Caldentey use original archival material to study the theoretical and policy evolution of Marriner S. Eccles in the United States and Raúl Prebisch in Argentina. As they show, the Great Depression created a need to rethink the principles of central banking, as with economics in general, drawing largely on the Keynesian Revolution. They show that "the role of the monetary authority as a fiscal agent of government and the abandonment of the view of the economy as self-regulated were the central changes in central banking" in the rich countries. Meanwhile, according to Vernengo and Pérez Caldentey, central banks in the periphery tried to insulate themselves from balance of payments crises through the use of capital controls and other measures. As they show, "Marriner S. Eccles, in the United States, and Raúl Prebisch, in Argentina, are paradigmatic examples of those new tendencies of central banking in the 1930s."

FINANCIAL HISTORY AND INSTITUTIONS

Part II, Financial History and Institutions, reflects a second area of Jane D'Arista's research and interest. Jane's classic study *The Evolution of US Finance: Restructuring Institutions and Markets* (D'Arista, 1994b) focuses on how government policy helps shape these financial institutions and their impacts on income distribution, financial stability and growth, for good or ill.

Robert McCauley's essay (Chapter 6) is a study in the D'Arista mold of the interaction between government policy and US securities firms, a topic obviously of great importance in light of the Great Financial Crisis of 2007 but one which has been largely neglected. McCauley shows the myriad ways in which the Federal Reserve and other government-connected institutions helped to nurture securities firms over the last 100 years. In many cases these efforts related to legitimate public policy purposes, such as helping the government sell US Treasury debt or helping finance foreign trade. However, too often these initiatives became entangled with efforts to support the profitability of particular institutions. And sometimes they may have contributed to significant macroeconomic problems, including those traceable to the asset-securitization practices that ultimately blew up the financial system in 2007–08. It is in this fascinating, richly detailed tale of public and private purpose that we see the work of Jane D'Arista so well reflected in Robert McCauley's chapter.

Ellen Russell's fascinating chapter (Chapter 7) on the origins of the Glass–Steagall Act is also an exercise in institutional financial history that bears the valuable marks of Jane D'Arista. Russell, as she puts it, "emulates [. . .] important attributes of D'Arista's contributions to the heterodox political economy of finance by exploring one of the most prominent examples of a sweeping regulatory reform in American financial history: the Glass–Steagall Act." Based on extensive archival research, she argues that Glass–Steagall's separation of commercial and investment banking, alongside other reforms in the Banking Acts of 1933 and 1935, "created a domestic regulatory framework which was supportive of the subsequent experiment with welfare state Keynesianism in the United States." She also contends that these reforms were crucial to the creation of:

> a long period of relative tranquility in financial markets, vigorous investment and the relative economic prosperity which characterized the "golden age" of the Keynesian welfare state. The erosion of this regulatory framework coincided with an era of increased domestic financial innovation and instability which culminated in the repeal of Glass–Steagall in 1999.

Robert Wade, in Chapter 9, provides a global perspective on the breakdown of the Glass–Steagall system that Ellen Russell depicted, and takes a snapshot of the global regulatory apparatus that prevailed just prior to the Great Financial Crisis. He describes the rise of what he calls the "Standards-Surveillance-Compliance System" (SSC), which was adopted in rich countries and imposed on developing countries. It was designed to open up and facilitate the harvesting of financial profits by financial institutions located primarily but not exclusively in the wealthy developed countries. Wade notes:

> The shift from "liberalize" to "standardize" is not just a tweaking of the "Washington Consensus." While the new consensus continued to accept the theory that markets allocate resources efficiently, it emphasised more than before the need for national and global *political* authorities to reshape and standardize markets, as distinct from government just getting out of the way. This amounted to turning classical liberalism on its head, because it gave normative sanction to a big *increase* in governmental and multilateral "intervention" to effect the standardization.
> [. . .]
> The central thrust of this effort was further to *constrain policymaking and institutional arrangements in developing countries in order to ensure they fitted the preferences of international investors* for full openness, arms-length relations between firms, banks, financial markets, and government, and no government guarantees to banks that might give them an "unfair" competitive advantage.
> [. . .]
> The SSC system [. . .] is just one part of a larger complex of international regimes, backed by the authority of the leading western states (often delegated upwards to interstate organizations), which helped to sluice opportunities and income towards (a) the financial sector, and (b) the top percentile of world income distribution.

While these policies worked to sluice income to the One Percent they pushed the economy off the precipice.

Gary A. Dymski makes related points in Chapter 8, but applies these in more detail to the United States and Latin America. Remaining true to the institutional specificity of Jane D'Arista's work, Dymski notes that the imperatives facing the US and Latin America are quite different. For developing Latin American countries, the constraints of the "Post-Washington Consensus" system described by Robert Wade substantially impact their capacity to manage their economies to avoid financial crises:

> The ability of financial regulators to control banking behavior is caught between the imperatives required for domestic stability and for reliable cross-border flows of bank loanable funds or bank capital. Specifically, the ability of these nations to impose rules that would pull banking systems in the direction of being more socially productive and economically functional is constrained

both by regional economic compacts (in the case of Mexico, NAFTA) and by having a large share of the domestic banking market operated by multinational banks.

The United States faces different dilemmas, according to Dymski: key among them is the "huge structural divide between Wall Street megabanks and the remainder of the US banking system." But the crisis creates possibility for change: "The 2007–08 global financial crisis provides a good opportunity for thinking anew about the economic functions and social impacts of banking and finance." Dymski proposes "a future that begins by renewing a broad-based discussion among all segments of society about the economic goals and social functions that financial institutions should meet."

Korkut Ertürk and Gökçer Özgür, in Chapter 14 (Part V), also analyze consequences of the massive financial changes that have occurred in the last 50 years. In doing so they tie together three key themes of Jane D'Arista's work: the role of financial liberalization; the rise of the "parallel" or "shadow" banking system; and the transformation of the monetary transmission mechanism that dramatically alters the way the central bank policy works. Describing the decline of the traditional banking system's role as a commercial-loan provider, Ertürk and Özgür note: "While traditional banking contracted, non-bank sources of credit experienced an explosive increase. It is no exaggeration to say that the very landscape of financial intermediation has been totally transformed in the last couple of decades as credit became increasingly market-driven rather than bank-driven." They then assess the implications of this transformation for post-Keynesian analysis of the money supply process, particularly "endogenous conceptions of money." They conclude that the central insight of endogenous monetary theory – namely "that credit creation causes monetary growth, makes much better sense that than the other way around" – should be revised to address two important issues:

> First, financial deregulation has fundamentally transformed bank behavior as it drastically altered what a bank is. Thus, it is hardly persuasive to depict credit creation as a passive, solely demand-driven process. Secondly, at the level of empirical analysis it can no longer be taken for granted that total bank credit "statistically" causes broad money.

In particular, activities such as "asset securitization and portfolio choice can no longer be ignored in understanding how the money supply process works," a lesson that Jane D'Arista has also made central to her work for many years. In particular D'Arista has long argued for regulatory adjustments to enhance the transmission belt for monetary policy in light of these and other financial changes.

GLOBAL FINANCE

Jane D'Arista has written extensively on global finance. Indeed, her earliest published work concerned US bank lending abroad (see Chapter 1). D'Arista pioneered the use of a flow of funds framework for understanding capital flows among countries; and she has written extensively about international monetary reform that would avoid the instability and deflationary biases of the privatized global financial system. In this part of the book, the authors explore a number of these themes.

In Chapter 10, Robert A. Blecker and Mario Seccareccia ask whether regional monetary arrangements are a promising avenue for solving domestic and regional financial problems, and, in addition, whether a collection of such arrangements can help solve global financial problems: these include real exchange rate misalignments, financial instability, and restrictions on the ability to use monetary and fiscal policy to address insufficient or excessive aggregate demand.

The recent experience of the euro does give pause to even the most ardent supporters of monetary unions. Well before the euro problems became so evident, Blecker and Seccareccia identified similar concerns about forming a "North American Monetary Union." Arguing against those who ascribe exchange rate over-valuation in Canada entirely to the so-called "Dutch Disease Problem" the authors identify the role of speculative financial flows as also significant. They also emphasize the constraints on monetary and fiscal policy that we now know can wreak havoc on the ability of countries to deal with recessions and depressions when they are part of a monetary union, as the Eurozone's current malaise demonstrates. In the end, Blecker and Seccaraccia counsel strongly against the formation of monetary unions. Instead, they adopt a position more closely aligned with Jane D'Arista's writings on these issues. They write: "What is needed is a more fundamental reform of the global payments system that would maintain intact the ability of national governments to pursue independent macroeconomic policies while still retaining their respective national currencies."

Thomas Palley's chapter (Chapter 11) raises fundamental questions about the nature of capital mobility in the modern global economy and what policy tools might be able to manage it. He explores and critiques the mainstream economics defense of "free" capital mobility and then analyzes the impacts of capital flows from the perspective of Keynesian, "neo-Walrasian" and Marxian perspectives. Palley concludes that these perspectives provide multiple explanations for unfettered capital mobility creating microeconomic, macroeconomic and distributional problems and they provide a strong rationale for capital flow management. Palley concludes with the important point that capital controls give nations a significant tool of macroeconomic management, but for them to be fully effective, international cooperation is required. In relation to Jane D'Arista's work and Chapter 9 by Robert Wade, Palley's chapter reinforces the idea that global financial reform is necessary to provide an appropriate context for effective national economic management.

Chapter 12, by Patrick Bond, views the Great Financial Crisis of 2007 through a global lens, with a focus on two sets of interactions: one, between the global "North" and "South"; and two, between financial accumulation and "real" accumulation. He notes that, "the expansion of the global economy's financial sector in the context of relative productive sector stagnation tendencies can be read as a classical over-accumulation crisis." Bond assesses the way in which elites and "policy makers" reacted to the crisis and argues that they did so "through 'devalorization' of large parts of the Third World alongside the write-down of selected financially volatile and vulnerable markets in the North (for example, dot.com, real estate and other derivatives bubbles)." He argues that the devalorization occurred through "intensified extra-economic coercion, including gendered and environmental stresses. The result is a world economy that concentrates wealth and poverty in more extreme ways, geographically, and brings markets and the non-market spheres of society and nature together in a manner adverse to the latter."

Bond goes on to ask whether the types of financial reforms advocated by Jane D'Arista (and many other authors in this book) will be sufficient to solve this complex set of problems; he concludes that they will not be sufficient:

> Is reform of the system possible? If so, Jane D'Arista's ideas for revitalized multilateral financial institutions, following various of Keynes' proposals, are worth revisiting. However, what such ideas "from above" require for consideration are states and socio-political movements "from below," like Ecuador (which defaulted) and Occupy, in order to change the many unhealthy relationships between society, state, economy, and financiers.

THEORETICAL CONSIDERATIONS: LIQUIDITY, CYCLES AND INCOME DISTRIBUTION

Most of Jane D'Arista's research and writing is grounded in a historical, institutional and empirical foundation; still, implicit in her approach is a strong theoretical commitment to certain key theoretical ideas which have their roots in Keynes, Kindleberger, Minsky and J.K. Galbraith. Part V gathers chapters that reflect this more theoretical orientation.

Lance Taylor links his theoretical essay (Chapter 13) explicitly to key themes in Jane D'Arista's work:

> The financial events beginning in 2007–08 underlined points that Jane D'Arista has always emphasized – that the behavior of the financial system is strongly influenced by its structure, that the structure can change in unexpected ways, and that the nature of regulation has a big effect on the direction and stability or instability of the changes.

Taylor pursues a set of themes underlying other chapters in this section, notably the role of liquidity and leverage in the generation of economic cycles and crashes. He draws on historical experience in the industrialized countries and more or less contemporary shifts in the developing economies to analyze the increasing role of liquidity in the financial system as it has evolved over time and space. Taylor notes: "More liquidity has historically been associated with greater leverage, and this linkage was a key factor underlying the crisis in the industrialized world. Its destabilizing effects were exacerbated by the pro-cyclical character of contemporary approaches to financial regulation." Taylor pays close attention to accounting principles in his work, drawing on the flow of funds account, again echoing an important aspect of D'Arista's work. Liquidity is defined by Taylor in the following way: "*Liquidity* is often interpreted as a measure of the financial flexibility of an individual actor, group of actors, or the financial system as whole. It constitutes 'wherewithal' – the resources readily available for purposes of capital formation or financial transactions."

Taylor develops a series of models in the form of stages showing how the co-evolution of liquidity creation and debt creation can lead to various forms of financial and real crises. He uses this Keynes–Minsky–Kindleberger–D'Arista framework to describe some of the key forces that led to the Great Financial Crisis. Lance Taylor then turns to policy alternatives. Acknowledging the important contributions by D'Arista, Taylor strongly criticizes the Basel frameworks of capital regulation showing, among other things, their highly permissive and pro-cyclical nature. In terms of a better regulatory framework, he suggests: "So how could the financial system be run more effectively, in particular for developing countries? A combination of capital controls, prudential regulations affecting cross-border flows, and long-term state-backed funds could be appropriate."

Chapter 13 ends on a cautionary note, especially ominous in light of the evident failure of post-crisis regulatory reforms to be adequately developed or implemented in the US or abroad:

> Prudential regulation has become much more difficult, and in the best of times it did not always work. It involves discretionary interventions (both quantitative and price-based), which may be subject to abuse. Information lacunae are rife and ever-changing. But as Jane D'Arista has always emphasized, an unregulated financial system is prone to crisis. It can truly turn into a weapon of mass destruction.

James Crotty and Gerald Epstein explore the uses and abuses of the term "liquidity" in the fight over financial reform and reconstruction in the aftermath of the Great Financial Crisis. Jane D'Arista has dealt with these issues extensively in her work with Stable, Accountable, Fair and Efficient Financial Reform (SAFER) and the Americans for Financial Reform (AFR) (see Chapter 1). In Chapter 16, James Crotty and Gerald Epstein dissect financiers' and mainstream economists' claims that financial regulations such as the Volcker Rule bans on proprietary trading, or proposed bans on naked credit default swaps, or other derivatives regulations, will necessarily limit the useful provision of "liquidity," and that, as a result, these regulations should be dramatically loosened or not implemented at all. Mainstream observers claim that more market liquidity is always better because it leads to lower asset trading costs and therefore a reduced cost of capital, and facilitates "price discovery." In discussions of policy, they almost always add a further proviso that more liquidity leads to assets being sold at the "appropriate price." Crotty and Epstein show that the mainstream view relies on vague and inconsistent definitions of liquidity, and cannot provide a convincing basis for the claims that recent proposed financial regulations harm the economy by reducing liquidity. By contrast, they discuss Keynes–Minsky (KM) perspectives on liquidity, showing that from a KM perspective there can be good and bad liquidity and that in general, the relationship between liquidity and capital accumulation is non-linear. Keynes argued that liquidity should be regulated, for example, through a financial transactions tax. The real solution, according to Keynes, is more social control over investment.

Perry Mehrling and Daniel Neilson, in Chapter 15, focus on a different aspect of "liquidity:" the liquidity "premium" that measures the value of liquidity. Their chapter goes into some institutional detail about how banks provide liquidity to futures markets to help offset mismatch and other risks. These are the kinds of services that Crotty and Epstein refer to as useful liquidity provision. In their analysis, Mehrling and Neilson show that this service provision by the banking system results in a residual liquidity premium in even the most "liquid" of markets, because the banks themselves cannot offset all the residual risk. In the Great Financial Crisis of 2007, however, the banks provision of "liquidity" services went well beyond trying to help others offset risks, as Jane D'Arista has shown in detail in her work with SAFER and AFR (see Chapter 1) and as indicated by Taylor and Crotty and Epstein in Part V.

In the final chapter, Codrina Rada analyzes the impact of demographic changes on income distribution. Writing in the tradition of Jane D'Arista, who always starts with concrete, important stylized facts to frame questions and analyses, Codrina Rada starts with some stark demographic arithmetic. She notes that: "Unprecedented demographic changes are set to unfold in most of the industrialized world. They are relevant not only because of the diminishing pool of workers, but also because of the increasing importance of retirees as an economic class." Rada then incorporates this stylized fact into a Kaldorian growth model to identify some key issues that may be important for growth and distribution. She argues that:

> Retirees' consumption and saving patterns can differ considerably from those of wage earners and capitalists, as retirees tend to consume more services and save less or in fact dis-save. From this perspective of changing aggregate consumption and saving patterns I argue that population aging together with existing constraints to growth and the institutional framework in place leads to a reconfiguration of income distribution and therefore to possible changes in the growth rate of the economy. Understanding how future income distribution may look like and the behavior of different economic classes, helps in designing the right policies to accommodate the demographic transition.

Though these considerations seem to be somewhat distant from those addressed by Jane D'Arista, in fact, throughout her career, D'Arista has maintained a razor-sharp focus on big issues that, as recent events have proven, will sooner or later come to dominate our economic lives. As Codrina Rada shows, demographics is such an issue and one that we ignore at our peril.

REFERENCES

D'Arista, Jane (1994a), *The Evolution of U.S. Finance, Volume 1: Federal Reserve Policy: 1915–1935*, Armonk, NY: M.E. Sharpe.

D'Arista, Jane (1994b), *The Evolution of U.S. Finance, Volume II: Restructuring Institutions and Markets*, Armonk, NY: M.E. Sharpe.

PART II

Federal Reserve Policy

3. From Milton Friedman to Jane D'Arista: the financial crisis and the dilemma facing the central banks[1]

James K. Galbraith

Twenty-five years ago, on a brilliant winter day at Alta, I skied off the top of the Sugarloaf lift and heard a familiar voice asking for directions. It was William F. Buckley Jr. I pulled off my hat and skied over to say hello. Buckley greeted me, then turned to a small man at his side wrapped in a quilted green parka topped with a matching forest-green stocking cap and wraparound sunglasses in the punk style. "Of course," Buckley said, "you know Milton Friedman."

In the fall of 2007, I received an invitation to deliver the 25th Annual Milton Friedman Distinguished Lecture at Marietta College. My first act was to notify Buckley, already then quite ill. I warned that he couldn't publish on it or the invitation might be revoked. The e-mail came back instantly, full of exclamation points, block caps, and misspellings. "Congratulations! What a wonderful opportunity to REPENT!"

But I went to bury Milton, not to praise him. I did so on the terrain that he favored, where he was strong and over which he ruled for many decades. This is the area of monetary policy, monetarism, the natural rate of unemployment, and the priority of fighting inflation over fighting unemployment. It is here that Friedman had his largest practical impact and also his greatest intellectual success. It was on this battleground that he beat out the entire Keynesian establishment of the 1960s, stuck as they were on a stable Phillips curve. It was here that he set the stage for the counterrevolution that has dominated academic macroeconomics for a generation, and that—far more importantly—also dominated, and continues to influence, the way in which most people think about monetary policy and the fight against inflation.

What was monetarism? Friedman famously defined it as the proposition that "inflation is everywhere and always a monetary phenomenon." This meant that money and prices were tied together. But more than that, Friedman believed that money was a policy variable—a quantity that the central bank could create or destroy at will. Create too much, and there would be inflation. Create too little, and the economy might collapse. There followed from this that the right amount would generate the right result: stable prices at what Friedman came to call the natural rate of unemployment.

The intent and effect of this line of reasoning was to defend a core proposition about capitalism: that free and unfettered markets are intrinsically stable. In Friedman's gospels, government is the lone serpent in Eden, while the task of policy is to stay out of the way. Just as this was the vulgar lesson of *Free to Choose*, so it turns out it was also the deep lesson of the larger structure of Friedman's thought. Friedman and Anna J. Schwartz's *A Monetary History of the United States, 1867–1960* (1963), for all its facts and statistics, carried a simple message: the market did not fail; the government did.

Friedman succeeded because his work was complex enough to lend an aspect of scientific achievement to his ideas and because those ideas played to the preconceptions of a particular circle. As John Maynard Keynes wrote of David Ricardo in his *General Theory of Employment, Interest, and Money* (1936):

> The completeness of [his] victory is something of a curiosity and a mystery. It must have been due to a complex of suitabilities in the doctrine to the environment into which it was projected. That it reached conclusions quite different from what the ordinary uninstructed person would expect, added, I suppose, to its intellectual prestige. That its teaching, translated into practice, was austere and often unpalatable, lent it virtue. That it was adapted to carry a vast and consistent logical superstructure, gave it beauty. That it could explain much social injustice and apparent cruelty as an inevitable incident in the scheme of progress, and the attempt to change such things as likely [. . .] to do more harm than good, commended it to authority. That it afforded a measure of justification to the free activities of the individual capitalist, attracted to it the support of the dominant social force behind authority.

Friedman's success was similar to Ricardo's, but not in all respects. Yes, he also explained away injustice and supported authority. But the logical superstructure was not vast and consistent. Rather, Friedman's argument was maddeningly simple, yet slippery. He would appeal to the short run for some effects and to the long run for others, shifting between them as it suited him. Once, at an American Economic Association meeting in San Francisco, I encountered him at the business end of a television camera. "Professor Friedman," the reporter inquired, "how will the economy do next year?" "Well," Friedman replied, "because of the slow money growth last year, there will be a terrible recession." "And what is your outlook for prices?" "Because of the fast money growth over the past several years, there will be a terrible inflation." "Professor Friedman," the reporter continued, "will the average American family be better off next year, or worse off than they are today?" "There is no such thing as the average American family. Some American families will be better off, and some will be worse off." As I said: he could be difficult to pin down. And while the practice resulting from the teachings was indeed austere and unpalatable, Friedman actually denied this. His money growth rules promised stable employment without inflation. Their promise was not austere, but happy. Ricardo was Scrooge. Friedman was more like the Pied Piper.

Friedman's success was consolidated in the late 1970s by facts: the strength of the monetarist regressions and the failure of the Keynesian Phillips curve. Stagflation happened. Robert Lucas called this "as clear-cut an experimental discrimination as macroeconomics is ever likely to see." At the same time, as a contemporary of Jane D'Arista's on the Banking Committee staff, I played a minor role in bringing monetarist ideas to the policy market. My responsibility was to design the Humphrey–Hawkins hearings on monetary policy from 1975 through their enactment into law in 1978. In a practical alliance with monetarists on the committee staff, we insisted that the Federal Reserve develop and report targets for monetary growth a year ahead. The point here was not to stabilize money growth as such; it was to force the Fed to be more candid about its plans. In this, we achieved an enduring success, far beyond our expectations. But the process certainly lent weight to monetarism.

It was on the policy battleground, shortly after, that monetarism collapsed. From 1979, the Federal Reserve formally went over to short-term monetary targets. The results were a cascading disaster: 20 percent interest rates; a 60 percent revaluation of the dollar; 11 percent unemployment; recession; deindustrialization throughout the Midwest; and, ultimately, the debt crisis of the Third World. In August 1982, faced with the Mexican default and also a revolt in Congress—which I engineered from my perch at the Joint Economic Committee—the Federal Reserve dumped monetary targeting and never returned to it.

By the mid 1980s, the rigorous monetarism Friedman had championed also faded from academic life. Money growth became high and variable, but inflation never came back. Perhaps inflation was "always and everywhere a monetary phenomenon," as he observed in 1963. But monetary phenomena could happen without inflation. This vitiated the use of monetary aggregates as an instrument of policy control. At the Bank of England, Charles Goodhart stated his law: When you try to use an econometric relationship for purposes of policy control, it changes. Friedman himself conceded to the *Financial Times*' Simon London in 2003: "The use of quantity of money as a target has not been a success. I'm not sure I would as of today push it as hard as I once did."[2]

What remained in the aftermath was a sequence of doctrines. All were far more vague and imprecise than monetarism, but they carried a similar policy message: the Fed should place inflation control at the center of its operations; it should ignore unemployment, unless that variable fell *too low*. Further, there was a sense that instability in the financial sector should be ignored by macroeconomic policymakers except when it could not be ignored any longer. The first of these doctrines, the "natural rate of unemployment" or "non-accelerating inflation rate of unemployment" (NAIRU), originated with Friedman and Edmund Phelps in 1968 and had the fatal attraction of incorporating expectations into a macroeconomic model for the first time. Macroeconomists fell for it wholesale. But it proved laughably defective in the late 1990s, when Alan Greenspan, bless his heart, allowed unemployment to fall below successive NAIRU barriers—6 percent, 5.5 percent, 5 percent, 4.5 percent, and, finally, even 4 percent. Nothing happened. No inflation resulted. This was good news for everyone except economists associated with the NAIRU, who were, or ought to have been, embarrassed. Some retreated from Friedman to Knut Wicksell: there was a brief vogue of something called the "natural rate of interest," an idea unsupported by any actual research or any theory since the demise of the gold standard.

And then we got Ben Bernanke and the ostensible doctrine of "inflation targeting." This idea—Dr. Bernankenstein's Monster—rests on something Marvin Goodfriend of Carnegie Mellon University calls the "new consensus monetary policy." The new consensus is a collection of ideas framed by the experience of the early 1980s but adapted, at least on the surface, to changing conditions since then. These are, first, that "the main monetarist message was vindicated: monetary policy alone [. . .] could reduce inflation permanently, at a cost to output and employment that, while substantial, was far less than in common Keynesian scenarios." Second, "a determined independent central bank can acquire credibility for low inflation without an institutional mandate from the government." And third, "a well-timed aggressive interest-rate tightening can reduce inflation expectations and preempt a resurgence of inflation without creating a recession."[3] Let us take up each of these alleged principles in turn.

First, is the proposition that monetary policy can reduce inflation permanently and at reasonable cost the "main monetarist message"? The idea is absurd. The main monetarist message was that the control of inflation was to be effected by the control of money growth. We have not even attempted this for a generation. Money growth has been allowed to do whatever it wants. The Federal Reserve stopped paying attention and even stopped publishing some of the statistics. Yet inflation did not return for over twenty years. The main monetarist message is plainly false. As for the question of cost, no one ever doubted that a harsh recession could stop inflation. But, in fact, the monetarists' recession of 1981–82 was by far the deepest in the postwar record. It was far worse than any inflicted under Keynesian policy regimes. In misstating this history, Goodfriend also completely overlooks the catastrophe inflicted by the global debt crisis on the developing world.

Second, is the anti-inflation "credibility" of a "determined central bank" worth anything at all? This idea is often asserted as though it were self-evident: that workers will restrain their wage demands because they recognize that excessive demands will be punished by high interest rates. There is some evidence for such a mechanism in the very specific case of postwar Germany, where a powerful union, the metalworkers, implicitly bargained with the Bundesbank for a period of some years. But in that case, the Bundesbank held a powerful, targeted weapon: a rise in interest rates would appreciate the Deutsche Mark and kill the export markets for German machinery and metal products. This was a credible threat. Such a situation does not exist in the United States, and there is no evidence that American labor unions think about monetary policy at all in their day-to-day work. It would not be rational for them to do so: in a decentralized system, restraint in one set of wages just creates an advantage for someone else. Moreover, there never existed any oil company that ever failed to raise the price of petroleum, when it could, because it feared a rise in interest rates might afflict someone else later on.

Third, can we safely state that a "well-timed aggressive interest-rate tightening" can avert inflation "without creating a recession"? That statement is surely the lynchpin of the new monetary consensus. It was published in the Fall 2007 issue of the *Journal of Economic Perspectives*—a flagship journal of the American Economic Association—in an article by Goodfriend titled "How the World Achieved Consensus on Monetary Policy." It therefore represents a statement of the highest form of expression of economic groupthink we are ever likely to find. Let me quote further, just so the message is clear. Goodfriend writes: "According to this 'inflation-targeting principle,' monetary policy that targets inflation makes the best contribution to the stabilization of output [. . .] [T]argeting inflation thus makes actual output conform to potential output." Further: "This line of argument implies that inflation targeting yields the best cyclical behavior of employment and output that monetary policy alone can deliver. Thus, and here is the revolutionary point delivered by the modern theoretical consensus—even those who care mainly about the stabilization of the real economy can support a low-inflation objective for monetary policy [. . .] [M]onetary policy should [therefore] not try to counteract fluctuations in employment and output due to real business cycles."

This statement was published, hilariously, around August 2007. It is the economists' equivalent of the proposition that the road to Baghdad would be strewn with flowers. For as of that moment, the Federal Reserve was at the crest of an "aggressive interest-rate tightening" that had been under way since late 2004, aimed precisely at "pre-empting inflationary expectations" while "averting recession." On July 19, 2006, Chairman Bernanke so testified before the Senate Committee on Banking, Housing, and Urban Affairs: "The recent rise in inflation is of concern to the FOMC [. . .] The Federal Reserve must guard against the emergence of an inflationary psychology that could impart greater persistence to what would otherwise be a transitory increase in inflation." On February 14, 2007, he repeated and strengthened the message: "The FOMC again indicated that its *predominant* policy concern is the risk that inflation will fail to ease as expected" (emphasis added). On July 19, 2007, this is again repeated: "With the level of resource utilization relatively high and with a sustained moderation in inflation pressures yet to be convincingly demonstrated, the FOMC has consistently stated that upside risks to inflation are its predominant policy concern."

Before the fall, Chairman Bernanke made occasional reference to developments in the financial sector. On May 23, 2006, these were actually enthusiastic. Bernanke testified: "Technological advances have dramatically transformed the provision of financial services in our economy. Notably, increasingly sophisticated information technologies enable lenders to collect and process data necessary to evaluate and price risk much more efficiently than in the past." And: "Market competition among financial providers for the business of informed consumers is, in my judgment, the best mechanism for promoting the provision of better, lower-cost financial products." As for consumers, education was Bernanke's recommendation and *caveat emptor* was his rule: "One study that analyzed nearly 40,000 affordable mortgage loans targeted to lower-income borrowers found that counseling before the purchase of a home reduced ninety-day delinquency rates by 19 percent on average."

On February 14, 2007, Bernanke was still optimistic: "Despite the ongoing adjustments in the housing sector, overall economic prospects remain good." And: "Overall, the U.S. economy seems likely to expand at a moderate pace this year *and next*, with growth strengthening somewhat as the drag from housing diminishes" (emphasis added). On March 28, 2007, he was less cheerful in testimony before the Joint Economic Committee: "Delinquency rates on variable-interest-rate loans to subprime borrowers, which account for a bit less than 10 percent of all mortgages outstanding, have climbed sharply in recent months." Still: "At this juncture, however, the impact on the broader economy and financial markets of the problems in the subprime market seems likely to be contained." Only on July 19, 2007, in his speech before the Senate banking committee, do we hear that previous assessments were a bit rosy. Only then do we hear that "in recent weeks, we have also seen increased concerns among investors about credit risks on some other types of financial instruments." That was three weeks before interbank lending markets collapsed on August 11, 2007.

What in the "new monetary consensus" led to a correct or even remotely relevant anticipation of the extraordinary financial crisis that broke over the housing sector, the banking system, and the world economy in August 2007 and that has continued to preoccupy central bankers ever since? The answer is, of course, absolutely nothing. You will not find a word about financial crises, lender-of-last-resort functions, or the nationalization of banks like Britain's Northern Rock, in papers dealing with monetary policy in the "new monetary consensus" traditions. What you will find, if you find anything at all, is a resolute, dogmatic, absolutist belief that monetary policy should not—should never—concern itself with such problems. That is partly why I say that the so-called new monetary consensus is an irrelevance. Serious people should not concern themselves with these ideas anymore. Meanwhile, central bankers caught in the practical realities of a collapsing financial system have had to reeducate themselves quickly. To some degree, and to their credit, they have done so. What they have not done is admit it.

What is the *relevant* economics? Plainly, as many commentators have hastily rediscovered, it is the economics of John Maynard Keynes, of John Kenneth Galbraith, of Hyman P. Minsky—and let me add, of Jane D'Arista—that is relevant to the current economic crisis. Let me say a word on each.

Here is Keynes, who wrote in 1931, in his "Consequences to the Banks of the Collapse of Money Values," that we live in:

> a community which is so organized that a veil of money is, as I have said, interposed over a wide field between the actual asset and the wealth owner. The ostensible proprietor of the actual asset has financed it by borrowing money from the actual owner of wealth. Furthermore, it is largely through the banking system that all this has been arranged. That is to say, the banks have, for a consideration, interposed their guarantee. They stand between the real borrower and the real lender [. . .] It is for this reason that a decline in money values so severe as that which we are now experiencing threatens the solidarity of the whole financial structure. Banks and bankers are by nature blind. They have not seen what was coming. Some of them have even welcomed the fall of prices towards what, in their innocence, they have deemed the just and "natural" and inevitable level [. . .] that is to say, to the level of prices to which their minds became accustomed in their formative years. In the United States, some of them employ so-called "economists" who tell us even today that our troubles are due

> to the fact that the prices of some commodities and some services have not yet fallen enough [. . .] A "sound banker," alas! is not one who foresees danger and avoids it, but one who, when he is ruined, is ruined in a conventional and orthodox way along with his fellows, so that no one can really blame him.

In *The Great Crash*: *1929* (1955), John Kenneth Galbraith rejects the idea, later embraced by Friedman, that bankers and speculators were merely reflecting the previous course of monetary policy. It is true, as he wrote, that "that in 1929, modifying a famous cliché, the economy was fundamentally unsound [. . .] Many things were wrong, [including] the bad distribution of income [. . .] the bad corporate structure [. . .] the bad banking structure [. . .] the dubious state of the foreign balance [and] the poor state of economic intelligence." And yet, that summer:

> there were no reasons for expecting disaster. No one could foresee that production, prices, incomes and all other indicators would continue to shrink for three long and dismal years. Only after the market crash were there plausible grounds to suppose that things might now for a long while get a lot worse.

John Kenneth Galbraith also wrote:

> To regard the people of any time as particularly obtuse seems vaguely improper, and it also establishes a precedent which members of this generation might regret. Yet it seems certain that the economists and those who offered economic counsel in the late twenties and early thirties were almost uniquely perverse.

On this point, he is now disproved. I refer you back to the "new monetary consensus."

Hyman Minsky taught that economic stability itself breeds instability. The logic is quite simple: apparently stable times encourage banks and others to take exceptional risks. Soon, the internal instability they generate threatens the entire system. Hedge finance becomes speculative, then Ponzi. The system crumbles and must be rebuilt. Governments are not the only source of instability. Markets, typically, are much more unstable, much more destabilizing. This fact is clear, in history, from the fundamental fact that market instability long predates the growth of government in the New Deal years and after, or even the existence of central banking.

What is to be done about it? The work of Jane D'Arista provides abundant guidance. Elements of the D'Arista doctrine include the reestablishment of effective quantity control over the extension of money and credit, through the application of reserve requirements to the entire universe of financial institutions and activities, based on assets rather than liabilities, and with repurchase agreements as the primary operating tool of monetary policy. The effective use of differential reserve requirements on assets of different types would give the central bank a powerful new regulatory tool against the concentration of financial investment that is the hallmark of bubbles, while the broad application of reserve requirements would equally extend the lender of last resort function, preventing the concentration of banking power that now characterizes financial crisis.

Now seven years have passed since the Great Crisis made a laughing stock of the New Monetary Consensus. The Dodd–Frank bill established the principle, broadly accepted, that the financial sector requires adult supervision. But in practice that supervision remains lacking, as does regular and efficient enforcement of norms and statutes against financial fraud. The wheel has turned, and Jane D'Arista has triumphed over Milton Friedman on the battleground of ideas. But on the battleground of action, of policy, of implementation and enforcement, the outcome remains uncertain and as time passes and memories fade, the outlook is not especially bright.

NOTES

1. This chapter is adapted from a paper delivered to a seminar at the European Parliament on June 24, 2008, itself adapted from the 25th Annual Milton Friedman Distinguished Lecture, entitled "The Collapse of Monetarism and the Irrelevance of the New Monetary Consensus," delivered at Marietta College in Marietta, Ohio on March 31, 2008 and published by the Levy Economics Institute.
2. Simon London (2003), "Targeting the Quantity of Money . . . Has Not Been a Success," *Financial Times*, June 9.
3. Marvin Goodfriend (2007), "How the World Achieved Consensus on Monetary Policy," *Journal of Economic Perspectives*, **21**(4): 47–68.

4. Federal Reserve priorities and the influence of capital: the evolution of monetary policy in the postwar period[1]

Martin H. Wolfson

Falling unemployment raises fears of rising wages, and may force the Federal Reserve to raise interest rates in order to head off inflation. This mantra was repeated over and over again by newspaper, TV, and radio correspondents in the 1980s and 1990s, conveyed to the public as if it were the obvious, and only, conclusion one could draw from the unemployment data. These commentators, either explicitly or implicitly, were basing their analysis on two important assumptions. The first is the non-accelerating inflation rate of unemployment, or NAIRU, the doctrine that asserts that inflation will accelerate if the unemployment rate drops below a fixed level, estimated in the early 1990s to be 6 percent. The second is that price stability, or zero inflation, is the only goal that the Federal Reserve should try to achieve with monetary policy. Thus, if the unemployment rate threatened to fall below NAIRU, the Fed would have no choice but to raise interest rates.

The unemployment rate did in fact drop below 6 percent in 1994, and the Federal Reserve responded by raising the federal funds rate from 3 percent in 1994 to 6 percent by early 1995 (see Figure 4.1). Interestingly, not only did the unemployment rate continue to fall, but the inflation rate remained remarkably stable, at approximately 3 percent. Adherents to NAIRU scrambled to reinterpret the concept, despite its obvious empirical contradiction.[2] With inflation showing no signs of accelerating, and even falling further in 1997 and 1998, the Federal Reserve kept the federal funds rate stable and seemed to turn its attention elsewhere.

In 1998 the Federal Reserve cut the federal funds rate three times, as the fallout from the Asian financial crisis threatened world financial markets. The Fed took back these interest rate cuts in 1999 and again pushed the federal funds rate up past 6 percent by early 2000, as inflation rebounded

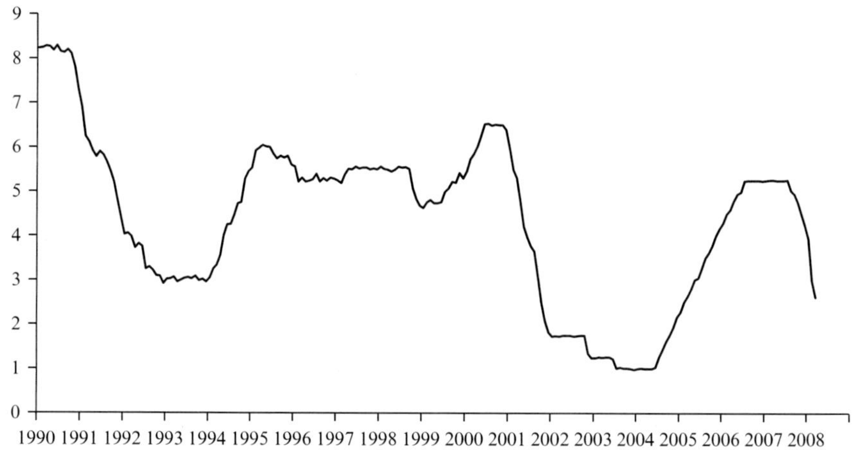

Source: Board of Governors of the Federal Reserve System, H.15 Statistical Release.

Figure 4.1 Federal funds rate

to the 3 percent range. However, when it became obvious in 2001 that the economy was entering a recession, the Fed changed gears once more and dramatically lowered interest rates. By late 2003 and early 2004, the Fed had reduced the federal funds rate to 1 percent, a level that had not been seen in 40 years.

The Fed then "took back" these interest rate cuts, raising the federal funds rate gradually but consistently, to a peak of 5.25 percent, from mid 2004 to mid 2006. It was motivated apparently by the desire to restore interest rates to more "normal" levels, not by any upsurge in inflation. After a year of interest-rate stability, the Fed then began to dramatically reduce the Fed Funds rate in 2007, reacting to the collapse of housing speculation and fears that the resulting financial crisis would dry up credit and usher in a serious recession. By April 2008, the federal funds rate stood at 2.25 percent, a full three percentage points below its recent peak in 2006.

Given this experience, is it still the case that the Federal Reserve's goal for monetary policy is price stability? I would argue that it is, although it has not always been, and at times the Fed has decided to temporarily focus on other goals. The Fed dramatically changed its goal to price stability in the early 1980s, and has maintained that goal since. I will argue in this chapter that it did so in reaction to institutional changes in the economy, changes that involved the relative power and priorities of financial institutions, nonfinancial corporations, and labor.

The chapter will trace these changes and indicate the ways in which they influenced the monetary policy goals of the Federal Reserve.[3] The first section discusses the methodology I use to approach this question. The second section analyzes the history of monetary policy in the postwar period in the United States, and addresses the relationship of Federal Reserve priorities to the requirements of capital, that is, the interests of major financial institutions and nonfinancial corporations. The final section reexamines the recent monetary policy experience from this perspective, and then concludes.

METHODOLOGY

There are two basic methodological perspectives that will be used in this analysis. The first is the political economy of central banking, or the influences that groups within society have on Federal Reserve policymaking. To understand these influences, I start with two general observations. The first is the special relationship that the Federal Reserve has with financial institutions. The Fed maintains close ties with financial market participants in order to gauge market expectations and reactions to its policies. It also regulates banking institutions and relies upon them for political support (Greider, 1987). The second is the structural influence that profit-making institutions have on policymakers in a capitalist economy. If policies are seen as threatening to profits, industry and finance can threaten to go on strike, that is, withdraw their capital from the economy until the offending policies are more to their liking.

I build here upon the excellent work of Raford Boddy and James R. Crotty, and Gerald Epstein and Juliet Schor. Boddy and Crotty (1975) raised early on the issue of Federal Reserve tightening in response to a decline in industrial profits. Epstein and Schor have developed the political economy of comparative central banking. Their analysis divides society into three groups—industrial capital, financial capital, and labor—and assumes that industrial and financial capital want monetary policy set so as to maximize their profit rates, and that workers want it to maximize their wage bill; also, monetary policy works by changing real interest rates (Epstein, 1992). They view the Federal Reserve as a contested terrain, in which central bank policy depends not only on the general need to be mindful of the profits of capital (in order to avoid a capital strike), but also on the relative power of finance, industry, and labor.

In general terms, financial capital, as a net creditor, favors a tight monetary policy to restrain inflation and protect the value of its loans and investments, whereas labor favors a looser policy that promotes the growth of output, employment, and wages. The attitude of industrial capital towards monetary policy is more complicated. Industry profits are subject to three effects: the Keynes process, which links strong aggregate demand with capacity utilization and a higher profit rate; the Wicksell process, in which nonfinancial corporations, as net debtors, benefit from inflation; and the Marx process, in which profits are affected by the ability of labor to raise wages (Epstein and Schor, 1990).

However, all of these attitudes towards monetary policy, and the monetary policy chosen by the central bank, can be influenced and constrained by structural factors that differ across countries. Epstein (1992) compares capital–labor relations, industry–finance relations, central bank independence, and role in the world economy for eight industrial countries. Focusing solely on the Federal Reserve in the United States, though, I develop the analysis not by comparing the conditions affecting central banks in different countries at a particular time, but rather by concentrating on how the conditions influencing the Federal Reserve have changed over time.

Thus the second methodological approach is a way of understanding this historical process. I argue that we can distinguish different stages over time in the way that finance, industry, and labor affect Federal Reserve policy. These stages are defined by institutional structures that are established, structures that are the outcome of capital–labor and intra-capital contradictions.

The stabilization of these contradictions can be either victory for one side over the other, or a compromise based on relative strength. In either case the outcome establishes an institutional structure that reflects the balance of forces. These institutional structures are relatively longlasting. Also, since there is a tendency for the principles underlying the various institutional structures to conform to one another, the stabilization of these contradictions, taken together, establishes a stage, or longlasting period of relative stability. In the post-World War II United States, there have been two stages: a period of regulated economic activity in the early period, and a neoliberal, or "free-market," stage, continuing up through the present.[4]

This methodology obviously owes much to the social structure of accumulation approach developed by David Gordon and his co-authors (1982). However, the emphasis here is on institutional structures that are based upon the stabilization of class conflicts rather than the requirements for economic growth (see Wolfson, 2003; Wolfson and Kotz, 2010).

The outcomes of these conflicts reflect relative power, and thus the relative ability to affect Federal Reserve policy. However, what type of monetary policy will be desired will also depend on the needs and objectives of the various groups, which can change from one stage to another. This implies that the monetary policy sought by capital during the regulated stage of U.S. postwar history could be very different from the one desired during the neoliberal period. In fact, that is exactly what an examination of U.S. history in the post-World War II period demonstrates.

HISTORY

The first stage in the postwar history extends from the end of the war through to the late 1960s and early 1970s. It was a period of relative stability and growth, sometimes referred to as the "Golden Age of Capitalism" (Marglin and Schor, 1990). After the Federal Reserve–Treasury "Accord" and establishment of Federal Reserve independence in 1951 (Epstein and Schor, 1995), the Federal Reserve adopted the "leaning against the wind" philosophy advocated by its Chairman, William McChesney Martin.[5] Under this philosophy, the Fed would lean against whatever seemed to be the most significant problem, raising interest rates if inflation was on the rise, and lowering interest rates in order to stimulate employment and output growth in more stagnant times.

In a transitional period in the 1970s, the Federal Reserve maintained the same general orientation towards monetary policy, but with worse results. The 1970s were a decade of stagflation, as unemployment and inflation both shot up sharply. In 1979, Paul Volcker was appointed Chairman of the Federal Reserve Board, and the Fed undertook a drastic campaign to restrain inflation. The results of that campaign were consolidated in the 1980s, when the economy entered the second postwar stage and the Fed's policy goal swung decisively to a permanent war on inflation, that is, a policy goal of price stability.

The Early Postwar Period

As a result of the turmoil of the 1930s, a postwar institutional structure was built that was able to moderate class conflict by restricting competition and regulating behavior. Industry recognized and bargained with the new industrial unions organized by the Congress of Industrial Organizations (CIO) on the basis of the Wagner Act framework and an informal capital–labor "accord" that ceded control of the workplace to management (Bowles et al., 1991). Intra-capitalist conflict was moderated by oligopolistic structures domestically and U.S. hegemony internationally. The Bretton Woods system regulated the international financial system, with the U.S. dollar as international reserve currency, and with capital controls in most industrial countries, except for the U.S. and Canada (Epstein and Schor, 1992).

The domestic financial system was regulated by "compartmentalization," which restricted competition by forcing financial institutions into specialized financial areas. For example, the Glass–Steagall Act of 1933 separated commercial and investment banking, and lending was carried out by depository financial institutions with defined areas: commercial banks made loans to business, savings and loan associations (S&Ls) specialized in mortgages, credit unions focused on consumer finance, and so on. Also, in response to what was seen as a destructive bidding war for deposits, legislation in the 1930s restricted competition by imposing ceilings on interest rates paid by banks. The government provided support for financial institutions by introducing federal deposit insurance. The resulting "system of financial regulation" reduced financial crises in the early postwar period (Wolfson, 1994), and brought a measure of stability to bank–corporate lending relationships.

In such a regulated environment, "leaning against the wind" was a monetary policy that fit in well with the objectives of industry, labor, and finance. The domestic oligopolistic structure, U.S. hegemony, and regulated collective bargaining with labor unions, along with strong productivity growth, provided for both steady real wage and profit gains and a safety valve of occasional price increases that did not imply a loss of competitive position. Thus, both industry and labor could benefit from a monetary policy that promoted growth in output and employment.

Financial institutions were willing to tolerate some growth, for two reasons. First of all, much lending by depository institutions like banks and S&Ls was still a relatively local and customer-oriented affair. Unlike all other industrial countries, the U.S. in the early postwar period had nearly twenty thousand small banks in communities all over the country, a legacy of the protective legislation of the 1930s. They identified with their customers and benefitted from the prosperity and profitability that postwar growth brought. Although individually these small banks obviously were not major players, together they constituted an important political force to which the Federal Reserve paid attention (Greider, 1987). The second reason that financial institutions tolerated some growth was that they knew that the Federal Reserve stood ready to raise interest rates if inflation threatened.

The 1970s

All of these relatively stable relationships began to fall apart in the late 1960s and early 1970s. U.S. economic and political hegemony was challenged by increasing competition from industrial countries like Japan and Germany, from oil exporters who joined together in the Organization of the Petroleum Exporting Countries (OPEC), and from developing countries demanding independence and autonomy. The war in Vietnam brought these contradictions to a head. By requiring an outpouring of dollars to finance operations in Southeast Asia and creating an overheated inflationary economy at home, the war was the last nail in the coffin of the Bretton Woods system. The dollar was allowed to float in 1973. Competition also increased domestically, posing challenges to oligopolistic structures (Bowles et al., 1991).

In the midst of the expanding economy of the late 1960s, workers used the opportunity of a strong demand for labor to push for higher wages and to resist corporate attempts at speedup. Given the increased competitive pressures on U.S. corporations in the context of the fixed exchange-rate system, corporations were unable to fully cover wage increases with higher prices. Although prices did rise, profits fell.

The Federal Reserve initially was reluctant to rein in this expansion because of the need to finance the Vietnam War (Dickens, 1995), but as prices increased and profits fell, they took more decisive action (Boddy and Crotty, 1975). Policy was tightened in 1969, and the economy entered a recession in December. The Fed eased somewhat as the recession took hold, but then supplied reserves much more liberally in response to the developing financial crisis in the commercial paper market in 1970 (Wolfson, 1994).

The "leaning against the wind" monetary policy was still in effect in the 1970s, and the Federal Reserve aggressively stimulated the economy in 1972 (perhaps influenced by the close association of the Federal Reserve Chairman, Arthur Burns, with President Nixon, who was running for re-election; Greider, 1987). In 1973, the OPEC oil embargo took effect, helping to set off another inflationary spiral. The Federal Reserve promptly tightened, and the economy went into recession, but inflation remained strong throughout the rest of the decade, and was not brought under control until the 1980s.

Given that "leaning against the wind" did not seem to be having much success against inflation, and given that the institutional basis for it, the regulated economy, had begun to erode, why did the Fed stick with its balanced policy throughout the 1970s? Why didn't it pursue a more aggressive attack on inflation? The answer may lie in the support of industry for the inflationary environment.

To understand this support, it is necessary to keep in mind that the OPEC price increases imposed a real tax on the economy. Because oil was so central to the U.S. economy, an increase in its price meant a real increase in costs and a decrease in income. Thus, in this context, industry concluded that if it could raise its prices faster than labor could raise its wages, it could protect its profits from the OPEC tax at the expense of labor.[6] Also, and significantly, because the dollar was set loose from its fixed-exchange-rate tether in 1973, the depreciation of the dollar that resulted from inflation allowed industry to maintain its competitive position internationally (Epstein, 1989).

However, financial institutions were more opposed to the inflationary environment. Those that had made fixed-rate loans, especially holders of long-term bonds and mortgages, suffered significant losses.[7] Although an increasing share of business loans were being made on an adjustable-rate basis, these loans posed their own problems for financial institutions. Despite the fact that these adjustable-rate loans shifted interest-rate risk from banks to borrowers, they increased the debt-repayment pressures on borrowers and increased the banks' credit risk (as has become painfully obvious in the recent sub-prime mortgage crisis).

The 1980s

Inflationary pressures continued to mount as the 1970s came to an end. A second OPEC price increase occurred in 1979, and inflation again hit double digits. President Carter replaced industrialist G. William Miller as Chairman of the Federal Reserve Board with the choice of the financial markets: Paul Volcker. Volcker proceeded to drastically tighten monetary policy. A recession began in March 1980,[8] and a second one followed in 1981–82. Again, the Federal Reserve eased policy when a financial crisis threatened in 1982.

It is significant to note, though, that "leaning against the wind" is still the best way to describe Federal Reserve policy up to 1982. Although Volcker pushed the federal funds rate up to 20 percent in 1981, he again abruptly, if temporarily, changed gears when the economy started to drop like a rock. Although the economy quickly rebounded and the Fed quickly reverted to raising interest rates, the episode is significant.

The real break with the "leaning with the wind" policy came in 1984. At that point the economy had begun to recover from the recession, and growth and employment were picking up. Although inflation had dropped by then to under 4 percent, and showed no signs of increasing, the Fed raised interest rates. Volcker explained to Congress that he wanted to avoid the "risks that could undercut much of what has been achieved [. . .] It is, in the end, the choice between building on the enormous progress of the past to achieve *sustained* growth in a framework of greater stability or a relapse into inflationary economic malaise" (Volcker, 1984: 635; emphasis in original). Raising interest rates to forestall what *might be* the inflationary implications of an expanding economy marks the decisive switch from "leaning against the wind" to a sole emphasis on inflation, in fact, to acceptance of the goal of price stability.

Why did the Federal Reserve make this major change in monetary policy? The hypothesis that will be explored here is that the economy had by 1984 moved into the second stage of postwar history. Major changes had occurred in the central contradictions of society so that the interests of *both* finance and industry were now oriented towards a goal of price stability for monetary policy.

By 1984, the financial landscape had changed dramatically. The stability of the regulatory environment of the early postwar years had been blown apart by the inflationary decade of the 1970s. The walls that had demarcated the lending areas of financial institutions had been breached, the ceilings that had limited interest-rate increases for depository institutions had been eliminated, and the importance of the small banks had been reduced. Failures and mergers of small banks and savings and loan associations had led to concentration in the banking industry, even as banks had begun to lose their dominant role in business lending. What had risen in importance were the institutional investors that formed the basis of what Hyman Minsky characterized as "money-manager capitalism": the pension funds, mutual funds, and other participants in the capital markets.

These money managers did not have the same kind of ongoing relationships with loan customers that the small banks (or even large banks) did. Bondholders in particular (who generally hold fixed-rate securities that lose value as a result of inflation) had suffered losses in the 1970s and early 1980s and were focused on preventing a return of inflation.

Corporations were also in favor of price stability by 1984. Their strategy of raising prices in the 1970s was only partly successful, since cost-of-living adjustments in union contracts were widespread, and workers' ability to maintain their wages was stronger than corporations would have liked. In any event, that strategy was foreclosed in 1984 because of the strong increase in the value of the dollar brought about by the high interest-rate environment of the early 1980s. The strong dollar hammered domestic manufacturing, but at the same time enabled—and encouraged—corporations to cut costs by closing down domestic factories and moving production offshore.

Runaway plants were one aspect of Corporate America's new strategy: to focus on reducing labor costs in order to restore profitability. A policy of price stability, by foreclosing the likelihood of tight labor markets that push up wages, was a suitable complement to this strategy.

The capital–labor accord of the early postwar period, in which industry bargained collectively with labor and accommodated steady gains in real wages, was based on international hegemony and unchallenged oligopolies.[9] These were gone by 1984. Corporations sought to avoid and attack unions, encouraged by the Reagan administration's hiring of permanent replacement workers in the air traffic controllers' strike in 1981. The overall deregulatory and "free-market" ideology in Washington enabled corporations to further press the attack by rolling back protective labor and environmental regulations.

By 1984, the regulatory stage of postwar U.S. capitalism had been replaced by a new "free-market" stage. And with it, the outlook of industrial and financial capital that had supported a relatively balanced approach to monetary policy in the early postwar period had swung decisively to a policy of stable prices.[10] By raising interest rates at the first signs of strong growth, the Federal Reserve gave up on a vibrant economy, but ensured low inflation for finance capital and a slack labor market that kept down wages for industrial capital. Labor, weakened by capital's increasing attacks, was not able to mount significant opposition to this policy.

IS PRICE STABILITY STILL THE FEDERAL RESERVE'S GOAL?

In 1994, the Federal Reserve again raised interest rates when growth picked up after the 1990–91 recession, even though there were no signs of an increase in inflation. This action is consistent with the policy discussed above, but other Federal Reserve actions since then do not seem to fit the pattern quite so easily. The three anomalous events, mentioned in the Introduction, are: 1) the three interest rate cuts in 1998 in response to turmoil in the international financial system following the Asian financial crisis; 2) the vigorous cutting of interest rates in 2001, and again in 2007–08, in response to the collapse of financial speculation and a gathering recession; and 3) the refusal to raise interest rates between 1995 and 1999, despite strong economic growth and a sharply falling unemployment rate.

The first two of these events are actually very consistent with traditional Federal Reserve policymaking. No matter what the goals of monetary policy have been, the Fed has always been concerned with limiting financial crises and financial instability. Throughout the postwar period, its role as lender of last resort has taken priority when financial crises threatened to disrupt the financial system and the economy, even though, ironically, it has often been the Fed's tight monetary policy that has pushed the economy towards financial crisis in the first place (Minsky, 1982).

A similar principle applies to the issue of recession. When it becomes clear that the economy has entered, or is about to enter, a recession, the

Fed has traditionally devoted its full attention to ending the recession and putting the economy back on a positive, even if restrained, growth track.[11]

The third event raises more controversial issues. It seems to directly contradict the Fed's actions in 1984 and 1994, when it raised interest rates in the face of low and stable inflation but vigorous output and employment growth. Has the Fed backed away from its relatively recent embrace of the goal of price stability? Some inflation hawks from the world of finance certainly are concerned that this is the case, but I think there is another interpretation.

In 1984 and 1994 the Fed, influenced by the NAIRU doctrine, was convinced that inflation would accelerate if it did not act. During the long expansion of the late 1990s, the validity of NAIRU was increasingly called into question. Also, Alan Greenspan was extolling the wonders of the New Economy, and claiming that the productivity gains from the use of information technology would moderate inflation pressures (Greenspan, 2000).

Receiving less attention were two other important considerations that reduced inflationary pressures. One was the overcapacity that existed in world markets, a major constraint on corporate pricing power and, ironically, in part a legacy of the neoliberal strategy of expanding production offshore (Crotty, 2000). The second was the fact that industry had made significant progress in holding down costs by reducing the power of workers and their unions. Although real wages did rebound to some degree during the long expansion, the ability of wages to challenge profits, and add to the pressure for price increases, was much diminished.

Thus, in the future industry might see less need to rely on tight monetary policy to repress labor, and there could be a divergence of opinion between industrial and financial capital about the degree to which the Fed can support economic growth. On the other hand, an increase in the power of labor could overturn the "free-market" environment altogether and usher in a new regulatory period more favorable to growth. Future Fed policy may also be influenced by the ability of the NAIRU doctrine to survive in the face of empirical evidence that undermines it. But we can be reasonably sure that policy will continue to be influenced by the contradictions among industry, finance, and labor, and the ways in which those contradictions are addressed.

NOTES

1. An earlier version of this chapter was originally presented at 'The Political Economy of Monetary Policy and Financial Regulation: A Conference in Honor of Jane D'Arista', Political Economy Research Institute Amherst, Massachusetts May 3, 2008. I would like to thank Beth Almeida, Jim Crotty, and Jerry Epstein for helpful comments.
2. For a thorough history and critique of NAIRU, see Baker (2002) and Galbraith (1997).

3. The analysis at this point is exploratory, more properly hypotheses than settled conclusions.
4. The phrase "free market" is put in quotation marks because there are many imperfections in the "freedom" of the current market system. Although beyond the scope of this chapter, there is support for the hypothesis that the goal of the "free-market" environment is not to achieve competitive markets, but rather to undermine worker protections, promote capital mobility and opportunities, enhance corporate bargaining power over labor, and improve the profitability of both industrial and financial capital.
5. With regard to monetary policy, it would certainly be possible to consider an additional period, from World War II until the Accord, when the Federal Reserve, at the direction of the Treasury, maintained low and stable interest rates. That approach will not be followed here, however, for two reasons. First, the historical comparison of monetary policy is more useful if focused on the consistent period of Federal Reserve independence. Second, although the episode involved a decisive victory for finance and industry over the interests of labor (Epstein and Schor, 1995), the period of central bank dependence in the 1940s was relatively brief and had much to do with the need to reduce the costs of financing the war.
6. As it turned out, industry was not as successful as it had hoped in its struggle with labor. In the 1970s, the power of labor was still sufficiently strong, so that neither side was able to achieve a significant victory in the battle to shift the costs of the OPEC tax. The outcome was a wage-price spiral and stagflation.
7. Indeed, companies and individuals who had taken out mortgages in the 1960s and earlier were among the biggest winners in the inflationary 1970s.
8. Interestingly, it took more than high interest rates to bring about the recession. Credit controls were used in March 1980, and they seemed to be more effective in stopping the expansion of credit and initiating the recession than high interest rates.
9. It was also helped by gains in productivity and a stable value of the dollar, both of which collapsed in the 1970s.
10. By the 1990s, a new development had reinforced the support of industrial capital for price stability: the increased financial operations of industrial corporations. Companies like General Electric (GE) were deriving a larger share of their profits from financial subsidiaries like GE Capital, and thus increasingly shared the financial institutions' outlook on price stability.
11. Of course, within the Fed controversies have existed over how vigorously the Fed should fight the recession, and how far and how fast the Fed should lower interest rates. But there has been agreement on the overall objective of ending the recession.

REFERENCES

Baker, Dean. 2002. The NAIRU Theory: A Rationale for High Unemployment. Paper presented at the ASSA Conference, Atlanta, Georgia. January.

Boddy, Raford, and James Crotty. 1975. Class Conflict and Macro-Policy: The Political Business Cycle. *Review of Radical Political Economics* **7**: 1–19.

Bowles, Samuel, David M. Gordon, and Thomas E. Weisskopf. 1991. *After the Waste Land: A Democratic Economics for the Year 2000*. Armonk, New York: M.E. Sharpe, Inc.

Crotty, James. 2000. Structural Contradictions of the Global Neoliberal Regime. *Review of Radical Political Economics* **32**(3): 361–8.

Dickens, Edward. 1995. The Great Inflation and U.S. Monetary Policy in the Late 1960s: A Political Economic Approach. *Social Concept* **7**(1): 49–82.

Epstein, Gerald. 1981. Domestic Stagflation and Monetary Policy: The Federal

Reserve and the Hidden Election. In: Thomas Ferguson and Joel Rogers (eds), *The Hidden Election: Politics and Economics in the 1980s Presidential Campaign*. New York: Pantheon Books, pp. 141–95.

Epstein, Gerald. 1989. Profit Squeeze, Rentier Squeeze and Macroeconomic Policy Under Fixed and Flexible Exchange Rates. Working Paper 1989–12. Department of Economics, University of Massachusetts Amherst.

Epstein, Gerald. 1992. Political Economy and Comparative Central Banking. *Review of Radical Political Economics* **24**(1): 1–30.

Epstein, Gerald and Juliet Schor. 1990. Corporate Profitability as a Determinant of Restrictive Monetary Policy: Estimates for the Postwar United States. In: Thomas Mayer (ed.), *The Political Economy of American Monetary Policy*. New York: Cambridge University Press, pp. 51–63.

Epstein, Gerald and Juliet Schor. 1992. Structural Determinants and Economic Effects of Capital Controls in OECD Countries. In: Tariq Banuri and Juliet B. Schor (eds), *Financial Openness and National Autonomy: Opportunities and Constraints*. Oxford: Clarendon Press, pp. 136–61.

Epstein, Gerald and Juliet Schor. 1995. The Federal Reserve–Treasury Accord and the Construction of the Postwar Monetary Regime in the United States. *Social Concept* **7**(1): 7–48.

Galbraith, James K. 1997. Time to Ditch the NAIRU. *Journal of Economic Perspectives* **11**(1): 93–108.

Gordon, David M., Richard Edwards, and Michael Reich. 1982. *Segmented Work, Divided Workers: The Historical Transformation of Labor in the United States*. New York: Cambridge University Press.

Greenspan, Alan. 2000. Structural Change in the New Economy. Speech at the National Governors' Association, 92nd Annual Meeting, State College, Pennsylvania, July 11.

Greider, William. 1987. *Secrets of the Temple: How the Federal Reserve Runs the Country*. New York: Simon and Schuster.

Marglin, Stephen A., and Juliet B. Schor. 1990. *The Golden Age of Capitalism: Reinterpreting the Postwar Experience*. Oxford: Clarendon Press.

Minsky, Hyman P. 1982. The Federal Reserve: Between a Rock and a Hard Place. In: *Can "It" Happen Again? Essays on Instability and Finance*. Armonk, New York: M.E. Sharpe, Inc, pp. 192–202.

Wolfson, Martin H. 1994. *Financial Crises: Understanding the Postwar U.S. Experience*. 2nd edn. Armonk, New York: M.E. Sharpe, Inc.

Wolfson, Martin H. 2003. Neoliberalism and the Social Structure of Accumulation. *Review of Radical Political Economics* **35**(3): 255–62.

Wolfson, Martin H. and David M. Kotz. 2010. A Re-conceptualization of Social Structure of Accumulation Theory. In: *Understanding Contemporary Capitalism: Social Structure of Accumulation Theory for the Twenty-First Century*. Cambridge, UK: Cambridge University Press, pp. 72–92.

5. Heterodox central bankers: Eccles, Prebisch and financial reform

Matías Vernengo and Esteban Pérez Caldentey*

INTRODUCTION

Central bankers have been defined as men that lend you an umbrella, and then want it back when it starts to rain. The Great Depression saw plenty of rain, so to speak, but some central bankers did not fit the stereotype. The reason is that the Great Depression led to a need to rethink the principles of central banking, as much as it led to the rethinking of economics in general, with the Keynesian Revolution at the forefront of the so-called "years of high theory," during which much of the rethinking was done (Shackle, 1967).

In the center the tenets of sound finance and the Gold Standard were threatened by the economic collapse, and the heightened social conflicts that followed rising unemployment. The conventional wisdom suggests that central bankers dismissed the so-called real bills doctrine, and developed an activist view of the central bank. In this view, the abandonment of the real bills doctrine allowed a more active control of money supply and credit. In contrast to that argument, we suggest that the role of the monetary authority as a fiscal agent of government and the abandonment of the view of the economy as self-regulated were the main changes in central banking. In addition, in the periphery, central banks changed to try to insulate the worst effects of balance of payments crises, and the use of capital controls became acceptable. Marriner S. Eccles in the United States, and Raúl Prebisch in Argentina, are paradigmatic examples of those new tendencies of central banking in the 1930s.

Heterodoxy in central banking was a feature of the times, and a direct response to the challenges wrought by the Great Depression. Central banks that had been the stalwart defenders of sound money, from at least the 1840s when the Currency School became dominant in the United Kingdom, were redesigned to stimulate, directly or indirectly, demand, and to maintain full employment. However, a neglected feature of the heterodoxy of central banking in the 1930s is the emphasis that was put on managing the conflict between debtors and creditors on the one hand, and the preoccupation with external shocks on the other, which came to be seen, among certain central bankers, as essential for demand management.

The remainder of this chapter is divided into five sections. The next section discusses the relevance of the abandonment of the real bills doctrine for the development of the new central banking practices during the 1930s. It is suggested that the abandonment of both the pre-Keynesian idea that the market was self-adjusting and the Gold Standard were more important than any particular position regarding the real bills doctrine. The two subsequent sessions discuss the main innovations in central banking during the 1930s taking the views of Eccles and Prebisch as paradigmatic of the new set of practices that came to dominate the period, which was referred to as "the decades of government control" by Charles Goodhart (2010). The fourth section describes the changes that occurred in Central Banking in Latin America in the 1940s and how Prebisch exported his Argentinean experience and views on Central Banking to the rest of the continent. The last section provides a few comments and draws some lessons for the current state of the art with respect to central banking.

The chapter is heavily influenced by Jane D'Arista's stance that to understand the challenges of economic policy in modern capitalist economies one must analyze the evolution of financial institutions.[1] Further, we believe that the interaction of ideas and policies shape the dynamic and shifting environment in which economic policy takes place. Last, but not least, we share with D'Arista the view that economic policies should be at the service of promoting a stable financial environment, and full employment.

RETHINKING CENTRAL BANKING IN THE 1930S

The real bills doctrine suggests that the central bank passively provides liquidity to the system.[2] The name of the doctrine results from the notion that banks only discount real bills, associated with the functioning of the economy, in particular for international trade that was essential in the 18th century when the doctrine was developed. In terms of central banking policy, the real bills doctrine fundamentally meant that there was no need to lean against the wind, and money supply should adjust to the needs of trade. It is generally presumed that in the 1930s a more activist position – leaning against the wind – was developed.

In particular, Meltzer (2003) seems to believe that the abandonment of the real bills doctrine was essential first for the collapse of the economy, which followed a great contraction of money supply, and then for the recovery from the Great Depression, since, in his view, the increase in money supply was the essential element in the recovery, rather than the New Deal policies.[3] This view, both of the recovery from the Depression and about central banking practices, has been generally accepted and is canonical among economists and policy makers.[4]

While it is true that some views within the Federal Reserve (Fed) in the 1930s, in particular those of Lauchlin Currie, were critical of the real bills doctrine, and believed that the collapse of money supply played an important role in causing the Great Depression (Sandilands, 1990), it is far from clear that this view dominated policy actions at the Fed.[5] The available evidence seems to indicate that the actions of the Federal Reserve Banks were rather guided by practical motives and different objectives. As an example, the rise in interest rates by some of the banks following the 1918 armistice in 1920 responded to inflation considerations while their subsequent decline was aimed at counteracting the 1921 recession.[6] At the same time, by 1921 Benjamin Strong was willing to actively use US monetary policy to support Europe's economic recovery efforts, underscoring the importance of international objectives and in some instances their preeminence over domestic ones.[7] While advocating the use of active monetary policy, Strong was also aware of the limitations of counter cyclicality as clearly expressed by his testimony in the Strong Bill Hearings (1926–27). The hearings were meant to clarify the relationship between Benjamin Strong's bank reserve stabilization policy (through open-market operations) with the price stability that characterized the US economy from 1922 to 1928. During the hearings Strong argued that the Federal Reserve Board should be credited with successfully administering credit to ensure price stability. However, he pointed out that: "In case there should be a gradual decline in prices, and if then business were unwilling to borrow, he doubted whether the system could do anything to raise the price level by forcing business men to use more credit" (Fisher, 1934, p. 165).[8]

The limits to monetary policy took a on a more central role within economic thinking in the 1930s and became by the middle of the decade the dominant view held at the Fed by the chairman Marriner S. Eccles, and also by Currie, a crucial advisor to Eccles on economic policy. Monetary policy was "like pushing on a string," and hence incapable of getting the economy out of the recession. Expansionary fiscal policy was then necessary to get out of the recession (Laidler and Sandilands, 2002; Vernengo, 2009).[9]

If the real bills doctrine was really abandoned, that should not be equated with an acceptance of the quantity theory of money, or the notion that money was exogenous, or more extremely an early version of monetarism.[10] At this point, it is important to understand a common misconception regarding the meaning and the role of the real bills doctrine in monetary policy.[11] The idea of money endogeneity, which is implicit in the real bills doctrine, does not per se suggest that the monetary shocks are irrelevant and money is not important. Further, and perhaps more importantly, the acceptance of the real bills doctrine, and of endogenous money, is sometimes held hand in hand with a view of the economic system as self-regulated in the direction of full employment. That was certainly the position that several post-Wicksellian and Austrian authors held in the 1930s.[12] But the view of a self-regulated market system is not equivalent to the real bills doctrine.

First, most authors that are critical of the real bills doctrine and suggest that it was central in causing the Great Depression argue that according to that doctrine monetary authorities cannot affect monetary equilibrium. Money supply being passive, in this view, is equated with an ineffective monetary authority, something that is seen as a quintessentially incorrect idea, and one that is behind the recessionary monetary contraction that caused the Depression. However, it is far from clear that the defenders of the real bills doctrine thought that the monetary authority was ineffective.[13] Their point seemed to be that printing money would not create an excess supply of money or per se activate the demand for credit. What this suggests is that the monetary authority might be incapable of getting the economy back on track in a downturn by changing the money supply exogenously. The easiness of credit is, in the real bills doctrine, measured by low interest rates rather than an expansionary monetary supply.[14]

Second, it is clear that at least some authors who defended the real bills doctrine did not believe that the system had a tendency towards full employment. The classical political economy authors, even when they accepted Say's Law, did not suppose that with price flexibility the system would move towards full utilization of resources. In other words, lower real wages or lower rates of interest would not lead to the functioning of the substitution principle and the increase in demand for the relatively cheap factor of production. Classical authors simply assumed that the level of output was given. Hence, classical authors that were anti-Bullionist, like Thomas Tooke, accepted the notion that the system could be stuck with significant amounts of idle resources.[15]

This is quite different from the so-called neo-Wicksellian model, which had a considerable following in the late 1920s and early 1930s, according to which money was endogenous, and the central bank set its interest rate on the basis of an unobservable natural rate of interest (Amadeo, 1989). Inflationary pressures were an indication of a bank rate that was too low with respect to the natural one, and vice versa in deflationary situations.[16] It is only in this case, when one has combined the idea of endogenous money, with the view that the system will mean revert, as a result of inflationary and deflationary forces, to full employment monetary equilibrium – to borrow the term used by Gunnar Myrdal about a situation in which the bank rate is equal to the natural rate – that one can suggest that real bills doctrine defenders would say that the central bank should do nothing beyond reducing the bank rate when deflationary pressures are present.[17]

However, during the 1930s the neo-Wicksellian model became increasingly less relevant after the onslaught of Keynesian ideas. The very idea that a natural rate regulated the equilibration of investment to the level of full employment savings was discarded. Contrary to the conventional view, the 1930s should not be seen as a decade in which central banks moved away from the real bills doctrine, a point that is considerably murkier and less clear than often suggested, but a decade in which they moved away from the neo-Wicksellian idea that the economic system is self-regulated towards full employment. The real bills doctrine would then only say that if central banks should contribute to reduce unemployment, they cannot do it by simply printing money to promote credit, since demand for credit depends on the needs of the real economy. But certainly that does not mean that central banks cannot do anything.

More importantly, the alleged vanquishing of the real bills doctrine for the understanding of the changes in central banking practices in the 1930s is the collapse of the Gold Standard, which gave an additional degree of freedom to central bankers, allowing the management of capital flows and a certain control over the evolution of the exchange rate. The rules of the game, as Keynes referred to the Gold Standard practices, implied that often interest rates had to be kept at very high levels to preclude capital flight, and in a situation in which price flexibility was incapable of producing a self-adjusting economy those rules might be the cause of permanent stagnation.

MARRINER ECCLES AND THE KEYNESIAN REVOLUTION

Marriner Stoddard Eccles (1892–1977) was a Republican banker in Ogden, Utah with a reputation for shrewd successful business experience and a few unusual ideas when he first went to work for the Treasury at the height of Franklin Delano Roosevelt's New Deal in 1934 (Hyman, 1976). He was subsequently appointed to the Federal Reserve and was influential in crafting the 1935 Banking Act, being appointed the first chairman of the board of governors, a newly created position that centralized power in Washington and away from the New York Fed (D'Arista, 1994).

Eccles's views on the Depression were developed fundamentally on the basis of his own experience as a businessman and banker, and were only to a lesser degree influenced by some underconsumptionist popular authors of the time (Vernengo, 2009). Eccles's views on the Great Depression tended to emphasize the role of underconsumption and unsustainable debt in promoting the collapse of the economy. He suggested to a gathering of the Utah State Bankers Convention in June 1932 that:

> The depression within our own country was primarily brought about by our capital accumulation getting out of balance in relationship to our consumption ability. [. . .] The difficulty is that we were not sufficiently extravagant as a nation. We did not consume what we were able to produce. (Marriner S. Eccles Papers, Box 72, Folder 2)

Also, he emphasized that international debt was an essential part of the Great Depression, for him "the matter of international debts is the commencement, I believe, of our problems," (ibid.) and he understood that a worldwide recovery was heavily dependent on a recovery in the United States. For him, "a revival in this country, a willingness to sit down and discuss world economy problems in the light of financial and business necessity would go a long way toward bringing the world out of this depression" (ibid.). Eccles was for the cancellation of inter-allied war debts, a debt jubilee so to speak, suggesting that an unpayable burden of debt would create a reduction in demand and perpetuate the depression.

In other words, the problems of what has been referred to as debt-deflation were very clear, and not just regarding international debt.[18] For that reason, Eccles was not only favorable to the New Deal programs to reduce the burden of debt on homeowner and farmer mortgages, but he was essential in the design of the new housing market, in particular the Federal Housing Authority (FHA), one of the key New Deal programs, with a particular preoccupation of making it easier for people to obtain loans to finance the construction of new residential and farm buildings. The plan proposed by Eccles was based on what most plans to deal with distressed debtors do, namely: it lowered interest rates and provided longer maturity. The plan also allowed for a higher percentage of the property value to be funded, increasing the number of families that would be able to come up with a down payment (Hyman, 1976).[19]

Furthermore, Eccles was clear that monetary policy was relatively inefficient as a way to get the economy out of a crisis when the rate of interest was close to zero and deflationary forces were persistent, and he famously popularized the expression that monetary policy in those particular circumstances was like "pushing on a string." During the hearings on the Banking Bill of 1935, in March of that year, he said:

> At the present time we are still in the depths of a depression and, beyond creating an easy money situation, there is very little, if anything, that the Reserve organization can do toward bringing about recovery. *One cannot push a string*. I believe, however, that if a condition of great business activity were developing to a point of credit inflation, monetary action could be very effective in curbing undue expansion. That would be pulling a string. (The Marriner S. Eccles Document Collection, FRASER Economic Library and Archives; Summary of Statements on the Banking Act of 1935, p. 17; emphasis added)

Monetary policy had asymmetric effects, being more effective as a tool for stopping a booming economy than for stimulating a sluggish one. This asymmetry did not mean that monetary policy became irrelevant, but the focus would have to be different since just increasing money supply would not stimulate credit. In Eccles' view:

> Every effort has been used to bring this about by the Reconstruction Finance Corporation and the Federal Reserve banks without result, demonstrating that extension of credit alone is not the solution. Credit is the secondary offensive when there is a basis of credit through the raising of the price level and an increase in the demand for goods requiring credit. Nor is the correction of our present difficulties to be found in a general scaling down of debts in an effort to bring them in relation to the present price levels. (The Marriner S. Eccles Document Collection, FRASER Economic Library and Archives; Testimony to Senate Finance Committee, February, 1933, p. 709)

Furthermore, Eccles thought that money supply was actually adequate even in the worst of the Depression, in part because the velocity of circulation could vary, and more importantly because the main problem was not the level, but the distribution of money supply. In his view:

> there is plenty of money today to bring about a restoration of prices, but the chief trouble is that it is in the wrong place; it is concentrated in the larger financial centers of the country, the creditor sections, leaving a great portion of the back country, or the debtor sections, drained dry. (The Marriner S. Eccles Document Collection, FRASER Economic Library and Archives; Testimony to Senate Finance Committee, February, 1933, p. 711)

Wall Street, so to speak, had plenty of money, but debtors were in a difficult position, and the solution depended on a rebalancing of debtor–creditor inequities.

That is why the solution was for government to spend money and provide debt relief for the unemployed. The increase in public debt would compensate the fall in private debt, caused by the negative effects of deflation on the net wealth of private agents. Further, Eccles argued that his program "can be financed in one of two ways – either through a Government bond issue, or through the issuance of currency by the Treasury which would be put into circulation through the Federal Reserve banks in payment of the projects proposed" (The Marriner S. Eccles Document Collection, FRASER Economic Library and Archives; Testimony to Senate Finance Committee, February, 1933, p. 720). Beyond increasing spending, Eccles favored increasing certain types of taxes (favoring higher income for the wealthy and inheritance taxes) that had a small impact on private spending.

Eccles did not suggest, however, that the Federal Reserve should necessarily finance government spending directly. His argument was that the Fed had a responsibility in:

> protecting the bond market from the pressure of new Government bond offerings at a time when it [was] desirable to preserve that market for the necessary Government financing required to meet its [. . .] operating deficit and provide for unemployment belief until the beneficial effects of the proposed emergency measures [were] realized. (Ibid., p. 722)

Monetary policy, during Eccles's tenure as chairman, was centered on the role of the Fed as fiscal agent of the government, maintaining a 2.5 percent interest on government bonds, and increasing the amount of bonds held by the banking sector, in particular the Fed. By the late 1930s, the Fed switched its portfolio to hold a greater amount of long-term bonds (7 years or more) instead of bills of shorter maturity (12 months or less).

Among other things that allowed the Fed to keep the rate of interest on long-term government bonds relatively low, which would become after the war and until the so-called Fed–Treasury Accord of 1951 an informal agreement with the Treasury to keep the rate within the 2.5 percent upper limit,[20] Eccles considered the role of the Federal Reserve as fiscal agent of the Treasury as the essential one, in a situation that only expansionary fiscal policy could turn the economy around.

Furthermore, it is important to note that Eccles's views were developed in an environment in which the idea that the economic system might be self-adjusting and government intervention would not be required had lost all intellectual currency. In fact, in his 1933 Senate Testimony, Eccles had called for a "national planning board, similar to the industries board during the war [World-War I], [that would be] necessary to the proper coordination of public and private activities of the economic world" (ibid., p. 731).

Eccles's views were in perfect harmony with the views of his advisors, in particular Currie. Currie's unpublished review of Keynes's *General Theory*, writing as an internal memo for the Board, was very perceptive and did not fall into the trap that many other early Keynesians fell – for example, Hicks and Modigliani, who were central in the development of the fix-price version of Keynesian ideas that would become known as the neoclassical synthesis – assuming that Keynes's main proposition rested on the notion of fixed wages. Currie clearly noted that "in a downturn wage reductions are likely to result in an expectation of further reductions, a fall in prices, a diminished prospective yield of new capital, and, hence, lessened investment and employment" (Marriner S. Eccles Papers, Box 111, Folder 1).

In addition, not only did Eccles believe that the economic system was not self-adjusting, but he did not seem to have completely discarded the real bills doctrine. In fact, according to Meltzer (2003, p. 470) Eccles "did not seem to share Currie's strong beliefs about the need to abandon the real bills doctrine [and] he preferred to rely on judgment and wanted a large measure of authority to do what he believed was in the public interest." In all likelihood, Eccles did not care much for the real bills doctrine, since he was fundamentally a pragmatic policy maker. But he did share the notion with endogenous money authors that credit conditions depended on the needs of the real economy. In this sense, the central change in the Fed policies during the 1930s was the increasing use of public debt to maintain low interest rates as a tool to support the fiscal expansion, within a broadly Keynesian view that the system could remain below full employment for a prolonged period.[21] The view that the Fed is responsible for the employment level and not just inflation, in the case of the United States, which was a legacy of the New Deal, has survived the onslaught of the era of the "triumph of markets," to use Goodhart's expression (2010), which has led in many other places to central banks concerned uniquely with inflation targeting.

RAÚL PREBISCH AND CENTRAL BANKING IN THE PERIPHERY[22]

Raúl Prebisch (1901–86) is mostly known for his long-run analysis and analysis of the development problems of Latin America, which he fully stated in "The Economic Development of Latin America and Some of its Principal Problems", (1949 [1950]), also known as his "Development Manifesto." Less well known is his role as the first general manager of the Central Bank of Argentina, an institution that was primarily designed by him (Dosman, 2008) and instituted coincidentally in 1935, the same year in which the Banking Act recreated the Fed in its modern guise.

The project for the bank was drafted by Prebisch himself in 1934 at the request of the minister of finance Federico Pinedo. It was conceived as an institution independent of the government ("It is not conceivable that a Central Bank be managed by governments"), permitting a more rational distribution of monetary functions and more efficient management of reserves, whose main objective was monetary stability along conventional lines. However, while it is true that by the mid 1930s Prebisch still believed that fiscal deficits could be inflationary, and that was an important reason for his defense of central bank independence, it is important to note that the design of the central bank was not particularly conventional. As noted by Dosman (2008, p. 98), Prebisch wanted to centralize several activities in the bank, including the management of the exchange control system, which allowed it to administer the exchange rate, to buy and sell bonds, regulate import controls and far-reaching regulatory powers, all in order not just to control inflation, but also manage the cycle.[23]

Contrary to the view of Prebisch as a conservative at the service of local elites and international financial interest, he seemed to be a pragmatic policy maker trying to manage the severe problems of the Great Depression in a peripheral country.[24] In other words, Prebisch saw monetary policy as an instrument to manage the cycle that was in the case of the periphery fundamentally associated to external shocks that affected the terms of trade, and the ability to import.

To this end, Prebisch thought that the Central Bank had a role to play in smoothing out the effects of the economic cycles although he found it illusory to think that it could offset the movements of the cycle. As he put it:

> To expect that undulatory movements in the economic activity of the country can be offset by the excellence of a monetary system would be to fall in the same illusion harbored by many economists of the United States with respect to the Federal Reserve, prior [. . .] to the [. . .] collapse. But it cannot be doubted that the amplitude of those movements could be cushioned by an efficiently run Central Bank. (Prebisch, 1991, Vol. II, p. 64)

It is important to understand that the cushioning of the fluctuations of the business cycle did not respond to the objective of maintaining domestic output stability but rather to that of maintaining the stability of prices and that of money. It is in this sense that the leaning against the wind monetary policy was, in essence, of an orthodox nature (see Prebisch, 1991, Vol. III, p. 90).

The leaning against the wind policy was reflected in one of the key objectives of the Central Bank, as set out in Prebisch's 1934 project: to ensure an adequate level of reserve accumulation as a precautionary motive of building buffer stocks to confront export shocks and sudden capital stops. As Prebisch put it: "The ascending movements are, in general, of a limited duration. The opportunity to repair the consequences of past wrongs and accumulate reserves for difficult times, whose return it is prudent to foresee, should not be then undermined" (Prebisch, 1991, Vol. II, p. 610–11).

As such, the first article of project proposal for the creation of a Central Bank in Argentina dealing with its functions stated: "The Bank will have as objective: a) The concentration of sufficient reserves to moderate the consequences of fluctuations in exports and the investments of foreign capital, on money, credit, commercial activities, in order to maintain the value of money" (ibid., p. 383).[25]

Following the creation of the Central Bank, the Argentine economy experienced expansion in economic activity lasting until 1937. During this time the Central Bank, in line with the orthodox spirit of its creation, used open-market operations, interventions in the foreign exchange market and moral suasion to avoid overexpansion and overheating of the economy (see ibid., pp. 64, 359, 610–22; Prebisch, 1991, Vol. III, pp. 88–119).

However, the force of events prompted by the beginning of the downward phase of the cycle in 1937 led the bank to progressively evolve into a less orthodox institution whose goal became more ambitious than just "cushioning" the phases of the business cycle to ensure their orderly occurrence and maintain the stability of money, something not completely dissimilar to the effects of the 1937 recession on the policies of the Roosevelt administration. The Central Bank of Argentina became aware that it had a double objective, price and output stability, and that the balance of payments was central for both.[26]

Initially in 1937, "the Central Bank [. . .] was predisposed to consider this contraction of domestic economic activity as a logical and natural event, indispensable to reduce imports and establish the equilibrium in the balance of payments" (Prebisch, 1991, Vol. III, pp. 101–2). Yet, as the contractionary effects wreaked havoc, the Central Bank decided to change and stabilize domestic activity. According to the 1938 Central Bank Report:

> Monetary policy can propose two objectives in the face of the economic cycle. The first consists in avoiding that the expansion of credit accentuates the intensity of the wave motion [. . .] The second objective goes further. It is not limited to avoid the aggravation of these fluctuations, but it intends, furthermore, to limit its amplitude and reduce the intensity of the variation of purchasing power during the cycle, in order to attenuate the consequences of its variations on the volume of domestic economic activity. (Prebisch, 1991, Vol. III, p. 104)

The need for countercyclical action resurfaced soon after the beginning of World War II, as Argentina was faced with a growing external imbalance, and the "perception of decline in business activity and in particular in the construction sector" leading to a fear of general economic stagnation (Prebisch, 1993, p. 156–7). The plan for countercyclical action (The Plan for National Reactivation) contemplated an expansionary monetary policy coupled with exchange rate controls, but it also for the first time developed the idea that industrialization was the key to a new development strategy for Argentina. More specifically, the plan sought to purchase agricultural surpluses to avoid price declines, increase construction activity and promote the finance of industrial development. It would have also created an industrial development bank, to promote the development of long-term capital markets, with the intention of stimulating industrial exports, to reduce balance of payments problems.

The plan was designed by Prebisch, but became known as the Pinedo Plan, as Pinedo had been reappointed briefly as finance minister, and included elements that would become associated with the economic policies of the Peronist government in subsequent years (Llach, 1984). However, Pinedo was dismissed and the plan floundered, which shows that the Argentine authorities of the time remained appreciably fond of orthodox economic thinking.

The Pinedo Plan was never approved. The force of events superseded it; in particular, the war effort of the United States, which led to an increase in internal demand and imports. As put by Prebisch: "The United States, which in 1940 had been absent in the market of certain Argentine products, starts to purchase very actively. This soothes our balance of payments concerns, allows a more flexible distribution of foreign exchange, increases domestic purchasing power and rapidly changes the context of the situation" (1993, p. 160).

The change in external conditions led to the suppression of import permits and the flexibilization of the exchange rate regime, even though a dual exchange rate remained in place. It is also important to note that in 1943 the central bank re-imposed exchange controls to deter the inflow of short-term capital and avoid its destabilizing effects and to stimulate foreign direct investment inflows instead. While this measure was in force only for three months, it is worth quoting Prebisch at length due to its current relevance:

> This capital [short-term capital] went to further inflate the categories of goods or assets that were already inflated, and did not translate, except in very rare occasions, in a real increase in the production of the country [. . .] the measures adopted by the government permit to make an exception, to allow the inflow of these capitals if it is shown that these are oriented towards the increase in real production. (Prebisch, 1993, p. 183)[27]

Prebisch viewed the change in external conditions after the start of World War II and its effects on Argentina as a validation of his business cycle approach. The business cycle and its phases were a recurrent and natural phenomenon. The phases were related and the more exaggerated the boom (expansionary) phase, the sharper the contraction. The change from boom (expansionary) to bust (contractionary) conditions occurred rapidly and unpredictably requiring flexibility in economic policy and more importantly moderation and prudence, and an active policy of neutralization.[28]

While Prebisch did recommend avoiding excessive fiscal spending and lax monetary policies, and increased savings during the boom (expansion) to face and weather the inevitable following contraction, he argued that a country like Argentina should not be forced to forego higher growth and improved material well-being during the upward phase of the cycle, only to face to consequences of a downturn.

Prebisch ultimately recommended shielding the domestic economy from the ups and downs by a process of substitution of domestic industry and production for foreign imports. This was a basis for arguing for the promotion and development of domestic industry and the expansion of internal activity.

These ideas were already embedded in Prebisch's book proposal, *Money and Economic Activity*, on which he began work in 1943, the year in which, as a result of a military coup marking the eventual ascendancy of Peronism, Prebisch lost his position in the administration, including his Central Bank appointment, that had been essential for the development of his ideas since the early 1930s.

In *Money and Economic Activity*, he argued that monetary and financial policy should have three main aims: (i) attenuate the incidences of the abrupt changes in harvest conditions and the fluctuations and external contingencies; (ii) create the monetary conditions that stimulate the development and maintenance of full employment of the working force; (iii) foster and support the highest possible rate of growth of economic activity.[29]

The successful achievement of these policies required an imports policy and fiscal reform. Thc imports policy consisted in the "rational modification of their composition to serve certain objectives rather than their systematic restrictions." Prebisch thought that a policy of autarky was as absurd as a policy of free trade and agreed that Argentina should participate to the extent of the possible in the international economy but to avoid a "constant subordination of the national economy to external movements and contingencies," the country needed to "develop inwardly, strengthening its internal structure and achieve an autonomous functioning of its economy." Prebisch's defense of national policy autonomy eventually took on a regional tone, as he became convinced that the Argentinean cycle and its features were not specific to Argentina but that they were rather the manifestations and characteristics of the workings of a global process, a universal cycle. In this sense, Prebisch argued that the Argentine cycle was a mirror, a reflection, of external of the international monetary cycle.

The global or universal cycle was triggered by developed countries and more specifically by what Prebisch termed to be the cyclical center. The cyclical center referred to the country (perhaps group of countries) whose economic repercussions due to its importance were transmitted to the rest of the world. In the 19th century and up until World War I, Great Britain held the cyclical center title only for it to be taken by the United States thereafter. The countries subject to the influence of the impulses of the center, the periphery, included all Latin American countries.

The universal or global cycle was thus divided into two phases with different characteristics, one affecting the center and the other the periphery. Moreover, since the periphery faced a binding external constraint while the center did not, it faced markedly different restrictions in the use of domestic policy space.

Faced with a contraction of economic activity and price declines the cyclical center could always resort to the use of monetary instruments, such as the money supply or interest rates, without regard for exchange rate parity or international reserve adequacy conditions. Contrarily, the periphery, bereft of the use of this privilege by the binding character of its external constraint, had to turn to the use of exchange rate variations or quantitative restrictions and controls (Prebisch, 1993, pp. 225–6).

Prebisch also contemplated a policy of reserve accumulation by the countries of the periphery. In fact he argued, very much in line with his earlier views, that the countries of the periphery had the responsibility to generate the financial resources during the upward phase of the cycle (including international reserves) to face and weather contractions (Prebisch, 1993, p. 232).

PREBISCH AND HETERODOX CENTRAL BANKING REFORM IN LATIN AMERICA

Following his termination at the Central Bank in 1943 and until 1948, Prebisch used his acquired policy experience to participate, assist, and promote banking reforms in Latin America.[30] He was instrumental in the reform process of the Central Banks and banking system of the Dominican Republic (1946), Guatemala (1945), Paraguay (1943–44) and Venezuela (1948).[31]

Prebsich's involvement benefitted to a great extent from the change in United States–Latin America relations that took place in the 1930s and 1940s. Under the leadership of F.D. Roosevelt, the United States began a Good Neighbor policy towards Latin America based upon non-intervention and non-interference with its domestic affairs. This policy evolved into one of active financial and economic cooperation. It included the support of trade expansion and development projects through loans from the Export–Import Bank and the Exchange Stabilization Fund; the compensation for the loss of European markets after the war through a series of financial schemes including the stabilization of commodity prices. Finally, the United States announced the creation of a publicly controlled Inter-American Bank to provide balance of payment support and long-term development finance (Helleiner, 2009).

As part of this overall policy, the United States embarked on providing technical assistance, which was provided in monetary matters at the request of Latin American governments. The first mission took place in Cuba in 1942, the goal to provide assistance in the establishment of a central bank. Cuba wanted its central bank to have a broad mandate including lending to the government, acting as a lender of last resort, and carrying out monetary policy to fulfill domestic development goals. Thereafter, under the lead of Robert Triffin, the United States provided technical assistance to the Central Bank of Paraguay, among others. Triffin, who had met Prebisch in Mexico, invited him to join the mission.

Triffin shared similar views to those of Prebisch on the role of central banks. Both men understood that the functions of a central bank were not only limited to maintaining nominal stability, reacting to external shocks, and balancing of payment difficulties. Central banks also had to follow a countercyclical stance and promote domestic objectives including growth and employment. Triffin was in favor of economic planning, a managed economy, infant industry protectionism, and was also sympathetic to state-guided industrialization.

In the Monetary and Banking Reform Reform in Paraguay (1947a, p. 72), Triffin made his point as follows:

> The Bank of Paraguay is authorized to carry out every type of banking operation [. . .] It possesses broad powers of monetary regulation, almost without precedent. The monetary issue is not regulated by rigid provisions linking it to gold or foreign exchange reserves, nor are there inflexible limitations upon the granting of credit to the State [. . .] the law departs form the traditional concepts which [. . .] have dominated the orthodox theory and practice of central banking [. . .] From their very initiation, many of the central banks established on this continent [. . .] suffered from a servile imitation of the monetary and banking regimes of the great financial centers of the world and from a consequent lack of adaptation to the economies they were to serve.

The main objective of the Bank of Paraguay involved not only the "creation of maintainance of a monetary and financial structure most favorable to the orderly development of the national economy," but also the adaptation of the means of payment and credit policy to the development of productive activities in line with the real bills doctrine discussed in the first section of this chapter.[32] The Central Bank of the Dominican Republic had a similar purpose in stimulating the development of the economy (see Wallich and Triffin, 1953).

The central bank of Paraguay, as in the case of the Dominican Republic, had a definite countercyclical objective illustrated by its mandate to accumulate international reserves as a precautionary balance of payments measure. Also in the case of the Paraguay Central Bank, regulation contemplated the intervention and regulation of "abnormal movements of capital" in order to prevent unwarranted disturbances in the domestic economy. For its own part, the Dominican Republic Central Bank Law postulated the use of anticyclical policy of credit stimulation through rediscounts and advances.

As part of monetary management Triffin proposed that central banks concentrate all banking activities of the state, including medium and long-term lending to agriculture and industry. In the particular case of the Dominican Republic, the central bank also had the role of allocating credit through a government development bank (Banco Agrícola e Hipotecario; Article 4a) 3) Central Bank Law [see Prebisch, 1991, p. 8]).

Finally, crucial to the whole central bank reform project was a framework for exchange controls. In general terms Triffin viewed exchange controls as nondiscriminatory "consisting in in an official exchange rate and a free, auction price of foreign currencies"; the former would be stable, the latter would fluctuate according to fluctuations in demand and supply. The low official rate would apply to: "easily controllable exports" (which the author thinks would be the overwhelmingly larger part of all exports); certain categories of "necessary or essential" imports; and approved capital exports. The higher auction rate would apply to other imports, to uncontrollable exports and other exchange proceeds of "unimportant or practically uncontrollable transactions" (Harbeler, 1947).

Triffin's ideas were partly influenced by Prebisch's own experience, as Triffin himself recognized. In particular in the case of Paraguay, Prebisch was instrumental in the design of "exchange controls."[33]

By the time Prebisch had ended his Latin American Central Banking period, he assigned a greater role to monetary policy in maintaining growth and employment. Indeed, in 1948, a year prior to his joining of the United Nations Economic Commission for Latin America and the Caribbean (ECLAC), Prebisch argued that a central bank should give hierarchical priority to the objective of maintaining stable growth consistent with the maximum possible employment of productive factors. This was the most important objective of monetary policy, an overarching objective which subsumed responding to external shocks, the accumulation of reserves for precautionary motives, and the lender of last resort functions (Prebisch, 1993, p. 376).

CONCLUDING REMARKS

The 1930s saw the collapse of the Gold Standard, and the slow transition from the British-centered international division of labor to the more complex arrangements of the Cold War era. Central banks, as almost all institutions of the period, went through significant changes. The Victorian dreams of a self-adjusting economy with a tendency to full employment and an orderly division of labor, where the periphery only produced commodities and imported manufactured goods, were utterly shattered by the harsh realities of the Great Depression.

In the United States, the Fed was re-organized by two banking acts and the dominant personality of Marriner S. Eccles, a Western banker in a progressive administration, who considered the role of the Federal Reserve as fiscal agent of the Treasury as the essential one, in a situation that only expansionary fiscal policy could turn the economy around, shaped the organization of the new monetary authority. In Argentina, Raúl Prebisch, a very young policy maker in a conservative government, designed the new central bank, with the view that an independent central bank could minimize the effects of external crises and smooth out the cycle, in particular. Both were more than willing to allow a more depreciated currency and the abandonment of the Gold Standard, but more importantly they both moved to an understanding that the central bank had an important role if the economy did not move automatically to full employment.

In other words, by the mid to late 1930s both Eccles and Prebisch did not consider that the only role of the central bank was to control inflation, even though they remained concerned about inflation. They envisioned an important role for the central bank in the creation and maintenance of full employment conditions, in the center, or higher growth rates, in the periphery. The embrace of this quintessential Keynesian understanding of the role of central banks was one of the most revolutionary aspects of the institutional transformations of the 1930s. In the following decade Prebisch went further and argued that the primary role of a central bank was to maintain a growth path consistent with the full utilization of resources.

This particular development of the 1930s was completely reversed with the combined effects of the Monetarist and New Classical counter-revolutions and the Great Inflation of the 1970s, and coalesced in a policy framework known as flexible inflation targeting. In a recent study by the

Committee on International Economic Policy and Reform (Eichengreen et al., 2011, p. 1) it is argued that the basic tenets of the framework developed remain "uncontroversial." Among those tenets are the ideas that there is "no permanent tradeoff between inflation and unemployment" and that central banks should aim "to stabilize inflation around its target but also minimize the output gap" (ibid.). In other words, the pre-Keynesian (or post-Wicksellian) ideas that predominated before the revision of central banking practices in the 1930s are back, and in spite of the current global financial crisis they remain very much in place.

NOTES

* The opinions here expressed are the authors' own and not necessarily those of the institutions with which they are affiliated. A preliminary version of this chapter was presented in May 2008 at the Political Economy Research Institute (PERI), University of Massachusetts Amherst, and at the European Society for the History of Economic Thought (ESHET) in November 2012 in Buenos Aires. We thank, without implicating, comments by conference participants, in particular Ivo Maes. We are grateful to Jane D'Arista for insightful and very valuable comments to an earlier version of the paper.

1. For a discussion of the importance of the evolution of the banking sector and how it affected financing practices and the process of growth and development over time, see Chick (1986).
2. The real bills doctrine (RBD) argues that money (bank notes) is "lent in exchange for title to real values or values in the process of creation." Hence, money cannot be issued in excess (that is, there cannot be an excess supply of money). Bank notes in excess of "real value" return to the issuer rather than inflate their nominal values. Adam Smith was an early proponent of the RBD. For a discussion of the RBD see Green (1987). For a discussion of Smith's views on monetary and banking principles see Laidler (1981).
3. Friedman and Schwartz (1963) is the *locus classicus* of the monetarist view of the Great Depression. For a recent view that suggests the RBD rather than Gold Standard is behind the Great Contraction, see Timberlake (2008). For Timberlake, the RBD has "bright" and "dark" sides. The bright side is the discounting of bills (or the issue of bank notes) for title to real value or value in the process of creation and conforms according to Timberlake to the "form and method of the gold standard" (ibid., p.305). The bright side is represented by Benjamin Strong, president of the Federal Reserve Bank of New York from 1914 until his death in 1928, whose policies, while conforming to the RBD, maintained a high degree of nominal stability from 1922 to 1928. The dark side of the RBD is the "condemnation of all monetary instruments used 'to support' bubbles," and in general, money and stock market exuberances. The dark side of the RBD is embodied by Adolph Miller, who replaced Strong as president of the Federal Reserve System and who managed to impose his views on monetary contraction as an antidote to stop stock market speculation.
4. For a critique of the conventional view about the role of the New Deal see Hannsgen and Papadimitriou (2009).
5. From a mainstream view, the Federal Reserve System (1913) and "monetary-institutional structure" of the United States reveals the contradictory influence of the RBD, but also that of the Gold Standard and the granting of "ample" discretion to the respective governors (Mints, 1950). See also Hester, 2008.
6. The Federal Reserve Bank of New York raised its discount rate by 244 basis points in 1920. Production levels declined by 35 percent in 1921 (Kuehn, 2012).

7. In 1920 the League of Nations endorsed the Ter Meulen Plan, which consisted of using government bonds as a guarantee for private credits for the financing of Europe's recovery. Strong suggested the participation of American financiers with the support of an active policy on the part of the US government. Strong's support of Europe earned him the enmity of Herbert Hoover who accused him of being a "mental annex to Europe," blaming him in part for the Great Depression. See Roberts (2000). Strong played an instrumental role in the restoration of the pound to a 4.86 par with gold, a key objective of England's central banker Montagu Norman. See Moggridge (1972) and Ahamed (2009).
8. Strong is often portrayed as an RBD proponent, a monetary policy activist and Gold Standard adherent, all at the same time (Roberts 2000; Timberlake, 2009). Hetzel (2008) argues that by 1923, Strong realized the invalidity of the RBD and began using open-market operations.
9. Laidler and Sandilands (2002) show how, in an early 1932 memorandum of three Harvard scholars, including Currie and Harry Dexter White, some non-Chicago economists were for both monetary and fiscal expansionary policies as a way out of the Depression. The Chicago memorandum also prioritized counter-cyclical fiscal policy. Prior to that, Senator Robert Wagner of New York introduced a bill for an Employment Stabilization Board that was supported by several economists including F. Knight, Sumner Slichter and Frank Taussig. For the differences between later Keynesian ideas and the Chicago Tradition that emphasized fiscal activism in the short run see Pérez Caldentey (2003).
10. Calomiris (2010) believes that the RBD was central in causing the Depression, but argues that the regulatory changes of the 1930s were designed to preserve it. In that case, it would be hard to argue that the Fed abandoned the RBD in the 1930s.
11. This is obviously not a new phenomenon. See, for example, Laidler (1984) for a harsh critique of the misuse of the real bills doctrine in modern discussions. Certainly the views arguing that the RBD involved a monetary contraction in order to stop speculation as sustained by Timberlake (see footnote 3 above) are, from our point of view, mistaken.
12. Some of the same issues of the confusion about the role of the RBD take place when discussing the role of the quantity theory in this same period, as in the famous debate between Milton Friedman and Don Patinkin on the so-called Chicago Tradition. Those confusions are the mirror ones, in a sense, of those related to the "Real Bills Tradition." For a recent take on the Chicago Tradition see Laidler and Sandilands (2010).
13. For example, Thomas Tooke, one of the main authors of the Banking School and a defender of the real bills doctrine, believed that interest rates, determined by the central bank, entered the cost of production, and, as a result, of this direct relation between interest rates and prices, central banks could be quite influential. See Pivetti (1998) and Smith (2008) for an analysis of Tooke's views and some of its implications.
14. And, as a matter of fact, short-term nominal interest rates were reduced immediately after the 1929 crisis. Of course, deflation, and the zero-bound limit to nominal rates, implied that real rates were relatively high.
15. The same can be said, inter alia, of other classical authors like Adam Smith, Henry Thornton and Karl Marx. For a discussion of classical views on money and output see Green (1992).
16. Neo-Wicksellian ideas were popular with: Cambridge economists like Dennis Robertson and Keynes in his *Treatise on Money*; Ralph Hawtrey, a Treasury man with Cambridge connections; Austrians like Friedrich Hayek. The neo-Wicksellian model has become popular again, as in the Taylor Rule, with the so-called new neoclassical synthesis. See Goodfriend and King (1997).
17. Charles Goodhart (2010, p. 2), in his otherwise excellent review of the different eras of central banking, confuses the RBD with the notion that the system is self-adjusting. He says: "The real bills doctrine is wrong [. . .] it assumes implicitly that the private sector is inherently self-stabilizing."

18. This understanding of the problems of debt deflation are made clear in a radio address in response to Senator Byrd in 1939: "From 1929 to 1935, total debts, both public and private, contracted by 14 percent. Yet at the same time national income fell by more than 50 percent. As a result, the private debt structure, even though contracted, was so large in relation to the diminished national income that debts became insupportable. Hence, our entire financial structure collapsed and general economic paralysis resulted" (The Marriner S. Eccles Document Collection, FRASER, Economic Library and Archives; Radio Address, 1939, p. 6). Further, Eccles knew that private debt was riskier than public debt, and that excessive private debt could lead to bankruptcy. Only public debt was free of default risk. In his words: "Individuals and corporations may become bankrupt, but no nation, having the human and material resources of the United States, need impoverish itself by borrowing from itself. The only way that we can impoverish ourselves is by failing to utilize our idle man power, resources, productive facilities and money in the production of real wealth" (ibid., p. 11).
19. Refinancing farm mortgages on a long-term basis at a low rate of interest was number four of Eccles's five-point program to recover from the Depression, which he presented in his testimony to the Senate Finance Committee in February, 1933. Eccles's program consisted of: increasing transfers to states; increasing federal government spending; implementing a program to control production and raise agricultural prices; refinancing mortgages on a long-term basis at low rates of interest; and bringing about a permanent settlement of inter-allied debts by promoting cancellation of debts (Vernengo, 2009). To achieve these goals, Eccles favored a unification and centralization of the banking system, which would take place with the 1935 Bank Act, high income and inheritance taxes, national child labor and minimum wage laws, and, finally, unemployment insurance and old age pension laws, which were enacted with the Wagner and Social Security Acts.
20. For a discussion of the meaning of the pre- and post-Accord policies and their meaning from the point of view of the political economy of debtor–creditor conflict, see Epstein and Schor (1995).
21. The resemblance of these policies with the quantitative easing (QE) policies pursued by the Fed after the Great Recession of 2007 is inescapable. For a description of the circumstances that require QE, see Bernanke and Reinhart (2004).
22. All the English translations of Prebisch's Works (Vols I to IV) are by the authors of this chapter.
23. Prebisch would emphasize that his views differed from the British advisor Otto Niemeyer, the British Treasury expert who provided advice to the Argentine government on the role the bank should play. Prebisch's views were more akin to John H. Williams, a Harvard professor influential in Eccles's Fed, who could understand the limitations under which the Argentine economy was operating, and the need for capital controls (Dosman, 2008, p. 122). It is worth noting that Prebisch translated one of Williams's books.
24. It is important to note that while Prebisch was developing Keynesian ideas adapted to the particular circumstances of peripheral countries, as a result of his participation in the conservative governments of the 1930s, his dismissal from the central bank by the government of the 1943 military coup, and his troubled relation with the Peronist government (1946–55), he would not be seen as particularly Keynesian or progressive, and his policy advice would be seen as contradictory to his international policy positions. Arturo Jauretche (1955), one of the organic intellectuals of the nationalist and popular left connected to Peronism, provides a scathing critique of Prebisch's economic plan for Argentina after the 1955 military coup. See Sikkink (1988).
25. In *International Currency Experience* (1944, pp. 85 and 194), Nurkse thought highly successful the policy of neutralization, mainly international reserve accumulation, pursued by the Central Bank of Argentina. Triffin also entertained a similar opinion praising non-orthodox instruments such as foreign exchange controls. Following a similar line of thought, in 1945 Prebisch helped to draft the legislation for the newly created Central

Bank of Paraguay and the reform to the existing system of foreign exchange controls. See also Helleiner (2009).

26. Prebisch had developed a theory of the foreign trade multiplier, which he saw as being in some respects similar to Keynes's analysis. Around 1935, Prebisch introduced the concept of the "coefficient of expansion" (Prebisch, 1991, Vol. III, pp. 249–98; 301–10; 335–42; 349–70). It measured the intensity with which an increment in income, resulting from a given increase in exports or financial flows, produced an expansion of greater amplitude in domestic economic activity. For further discussion see Pérez Caldentey and Vernengo (2011).
27. Nowadays, in Latin America and elsewhere, proponents of capital controls base their case precisely on the argument put forward by Prebisch, that is, the change in the composition of financial inflows from short-term to long-term investment.
28. As he explains: "We are exposed, in our country, to rapid and unpredictable changes in the economic situation. We pass in a few months of transition from a moment of somber perspectives, such as in 1940, to the opposite situation [. . .] It suffices to reflect on what would have happened if the plan for construction [under the National Plan for Reactivation] would have been launched and to the resulting purchasing power would have been added a new purchasing power derived from the increase in exports: circulation would have expanded in an exaggerated manner, with the pernicious consequence that always follow" (Prebisch, 1993, p. 160).
29. Note that contrary to mainstream theory and practice on inflation, a low and stable rate of inflation is not included as part of the aims of monetary policy. Nonetheless, maintaining full employment and the highest possible rate of growth of output does inevitably lead to situations of inflation and output trade-offs. Throughout the period covered in this chapter, Prebisch never abandoned the orthodox belief that inflation is the product of fiscal deficits. See Prebisch, 1993, p. 229.
30. Following his demise from the Central Bank in 1943 and until his ECLA appointment, he remained committed to teaching and was also an international consultant. According to him, he began at this time to re-think his past experiences and develop his periphery–center and development theories.
31. The particular examples in this section draw on the Paraguay and Dominican Republic cases.
32. See Article 3 and 4 of the Decree-Law No. 5130 (September 1944) which created and organized the Bank of Paraguay.
33. According to Helleiner (2009, p. 18): "Triffin frequently cited his debt to Prebisch's 'pioneering work' in his publications." Triffin thought that Prebisch's proposal on exchange controls was novel and interesting and of great value to the Federal Reserve mission in Paraguay. Haberler (1947) argued that Triffin's exchange control proposal wasn't an "exchange control" but rather a "temporary currency depreciation." He attributes the invention of non-discriminatory exchange control to Prebisch. See also Triffin (1947b).

REFERENCES

Ahamed, Liaquat (2009), *Lords of Finance: The Bankers Who Broke the World*, New York: Penguin.

Amadeo, Edward (1989), *Keynes's Principle of Effective Demand*, Aldershot, UK and Brookfield, VT, USA: Edward Elgar.

Bernanke, Ben, and Vincent Reinhart (2004), "Conducting Monetary Policy at Very Low Short-Term Interest Rates," *American Economic Review*, **94** (2), 85–90.

Calomiris, C. (2010), "The Political Lessons of Depression-era banking reform," *Oxford Review of Economic Policy*, **26** (3), 540–60.

Chick, Victoria (1986), "The Evolution of the Banking System and the Theory of Saving, Investment and Interest," in Philip Arestis and Sheila C. Dow (eds), *On Money, Method and Keynes: Selected Essays by Victoria Chick*, Basingstoke, UK: Palgrave Macmillan.
D'Arista, Jane (1994), *The Evolution of U.S. Finance: Federal Reserve Monetary Policy, 1915–1935*, Armonk, NY: M.E. Sharpe.
Dosman, Edgar (2008), *The Life and Times of Raul Prebisch, 1901–1986*, London: McGill-Queen's University Press.
Eccles, Marriner S. (1890–1977), *The Papers of Marriner S. Eccles*, Special Collections Department, University of Utah Libraries, Salt Lake City, UT.
Eichengreen, B., M. El-Erian, A. Fraga, T. Ito, J. Pisani-Ferry, E. Prasad, R. Rajan, M. Ramos, C. Reinhart, H. Rey, D. Rodrik, K. Rogoff, H.-S. Shin, A. Velasco, B. Weder di Mauro and Y. Yu (2011), "Rethinking Central Banking," Committee for International Economic Policy and Reform (CIEPR) and Brookings Institution, Washington, D.C.
Epstein, Gerald and Juliet Schor (1995), "The Federal Reserve–Treasury Accord and the Construction of the Post-War Monetary Regime in the United States," *Social Concept*, **7** (1), 7–48.
Fisher, Irving (1934), *Stable Money*, New York: Adelphi Company.
Friedman, Milton and Anna Schwartz (1963), *A Monetary History of the United States, 1867–1960*, Princeton, NJ: Princeton University Press.
Goodfriend, Marvin, and Robert King (1997), "The New Neoclassical Synthesis and the Role of Monetary Policy," *NBER Macroeconomics Annual*, **12**, 231–83.
Goodhart, Charles (2010), "The Changing Role of Central Banks," Bank of International Settlements, Working Paper No. 326.
Green, Roy (1992), *Classical Theories of Money, Output and Inflation*, London: St. Martin's Press.
Green, Roy (1997), "Real Bills Doctrine," in John Eatwell, Murray Milgate and Peter Newman (eds), *The New Palgrave Dictionary of Money and Finance*, New York: Macmillan.
Haberler, Gottfried (1947), "Comments on National Central Banking and the International Economy," in Board of Governors of the Federal Reserve System (U.S.), Haberler, Gottfried, Metzler, Lloyd A. and Triffin, Robert, *Postwar Economic Studies No. 7 – International Monetary Policies*, Washington D.C., pp. 82–99.
Hannsgen, Greg and Papadimitriou, Dimitri (2009), "Fiscal Stimulus, Job Creation and the Economy: What are the Lessons of the New Deal?", Levy Economics Institute Policy Note no. 2009/10.
Helleiner, Eric (2009), "Central Bankers as Good Neighbours: US Money Doctors in Latin America During the 1940s," *Financial History Review*, **16** (1), 5–25.
Hester, Donald, D. (2008), "Federal Reserve System," in Steven N. Durlauf and Lawrence E. Blume (eds), *The New Palgrave Economics Collection*, New York: Palgrave Macmillan.
Hetzler, Robert (2008), *The Monetary Policy of the Federal Reserve: A History*, Cambridge: Cambridge University Press.
Hyman, Sidney (1976), *Marriner S. Eccles: Private Entrepreneur and Public Servant*, Stanford, CA: Stanford University Graduate School of Business.
Kuehn, Daniel (2012), "A Note on America's 1920–21 Depression as an Argument for Austerity," *Cambridge Journal of Economics*, **36** (1), 15–60.

Laidler, David (1984), "Misconceptions About the Real Bills Doctrine: A Comment on Sargent and Wallace," *Journal of Political Economy*, **92** (1), 149–55.
Laidler, David and Sandilands, Roger (2002), "An Early Harvard Memorandum on Anti-Depression Policies: An Introductory Note," *History of Political Economy*, **34** (3), 515–52.
Laidler, David and Sandilands, Roger (2010), "Harvard, the Chicago Tradition, and the Quantity Theory: A Reply to James Ahiakpor," *History of Political Economy*, **42** (3), 573–92.
Llach, Juan José (1984), "El Plan Pinedo de 1940, su significado histórico, y los orígenes de la economía política del Peronismo," *Desarrollo Económico*, **23**, 515–58.
Meltzer, Allan (2003), *A History of the Federal Reserve, 1913–1951*, Volume I, Chicago: University of Chicago Press.
Mints, Loyd W. (1950), *Monetary Policy for a Competitive Society*, New York: McGraw-Hill.
Moggridge, Donald E. (1972), *British Monetary Policy, 1924–1931: The Norman Conquest of $4.86*, Cambridge: Cambridge University Press.
Nurkse, Ragnar (1944), *International Currency Experience: Lessons of the Inter-War Period*, Geneva: League of Nations.
Pérez Caldentey, Esteban (2003), "Chicago, Keynes and Fiscal Policy," *Investigación Económica*, **LXII**, 15–45.
Pérez Caldentey, Esteban and Matías Vernengo (2011), "Understanding the Business Cycle in Latin America: Prebisch's contributions," *serie Estudios y perspectivas*, N° 127 (LC/MEX/L.1011), México, D.F., Sede Subregional de la CEPAL en México. Publicación de las Naciones Unidas, N° de venta: E.11.II.G.51.
Pivetti, Massimo (1998), "Thomas Tooke and the Influence of the Rate of Interest on Prices: Implications for Distribution," *Contributions to Political Economy*, **17**, 389–52.
Prebisch, Raúl (1943), *La moneda y el ritmo de la actividad económica*, Inédito.
Prebisch, Raúl (1991), *Obras 1919–1948*, Volumes 1 to 3, Buenos Aires: Fundación Raúl Prebisch.
Prebisch, Raúl (1993), *Obras 1919–1949*, Volume 4, Buenos Aires: Fundación Raúl Prebisch.
Roberts, Priscilla (2000), "Benjamin Strong, the Federal Reserve, and the Limits to Interwar American Nationalism," *Federal Bank of Richmond Economic Quarterly*, **86** (2), 61–98.
Sandilands, Roger (1990), *The Life and Political Economy of Lauchlin Currie: New Dealer, Presidential Adviser, and Developing Economist*, Durham, NC: Duke University Press.
Shackle, George Lennox Sharman (1967), *The Years of High Theory: Invention and Tradition in Economic Thought, 1926–1939*, Cambridge: Cambridge University Press.
Sikkink, Kathryn (1988), "The Influence of Raúl Prebisch on Economic Policy-Making in Argentina, 1950–1962," *Latin American Research Review*, **23** (2), 91–114.
Smith, Matthew (2008), "Thomas Tooke on the Bullionist Controversies," *European Journal of the History of Economic Thought*, **15** (1), 49–84.
Timberlake, Richard, H. (2009), "The Federal Reserve's Role in the Great Contraction and the SubPrime Crisis," *Cato Journal*, **28** (2), 303–12.
Triffin, Robert (1947a), *Monetary and Banking Reform in Paraguay*, Board of Governors of the Federal Reserve System: Washington, D.C.

Triffin, Robert (1947b), "National Central Banking and the International Economy," in Board of Governors of the Federal Reserve System (U.S.), Haberler, Gottfried, Metzler, Lloyd A. and Triffin, Robert, *Postwar Economic Studies No. 7 – International Monetary Policies*, Washington, D.C., pp. 49–76.
Vernengo, Matías (2009), "A Hands-off Central Banker? Marriner S. Eccles and the Federal Reserve, 1934–51," in Robert Leeson, *American Power and Policy*, Gordonsville, VA: Palgrave Macmillan, Chapter 3.
Wallich, Henry C. and Triffin, Robert (1953), *Monetary and Banking Legislation of the Dominican Republic 1947 with Reports and Letter of Transmittal*, Federal Reserve Bank of New York.

PART III

Financial History and Institutions

6. Nurturing US securities firms: a century of public policy[1]

Robert N. McCauley[2]

INTRODUCTION

In rapid succession in March 2008, the Federal Reserve extended its securities lending facility to permit securities firms to exchange illiquid securities for Treasury securities, rescued Bear Stearns' creditors and welcomed certain securities firms to something like its discount window. These may not be the last public policies adopted to sustain the US securities industry. But these moves were by no means the first.

For almost a hundred years, law and practice favoured the development of securities markets and the evolution of a securities industry distinct from the banking system as a means to distribute government debt. This tilt did not start in the 1930s with the passage of Glass–Steagall Act separating the securities industry from commercial banking. Neither did the tilt disappear in the 1990s with the effective repeal of that Act. Bear Stearns' tombstone, "born 1923, died 2008", provides a better clue to the span of the public policy favouring the securities industry than does that of Glass–Steagall.

This chapter reviews how public policy over the last nearly one hundred years nurtured the US securities industry. The approach is chronological. The next section considers how the Federal Reserve Act and early Federal Reserve operations sought to build up the securities market in New York at the expense of the established market in London and in the process nurtured independent securities firms. The third section discusses the period from the end of World War II (WWII) until the summer of 2007 during which the primary dealer system developed and government-sponsored guarantees moved home mortgages into the securities market. The final section analyses how the Federal Reserve has responded to financial turbulence since the middle of 2007 in ways that both support the securities industry and work around it.

1913 TO WWII

There were two motivations for a public policy supportive of the development of securities markets and securities firms. First was to build financial markets that could compete with London, and relatedly, to reduce costs of international trade and to avoid a currency mismatch. Second was the US Treasury's well-founded concern that it not be too dependent, or seen to be too dependent, on major US banks in financing itself. For instance, the Treasury's private sale of bonds to the Belmont–Morgan syndicate in 1895, and the profit realised by that syndicate, not only outraged populists (Chernow, 1990: 71–7). In addition, the US Treasury could have only concluded that the market power demonstrated by the syndicate in protecting the Treasury's gold reserve (Simon, 1968) could also be used against the Treasury. When a subsequent issue of $100 million in bonds was put up for public auction in 1896, J.P. Morgan won $38 million of the issue (Markham, 2002: 361), an outcome that would not have been entirely comforting. Twenty years later, "after the United States entered the war [WWI], the House of Morgan expected to be repaid a $400 million loan to Britain from the proceeds of the first Liberty Loan drive" (Chernow, 1990: 201), which Morgan had supported. The controversy arising from such debt issues and the risk of facing a money trust encouraged Treasury officials to nurture an alternative financing channel to the banking system.

American public policy favoured the growth of the securities industry in the period between the founding of the Federal Reserve and WWII in three ways. First, the Federal Reserve Act gave a fiscal incentive to repatriation from London of the short-term money market used to finance US trade. Second, the Federal Reserve decided to conduct monetary policy mainly through open market operations in short-term securities rather than through the discount window. Third, the Federal Reserve innovated repurchase operations to fund thinly capitalised securities dealers at times of money market strains. The first two policies supported securities firms indirectly by supporting the development of the money market. The third policy supported securities firms directly.

The Original Federal Reserve Act Support for the Bankers' Acceptance Market

The 1913 Act sought to develop a market in the United States for the financing of US foreign trade. Theretofore, US trade was financed in Europe, mostly in London. This was thought to be an undesirable state of affairs both from the standpoint of the cost and from the standpoint of currency exposure, since London acceptances were denominated in sterling (LaRoche, 1993).[3]

The Act provided two incentives for the repatriation of the financing of US trade. It gave a fiscal incentive for banks to create marketable securities out of private debts by promising to pay trade bills at their maturity. In particular, the Act exempted the promise to pay (the "acceptance liability") from reserve requirements. Thus banks could in effect guarantee trade paper, especially the obligation of importers to pay exporters, more cheaply because unremunerated reserves did not have to be held against the liability of future payment. This cost saving to the bank would encourage banks to create and sell into the money market the "two-name" paper, which would trade on the basis of the credit-worthiness of the bank. In addition, the Act made bankers' acceptances (BAs) eligible for discount or outright purchase by the new Federal Reserve. The use of the latter power is discussed in the next section. In sum, the Federal Reserve Act provided an incentive for securitisation of short-term obligations connected to the shipment and holding of goods.

The fiscal incentive, in conjunction with Federal Reserve operations and holdings described below, worked. By the late 1920s, BAs came to finance a third to a half of US imports and exports (LaRoche, 1993: 134).

Monetary Operations in the Money Market Rather than Through the Discount Window

The early evolution of Federal Reserve operations away from the discount window and toward money market operations favoured the development of the money markets. This illustrates the general principle that the choice of operating instruments by a central bank tends to have positive external effects on the liquidity of the chosen market. This point came into focus when there was a prospect, all too transitory in retrospect, of the US Treasury running surpluses to such an extent that the Federal Reserve would have had to change its operating procedures' reliance on Treasury securities (Broaddus and Goodfriend, 2001; Federal Reserve System, 2002; Kohn, 2002; Marshall, 2002; McCauley, 2002).

Now it is difficult to imagine a Federal Reserve for which open market operations do not predominate. But the 1913 Act presumed that Federal Reserve banks discounting eligible paper would be the principal operating instrument of monetary policy (Hanson and Kim, 2002). Open market operations were assigned a secondary and supporting role. An expression of this minor role was that Federal Reserve notes could not be backed by assets purchased in the open market. This was consistent with the real bills doctrine, which took monetary expansion based on the self-liquidating trade paper acquired through the discount window to be healthy and non-inflationary, but monetary expansion based on purchases of government paper in the open market to be potentially unhealthy and inflationary.

D'Arista (1994) has told the story of how in practice the Federal Reserve came to rely on open market operations rather than the discount window. Among the options for open market operations, the Federal Reserve favoured BAs over Treasury bills in times of peace and prosperity. It both bought BAs outright and entered into repurchase agreements against them, holding on average a third of the outstanding stock and at times half. These Federal Reserve holdings of private paper bulked larger than its holdings of Treasury paper before the war in 1923, 1926 and 1928 (Figure 6.1).

The Federal Reserve Bank of New York also purchased acceptances for the account of foreign central banks. By adding its signature, it in effect made the private paper into a government obligation. Federal Reserve support for the bankers' acceptance market resumed in 1955 but never reached the levels seen between the world wars.[4]

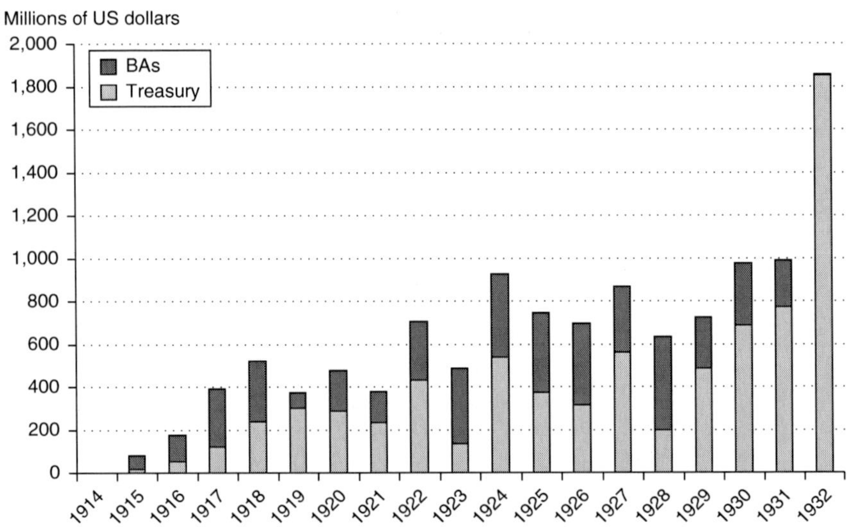

Note: Holdings of BAs in the early years include purchases under repo agreements.

Source: Meulendyke (1998: 22).

Figure 6.1 Federal Reserve holdings: Treasuries and bankers' acceptances

Repurchases at the Initiative of Securities Dealers

The evolution of the Federal Reserve's interaction with money-market dealers in the early days has not to the author's knowledge been the subject of systematic study. What follows depends on passing references in descriptions of Federal Reserve operations. That the Federal Reserve accepted small firms as counterparties is suggested by Sobel (1986: viii), the historian of Salomon Brothers, then a five or so man firm: "In 1914, the house was one of the first to recognize the promise offered by the new Federal Reserve System and quickly registered to become an active participant."

For some time, the Federal Reserve has operated in repos to fine-tune the availability of bank reserves.[5] The long-standing argument for the use of repos is that short-term reversed operations do not affect the prices of the underlying securities. But the original use of repo operations seems to have had more to do with market development in general, and the financing of non-bank securities dealers in times of stress, in particular.

The Federal Reserve's repo operations in its first 60 years were predominately a means to provide liquidity to non-bank dealer firms. Lumpkin (1993: 69) reports that the Federal Reserve did repos in 1917 with member banks, but these were discontinued "a few years later" until 1975 when bank dealers were made eligible as repo counterparties. In the 1920s and early 1930s repos were "infrequently" done with non-bank dealers. Meulendyke (1998: 27) reports that repos against Treasury securities and BAs would be arranged at the initiative of the dealers for periods of up to 15 days, with early repayment permitted. At the systemic level, Meulendyke highlights the safety-valve function of such dealer-initiated operations, in that they relieved shortages caused by Treasury cash management or other autonomous factors. In addition, to the dealers and their customers, such collateralised borrowing from the central bank at times of "temporary credit stringency" must have been reassuring.

In his chapter "Bankers for the Government", Burgess (1936) describes the practice more narrowly. In his account, the Federal Reserve stood ready to buy Treasury paper from dealers at times of tight credit and negative carry to encourage the development of an open market in such paper.

> Dealers were encouraged to buy and sell Treasury certificates and in so doing were given the support of the Federal Reserve Banks, which adopted a policy of standing ready to purchase Treasury certificates from dealers for short period from time to time whenever the market became congested or money rates rose to such high points that dealers could not obtain the call loans they required to carry their portfolios of certificates at rates approximating the rates borne by the certificates.

> The way this worked out was that when call money rates were temporarily high, or when the supply of Treasury securities was much larger than the demand, dealers sold some of these securities to the Federal Reserve Banks under an agreement to repurchase them within fifteen days. The dealers repurchased the securities as soon as the temporary condition was passed, usually well before fifteen days had passed. (Burgess, 1936: 122)

After a lull during World War II, repo operations were resumed in mid 1949 (Lumpkin, 1993: 70) or 1951 (Meulendyke, 1998: 37). The latter notes a shift to operations done at the Fed's initiative "to provide temporary, but immediate, reserve assistance to the central money market at times of unusual strain on that market" (quoting the New York Fed's report on operations in 1953 to the Federal Open Market Committee [FOMC]).

> Until the 1970s, RPs were done only with nonbank dealers at preannounced rates—usually at or slightly below the discount rate—although beginning in 1968, the RP rate was occasionally set slightly above the discount rate. The practice of arranging RPs only with nonbank dealers was a holdover from the earlier view that RPs served primarily to finance dealer positions in securities. On occasion during the 1950s and 1960s, an RP would still be arranged at the request of dealers facing difficulties in financing their positions in the markets. In discussing repurchase operations at [one of] the FOMC's annual reviews [in 1961] Governor J.L. Robertson objected to the FOMC's use of the instrument, arguing that RPs were not security purchases in the open market, as authorized by the Federal Reserve Act, but were actually loans to dealers . . . Governor Robertson was particularly troubled by the practice at the time of lending through RPs only to nonbank dealers and at rates below the discount rate . . . Most members disagreed. They considered RPs to be an appropriate instrument that had proved to be of inestimable value in the implementation of monetary policy; their continued use was authorized.[6]

Thus, before repos became the main Federal Reserve instrument they served to nurture non-bank securities dealers. Into the 1960s these could approach the Federal Reserve for financing of their government securities. Whether the rate at which the transaction could be done was in some sense favourable must have often been a secondary consideration. The more important impact would have been on the financial management of the primary dealers and even more on their customers' assessment of the counterparty risk of the dealer.

In sum, the Federal Reserve sought with its operational choices to encourage the development of short-term securities markets in the United States. In doing so, it was fulfilling the broad intention of framers like Paul Warburg (Federer, 2003), if not the vision of a passive discounting of self-liquidating paper held by some adherents to the real bills doctrine. Tellingly, the support for the development of the securities market extended to financing securities dealers' inventory at their initiative at times of credit stringency.

Thus, public policy supportive of securities markets and separate securities firms preceded the 1933 Glass–Steagall Act, which split the securities and banking businesses. A sign of the success of the long-standing policy to nurture a separate securities industry came after the passage in the same year of the Securities Act. Wall Street refused to bring securities to market under the new issuance rules established by the Joseph Kennedy-headed Securities Exchange Commission. "Salomon Brothers broke the 'Wall Street strike' against the new securities regulation by serving as the sole selling agent for a $43 million issue by Swift & Co. in 1934" (Sobel, 1986: 49).

FROM WWII TO 2007

Major public policies that supported the securities dealers after World War II included the development of the primary dealer system, and the launching of government-sponsored enterprises to securitise mortgages.

The Primary Dealer System

After World War II, the Federal Reserve's repurchase operations became more symmetrical, more competitive and more inclusive. In particular, the introduction of matched sale-purchase transactions in 1966 meant that repos could drain as well as inject liquidity. Then, the introduction of the "competitive go around" technique of contacting all the primary dealers at once in 1972 rendered the operation more competitive. Finally, the addition of bank dealers to the list of eligible counterparties in 1975 made the operations more inclusive.

The criteria and procedures for becoming a primary dealer in 1988 emphasise the obligations put on primary dealers (US Treasury et al., 2002: E-11–16). These included making markets in a wide range of government securities for a diverse customer base, meaningful participation in Treasury auctions, facilitation of Federal Reserve operations and provision of information on market developments. The dealer was expected to run a sound business: strong management and risk controls, reasonable profitability, and adequate capital. Nevertheless, market participants were not to make too much of the designation:

> The designation is not an endorsement, is not conferred upon regulatory authority, and does not entail official supervision by the Federal Reserve. The Federal Reserve does monitor dealer activities to determine that the primary

> dealer performance standards are being met and to obtain information about market developments. The process is not designed to assist the public in determining dealer creditworthiness. (US Treasury et al., 2002: E-11)

Quantitative tests were employed, although only as minima and only in conjunction with the more qualitative requirements. These included 1% of market-wide customer transactions and competitive bidding in auctions proportional to the share of customer transactions. The focus was on capital relative to risk, but a capital of less than $50 million was seen as inconsistent with prudent functioning.

Rights or privileges corresponding to these obligations were conferred by the Federal Reserve, the Treasury and, importantly, by other market participants. Primary dealers serve as counterparties to the Federal Reserve Bank of New York in its operations. Among non-depository institutions, only primary dealers could submit bids in Treasury auctions on behalf of other market participants. Seeing customer bids may offer informational advantages in an auction. The Treasury tended to consult on possible changes to its borrowing strategy with the primary dealers. Market practice within and outside the government securities market probably conferred most of the franchise value of designation as a primary dealer.

Within the market, primary dealers accepted so-called blind brokerage, wherein they were prepared to deal with each other without knowing the identity of the counterparty. This was preferred so as not to give away to the counterparty information from which trading strategies of a particular firm might be inferred. Consistent with this practice, the interdealer brokers allowed only the primary dealers access to their screens.

Market practice on the part of customers in the government securities market could vest arguably greater franchise value in the primary dealer designation. Lumpkin (1993: 67) cites the attraction of repos subject to "prudent investor" or other types of asset restrictions, such as public bodies required to invest tax receipts or the proceeds of bond issues in Treasury securities. These can invest in repos against Treasury securities instead of buying them outright. In some cases, such investments would be restricted to repos with primary dealers designated by the Federal Reserve.

> Money market mutual funds are also major participants in the RP market. [. . .] Because RPs are deemed to be loans under the Investment Company Act of 1940 and carry risks not typically associated with direct security investments, mutual funds often limit their RP investments to RPs with maturities of seven days or less that are arranged with member banks of the Federal Reserve System or dealers on the Federal Reserve Bank of New York's list of reporting dealers. (Lumpkin, 1993: 67)

In the early 1980s, the failure of several government securities dealers that were not primary dealers brought legislative attention to the informational advantage of the primary dealers. Hearings that led to the Government Securities Act of 1986 aired criticism of the restricted access to the interdealer broker screens: "Primary dealers can see 5 major and 2 specialized inside dealer screens. The interdealer brokers determine who may have the inside screens. The biggest differences between inside and public screens are how many issues are quoted, how much basis information they offer, and how much financing information they provide" (Schap, 1990).

In 1991, it was learned that Salomon Brothers, a major dealer, had entered false customer bids in a Treasury auction. Ironically, the violation concerned the limit on a single firm's share of an auction, a rule that recalled the 38% of the House of Morgan in the auction of 1895. This behaviour by a firm that had long benefited from public policy, not least the government support of mortgage securitisation described below, led to changes in Treasury auction procedures and the administration of the primary dealer system by the Federal Reserve Bank of New York. All Securities and Exchange Commission (SEC)-registered dealers were permitted to enter customer bids in Treasury auctions (US Treasury et al, 2002: xiii). The Treasury began to consult with a wider group of market participants on possible changes to its borrowing strategy.

For its part, the Federal Reserve Bank of New York made changes to make the primary dealer system more "open" (Corrigan, 1991–92). In particular, the market share test was dropped in favour of a "straightforward and objective" capital standard. In order to counter "moral hazard" and to underscore that the Federal Reserve does not regulate the primary dealers, the "dealer surveillance" unit of the Federal Reserve Bank of New York was disbanded. Instead, market surveillance as it evolved focused on identifying possibly manipulative practices akin to cornering particular Treasury issues in high demand (Fisher, 1996). Despite the changes, primary dealer obligations remained to "make reasonable markets for Fed open market operations", "participate meaningfully in Treasury auctions", and "provide the Fed with meaningful market intelligence".

Government Support of Mortgage Securitisation

Government support of the market for home mortgages turned illiquid bank assets into assets that could be turned into securities and traded. While the intended beneficiaries of the government support for the mortgage market were homeowners and the home construction business, there can be no doubt that the securities industry benefited as well. Homeowners got narrower spreads over US Treasury bonds on fixed-rate mortgages;

home builders experienced demand for homes less subject to being cut off by rising interest rates; and the securities industry got an extension of the bond market ultimately larger than the market for US Treasury securities. To be sure, there is a logic to securitisation in the absence of government guarantees (Cumming, 1987). And house mortgages can be securitised without government guarantees, as in Australia (Chan et al., 2006). But there can be no doubt that government and quasi-government guarantees jump-started home mortgage securitisation, and securitisation more generally.

The Reconstruction Finance Corporation, founded in 1932, marked the entry of the government into the mortgage market (Jones, 1951). The norm of medium-term balloon mortgages had led to the threat of foreclosures amidst declining house prices and tightened bank credit in the Depression. Government intervention established a new norm, the 30-year, amortising, repayable mortgage. Agencies spawned to guarantee and finance home mortgages outlived the RFC into the postwar period.

In the late 1960s, a court accepted the argument that indebtedness associated with these agencies should be counted as federal debt. This led to a Commission on Budget Concepts that articulated ownership and governance tests for government-sponsored enterprises (GSEs) to be kept off budget. This in turn led to the separation of off-budget Federal National Mortgage Agency (FNMA or Fannie Mae) from the Government National Mortgage Agency (GNMA). Later, Freddie Mac would join Fannie Mae as a GSE.

In the 1970s, there was an argument whether the government mortgage agency, the Federal Housing Administration (FHA), should sell straight bonds or so-called pass-through bonds to finance itself. The latter would leave the investor to cope with the variability of principal repayments on a pool of mortgages, including faster or slower repayments as homeowners responded to lower or higher long-term interest rates. Ironically, William Simon of Salomon Brothers, later Treasury Secretary, opposed pass-through securities on the grounds that investors could not deal with their complexity (Sobel, 1986). In the end, the FHA issued pass-through securities. Salomon Brothers eventually recognised the potential of the new securities and started a separate department to make a market in the initially illiquid securities. Lewis Ranieri would leave his mark on US finance in leading this effort.

Over a generation, US home mortgages shifted from the books of banks, thrifts and credit unions to backing mortgage securities. Federal Reserve Board flow of funds data aggregate mortgages backing "agency" securities, where agencies include the government bodies and the GSEs. The share of mortgages backing agency securities rose from less than 1% in

1969 to almost one half in 2002 (Figure 6.2). This share grew particularly quickly in the 1980s after the rise in long-term interest rates left thrifts in distress. Banks and thrifts benefited from the greater liquidity of their mortgage assets. They did not benefit, however, from the lower spreads on mortgages that arose from the wider market and competition from mortgage brokers who could originate without any capacity to hold. The share of mortgages held by depository institutions fell from 70–75% to less than a third.

Relieved of coping with credit risk by the government and quasi-government guarantees, the securities industry innovated ways to deal with the prepayment risk. Pools of mortgages were sliced into tranches, with prepayment risk concentrated in some and not others. Expected duration could thereby differ across the new securities, although the variability remained (Estrella and Silver, 1984). At the limit, mortgage pools were sliced into interest-only securities and principal-only securities. While securities firms and investment pools periodically blew up when they mis-estimated how interest rate changes would affect these complicated securities, these blow-ups never rose to the level of systemic risk.

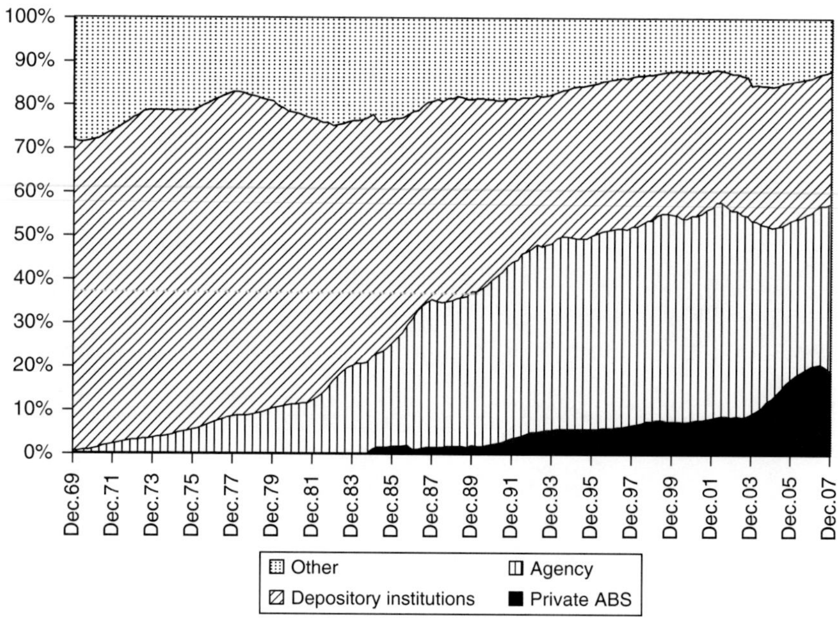

Source: Board of Governors of the Federal Reserve System, Flow of funds accounts.

Figure 6.2 Market share in holdings of home mortgages

Once the pump of securitisation had been primed with government and quasi-government guarantees, its techniques were applied to other assets, such as credit card loans. These did not benefit from any government guarantee, but with relatively high interest rates, they could in effect insure themselves against expected and unexpected credit losses. Given the dollar limits on mortgages that could benefit from government and GSE guarantees and house price inflation, so-called jumbo mortgages came to be securitised by so-called private label mortgage-backed securities. Such loans backed what the flow of funds data label asset-backed securities (ABS).

The securities industry drew the portentous lesson that mortgages could be securitised without the help of the government and GSE guarantees. Instead, the techniques of securitisation developed for credit cards and the like were applied. Eventually, the slicing and dicing that had been applied to the duration problem was applied to credit risk.

The growth of market share of the ABS was gradual until the early years of this century. Figure 6.3 focuses on home mortgages other than home equity loans, in which banks have kept a high market share (and where agencies do not compete). Private ABS represented less than 2% of the market at

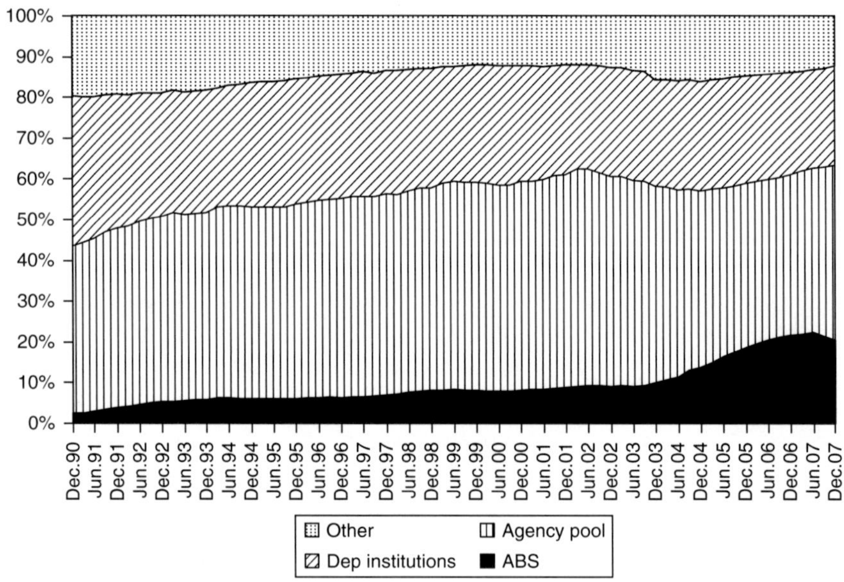

Source: Board of Governors of the Federal Reserve System, Flow of funds accounts.

Figure 6.3 Market shares of holders of home mortgages other than home equity loans

the beginning of the 1990s, and claimed about 1% a year larger share of the home mortgage market per year in that decade. Prime loans represented half the collateral for the privately issued MBS as late as 2001 (Frankel, 2006: 68). Then, against the backdrop of 1% policy interest rate, the share lifted off in 2003, and reached a peak of 22% in early 2007. Issuance of private label mortgage-backed securities rose from less than a third of agency mortgage-backed securities to an amount greater than agency securities in 2005.

The growth in ABS came as the securities industry found it possible not only to securitise jumbo mortgages but also mortgages that did not meet the underwriting standards of the agencies. Loans that had high loan-to-value ratios (up to 100%) and loans where the documentation was not up to standards became possible to bundle into securities. Such loans allowed borrowers who might have otherwise qualified for "conforming" loans from Fannie and Freddie to take out bigger or faster loans. In their unique study of "homeowner experiences", Foote et al. (2008) find that many subprime and "Alt-A" mortgages were extended to borrowers whose credit scores were high enough to allow them to qualify for conforming mortgages that could have been guaranteed by the GSEs. In addition, many homeowners refinanced from conforming loans into subprime loans, extracting so much equity or offering so little documentation to turn a low spread mortgage into a high-spread mortgage. In this manner, the securities industry sought and gained market share from the agencies (Smith et al., 2006: 16–18). Innovations in mortgage markets not only widened the market, by making loans available to borrowers with shaky credit histories, but also deepened it with riskier mortgages to those already in the market, by allowing more leverage and weaker documentation. The market share of the agencies actually declined in the five years 2002–07.

It appears that US securities firms led the competition in laxity to create risky mortgage assets. To be sure, big banks, too, originated mortgages in order to bundle them into securities. Big banks typically had a nonbank mortgage originator under the holding company. Securities firms not affiliated with big banks may have depended more on independent originators (in many cases funding them, and in some cases owning them). In part because of the additional layer,[7] the nexus of independent mortgage originators and securities firms seems to have led the decline in underwriting standards. In particular, Morgenson (2008) reported that the Bear Stearns private "Alt-A" mortgage-backed securities as of February 2008 showed a worse record of delinquency or foreclosure at 15% than the industry average of 8.4%. Mian and Sufi (2008: Table 5) find that higher defaults were associated with a higher fraction of mortgages sold to non-bank financial firms, and lower defaults were associated with a higher fraction to affiliates.

Stepping back, securities firms capitalised on government and quasi-government guarantees to create a segment of the securities market larger than the US Treasury market. As they learned to securitise mortgages too large for such guarantees, and applied the slice and dice techniques developed to handle prepayment risk to credit risk, they bid away mortgages from the government and GSEs with easier terms. This market share gain went into reverse after mid 2007, amid huge losses on the part of holders of the private-label mortgage securities.

SUMMER 2007–SUMMER 2008

It is too early to tell how public policy toward a separate US securities industry shifted over the last year on balance. This uncertainty prevails not only because changes in the law typically follow a financial crisis. Changes in practice alone leave the net effect hard to call. In chronological order, two changes in practice tended to allow policy to work around the securities industry, or at least the part of it not affiliated with banks. In March 2008, policy underscored the role of securities firms in the financial system.

Bank-owned Securities Firms' Funding

Little-noticed in August 2007, the Federal Reserve relaxed limits on funding of securities affiliates within several bank holding companies that it regulates (Board of Governors, 2007). In particular, Bank of America, Citibank and Wachovia were allowed to advance funds to their securities affiliates. The securities affiliates were required to pass through the credit from the bank to customers in the form of securities financing. The rationale was that the public interest in the proper functioning of the repo market would be well served by the flow of funds from the banking system.

From a public policy standpoint, it was a virtue of the demise of Glass–Steagall that credit could flow from the banking system to the repo market without having to overcome the asymmetric information between lender and borrower. But from the standpoint of the securities firms without a bank holding company parent, this was mixed news. Such firms would benefit from any increase in the liquidity of repo markets. But at the same time, they would ask whether competitors had derived strength from their bank holding company parent. The rationale in the first place for the limits on credit flowing from the bank to the securities affiliate was that the safety net—deposit insurance and the discount window—should not be available to support the securities affiliate. Otherwise, competition with other securities firms that did not have such a source of strength might be distorted. In retrospect, in relaxing its rules, the Federal Reserve was making the judgement that the proper functioning of the repo market should benefit from the discount window.

The Term Auction Facility

The other change in Fed practice was also introduced as a short-term exigency, but it is explicitly under consideration to become standard practice. Announced on 12 December 2007, the term auction facility (TAF) allowed the Federal Reserve to widen its open market operations in two different dimensions: counterparty and collateral. The rationale cited in the press release is to "promote the efficient dissemination of liquidity when the unsecured interbank markets are under stress". All depository institutions with access to the discount window, thousands in number, can bid for discount window advances of a maturity of 28 or 35 days. And as is usually the case with discount window advances, all manner of collateral would be acceptable, including not only asset-backed securities but bilateral loans.

To understand the potential significance of this experiment, it is helpful to go back into history. Recall from the first section above that the earliest operations of the Federal Reserve through the discount window were supplanted by unified operations in the form of outright or reversed transactions against securities. The experiment with the TAF in some ways returned to the fork in the road between the discount window or securities market transactions as the Federal Reserve's main operation.

Its provenance suggests that the experimental TAF might prove to have some staying power. When there was a serious prospect of the disappearance of the US Treasury debt, the Federal Reserve's consideration of alternatives to traditional Treasury operations (Federal Reserve System, 2002) devoted 26 pages to the analysis of buying different assets (agency paper, municipal bonds, corporate bonds, and so on) but 93 pages to the analysis of using the discount window to provide Federal Reserve credit. An auction facility not very different from what has been introduced is described in pages 3–3 to 3–7 and 3–35 to 3–40.

The Term Securities Lending Facility

From its origins as a means to finance the securities industry's inventory of short-term private paper and Treasury securities, the repurchase market evolved into a huge market that financed long-term asset backed securities whose pricing and liquidity had not been tested in adverse market circumstances. By the time that the term securities lending facility was introduced in mid March, counterparties were offering to finance a lower fraction of the market value of such packaged home and commercial mortgages and credit cards ("demanding higher haircuts"). This in turn was building pressure for liquidations, which in turn was putting pressure on prices and leading to higher haircuts. The new facility auctioned the right for primary dealers to exchange high-rated asset-backed securities for Treasury securities. These in turn could be used as collateral for cash in the Treasury repo market.

Two months later, Bill Dudley, the head of markets at the Federal Reserve Bank of New York, described the rationale for this facility as follows:

> The Fed can reduce bank funding risks by providing a safe harbor for financing less liquid collateral on bank and primary dealer balance sheets. Reducing this risk may prove helpful by lessening the risk that an inability to obtain funding would force the involuntary liquidation of assets. The ability to obtain funding from the Fed reduces the risk of a return to the dangerous dynamic of higher haircuts, lower prices, forced liquidations, and still higher haircuts that was evident in March.
>
> In essence, the Federal Reserve's willingness to provide liquidity against less liquid collateral allows the reintermediation and deleveraging process to proceed in an orderly way, which reduces the damage to weaker counterparties and funding structures. One can think of the Federal Reserve's actions as smoothing and extending the adjustment process—not preventing it—so that the adjustment causes less damage to the financial system and less pernicious macroeconomic consequences. (Dudley, 2008)

Bear Stearns

Timothy Geithner, President of the Federal Reserve Bank of New York, looked back three months and provided this account of the intervention in Bear Stearns:

> The Fed made the judgment, after very careful consideration, that it was necessary to use its emergency powers to protect the financial system and the economy from a systemic crisis by committing to facilitate the merger between JPMorgan Chase and Bear Stearns. We did this with great reluctance, and only because it was the only feasible option available to avert default, and because we did not believe we had the ability to contain the damage that would have been caused by default.
>
> Our actions were guided by the same general principles that have governed Fed action in crises over the years. There was an acute risk to the stability of the system; we were not confident that the damage could be contained through other means; we acted only to help facilitate an orderly resolution, not to preserve the institution itself; and the management of the firm and the equity holders of the institution involved suffered very substantial consequences.

> Although we assumed some risk in this transaction, that risk is modest in comparison to the risk of very substantial damage to the financial system and the economy as a whole that would have accompanied default. (Geithner, 2008)

While market commentary has often focused on Bear Stearns' outstanding swap portfolio, especially its book of credit default swaps, as the risk to the system, the damage threatened by Bear's demise could have been heavy in a market of long-standing importance. The repo market, the nexus between the Federal Reserve and the primary dealers, could have suffered a withdrawal by placers of funds. The difficulty that Bear Stearns had experienced in accessing credit in the repo market (Boyd, 2008: 58; Kelly, 2008) could have become general were lenders of cash in this market to re-examine the list of eligible counterparties on their triparty repo agreements, which totalled $2.5 trillion (Geithner, 2008).

The Primary Dealer Credit Facility

For years, executives of the major securities firms have understood their vulnerability to a run. For instance, the Undersecretary of the Treasury is reported to have approached the head of Salomon Brothers in 1987 to obtain his support for a financial services reform that would presumably include an end to Glass–Steagall. John Gutfreund is said to have asked for access to the Federal Reserve's discount window and payments system, as well as tax-free repatriation of earnings retained in Switzerland (Mayer, 1993: 223–4).

Under conditions of extreme market stress, on 16 March 2008 the Board of Governors authorised the extension of overnight credit to the primary dealers. This depended on the broad authority of Section 13.3 of the Federal Reserve Act.

> In 1932 enactment of section 13.3 authorized Reserve Banks to *discount* eligible paper for individuals, partnerships and corporations (IPCs) in unusual and exigent circumstances. Originally, this authority was limited to discounting only those notes, drafts, and bills of exchange of the kind that Reserve Banks could discount under section 13, but section 13.3 was amended in 1991 to permit Reserve Banks to discount notes of the IPCs "secured to the satisfaction" of the Reserve Banks. (Hanson and Kim, 2002: I-23)

Before the 1991 amendment, the limitation to eligible paper was, according to Hackley (1973: 128–9), "an important limitation": "Nonbank financial institutions [. . .] ordinarily do not hold customers' paper of the kind that would be eligible for discount." The market response to the Salomon Brothers bidding irregularities had highlighted the potential for a securities firm to suffer illiquidity with potential for systemic disruption. The 1991 amendment permitted the collateral for the primary dealer credit to be set as investment-grade corporate securities, municipal securities, mortgage-backed securities, and asset-backed securities for which a price is available. With the 1991 amendment, Congress made Section 13.3 broad enough to permit liquidity support for a securities firm.

Thus it is not strictly speaking correct to say that the primary dealer credit facility has given securities firms access to the discount window. As noted, the facility draws on an authority that is wider than what applies to the discount window with regard to acceptable security. At the same time, it should be stressed that the terms of the new facility are in other respects not as favourable as those that apply to the discount window. In particular the primary dealer loans are overnight only (instead of up to 90 days), cannot be collateralised by assets with no market prices, like the loans that can be presented by banks at the discount window, and the cost will rise with repeated use (Dudley, 2008; Federal Reserve Bank of New York, 2008).

On the third day of the new primary dealer facility, Morgan Stanley's Chief Financial Officer, Colm Kelleher said in an interview: "We have tested the window because we want to remove the stigma from the window [. . .] It's meant to be there for normal business. It's not meant to be there as a last-recourse thing" (Onaran and Harper, 2008).[8] Goldman Sachs took a more private view:

> 'We think the Fed window provides a good alternative to the secured funding markets and we welcome the initiative', a Goldman spokesman said in an emailed statement. 'We're testing it this week and will certainly use it if doing so makes sense from an economic and funding diversification point of view.' (Batt, 2008)

Lehman referred to showing leadership in drawing on the facility, distancing itself from the fears in the market that had seen its share price halve from a close of about $40 on Monday 17 March to a low of $20 on Tuesday 18 March. The Federal Reserve H.4.1 release of 20 March showed outstanding drawings as of the previous day of $28.8 billion, which had declined to $22.6 billion by 23 April.[9] The future and consequence of this facility remain a subject of discussion (Geithner, 2008; Kohn, 2008).

CONCLUSIONS

American public policy has for almost a century nurtured a securities industry separate from the banking system. The Federal Reserve Act sought to build up the securities market in New York at the expense of the established market in London. The shift of Federal Reserve operations from the discount window to reliance on open market operations in private and public securities and using repurchase agreements built up both the securities markets and industry. The repurchase market seems to have evolved at least in part as a means to finance securities firms in times of financial stringency.

In the period from the end of World War II until the summer of 2007, the securities industry benefited from government-sponsored guarantees of home mortgages and the development of the primary dealer system. In retrospect, the most important legal change in this period for the development of the securities industry was the broad expansion of quasi-public guarantees of mortgages. Guarantees by Fannie and Freddie allowed the securities industry to turn some of the banking industry's best assets into tradeable securities. More directly, the Treasury and Federal Reserve aligned debt management policy and operating procedures to produce a primary dealers' system that combined underwriting of government debt with dealing with the Federal Reserve, mostly through repurchase agreements. The Salomon Brothers auction bidding scandal of 1991 ultimately had a limited effect on the law or practice, though it did ultimately set the stage for the merger of Salomon with Citibank.

The Federal Reserve has responded to financial turbulence since the middle of 2007 in ways that both support the securities industry and work around it. The impression conveyed by the Federal Reserve moves in March 2008 might be that public policy has only become more supportive of the securities industry. But earlier relaxation of limits on the extension of credit within bank holding companies to securities affiliates and Federal Reserve experiments with auctions of discount window credit worked around rather than through the securities industry.

The securities industry seems to have taken the lead in the creation of the financial structures whose leverage, maturity mismatches, obscurity and complexity led to the financial turmoil that began in mid 2007. It might seem, then, that public policy should be indifferent to the prospect that the remaining four big US securities firms go the way of Salomon Brothers and Bear Stearns. Still, as long as the US Treasury has debt to sell, the original reasons for a public policy in support of a more diverse financial system may have some weight.

AUTHOR'S POSTSCRIPT

A full update of this chapter would add a section on the crisis and another on the legislative response represented by Dodd–Frank. The list of references could double. In terms of the historical argument, the most important addition would be Eichengreen and Flandreau (2010). For now, the following three paragraphs must serve as the tombstone for the major securities firms.

After this chapter was written in mid 2008, a major US securities firm, Lehman Brothers, failed in September 2008, setting off a global financial crisis. Historians will have to apportion responsibility to management missteps, the political reaction to the assisted purchase of Bear Stearns, miscalculation by would-be acquirers of Lehman and errors of policy-makers. A memorable line is that of Congressman Frank, who said that the United States conducted a 24-hour experiment in market discipline.

In the event, Merrill Lynch was shortly thereafter absorbed by Bank of America, a deal that provoked ongoing litigation. In late September 2008, Goldman Sachs announced a $5 billion investment by Berkshire Hathaway and Morgan Stanley announced a $9 billion investment by Mitsubishi UFJ Group bank and both received Federal Reserve permission to become bank holding companies. Large non-bank US securities firms ceased to exist.

Management of Goldman and Morgan Stanley may have had some second thoughts after the inclusion of the Volcker Rule limiting proprietary trading at US banks in the Dodd–Frank legislation. However, management cannot go back to the status quo ex ante since that legislation also amended Section 13.3 of the Federal Reserve Act to limit it to a "program or facility with broad-based eligibility", thereby constraining future assistance to a non-bank.

NOTES

1. Paper presented to the conference in honour of Jane D'Arista, University of Massachusetts Amherst, 2–3 May 2008.
2. Thanks are due to Jane D'Arista. The views expressed are those of the author and not necessarily those of the Bank for International Settlements.
3. By the 1980s, much of Japanese external trade was financed with US BAs. One of the aspirations of those who sought to internationalise the yen was to build up the yen bankers' acceptance market. See Sakakibara and Kondoh (1984).
4. In the 1970s the Federal Reserve concluded that the market could stand on its own and ceased endorsing acceptances for its foreign correspondents. In 1977 outright purchases ceased and in 1984 repos against BAs ceased. The exemption of BAs from reserve requirements boosted outstandings in the high-inflation and high-interest rate years of the late 1970s and early 1980s. The subsequent reduction of reserve requirements for large certificates of deposit and Eurodollars in 1990 left BAs little advantage over commercial paper and other means to finance trade and the market has languished.
5. In 1992, its daily transactions amounted to $1.5–$6 billion, compared to daily total transactions of $629 billion then reported by the primary dealers (Lumpkin, 1993: 70 and 73).
6. Meulendyke (1998: 37, with interposed footnote 39 from page 230) added the Robertson

objection to the 1998 edition; perhaps research arising from the Salomon Brothers scandal brought this discussion to her attention.

7. The Financial Stability Forum (2008: 7) highlighted another difference: "Weak government oversight of these entities [mortgage originators and brokers] contributed to the rise in unsound underwriting practices, especially by mortgage companies not affiliated with banks."
8. Morgan signing up for government support recalled J.P. Morgan's receiving the first injection of preferred shares from the Reconstruction Finance Corporation in 1933 (Jones, 1951: 35).
9. It also showed average drawings of $13.4 billion. See www.federalreserve.gov/releases/h41/Current/.

REFERENCES

Batt, Alistair (2008). "Top brokerage firms borrow from Fed's new facility: Morgan Stanley, Lehman borrow small amounts; Goldman testing program", *DowJones MarketWatch*, 19 March.

Board of Governors of the Federal Reserve System (2007). Letter from Robert DeV Frierson to Patrick S. Antrim, Bank of America, 20 August, www.federalreserve.gov/boarddocs/legalint/FederalReserveAct/2007/20070820a/20070820a.pdf.

Board of Governors of the Federal Reserve System (2008). "Flow of funds accounts", http://www.federalreserve.gov/releases/Z1/about/kennedy-fof-20120628. pdf.

Boyd, Roddy (2008). "The last days of Bear Stearns", *Fortune*, 14 April, pp. 56–8.

Broaddus, J. Alfred and Marvin Goodfriend (2001): "What assets should the Federal Reserve buy?", *Federal Reserve Bank of Richmond Economic Quarterly*, **87** (1) (Winter), 7–22.

Burgess, W. Randolph (1936). *The Reserve Banks and the Money Market*. Revised edition. New York: Harper Brothers.

Chan, Eric, Michael Davies and Jacob Gyntelberg (2006). "The role of government-supported housing finance agencies in Asia", *BIS Quarterly Review*, March, 71–83.

Chernow, Ron (1990). *The House of Morgan: An American Banking Dynasty and the Rise of Modern Finance*. New York: A Morgan Entrekin Book/Atlantic Monthly Press.

Corrigan, E. Gerald (1991–92). "Changes in the Government securities market", *Federal Reserve Bank of New York Quarterly Review*, Winter, 6–11.

Cumming, Christine (1987). "The economics of securitization", *Federal Reserve Bank of New York Quarterly Review*, Fall, 11–23.

D'Arista, Jane W. (1994). *The Evolution of U.S. Finance, Volume 1: Federal Reserve Monetary Policy, 1915–1935*. Armonk, NY: M.E. Sharpe.

Dudley, William (2008). "May you live in interesting times: the sequel", remarks at the Federal Reserve Bank of Chicago's 44th Annual Conference on Bank Structure and Competition, Chicago, 15 May, www.newyorkfed.org/newsevents/speeches/2008/dud080515.html.

Eichgreen, Barry and Marc Flandreau (2010). "Central banks as architects: The Federal Reserve, the Bank of England, and the rise of the dollar as an international currency, 1914–1939", BIS Working Papers 328, November.

Estrella, Arturo and Andrew Silver (1984). "Collateralized mortgage obligations:

Do they reduce cash flow uncertainty?", *Federal Reserve Bank of New York Quarterly Review*, Summer.
Federal Reserve Bank of New York (2008). "Primary dealer credit facility: Frequently asked questions", http://www.newyorkfed.org/markets/pdcf_faq.html.
Federal Reserve System, Study Group on Alternative Instruments for System Operations (2002). "Alternative instruments for open market and discount window operations", December.
Federer, J. Peter (2003). "Institutional innovation and the creation of liquid financial markets: The case of bankers' acceptances, 1914–1934", *Journal of Economic* History, **63** (3) (September), 666–94.
Financial Stability Forum (2008). "Report of the Financial Stability Forum on enhancing market and institutional resilience", April.
Fisher, Peter R. (1996). "The desk and the bond market: An operational view", remarks before the Money Marketeers of New York University, 8 October, http://www.newyorkfed.org/newsevents/speeches/1996/pf961008.html.
Foote, Christopher L., Kristopher Gerardi, Lorenz Goette and Paul S. Willen (2008). "Subprime facts: What (we think) we know about the subprime crisis, and what we don't", Federal Reserve Bank of Boston Public Policy Discussion Papers 08–02, May.
Frankel, Allen (2006). "Prime or not so prime? An exploration of US housing finance in the new century", *BIS Quarterly Review*, March, 67–78.
Geithner, Timothy F. (2008). "Reducing systemic risk in a dynamic financial system", speech to the Economic Club of New York, 9 June, www.ny.frb.org/newsevents/speeches/2008/tfg080609.html.
Hackley, Howard M. (1973). *Lending Functions of the Federal Reserve Banks: A History*. Washington, DC: Board of Governors of the Federal Reserve System.
Hanson, Joyce M. and HaeRan Kim (2002). "Legislative history of the Federal Reserve Act as it relates to the discount window and open market operations", in Federal Reserve System, Study Group on Alternative Instruments for System Operations (ed.), *Alternative Instruments for Open Market and Discount Window Operations*, December, pp. I-17–23.
Jones, Jesse H., with Edward Angly (1951). *Fifty Billion Dollars: My Thirteen Years with the RFC*. New York: Macmillan.
Kelly, Kate (2008). "The fall of Bear Stearns: Fear, rumors touched off fatal run on Bear Stearns", *Wall Street Journal*, 28 May, p. 1.
Kohn, Donald L. (2002). "Panel: Implications of declining Treasury debt: What should the Federal Reserve do as Treasury debt is repaid?", *Journal of Money, Credit and Banking*, **34** (3), part 2 (August), 941–5.
Kohn, Donald L. (2008). "The changing business of banking: Implications for financial stability and lessons from recent market turmoil", speech at the Federal Reserve Bank of Richmond's Credit Market Symposium, Charlotte, NC, USA, 17 April.
LaRoche, Robert K. (1993). "Bankers acceptances", in *Instruments of the Money Market*. Richmond, VA: Federal Reserve Bank of Richmond, pp. 128–38.
Lumpkin, Stephen A. (1993). "Repurchase and reverse repurchase agreements", in *Instruments of the Money Market*. Richmond, VA: Federal Reserve Bank of Richmond, pp. 59–74.
Markham, Jerry W. (2002). *A Financial History of the United States, Volume 1*. Armonk, NY: M.E. Sharpe.
Marshall, David (2002). "Origins of the use of Treasury debt in open market

operations: lessons for the present", *Federal Reserve Bank of Chicago Economic Perspectives*, Q1, 45–54.

Mayer, Martin (1993). *Nightmare on Wall Street: Salomon Brothers and the Corruption of the Marketplace*. New York: Simon and Schuster.

McCauley, Robert N. (2002). "Panel: Implications of declining Treasury debt: International market implications of declining Treasury debt", *Journal of Money, Credit and Banking*, **34** (3), part 2 (August), 952–66.

Meulendyke, Anne-Marie (1998). *US Monetary Policy and Financial Markets*. New York: Federal Reserve Bank of New York.

Mian, Atif and Amir Sufi (2008). "The consequences of mortgage credit expansion: Evidence from the 2007 mortgage default crisis", National Bureau of Economic Research Working Paper No. 13936, April.

Morgenson, Gretchen (2008). "Rescue me: A Fed bailout crosses a line", *New York Times*, 16 March.

Onaran, Yalman and Christine Harper (2008). "Goldman, Morgan Stanley use Fed's Wall Street window", *Bloomberg*, 19 March.

Sakakibara, Eisuke and Akira Kondoh (1984). "Study on the internationalisation of Tokyo's money markets", Japan Center for International Finance Policy Study Series, no. 1 (June).

Schap, Keith (1990). "Do inside dealer screens provide a clear trading edge?", *Futures*, **19** (8) (July), 42–4.

Simon, Matthew (1968). "The Morgan–Belmont syndicate of 1895 and intervention in the foreign-exchange market", *Business History Review*, **42** (4) (Winter), 385–417.

Smith, Valerie, Forrest Pafenberg and Laura Goren (2006). "Mortgage markets and the Enterprises", Office of Federal Housing Enterprise Oversight Research Paper, September.

Sobel, Robert (1986). *Salomon Brothers, 1910–1985: Advancing to Leadership*. New York: Salomon Brothers.

US Treasury, Securities and Exchange Commission and Board of Governors of the Federal Reserve System (2002). "Joint Report on the Government Securities Market", January.

APPENDIX 6A.1: LIST OF THE PRIMARY GOVERNMENT SECURITIES DEALERS REPORTING TO THE GOVERNMENT SECURITIES DEALERS STATISTICS UNIT OF THE FEDERAL RESERVE BANK OF NEW YORK

BNP Paribas Securities Corp.

Banc of America Securities LLC

Barclays Capital Inc.

Bear Stearns & Co., Inc.

Cantor Fitzgerald & Co.

Citigroup Global Markets Inc.

Countrywide Securities Corporation

Credit Suisse Securities (USA) LLC

Daiwa Securities America Inc.

Deutsche Bank Securities Inc.

Dresdner Kleinwort Wasserstein Securities LLC.

Goldman, Sachs & Co.

Greenwich Capital Markets, Inc.

HSBC Securities (USA) Inc.

J.P. Morgan Securities Inc.

Lehman Brothers Inc.

Merrill Lynch Government Securities Inc.

Mizuho Securities USA Inc.

Morgan Stanley & Co. Incorporated

UBS Securities LLC.

Notes: This list has been compiled and made available for statistical purposes only and has no significance with respect to other relationships between dealers and the Federal Reserve Bank of New York. Qualification for the reporting list is based on the achievement and maintenance of the standards outlined in the Federal Reserve Bank of New York's memorandum of January 22, 1992.
Italics indicate dealer unaffiliated with bank; italics added by author.

Source: Government Securities Dealers Statistics Unit Federal Reserve Bank of New York, 30 November 2007.

APPENDIX 6A.2

Table 6A.1 Forms of Federal Reserve lending to financial institutions (Federal Reserve Bank of New York, March 2008)

	Regular OMOs	Single-Tramohe OMO Program [announced March 7, 2008]	Discount Window[1]	Term Discount Window Program [announced August 17, 2007]	Term Auction Facility [announced December 12, 2007]	Primary Dealer Credit Facility [announced March 15, 2008][2]	Securities Lending	Term Securities Lending Facility [announced March 11, 2008]
Who can borrow?	Primary dealers	Primary dealers	Depository instructions	Primary credit-eligible depository institutions	Primary credit-eligible depository institutions	Primary dealers	Primary dealers	Primary dealers
What are they borrowing?	Funds	Funds	Funds	Funds	Funds	Funds	U.S. Treasuries	U.S. Treasuries
What collateral can be pledged?	U.S. Treasuries, agencies; agency- MBS	U.S. Treasuries, agencies; agency- MBS	Full range of Discount Window collateral	Full range of Discount Window collateral	Full range of Discount Window collateral	U.S. Treasuries agencies. agency MBS. investment grade debt scarifies[3]	U.S Treasuries	U.S. Treasuries agencies. agency MBS. AAA (Aaa rated private-table RMBS and CMBS agency CMO
Is there a reserves impact?	Yes	Yes	Yes	Yes	Yes	Yes	No (loans are bond-far-bond)	No (loans are bond-far-bond)

What is the term of loan?	Typically, term is overnight–14 days[4]	28 days	Typically overnight but up to several weeks	Up to 90 days	28 days[4]	Overnight	Overnight	28 days
Is prepayment allowed if term is greater than over overnight?	No	No	Yes	Yes	No	N/A	N/A	No
Which Reserve Banks conduct operations?	FRBNY	FRBNY	All	All	All	FRBNY	FRBNY	FRBNY
How frequently are operations conducted?	Typically once or more daily	Typically weekly	As requested	As requested	Every other weeks	As requested	Daily	Weekly
Where are: statistics reported publicly?	Temporary OMO activity	Temporary OMO activity	H.4.1 Factors Affecting Reserve Balances	H.4.1 Factors Affecting Reserve Balances	H.4.1 Factors Affecting Reserve Balances	H.4.1 Factors Affecting Reserve Balances	Securities leading activity	Term Securities leading activity

Notes:
1. Discount Window includes primary, secondary and seasonal credit programs.
2. The PDCF will remain in operation for a minimum period of six months and may be extended as conditions warrant.
3. Investment grade debt securities include corporate securities, municipal securities, mortgage-backed securities and asset-backed securities.
4. Open market operations are authorized for terms of up to 65 business days.
5. 28-day term may vary slightly to account for maturity dates that fall on Bank holidays.
6. Primary credit loans are generally overnight. Loans may be granted for term beyond a few weeks to small banks subject to additional administration.
7. Maximum maturity of term increased from 30 to 90 days on March 16, 2008.
8 Data only available on days when 28-day RP operations are conducted.

Source: http://www.newyorkfed.org/markets/Forms_of_Fed_Lending.pdf.

7. Lessons from the Glass–Steagall Act

Ellen D. Russell

INTRODUCTION

Jane D'Arista's outstanding contributions to the study of financial markets have been a cornerstone for scholars and policy makers seeking to reform the financial sector. Her vast knowledge of the evolution of financial practices, instruments and institutions has been a critical source of insight for those wishing to design financial regulation that anticipates and responds to the dynamism of financial markets. Perhaps most importantly, D'Arista has always addressed financial reform as a component of larger progressive economic agendas. During years when advocates for progressive economic change had largely overlooked the domestic financial sector, D'Arista insisted that heterodox scholars and activists focus on the relationship between financial reform and the pursuit of larger economic aspirations.

Progressive political economists began to delve more deeply into the study of financial regulation when the Bretton Woods arrangements that had prevailed during the golden age of Keynesian welfare state capitalism began to unravel.[1] While critics of neoliberalism focused on the increasingly pervasive influences of international finance, the heterodox analysis of domestic financial markets lagged behind. Fortunately, D'Arista's work for the US Congress (at the House Banking Committee and the Telecommunications and Finance Committee), and her scholarly contributions (such as her classic *The Evolution of U.S. Finance*) documented the destabilizing dynamics and other perverse economic tendencies that emanate from neoliberal deregulation in the domestic financial sector. Certainly since the beginning of the financial crisis in 2008 (if not before), it has become painfully evident that D'Arista's prescient focus on domestic financial regulatory issues is an important strategic and theoretical component of critical political economy.

D'Arista's research is also distinctive for its detailed attention to the historically and institutionally specific characteristics that animate financial markets. In a discipline that often occludes contextual influences behind abstract models, D'Arista has generated original contributions to theoretical and policy debates that would be unavailable to historically and institutionally unsophisticated analysis. D'Arista's work makes a persuasive case that analysis of this historical and institutional complexity is imperative if financial reform is to navigate the complex pressures of financial markets.

This chapter emulates these important attributes of D'Arista's contribution to the heterodox political economy of finance by exploring one of the most prominent examples of a sweeping regulatory reform in American financial history: the Glass–Steagall Act.[2] We will make the case that Glass–Steagall's separation of commercial and investment banking, alongside other reforms contained in the Banking Acts of 1933 and 1935, created a domestic regulatory framework which was supportive of the subsequent experiment with welfare state Keynesianism in the United States. This Glass–Steagall financial regulatory architecture presided over the era of "*pax financus*" (Hayes, 1978, 2), in which finance has been depicted as the "'servant' rather than the 'master' in economic and political matters" (Helleiner, 1994, 5). Thus in contrast to contemporary portrayals of finance as a hegemonic and destabilizing influence, New Deal financial reform was conducive to a long period of relative tranquility in financial markets, vigorous investment and the relative economic prosperity which characterized the "golden age" of the Keynesian welfare state. The erosion of this regulatory framework coincided with an era of increased domestic financial innovation and instability, which culminated in the repeal of Glass–Steagall in 1999.

As is the case with D'Arista's financial scholarship, this chapter is not prompted solely by retrospective interest. As financial crises and their destructive repercussions have become increasingly commonplace, heterodox financial scholars may look to the New Deal reforms as a precedent in which regulatory response to financial crisis dramatically reconfigured the financial landscape. Despite the many differences between the 1930s and today's financial environment, this chapter makes the case that lessons from the Glass–Steagall Act provide important insights for contemporary projects of progressive financial reform.

THE HISTORICAL AND INSTITUTIONAL PRELUDE TO THE NEW DEAL BANKING REFORMS

From the many factors that combined to produce the stock market crash of 1929 and the banking crises of the Great Depression, this chapter pays particular attention to the situation confronting commercial banks. In the 1920s (as was the case prior to the 2008 financial crisis) commercial banks were under considerable competitive pressure both from within the banking sector and from other financial institutions. As new financial institutions and practices impinged on the traditional roles of depository banks, banks responded to these competitive challenges by seeking deregulation which enabled them to participate more fully in the booming stock market of the late 1920s.

After the crash of the stock market, the economy was paralyzed by waves of bank failures in the early 1930s. The Pecora hearings (1932–34) exposed scandalous activity by the most prominent financial institutions, and the proposition that the increasingly speculative tendencies of banks had played an important role in destabilizing the financial system became influential. New Dealers sought to understand how the prominent banks had been enticed to participate in the financial speculation and dubious financial practices that flourished in the late 1920s by focusing on the competitive pressures that encouraged the migration of depository banks into investment banking activities. In particular, they highlighted the conflicts of interest and moral hazard problems that ensued once commercial banks were allowed to engage in investment banking.

Several institutional and historical issues are relevant to the New Dealers' analysis of the competitive conditions facing commercial banks in the 1920s. In particular, it is important to note that the US banking system has been characterized by a relatively large number of commercial banks. The National Banking Act of 1863 (and other previous state banking laws) embraced "free banking," the principle that the any firm should be allowed to enter commercial banking so long as it satisfied certain rather minimal general conditions that were uniformly applied to all market entrants.[3] The principle of free banking was later criticized as encouraging lenient capital requirements that contributed to dubious bank solvency and sometimes notorious banking practices.[4]

The large numbers of commercial banks – and the tendency towards lighter regulation of these banks – was also encouraged by the United States' dual banking system, in which commercial banks may be organized at the state or national levels (with the Office of the Comptroller of the Currency regulating national commercial banks and various state authorities, and the Federal Reserve – to various extents over time – regulating state banks). Multiple regulatory jurisdictions provide an incentive for regulators to charter banks (thereby enhancing the *raison d'être* of the regulators and garnering tax and other revenues for their jurisdiction). Multiple regulatory authorities also provide banks with the opportunity to threaten to change the jurisdiction in which they are chartered to compel regulators to match or exceed the permissiveness of rival jurisdictions. As regulatory agencies compete with each other to charter and regulate commercial banks, this creates what F.G. Awalt, acting Comptroller of the Currency, described in 1932 as a "competition in laxity" (Wheelock, 1992, 6).[5]

The proliferation of commercial banks was further encouraged by various regional and political factors that protected state and local banking structures. A long-standing suspicion of the big banks associated with the "money trust" galvanized an effective lobby thwarting interstate banking. Regional banks and their advocates opposed interstate banking on the grounds that larger banks would destroy local competition and drain savings into the large financial centers, thus depriving the local economy of funds. In some jurisdictions, this commitment to local banking resulted in unit banking laws (the prohibition on a bank having multiple branches).

Between the turn of the century and 1920, the number of incorporated banks grew from 8,320 to 28,695. In their examinations of the factors contributing to the 1930s banking crises, many regulatory authorities argued that this "over-banking" problem generated competitive pressures that enticed banks to migrate towards heightened risks. J.F.T. O'Connor, a prominent financial regulator privy to the high-level policy debates of the New Deal era,[6] claimed that "banks became too numerous; competition too great; necessity for profit too urgent" (O'Connor, 1938, 7).[7]

The crowded banking market was not the only dilemma faced by commercial banks in the 1920s. Banks were losing ground in the lucrative business of providing loans to businesses thanks to the increasingly attractive option of accessing investment capital by selling securities in booming financial markets. Under these circumstances, the "Decline of the Commercial Loan" was heralded in the pages of the *Quarterly Journal of Economics* by Lauchlin Currie in 1931. Currie reported that commercial loans expressed as a percentage of the total earning assets of national banks declined from 57.5 percent in 1920 to 37 percent in 1929.[8] Parker Willis, a prominent proponent of the Glass–Steagall Act, argued that:

> A "new era" had arrived in the years 1921–1929 in which corporations came more and more to avoid borrowing at banks, and to substitute therefore the practice of providing themselves with working capital in the stock market. [. . .] This new era was to be one in which the business enterprise would no longer be dependent upon the bank and would resort to the public in order to satisfy its needs for capital. (Willis, 1934, 35)

As the 1920s progressed, the banks were under pressure both from competition within the commercial banking sector and competition from investment banks (and trust companies[9]) as securities markets gathered momentum. In this context, profitable opportunities associated with the booming stock market were enticing,[10] and commercial banks sought entry into investment banking. Banks' previous attempts to expand into securities underwriting had been curtailed by the regulator of the nationally chartered commercial banks, the Comptroller of the Currency (Carosso, 1970, 97).[11] Commercial banks attempted to circumvent these restrictions via securities affiliates, but the growth of these securities affiliates was constrained because of legal disputes, regulatory uncertainties, and potential anti-trust concerns. By the mid-1920s, many state jurisdictions had been prevailed upon to allow state-chartered commercial banks to migrate into investment-banking activities. In 1927, the remaining regulatory obstacles were surmounted by the passage of the McFadden Act, which enabled nationally chartered banks to fully engage in securities underwriting via the creation of securities affiliates.[12] The passage of the McFadden Act marked the full-scale regulatory embrace of diversified financial conglomerates and the repudiation of the long-standing precept in English banking theory that commercial banking should be sealed off from the inherent risks of investment banking.[13] A surge of mergers among commercial banks and free-standing investment banks followed, and by 1929 nearly every large urban commercial bank had one or more securities affiliates (Carosso, 1970, 278).

From the perspective of the New Dealers, this entry of commercial banks into investment banking contributed to the financial disarray of the 1930s. One recurrent theme of this critique was that the blending of commercial and investment banking created conflicts of interest that influenced the commercial banks' lending activities in ways that were deleterious to bank stability. The general outlines of these critiques are resonant today. A commercial bank may be less vigilant about the quality of its loans if it believes that it can use its investment-banking arm to relieve it of dubious borrowers. For example, the investment-banking arm might enable problem borrowers to issue securities and thereby repay their bank loans.[14] A commercial bank may also be compelled to use its lending portfolio to further the agenda of its investment bank. Loans may be advanced to finance the purchase of securities (possibly with the securities themselves acting as collateral).[15] Investment banks may be better situated to attract underwriting business if they can lend funds to firms in the period prior to the issuance of securities. It is also possible (although often illegal) to engage in "loan-tying" (making the availability of credit conditional on other business interactions, such as the issuance of securities). Loans might be made to the investment-banking arm itself (or, if this is prohibited, less overt means of accomplishing the same thing may be devised) to finance the carrying of inventories of securities or to enable the investment bank to trade "on its own account".

The growing tendency of Federal Reserve member banks to make loans on securities while they were becoming more involved with investment banking is suggestive of the many ways in which banks' lending activities were being influenced by investment-banking concerns (see Figure 7.1). When the stock market crashed, many of these loans were highly compromised, particularly in situations in which corporate securities themselves served as collateral for the initial loans.[16] To the degree that commercial bank loan portfolios were dependent on the performance of stock markets, instability in securities markets was transmitted to the commercial banking system.

The Pecora–Gray hearings publicized many notorious activities alleged to have occurred thanks to the conflicts of interest and speculative excess encouraged by the blending of commercial and investment banking. For example, National City Bank (the world's second largest bank at the time and predecessor of today's Citigroup) and its securities affiliate, National City Company (the US's largest investment bank in the late 1920s), stood publicly accused of all sorts of dubious and possibly illegal practices stemming from the interaction of their commercial and investment-banking arms. In one noteworthy episode, National City Company rescued its parent bank from the consequences of its disastrous Cuban Sugar loans by selling stocks in the failing sugar company to investors (who were not apprised of the dubious quality of these stocks). The proceeds of this public offering allowed National City Bank to avoid a large loan loss, but left stockholders with next to nothing (Pecora, 1939, 122). Its

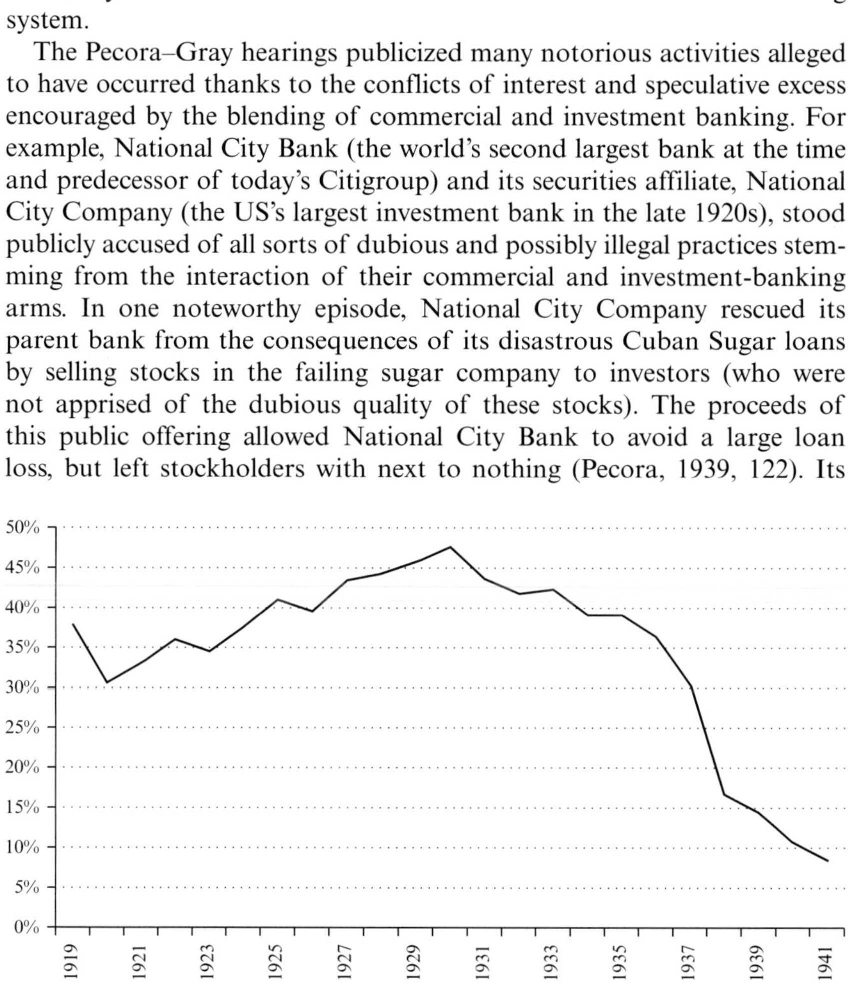

Source: Banking and Monetary Statistics.

Figure 7.1 Commercial bank loans made on securities as a percentage of total commercial bank loans

questionable securities underwriting included bonds issued by borrowers that were earlier described by bank officials as "lax, negligent, and entirely uninformed about the responsibilities of a long-term borrower" (Carosso, 1970, 330). National City was also suspected of manipulating copper prices to protect itself from losses on the large amount of Anaconda Copper Company stocks it held (Kotz, 1978, 51).

Contemporary financial reform advocates are well aware that the intertwining of commercial and investment banking poses moral hazard concerns that can encourage increasingly risky behavior by banks. Governments provide a safety net for depository banks (in the form of lender of last resort support) to stabilize the banking system because commercial banks are structurally vulnerable to bank runs (given the highly leveraged nature of depository banking), and bank failures can have contagion effects (if the failure of a large or important bank jeopardizes other banks in a highly interlinked banking system). To deter contagion effects, the state can extend its lender of last resort support to banks to restore confidence in the banking system's stability.

However, if depository banks are engaged in financial market (or even commercial) activities outside of the traditional business of taking deposits and making loans, it is possible that the intended "narrow" linkage between depository banking and lender of last resort support may be expanded (see Corrigan, 2000). In the event that problems in securities markets are transmitted to commercial banks, authorities may fear that a crisis originating outside the banking system proper may destabilize the banking system. For example, if a crisis in investment-banking activities threatens the commercial bank housed within the same firm, then the government may be compelled to provide support lest the crisis elsewhere in the firm destabilize its commercial banking arm and thereby provoke contagion in the banking system. Moreover, if commercial bank lending portfolios have become highly oriented to securities markets, the state may be obliged to regard entire non-banking financial markets as "too-big-to-fail."

To the extent that the government's safety net is broadened, moral hazard concerns are exacerbated. Incentives exist to increase risk exposure in the investment-banking affiliates of commercial banks if investment bankers perceive that their firms would be likely to impinge upon the safety net in a crisis. Of course, internal firewalls and other restrictions may be constructed to insulate the banking system from these pressures. But such mechanisms are always in jeopardy if their breach opens profitable opportunities for both synergies between the commercial and investment banking and new opportunities to impose upon the safety net.

Carter Glass, a recognized authority in banking matters owing to his role in the creation of the Federal Reserve System, was deeply suspicious that the blending of commercial and investment banking had contaminated the banking system with "stock gamblers" (Glass, 1929) resulting in the "misapplication" of credit for speculative purposes which deprives "legitimate business" of funds (see Willis, 1934, 53). The extensive study co-authored by Glass' confidante Parker Willis depicts a slippery slope in which the investment banking arms of commercial banks created increasing pressure to intertwine commercial bank-loan portfolios with the fortunes of securities markets during the 1920s. Ultimately, Willis concludes that the blending of commercial and investment banking was an ill-advised experiment in American finance:

> Accordingly, the tendency of investment banking to develop as a parasitic growth, drawing its support from commercial banking and constituting a diversion of the funds of the latter, notwithstanding that they were normally called-for as a means of liquidating demand obligations, presented numerous elements of danger, which did not, however, secure recognition at an early date. As often happens in financial development, it was an incidental phase of investment banking which originally operated to bring to the front the hazards that were involved in the maintenance of commercial and investment banking as phases of the activity of the same institution. (Willis and Chapman, 1934, 178)

This growing critique of the destabilizing consequences of the blending of commercial and investment banking gained political traction in the period leading up to the New Deal financial reforms. Financial conglomerates, tainted by the long-standing antipathy towards the reviled money trust, became emblematic of the abuses of financiers. Indeed, Roosevelt reflected this anti-finance sentiment in his inaugural address.[17] Thus the Roosevelt administration had the political opportunity to intervene in the re-organization of the financial sector in ways that might have been considered far too radical in the absence of public animosity towards finance. Moreover, the apparent inability of the banking sector to resolve its difficulties was a persuasive indication that the government was justified intervening in a broken system. Despite considerable opposition to the "creeping socialism"[18] of New Deal measures, finance largely acquiesced to these reforms, possibly because they feared even less appealing alternatives such as the nationalization of banks.[19]

By the time of Roosevelt's inauguration, the banking system was facing imminent collapse. In an environment of falling incomes and widespread unemployment, defaults on loans and the devaluation of the collateral backing those loans contributed to an acute crisis in commercial banking. A downward spiral was generated as the loss of confidence in bank solvency instigated bank runs, which in turn provoked bank failures and intensified the downward cycle further. State and nationally chartered commercial banks in operation dropped from 24,258 in 1929 to 15,021 by 1934. Deposits held in Federal Reserve member banks declined continuously from their high point prior to the stock market crash (see Figure 7.2). When Roosevelt received word that the states of New York and Illinois were poised to suspend banking operations, he was immediately obliged to declare (and later extend) a national bank holiday.

NEW DEAL BANKING REFORMS

Given the existence of a banking crisis and a general economic depression, the architects of New Deal banking reforms faced several simultaneous challenges. A banking system in collapse threatens credit and transactions in the general economy, thus it was imperative to restore the stability of the banking sector, and the financial system in general. Yet it was important to reform the banking sector in a manner that would be conducive to overall economic recovery. It would have sabotaged the larger New Deal agenda for economic recovery if banks had been stabilized in a manner that was deleterious to the promotion of economic growth. This section makes the case that – deliberately or fortuitously – New Deal banking reforms stabilized the banking system while ensuring that the banking system was structured in a manner conducive to economic growth. But despite the dexterity with which these financial reforms pursued these objectives, they also set in motion tensions that contributed to undermining the New Deal regulatory framework with the passage of time.

The Banking Act of 1933 emphasized the deterrence of speculation as a requisite of bank stability,[20] and its Glass–Steagall provisions were largely viewed as the protecting the banking system from contamination by the speculative pressures that may emerge when depository banks involve themselves in securities markets.[21] Section 20 of the Act required commercial banks belonging to the Federal Reserve System to divest themselves of their securities affiliates within one year. In combination with several other subsections of the Act,[22] this ended the combination of commercial and investment banking in the United States (until the mergers and acquisitions of the late 1990s that occurred in anticipation of the ultimate the repeal of Glass–Steagall in 1999).[23] The tearing apart of the financial conglomerates associated with the reviled money trust helped to appease public anger towards financiers, and enhanced Roosevelt's credibility as a president willing to act on his admonitions to the financial sector.

Roosevelt's vilification of speculation was no doubt cathartic for an angry population, but the Glass–Steagall separation of commercial and investment banking did little to address the precarious position of commercial banks. Surviving banks confronted an acute profitability crisis: the return on assets[24] hovered between 0.99 percent and 1.19 percent throughout the 1920s, but it had dipped to −1.07 percent by 1933 (see Russell, 2008, 54). So long as banking profitability was under such pressure, fragility in the banking sector would persist. Ironically, the Glass–Steagall Act placed further constraints on commercial banks profitability, insofar as the separation of commercial and investment banking largely foreclosed the possibility that banks might supplement their profitability via non-banking financial activities. Thus, Glass–Steagall forced banks to rely on commercial banking at a time when commercial banking was in crisis.

There are many reasons why an unprofitable banking system cannot be resilient, but profitability problems also had other ramifications that threatened the larger economic recovery. For example, Epstein and Ferguson (1984) argue this commercial bank profitability problem thwarted expansionary monetary policy. Prior to the Banking Act of 1933, commercial banks paid interest on demand deposits. This represented a serious burden to commercial banks facing both substantial loan losses and dismal earnings on their loan portfolios. In response to this dilemma, and to enhance their liquidity in the event of further banking panics, banks increasingly held short-term government securities. By 1932, "investments" (mostly in government securities) comprised 50 percent of bank earning portfolios among members of the Federal Reserve System (Epstein and Ferguson, 1984, 969). Bank reliance on income from their holdings of government securities created an important obstacle to expansionary monetary policy. Epstein and Ferguson argue that the Federal Reserve briefly experimented with open market operations to increase the money supply, but this policy further squeezed banks' earnings on their government securities.[25] Alarmed by this additional drag on their profitability, commercial banks succeeded in pressuring the Federal Reserve to abandon expansionary monetary policy.[26]

The Banking Act of 1933 included a number of provisions that worked synergistically to enhance the profitability of commercial banks. The Act created federal deposit insurance, which buttressed public confidence depositors and slowed bank failures precipitously.[27] This renewed trust encouraged depositors to return to banks to store their savings. Between 1933 and the end of the decade deposits grew 8.1 percent (Figure 7.2). The Banking Act also permitted the implementation of limits on the payment of interest on deposits,[28] and the interest paid to secure a dollar of deposits plummeted (see Figure 7.3). Despite the dramatic increase in the funds on deposits, the total interest paid by Federal Reserve member banks on deposits declined from $287 million in 1933 to just under $160 million by 1939 (see Figure 7.4). New Deal interest rate controls represent an implicit

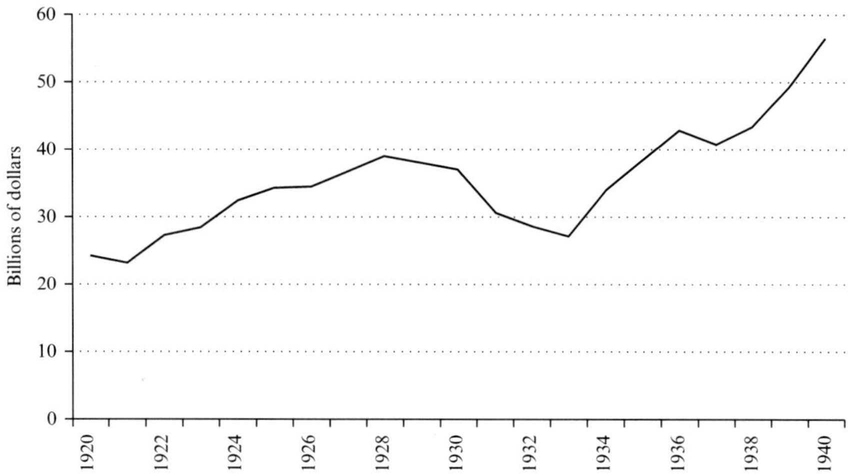

Source: Banking and Monetary Statistics.

Figure 7.2 Bank deposits, Federal Reserve member banks, 1920–41

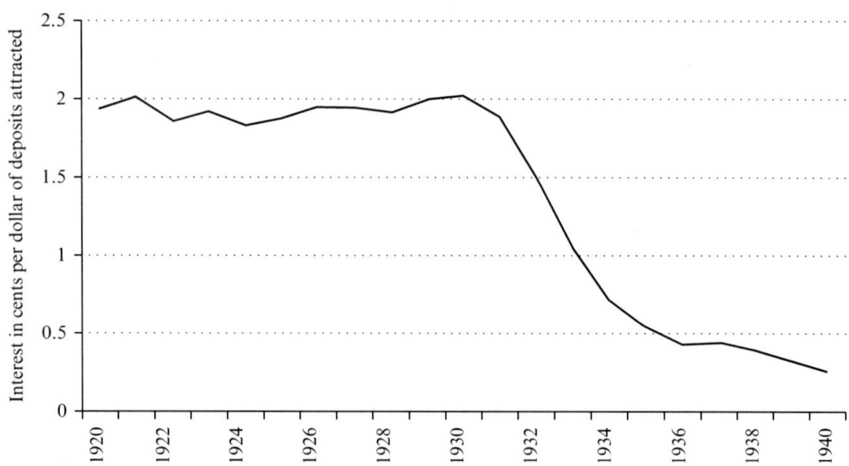

Source: Banking and Monetary Statistics.

Figure 7.3 Interests paid on deposit per dollar of deposits attracted at Federal Reserve member banks

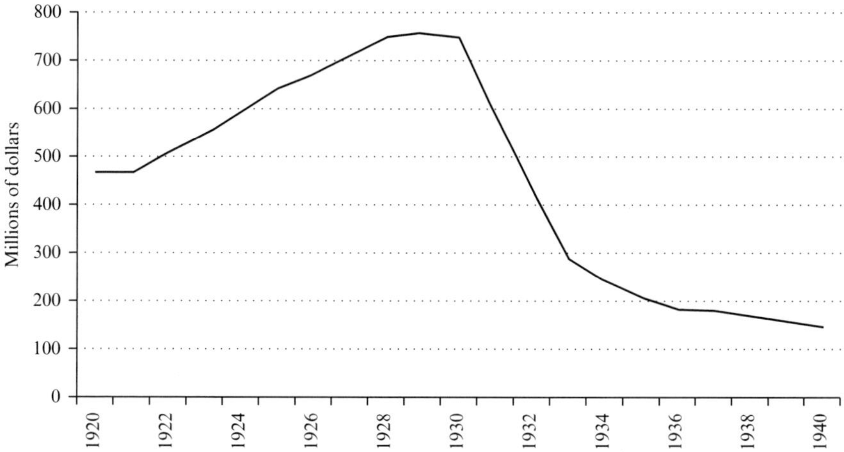

Source: Banking and Monetary Statistics.

Figure 7.4 Total interest paid on deposits at Federal Reserve member banks

subsidy to banks (since depositors gave up interest income on their deposits), but depositors were compensated for this loss by the security conferred by deposit insurance. Thus the Banking Act supported commercial bank profitability by ensuring that banks would have ready access to deposited funds (thanks to deposit insurance) at low cost (thanks to interest rate controls).

However, the concern with over-banking persisted, given that the ban on interstate banking continued, and Senator Glass's efforts to increase state-wide branching failed (see Russell, 2008, 73–4). The Federal Deposit Insurance Corporation (FDIC) became an important advocate for the elimination of "unfettered" competition among banks, and instead sought to create conditions of "rightful competition" in commercial banking (FDIC, 1998, 33). This culminated in the elimination of free banking in the Banking Act of 1935. The Act gave chartering bodies a degree of discretion over entry into commercial banking, and one of the criteria that had to be met before a new commercial bank could be chartered included regulatory consideration of the "future earnings prospects" of the bank.[29] This legal obligation imposed on banking regulators stood as an explicit acknowledgment that the profitability of commercial banks should be a guiding consideration.

Following the passage of the New Deal Banking reforms, commercial bank profitability recovered dramatically. As Figure 7.5 indicates, the "return

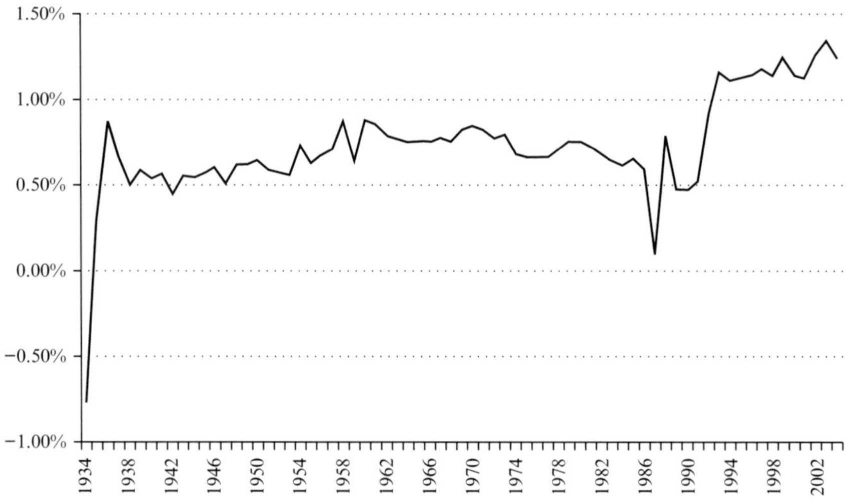

Sources: FDIC (2008); HSOB, Tables CB04 and CB09.

Figure 7.5 Return on assets 1933–99, FDIC-member commercial banks

on assets" of commercial banks jumped sharply following the passage of the Banking Act of 1933, and it had stabilized between 0.5 percent and 1 percent until the deregulatory era of the 1980s gathered momentum.

THE NEW DEAL FINANCIAL ARCHITECTURE AND THE RISE OF THE KEYNESIAN WELFARE STATE

While a banking sector in crisis certainly undermined any larger project for economic recovery, a stable and profitable banking sector does not necessarily conduct itself in a manner most conducive to economic growth. Banks, and the larger financial sector, must play a critical role in promoting economic growth by providing access to the investment capital necessary to spur economic growth. Conceivably, the creation of a protected banking sector that benefited from several sources of government support might enable banks to exploit this advantageous regulatory environment in ways that are not conducive to the promotion of vigorous investment. This section explores the ways in which the New Deal financial reforms militated against this possibility, and in so doing created a regulatory framework that was hospitable to the subsequent evolution of Keynesian welfare state capitalism.

While welfare state Keynesianism has many requisites (such as activist monetary and fiscal policy), this analysis is focused on the proposition that the viability of Keynesian-style aggregate demand stimulus is supported by a particular relationship between productive and financial capital. The pro-investment posture of welfare state Keynesianism is assisted to the extent that investment capital is forthcoming from the financial sector at low cost to promote economic growth. In addition to the other factors that shape the costs of accessing investment capital, the relative bargaining power of financial sector firms and those firms seeking access to funds to invest will influence the negotiation over the costs of accessing investment capital.

To understand how the Glass–Steagall Act influenced the relative bargaining power of providers and demanders of investment capital, consider the process through which a private sector firm secures external funds to finance an investment project. For present purposes, we shall assume that a firm in need of external sources of investment capital may approach the financial sector to secure funds through bank loans or via the sale of securities. The cost the firm must pay to secure funds depends on many factors, but we focus here on the relative bargaining power of the firms wishing to invest and the suppliers of funds. To the extent that the firm seeking funds for investment is in a good bargaining position relative to the providers of funds, this will exert downward pressure on the price of investment capital. In other words, any regulatory change that limits the bargaining power of financial sector firms *vis-à-vis* firms wishing to invest will limit the ability of financial sector firms to exploit an advantageous regulatory environment to increase the cost of securing investment funds.

The Glass–Steagall Act promoted the bargaining power of investing firms relative to the suppliers of investment capital. When financial sector firms are engaged in both investment and commercial banking, the two arms of the same firm are not likely to undercut each other to the advantage of the firm seeking investment capital. Moreover, there may be other considerations (such as a previous relationship between the financial sector firm and the firm in search of funds that mitigates information problems) that make it difficult for a firm seeking capital to leave a financial institution with which it has already established a reputation. Thus the combination of investment and commercial banking within a single financial sector firm tends to erode the bargaining power of firms seeking an infusion of capital to fund investment in productive capacity.

By separating investment banks, commercial banks, and other types of financial sector firms, Glass–Steagall enhanced competition among providers of investment capital. Thanks to Glass–Steagall, a firm contemplating an investment was better positioned to pit investment banks against commercial banks in order to bid down the costs of accessing investment capital. In this way, these New Deal reforms deterred upward pressure on the costs of securing investment capital while at the same time stabilizing and supporting the banking system.

Glass–Steagall set the stage for a domestic financial framework that prevailed throughout the era of the postwar Keynesian welfare state. Under Glass–Steagall's influence, American finance became characterized by "financial compartmentalization," in which commercial banks, investment banks, pension funds, mutual funds and insurance companies were placed in separate regulatory categories. These financial sector firms could provide investment capital, thus stimulating competition that tends to bid down its price. Yet each regulatory category was protected from cross-category competition in the particular manner in which they accessed funds (that is, only commercial banks could offer insured deposits, while only pension funds could receive pension contributions, and so on). Each category of financial sector firm was made more profitable by the protected access they enjoyed by acquiring funds in the manner particular to their regulatory category. For decades, this domestic financial regulatory framework encouraged the relative financial stability and low interest rates characteristic of the "golden age" of Keynesian economics in the United States. As the deregulatory impulses of a resurgent neoliberalism gathered steam, several provisions of the New Deal Financial reforms were either undermined or repealed in the 1980s and 1990s, culminating in the repeal of the Glass–Steagall provisions in 1999.

THE DÉNOUEMENT OF THE NEW DEAL REGULATORY FRAMEWORK

This New Deal domestic financial regulatory framework presided over a period of relative stability in the banking system combined with the low real interest rates that characterized the golden age of Keynesian welfare state capitalism in the United States. But it nonetheless set in motion tensions that ultimately undermined this regulatory framework. The functional segregation of financial intermediaries necessarily bestows an uneven assortment of both prerogatives and disadvantages to financial firms of different regulatory categories. This creates incentives to subvert these categories as firms of a given category seek to avoid the restrictions of their category while attaining the advantages enjoyed by firms in other regulatory categories. At the same time, firms in each category seek to maximize the advantages they enjoy under this framework while preventing any extension of their distinctive privileges to firms of other categories.

These tensions may be latent under some circumstances, but the potential for internecine struggle inheres in a regulatory framework that necessarily creates a patchwork of strictures and perquisites. Amidst a particular historical confluence of factors, financial sector firms were compelled to abide by the restrictions on their activities implied by financial compartmentalization. However, as these contextual circumstances evolved, new and profitable opportunities to subvert regulatory categories proved irresistible. Ultimately, the New Deal regulatory framework was undermined as conditions during the dénouement of the welfare state (such as the acceleration of inflation) set the stage for financial innovations designed to manipulate the mosaic of competitive advantages or disadvantages created by financial compartmentalization.

Jane D'Arista's research on domestic finance illuminates many of the strategies employed as banks and non-banks struggled to subvert the Glass–Steagall regulatory categories. Non-banks sought to intrude on traditional banking activity via a variety of financial innovations that siphoned savings out of the commercial banking system and used these funds to out-compete commercial banks as providers of funds. Even non-financial corporations such as automobile manufacturers were able to access funds and make loans (initially for the purchase of the parent company's product) by intermediating funds outside of traditional banking channels in a development that D'Arista and Schlesinger have called the "parallel banking system" (1997).

Banks responded to this competitive pressure by pursuing financial innovations intended to enhance their profitability in both their traditional activities and new lines of business. Their competitive advantages – explicit access to lender of last resort support and the ability to offer insured deposits – were attributes to exploit in their competitive strategies. And to assist them in these efforts, banks attacked regulation impediments that disadvantaged them *vis-à-vis* non-bank competitors (for example, banks succeeded in having required reserves reduced), which ultimately had repercussions for commercial bank stability. Moreover, banks were emboldened to take a variety of risks given the moral hazard that animates their special relationship to the state, and this migration into riskier activities also had implications for financial stability. As the stock market bubble in the late 1990s gained momentum, it was again intolerable to banks that they were excluded from the profitable opportunities open to other financial firms, and in 1999 they succeeded in removing the Glass–Steagall impediments to their full-scale entry into commercial banking.

CONCLUSION

As the most recent financial crisis has intensified demands for financial reregulation, some Glass–Steagall Act precepts are again in circulation. For example, the so-called Volker Rule (restricting proprietary trading by banks) is reminiscent of Glass–Steagall in its attempt to prevent banks from exposing themselves to the risks of trading securities on their own accounts. However, this chapter's reconsideration of New Deal financial reforms is not offered as endorsement of any project to reinstitute financial reforms of the past. Indeed, the D'Arista legacy of insisting on regard for historical and institutional context obliges us to consider the dramatic difference between the current financial environment and that of the 1930s. Many particular contextual circumstances contributed to the resilience of Glass–Steagall (limited international capital mobility, relatively stable interest rates, technological limitations of the times, and many other factors). Certainly, securities markets may now be intertwined with banking, and contagion effects can spread to and from the depository banking system, in ways never foreseen by the authors of the New Deal banking reforms. Given these dynamics, and the pervasive challenge of moral hazard problems in the wake of the 2008 financial crisis, the Glass–Steagall regulatory architecture would face important challenges in the contemporary context.

Financial reform inspired by Glass–Steagall cannot rely on nostalgia for a simpler time in which banking, and the financial sector generally, was confined to its modest role as a servant to the larger economy. Depository banks confined to the "plain vanilla" business of taking deposits and making loans to fund useful economic activity will be enticed to breach these walls so long as other financial activities overshadow the profitability of this most basic function of financial intermediation. Indeed, in the aftermath of 2008, banks understand the competitive advantage they enjoy thanks to their "too big to fail" status, which both reduces their cost of funds and creates powerful incentives to locate risk-taking activities within a bank.

The New Deal experience suggests that – so long as regulatory reforms prohibit certain activities – there will be pressure to subvert these reforms if circumstances emerge that renders these prohibited activities profitable. Indeed, much of financial innovation is inspired by the attempt to circumvent regulatory restrictions, thus obliging the state (assuming the state is motivated to do so) to devote monumental resources to the policing of regulatory boundaries in the perpetual task of attempting to preserve the spirit of the restriction. To avoid the sabotage of regulatory restrictions, the financial reforms must make it profitable for banks to do what regulators wish them to do, otherwise (when circumstances present themselves) the temptations to do otherwise will prove too great.

This presents some intriguing implications. Some advocates of financial reforms prefer seemingly modest, incremental measures, which may be intended to set the stage for further progressive economic intervention. But it can prove very challenging to design even modest measures that both meaningfully contribute to financial stability and are both sufficiently attractive to banks to secure their complicity and feasible to enforce by resource-constrained governmental authorities. Moreover, it is indeed demoralizing for advocates of progressive economic change to be obliged to design their reforms around the necessity of securing the consent of those entities responsible for many of the destabilizing financial pressures.

Alternatively, we might seek more ambitious alternatives. If moral hazard dilemmas are such that depository banks cannot be persuaded to relinquish the activities that invite systemic crisis, then perhaps we should consider whether basic banking functions should be executed for profit by capitalist firms (Russell, 2012). Or perhaps these functions must be allocated to small-scale community banks that are sufficiently numerous and insulated from securities market functions that the "too big to fail" problem is alleviated. These options are decidedly out of the realm of a modest economic reform that can portray itself as an incremental measure (and thus it will provoke immediate objections on the part of banks). Even if such a project were accomplished, new tensions emanating from that arrangement must be anticipated – although theorizing the tensions in a context that differs so significantly from the present context is indeed challenging.

Any way of proceeding is fraught with difficulties. That alone should not deter us (the status quo is also fraught with difficulties). The relative success and longevity of the New Deal financial reforms contradict the presumption that it is not possible to dramatically reshape the financial sector as part of an agenda of progressive economic reform. The ambitious scope of New Deal financial reforms – including dismantling financial empires such as J.P. Morgan's that had epitomized the power of finance in America – was possible given the particular confluence of factors in the 1930s. These factors include the widespread suspicion that the dubious practices of financiers bore large responsibility for the financial and economic crisis.[30]

Perhaps a time may transpire when it is politically possible to impose financial reforms which have previously been unthinkable. New Deal banking reforms offer some historical precedent to suggest that it may again be possible to seize on public condemnation of the financial system to support progressive change. As I write (August 2011), Standard & Poor's has just downgraded US debt, which serves as a helpful reminder that momentous events transpire that may have seemed entirely impossible in the not very distant past. Sometimes, as in the case of the New

Deal, circumstances are such that bold experiments are possible. Indeed, D'Arista, and others who have shared her concern for progressive financial reform, have toiled in preparation for just such a moment.

NOTES

1. Thanks to the influence of Mundell–Fleming's analysis of the "irreconcilable trinity", Bretton Woods was seen as enabling nations to navigate this trilemma by enabling them to impose capital controls, thus creating the opportunity to pursue full employment or other economic agendas characteristic of the Keynesian welfare state era (see Eatwell and Taylor, 2000, 35).
2. Subsections 16, 20, 21 and 32 of the Banking Act of 1933 are widely referred to as the "Glass–Steagall Act."
3. Free banking was a reaction against the bank chartering process of the late 1700s and early 1800s. At that time a special legislative act was required to permit entry into commercial banking. This element of discretion afforded officials the opportunity to demand financial or political favors in return for permission to open a bank.
4. For example, the highly influential Bray Hammond reinforced the association between free banking and unsound banking practices in his description of egregious banking conduct during the free banking era (1941, 9).
5. For example, in March 1900, the Comptroller of the Currency responded to pressure from nationally chartered commercial banks to reduce capital requirements from $50,000 to $25,000 for commercial banks in smaller communities (so that they could compete with state-chartered commercial banks). In turn, many states lowered capital requirements below $25,000. In the six months following the Comptroller of the Currency's decision, 509 new national commercial banks were approved, which represents a 14 percent increase in the number of nationally chartered commercial banks (Fischer, 1968, 192; Wheelock, 1992, 6; and author's calculation).
6. O'Connor was Comptroller of the Currency between 1933 and 1938, a member of the Federal Reserve Board between 1933 and 1935, and the first vice-chairman of the Federal Deposit Insurance Corporation (FDIC).
7. For example, a report of a survey of banking conditions in Indiana claimed that these highly competitive conditions eroded profits (O'Connor, 1938, 85):

   > Competition for deposits drove interest rates up to fantastic figures and resulted in all types of free services being offered. Competition for loans was so great that conservative credit principles were abandoned in an effort to secure business. [. . .] Exhaustive studies that have been made on this subject all agree that the over-banked condition of the state was, in a considerable measure, responsible, both directly and indirectly, for the large number of failures which occurred among banks in Indiana in the decade of the '20s and in the early '30s.

8. Currie's category of "commercial" loans is actually "all other loans," which he regards as commonly equated with commercial loans. He reports that commercial loans in the strict sense (loans eligible for rediscount) declined relative to other assets of national banks from 21.1 percent in 1923 to 13.9 percent in 1929 (Currie, 1931, 698). Peach (1941) provides a similar account.
9. Perkins (1971) provides a concise overview of the evolution of trust companies and their involvement in both securities markets and depository banking.
10. As Melvin Traylor of First National Bank of Chicago testified (in Peach, 1941, 25, footnote): "In the purely banking business, where you accept deposits and make loans,

the pickings, in the language of the street, got short and that led to the development of the trust business and security business."

11. Kaufman and Mote (1992) claim, contra many authorities in the field, that the Comptroller of the Currency issued no formal ruling in 1902 specifically prohibiting nationally chartered commercial banks from dealing in securities. They claim that these banks could only engage in investment-banking activities via the "incidental powers provision" of the National Bank Act, while state chartered commercial banks often had explicit authorization to engage in investment banking. Thus the more permissive regulatory climate enjoyed by state chartered commercial banks enhanced their ability to engage in investment banking activities, and the McFadden Act was demanded to equalize the status of national and state commercial banks in this respect.
12. The McFadden Act is perhaps more often remembered for its strengthening of the prevention of banking across state lines, thereby contributing to the perpetuation of the over-banking dilemma.
13. D'Arista explores the rationale for the "needs of trade" approach to commercial banking in English banking theory (1993, 63–4).
14. A more contemporary example is the possiblity that the commercial bank dilutes its lending standards – for, say, home mortgages – insofar as it intends to pass these loans on to be securitized.
15. Securities may serve as collateral for loans in commercial banks that have no connections with investment banks. However, the concern is that this activity will be more prevalent in firms where conflicts of interest exist between commercial and investment banking functions.
16. Willis and Chapman (1934, 556) indicate that in 1926 (prior to the passage of the McFadden Act), 30.1 percent of the loans of national banks were secured by stocks and bonds. By 1930, 37.8 percent of the loans of national banks were secured by stocks and bonds.
17. Roosevelt's inaugural address (1933) famously condemned the "unscrupulous money changers" who now stood "indicted in the court of public opinion, rejected by the hearts and minds of men". He continued to say:

> Stripped of the lure of profit by which to induce our people to follow their false leadership, they have resorted to exhortations, pleading tearfully for restored confidence. They know only the rules of a generation of self-seekers. They have no vision, and when there is no vision the people perish. The money changers have fled from their high seats in the temple of our civilization. We may now restore that temple to the ancient truths. The measure of the restoration lies in the extent to which we apply social values more noble than mere monetary profit.

18. Ironically, aspects of the New Deal banking reforms that first elicited opposition as "socialist" were later embraced by bankers. Deposit insurance was initially seen as "socialist," and later viewed as the savior of the banking system. Consider the initial opposition of Percy Johnson (Chemical Bank and Trust Company of New York), who testified at the Banking and Currency hearings of the US Senate that (in Burns, 1974, 67): "I do not think [a guarantee should be made to bank depositors], unless we are going to guarantee all elements of society against misfortunes and evils of all kinds. Of course, if we are going to have socialistic government, then we ought to guarantee everybody against all manner of things."
19. Rumors of nationalization were occasionally inflamed by comments such as those of Albert Agnew, General Counsel for the Federal Reserve Bank of San Francisco, who warned ominously from the pages of a banking periodical (in Burns, 1974, 73): "Either the bankers of this country will realize that they are guardians of the moneys committed to their charge, and will conduct themselves accordingly, or banking will cease to be a private enterprise and will become a purely government function."

20. The preamble indicates that it is "an act to provide for the safer and more effective use of the assets of banks, to regulate interbank control, to prevent the undue diversion of funds into speculative operations" (in Kross, 1969, 2758).
21. Other aspects of the Act addressed speculation. For example, the Act also required that loan portfolios be scrutinized in order to prevent the allocation of bank credit for speculative purposes. Section 3(a) required that:

    > each Federal Reserve Board shall keep itself informed of the general character and amount of the loans and investments of its member banks with a view to ascertaining whether undue use is being made of bank credit for the speculative carrying of or trading in securities, real estate, or commodities, or for any other purpose inconsistent with the maintenance of sound credit conditions.

    The Act goes on to say that a bank judged to be making "undue" use of bank credit in the judgment of the Federal Reserve Board could be suspended from the use of the credit facilities of the Federal Reserve System.
22. Section 16 prohibited commercial banks from purchasing equities and underwriting securities on their own behalf (with the exception of US Treasuries and general obligations of states and political subdivisions); Section 21 prohibited investment banks from accepting deposits; and Section 32 prohibited interlocking directorates between commercial and investment banks.
23. An exception was made to enable commercial banks to engage in the underwriting and dealing of certain government securities.
24. Note that the return on assets must be multiplied by the so-called "equity multiplier" (a leverage factor) to derive the return on equity, a measure which is frequently used to evaluate profitability. Hence return on assets is typically a much lower number than the return on equity (see Sinkey, 2002, 131).
25. Epstein and Ferguson (1984, 970) state that rates on short-term Treasury notes dropped from 3.4 percent in 1929 to 0.34 percent in 1932. They claim that as interest rates fell, commercial banks were unable to realize capital gains from these government securities because of the shortness of the banks' portfolios (ibid.).
26. Epstein and Ferguson conclude that (1984, 982–3):

    > The capitalist organization of finance implies that interest rates may fail to drop low enough to revive an economy because bank earnings might not permit it in an acute Depression. Moreover, contemporary students of money and banking have not reconciled a fundamental problem of the current system of bank regulation: that the Federal Reserve system is charged with performing two often incompatible tasks – that of advancing the interests of a specific industry while simultaneously overseeing the protection of other business and the public at a large.

27. For information on numbers of bank failures prior to and following the Banking Act of 1933 see Russell (2008, 55, 70).
28. Maximum interest rates were set on savings accounts and the previously common practice of paying interest on checking accounts was forbidden.
29. Officials were directed in the Act to consider "the financial history and condition of the bank, the adequacy of its capital structure, its future earnings prospects, the general character of its management, the convenience and needs of the community to be served, and whether or not its corporate powers are consistent with the purposes of this section" (in Hammond, 1941, 60–61).
30. "Yet our distress comes from no failure of substance. We are stricken by no plague of locusts. [. . .] Primarily this [distress] is because rulers of the exchange of mankind's goods have failed through their own stubbornness and their own incompetence, have

admitted their failure, and have abdicated. Practices of the unscrupulous money changers stand indicted in the court of public opinion, rejected by the hearts and minds of men" (Roosevelt, 1933).

REFERENCES

Board of Governors of the Federal Reserve System. 1943. *Banking and Monetary Statistics*. Washington, DC: Federal Reserve.

Burns, Helen. 1974. *The American Banking Community and the New Deal Banking Reforms, 1933–1935*. Westport, CT: Greenwood Press.

Carosso, Vincent. 1970. *Investment Banking in America: A History*. Cambridge, MA: Harvard University Press.

Currie, Lauchlin. 1931. "The Decline of the Commercial Loan," *The Quarterly Journal of Economics*, **45** (4) (August): 698–709.

D'Arista, Jane. 1993. *The Evolution of US Finance: Volume Two*. Armonk, NY: M.E. Sharpe.

D'Arista, Jane and Tom Schlesinger. 1997. "The Emerging Parallel Banking System," in Clifford Kirsch (ed.), *The Financial Services Revolution*, Chicago, IL: Irwin Professional Publishing, 485–504.

Eatwell, John and Lance Taylor. 2000. *Global Finance at Risk: The Case for International Regulation*. New York: The New Press.

Epstein, Gerald and Thomas Ferguson. 1984. "Monetary Policy, Loan Liquidations and Industrial Conflict: The Federal Reserve and the Open Market Operations of 1932," *The Journal of Economic History*, **44**: 957–83.

Federal Deposit Insurance Corporation. 1998. *A Brief History of Deposit Insurance in the United States*, http://www.fdic.gov/bank/historical/brief/brhist.pdf (accessed February 21, 2007).

Federal Deposit Insurance Corporation. *Historical Statistics on Banking*. http://www2.fdic.gov/hsob/SelectRpt.asp?EntryTyp=10 (accessed November 5, 2006).

Fischer, Gerald. 1968. *American Banking Structure*. New York: Columbia University Press.

Kaufman, George and Larry Mote. 1992. "Commercial Bank Securities Activities: What Really Happened in 1902: Note," *Journal of Money, Credit and Banking*, **24**: 370–74.

Glass, Carter. 1929. "Stock Gambling," *New York Times*, August 21.

Hammond, Bray. 1941. "Historical Introduction," in Members of the Staff of the Board of Governors of the Federal Reserve System (eds), *Banking Studies*, Baltimore, MD: Waverly Press, 39–64.

Hayes, Samuel. 1987. "Introduction," in Samuel Hayes (ed.), *Wall Street and Regulation*, Boston, MA: Harvard Business School Press, 1–6.

Helleiner, Eric. 1994. *States and the Reemergence of Global Finance*. Ithaca, NY: Cornell University Press.

Kotz, David. 1978. *Bank Control of Large Corporations in the United States*. Berkeley, CA: University of California Press.

O'Connor, J.F.T. 1938. *The Banking Crisis and Recovery under the Roosevelt Administration*. Chicago, IL: Callaghan and Company.

Peach, Nelson. 1941. *The Security Affiliates of National Banks*. Baltimore, MD: The John Hopkins Press.

Pecora, Ferdinand. 1939. *Wall Street Under Oath*. New York: Simon and Schuster.

Perkins, Edwin. 1971. "The Divorce of Commercial and Investment Banking: A History," *The Banking Law Journal*, **88**: 483–528.

Roosevelt, Franklin D. 1933. "Inaugural Address," http://www.presidency.ucsb.edu/ws/?pid=14473 (accessed March 10, 2007).

Russell, Ellen. 2008. *New Deal Banking Reforms and Keynesian Welfare State Capitalism*. New York: Routledge Press.

Russell, Ellen. 2012. *No More Swimming Naked: The Need for Modesty in Canadian Banking*. Ottawa: Canadian Centre for Policy Alternatives.

Sinkey, Joseph. 2002. *Commercial Bank Financial Management*, 6th ed., Upper Saddle River, NJ: Prentice Hall.

Wheelock, David. 1992. "Government Policy and Banking Instability: Overbanking in the 1920s." Federal Reserve Bank of St. Louis Working Paper 1992–007A. http://research.stlouisfed.org/wp/1992/92–007.pdf (accessed December 31, 2006)

Willis, Parker. 1934. "A Crisis in American Banking," in Parker Willis and John Chapman (eds), *The Banking Situation: American Post-War Problems and Developments*, New York: Columbia University Press, 103–18.

Willis, Parker and John Chapman (eds). 1934. *The Banking Situation: American Post-War Problems and Developments*, New York: Columbia University Press.

8. The financial trilemma and the future of American banking

Gary A. Dymski*

INTRODUCTION

While banking crises have provided front-page drama for the past five years, when one takes a historical perspective it quickly emerges that banking systems have been in crisis in one part of the world or another during much of the last 30 years. Focusing only on the Americas, our central concern here gives a lengthy list: the disintermediation crisis and massive deregulation of US banks in 1980; the 1982 Latin American debt crisis; the US savings and loan crisis; the 1994–95 Tequila crisis; the 1998 Long-Term Capital Management (LTCM) crisis and its fallout; the Argentine crisis of 2001; the "sudden stop" of foreign financial inflows to Latin America in 2002; then the 2007–08 subprime crisis; and the still-unfolding impacts on American banks of the Eurozone crisis.

The impact of these successive crises in the US and Mexico include reduced financial-sector employment, bank closures, banks' failure to meet legitimate business and household credit demand, and financial institutions' continuing experimentation with predatory loan products.[1] Beyond this, however, the evolution of financial systems in much of the Americas, including these systems' crises and the reactions thereto, has created a huge, unresolved regulatory problem, which is termed here the "financial trilemma."

In Mexico and in the remainder of Latin America, this trilemma involves a regulatory policy quandary similar to the macroeconomic-policy trilemma that smaller nations confront in the global economy.[2] The ability of financial regulators to control banking behavior is caught between the imperatives required for domestic stability and for reliable cross-border flows of bank-loanable funds or bank capital. Specifically, the ability of these nations to impose rules that would pull banking systems in the direction of being more socially productive and economically functional is constrained both by regional economic compacts (in the case of Mexico, North American Free Trade Agreement [NAFTA]) and by having a large share of the domestic banking market operated by multinational banks.

For the US, the financial trilemma has different elements. The key structural problem for regulators is the huge structural divide between Wall Street megabanks and the remainder of the US banking system. The ambitions, modes of operation, and economic effects of these two different elements of US banking are quite different. The success – if not survival – of one element depends on the creation of a regulatory atmosphere and set of enabling federal government subsidies or supports that is inconsistent with the success – or survival – of the other element. In effect, when attempting to control a system comprised of megabanks and smaller banks, regulators cannot generate rules that ensure a banking system that is economically functional, globally competitive, and safe and sound. And the members of the US banking population whose failure could create the largest systemic losses and financial chaos are precisely those who claim that any constraints on their behavior will compromise US global competitiveness.

Since it is largely the megabanks that are crossing borders to make loans or establish subsidiaries, it follows that the incapacity of US regulators to adequately regulate and control their domestic megabanks' behavior in their home markets creates an implicit threat (by the same institutions) to the stability and economic functionality of banking markets elsewhere in Latin America. Brazil, of course, stands as the exception; but it has to be noted that Brazil is not a member of a regional economic compact that includes US megabanks.

The idea that regulatory authority might be damaged by structural constraints, thus compromising both the stability of a financial system and its capacity to play a productive role in economic reproduction, cuts against an orthodox view that has become deeply embedded in financial economics in the past 30 years. Regulatory oversight of banking safety and soundness has shifted during the neoliberal era from balance-sheet standards (such as capital/asset ratios) to the self-monitoring of risks (via "black-box" calibrations of interest-rate shocks) to the idea that the financial markets themselves are the arbiter of value and soundness. Prior to the subprime crisis, the response of international financial institutions – especially the International Monetary Fund (IMF) – to financial crises in the Americas (elsewhere than in the US) was predictable: open markets, regulate better, eliminate fiscal deficits. Governments' loss of credibility and need to be disciplined was matched by markets' efficiency and thus capacity to properly discipline. Post-crisis, things are far less clear. The IMF has indicated a willingness to be flexible (Ambrose, 2009). Markets continue to define what "discipline" is and to punish undisciplined governments; but these markets have now cut megabanks' asset prices to record low levels. In global markets, confusion reigns.

This is thus an opportune moment to reshape banking systems in the Americas. This reshaping begins with a recognition that these systems have failed – either because many individual banks have become insolvent and been closed, or because they have ceased to fulfill the crucial economic roles that any functional financial system must provide: access to affordable credit in sustainable amounts for economic units that must borrow; and ready, cost-efficient access to means of exchange and payment. This chapter contributes to this reshaping by engaging in some rethinking, using the lens provided by the work of Jane D'Arista. Over the past several decades, D'Arista has elaborated a historically informed view of the evolution of the US and international financial systems. In the very same years that most analysts were proclaiming that the emergence of an efficient market in financial services was making regulation redundant, D'Arista was writing soberly about the possible operational and monetary-policy risks that were posed by developments in the increasingly unregulated banking system. Her prescient warning was ignored; and indeed, continued deregulation doubled down on the risks being taken, leading to the systemic failure of the late 2000s. And while the crisis of banking solvency has been at least temporarily stymied, the mismatch that Jane D'Arista pointed out in the 1990s, between structures and strategies in financial markets and regulatory capacity, has yet to be resolved.

This chapter thus focuses on how inattention to the dangers implicit in the parallel banking system of the 1990s has led to the unresolved financial trilemmas of the 2000s. Part of the story to be told involves understanding how different structural configurations can bind regulators' scope of action, leading to further changes that ultimately threaten the banking system's economic functionality. But structural circumstances alone cannot explain the creation of a system dominated by too-big-to-fail, leverage-addicted megabanks. One key element in arriving at the conjuncture is a crisis of vision. The notion that it is possible to create a financial system so efficient as to make its own history irrelevant can only be maintained by those who have forgotten – willfully or not – history's lessons. Jane D'Arista's own examination of the creation of US financial structure (1994a) clearly shows how structures inherited from the past combine with theoretical ideas to mold bank regulatory policies and monetary policy itself. In the spirit of her inquiry, this chapter tries to develop a critical, historically informed vision of the recent past and possible futures of banking in the Americas.

DIAGNOSING FINANCIAL CRISES: MORAL HAZARD CLEANSED BY EFFICIENT-MARKET FLOODWATERS

The frequent financial crises that have afflicted one or another part of the Americas have provided many opportunities for considering anew how banking and banking systems work, how they malfunction, and what to do about it. It will be useful to briefly recount the trajectory of thinking among economists about the causes of crises.

In the postwar period through to the mid 1960s, discussions of this kind were grounded in an economic development literature that acknowledged national economies' unique financial institutions and markets, each the product of a distinct history. Gerschenkron (1962), for example, argues that developing nations' "leaps forward" are often linked to the creation of new financial institutions that permit the channeling of wealth from embedded traditional uses to new sets of entrepreneurs. But in the mid 1960s, the reference point for discussions of banking shifted toward adoption of the core concepts of the efficient-market hypothesis (EMH), then emerging in finance theory. The basic premise of this approach is that one size fits all: specifically, financial markets are most efficient in allocating available resources when flows of credit and capital among wealth-holders, debtors, and financial intermediaries are given complete freedom of choice about how and where to borrow and/or to invest. This vision, of course, is embedded in the World Bank's and IMF's models of how financial markets should work; and it provides a benchmark for how these markets should be reformed when crises afflict them.[3]

In the 1980s, financial crises emerged in Latin America, as well as in the US savings and loan industry and in some US banking markets. This led economists to seek out a common factor that explains these different instances of credit-market malfunction. What lay readily at hand were explanations based on the existence of asymmetric information in the lending/borrowing process (Dymski, 2011b). The presence of asymmetric information (with the information advantage going to the borrower) precludes the attainment of first-best equilibrium in financial (or other) markets. The asymmetric-information framework is very malleable, with optimal outcomes depending on parameters chosen. So Eaton et al. (1986) used it to assert that Latin American countries had defaulted because the penalty for default was set too low. Meanwhile, Kane (1989) asserted that the savings and loan crisis was readily explained by the interaction of three sets of agents: regulators who hoped to cash in by working in the financial industry; bank managers whose remuneration was linked to institution size or risk; and depositors whom deposit insurance had made indifferent to risk-taking at the banks where they held their money. In effect it was easy to show how different parameterizations of the information-risk nexus could create a variety of problems in credit markets.

While these problems were unfolding, deregulation and technological change (especially the growth of high-speed communications and computing capacity) was transforming Wall Street. Indeed, the crises of traditional lenders accelerated the growth of securitization and of secondary markets for bundled debt, and led to the creation of innovative spot, futures, and derivatives markets that allowed ever more precise risk-bearing, risk-shifting, and risk-sterilization – all for a price. This continual transformation, linked to the steady influx of funds into US financial markets as a consequence of the US economy's chronic trade deficit, made it appear that moral-hazard problems in financial markets were the equivalent of temporary eddies and blockages in flowing financial streams. What was needed to sweep away the inefficiencies generated by one or another moral-hazard problem was precisely to expose these eddies and blockages to rushing waves of unchecked financial inflows.

So while asymmetric-information models were used to expose what had gone wrong in credit flows, with many disagreements among proponents of different modeling approaches, most financial economists shared the view that eliminating regulatory barriers domestically and abroad would maximize both US banks' global position and national welfare. Saunders and Walter wrote, for example (1994, p. vi):

> Overall, we suggest that barriers to market access, whether geography- or market-based, erode the static and dynamic efficiency and global competitiveness of the U.S. financial system and its contribution to national economic welfare. The barriers also erode the financial system's stability, by limiting financial institutions' access to capital and their ability to effectively diversify exposures and profit streams, thereby placing the taxpayer at risk [. . .] the existing U.S. bank regulatory structure seems to embody a triple threat to the national interest in being comparatively inefficient, uncompetitive, and unsafe, all at the same time.

This sentiment was broadly embraced by monetary economists in the 1980s and 1990s, both those who believed that moral hazard problems mattered in credit-market outcomes, and those who were fully under the sway of efficient-market thinking. Fama (1980) provided the logical bridge between the two views: in efficient financial markets with zero transaction costs, banks can only make credit commitments that would otherwise be made by non-bank lenders, unless distortions in market incentives or non-competitive market structures (such as banks' price-setting in loan markets) existed; as those distortions and barriers to fully competitive markets were eliminated, so too would inefficiencies in credit allocation. The fact that eliminating regulations and barriers to entry, while encouraging market consolidation, would permit a small number of financial intermediaries to emerge as positionally powerful megabanks with considerable market power and reach, did not enter into most economists' thinking.

To the contrary – the push was continually for more market entry. Not coincidentally, the formation of compacts such as the European Monetary Union (EMU), NAFTA, and the World Trade Organization (WTO) all involved shifts toward financial openness, and hence to entry by overseas firms (among which US firms were often first in line). The many financial crises during the neoliberal period also led to agreements to open markets, often reached under force. Not coincidentally, large Wall Street firms moved into the lead in numerous areas of "global financial services," and indeed the Wall Street megaplex became seen as a key source of competitive advantage for the United States (Franko, 2004).

WHAT WENT MISSING: THE NEED FOR STRUCTURALLY CONSISTENT NATIONAL REGULATION

These analyses, in focusing on micro-mechanisms and efficient markets, only partially encompassed the problem of national financial regulation. The micro-mechanism approach emphasized how the presence (deposit insurance) or absence (the lack of pre-agreed non-payment penalties) of regulations could inadvertently create incentives for behavior that would eventually generate large social costs; efficient-markets models postulated a post-regulation world as invariably more efficient than a world with financial regulation. But there was a missing middle in these diagnoses of how credit-market outcomes went wrong: a lack of attention to the systemic structures of financial intermediation, and the need for consistent regulation of these structures by national regulators.

There were several reasons for the invisibility of structural regulation by national authorities. For one thing, as Akyüz (2007) points out, macroeconomic modeling was increasingly dominated by dynamic equilibrium models, which described the behavior of representative agents; consequently, inherently complex questions (Roubini, 2001) such as maintaining a sustainable debt load are reduced to simple problems of time-consistent behavior by "representative agents."

Micro-behavioral models are similarly ineffective in making national regulation of systemic financial structures analytically visible. In the late 1990s and 2000s, Joseph Stiglitz was at the forefront of defending the need for regulation in finance. For example, he asserted that developing economies' financial systems would function better when public authorities made decisions that avoided moral hazard traps in credit and capital markets (Stiglitz, 2002). While Stiglitz' analytical results pertained to the case of Korea (among other nations), they were derived in very sparsely detailed models in which, in particular, a national regulator does not appear as an agent. This is explained by the fact that Stiglitz (like all economic theorists) faces the imperative of building models that deviate as little as possible from the competitive-market ideal – in effect, from efficient financial markets (Dymski, 2011a). This means that adding a regulatory sector would not only be unnecessary; it would deter from, not augment, the model's effectiveness in communicating with its target audience. But precisely because micro-behavioral models are specified in such an economical way, the results obtained from there are very plastic, and contingent on how parameters are specified. For example, in contrast to Stiglitz's result, other economists have shown how government-controlled credit allocation can worsen (not improve) moral hazard (and adverse selection) problems. So these economists' models tend to look for the sources of financial crises in the institutions that Stiglitz and his co-thinkers are trying to protect; they advocate measures such as privatizing public banks, eliminating state planning agencies and development banks, and opening financial and banking markets to foreign entry – all measures fiercely opposed by Stiglitz.

A deeper reason for the invisibility of structural regulation in economic debates is that the implicit autonomy of the nation-state has been challenged by events. Indeed, the increasing freedom of financial movement across national borders in the 1980s and 1990s led to a remapping of the implicit links between the rights of states and the prerogatives of markets. Financial market flows had always been seen as an accompaniment to or consequence of a process of economic policy-making over which governments exercised full control. The reason that the Mundell–Fleming impossibility result drew such attention in the 1960s was precisely its demonstration that the prerogatives of public authorities to determine the full scope of macroeconomic policy might be compromised.

But this view began to erode under the weight of recurrent financial crises in the neoliberal era. The Latin American debt crisis in particular opened up a broad-ranging discussion about whether the nation-states that could not meet their payment obligations were illiquid or insolvent – a discussion which included a calculation of national solvency on the basis of a given country's natural and other assets. History mattered, as the underpinning for this discussion. This notion that a country's national assets could be priced and sold, of course, represented the reassertion of rights of property in formerly colonized countries by international agencies acting on behalf of lenders in formerly colonizer countries. In effect, the colonizers were discussing how to take possession of what was rightfully – post-default – theirs.[4]

In any event, the absence of attention to the gut problems posed by regulation – how to manage a structured system of finance that interacts with other structured systems of finance – led to these models' irrelevance. The notions that financial crises represented either punishments for systems prone to moral hazard abuses or implosions for countries with unsustainable macroeconomic policies was eventually set aside. Experiences of financial crises in apparently "virtuous" countries suggested even to IMF-affiliated economists that financial crises could arise because of sunspots.[5] Economists studying Latin American banking and finance came to the realization that the completely boundaryless world of efficient-market theory, in which investors immediately recognize and fund the virtuous, was not the world they lived in. Recently, even economists inclined to accept the notion that market efficiency should guide decision-making have demonstrated caution. For example, Cavallo and Izquierdo (2009) warn about the need to guard against "sudden stops" in capital or credit flows to Latin America – "stops" unrelated to fundamentals. Chortareas et al. (2011) worry about whether the banking concentration that has resulted in many Latin American countries from years of crisis and foreign entry has subjected financial consumers to market power. In a 2007 World Bank volume, de la Torre and Schmukler describe the results of decades of reform and opening of Latin American capital markets as "disappointing." They argue that policy analysts' suggestions can be summarized by two summary statements: "be patient and redouble the effort" or "get the sequence right." Frustrated by what they regard as the fruitless to-and-fro between proponents of these views, they advocate a third approach: "revisit basic issues and reshape expectations."

These authors' conclusion goes right to the heart of the basic problem. Analysts have become increasingly skeptical of the premises of the efficient-market approach, and all of its warnings about moral hazard traps when allocation mechanisms take account of market imperfections, rigidities, and even national development priorities. But this slow stepping-away from efficient markets has come only after the devastating 2007–09 crisis period, too late to avoid paying the price for not incorporating the "missing middle" into analyses of the causes of financial crises.

This inattention to the problem of structurally consistent national regulation is ironic, given that Jane D'Arista's work on financial issues in these same years was centered on precisely this theme. Many of her essays and chapters illustrate this running motif. Here we focus on just two.

First, D'Arista and Griffith-Jones co-authored a 2001 essay examining the regulatory implications of the heightened cross-border portfolio flows that had emerged in the previous two decades, and which had led to the Latin American and East Asian debt crises, among others. These authors focus on a regulatory dimension of these crises that every other analyst has overlooked: while "it has become accepted that regulation by recipient countries of excessive surges of capital can be a desirable policy" (D'Arista and Griffith-Jones, 2001, p. 61), "no complementary action by source countries has been taken to regulate in any way potentially volatile flows from them" (ibid.). The authors point out that when financial flows into one country emanate from another whose financial markets and balance sheets are growing much faster, due to deregulation and/or a euphoric boom, then it is likely both that investors in the source country will be exposed to losses and that the recipient country's domestic financial markets will ripped by crisis. Correa and Vidal (2006) show that this is exactly what happened in Mexico after its crises – its development bank was closed, its businesses and banks became insolvent, and so on.

The second case involves the evolution of the US financial system itself. D'Arista began warning of the emergence of a "parallel banking system" in the late 1980s and early 1990s. Specifically, she was referring to "a parallel system divided intermediation between two separate entities, each of which dealt directly with the public through only one side of the balance sheet" (D'Arista, 1994b, p. 418). Because, under US law, only financial firms that conduct banking activities on both sides of their balance sheets (that is, loan making and deposit taking) are classified as banks, these "parallel" institutions were not regulated as banks, nor required to meet the various safety and soundness metrics to which banks are held; nor were they subject to the Community Reinvestment Act, the Glass–Steagall Act, and so on.

The notion of a "parallel banking system" is, of course, a precursor to the term "shadow banking system" in use today. In the mid 1990s, the focus of D'Arista's attention was on finance companies owned by industrial corporations (GMAC, FMCC, GECC, and so on). These companies were making many speculative loans, for example to finance highly leveraged transactions and commercial real estate acquisition and development; these were the kinds of loans that had led to insolvency for many thrifts in the previous decade. These institutions relied on the commercial paper market for the majority of their funding, and often sought guarantees or credit from banks. When these parallel banks got into trouble, they would generate cash by securitizing their receivables.

You didn't have to be a weatherman to know which way these winds were going to blow; this portrait foreshadows in many details the buildup of subprime-loan-backed securities that would soon enough nearly destroy the US banking system. D'Arista wrote the following summary of the challenges this situation posed for regulation (1994b, p. 418):

> The immense volume of bank guarantees to the parallel banking system has placed banks in a no-win situation in which they are weakened by the support they provide already advantaged competitors and are faced with greater risks if the parallel system falters. Clearly, the risk to the banks creates risk for the lender of last resort. The symbiotic relationship between commercial banks and their rivals in the parallel banking system leaves the Federal Reserve with much less room for discretion in exercising that role.

The danger here arises precisely because of the structural inconsistency in regulation: a regulator who cannot check the behavior of intermediaries that are luring regulated banks into danger cannot effectively govern. If this warning went unheeded by economists, the banks themselves were paying attention – especially the banks put most at risk by this situation – the (surviving) money-center banks. Within five years, they succeeded in repealing the Glass–Steagall Act and thus winning the opportunity to run parallel banks of various kinds as their subsidiaries.

Just over a decade after D'Arista warned of the regulatory incoherence generated by the unchecked growth of a parallel banking system, that system had matured an asymmetrically regulated, unchecked, hyper-leveraged system of exploitative lending and speculative position taking, reliant as in the 1990s on financing by the commercial paper market. Once this system collapsed in the subprime crisis, deep popular anger at the Wall Street megaplex-based financial system was unleashed. And there were again (as in the wake of the Latin American and East Asian debt crises) calls for improved regulation. But these calls resulted in a cautious reform bill whose implementation has been delayed by the foot dragging of appointees and regulators beholden to financial interests. As in previous debt crises, moral hazard arguments have been used to argue that any of a large cast of possible culprits – government regulators, subprime borrowers, securities insurers, rating agencies, and so on – might be at fault. With rare exceptions (see Acharya et al., 2011), post-crisis discussion of regulatory reform has not delved into the systemic structural issues that D'Arista has always made central in her work. Consequently, there has been little or no debate about how this existing system might be better regulated (less leverage, more transparency, and so on). There has been no debate among politicians or economists about how balanced, structurally consistent national banking regulation can be put in place – much less about the merits and flaws of an alternative approach to financial-system design. Engaging in this needed deeper debate would require, first of all, an awareness of the need to take a hard second look at the history of the financial system we have today, and second, a willingness to examine whether and how the current institutional arrangement is fulfilling the basic economic functions of a banking system. This double lack – of awareness and of willingness – has created a situation in which banking systems across the Americas are vulnerable to financial trilemmas that have gone largely unrecognized.

THE FINANCIAL TRILEMMA IN THE AMERICAS

We now turn from the absence of an adequate diagnosis of flaws in financial design to a brief elaboration on the regulatory challenges faced by banking systems in the Americas. These challenges differ for the US and for nations elsewhere on the continent. Our point of entry in identifying the problems that exist is to ask a fundamental question about financial regulation: How much autonomy of action and control do any nation's regulatory authorities possess, and how has this been affected by the global financial and economic crisis?

Autonomy is problematic for every American nation other than the US. Structural impediments and asymmetries of power in markets have created a bank regulatory trilemma, which parallels the familiar Mundell–Fleming macroeconomic trilemma.

We begin with the familiar case. During the neoliberal era, virtually all Latin American financial systems have experienced one or more crises linked to the Mundell–Fleming trilemma. According to this set of postulates, a country cannot simultaneously maintain independent monetary policy, stable exchange rates, and financial integration with the rest of the world. Financial crises, IMF intervention, and changing domestic balances of political power led many Latin American economies away from rejecting financial integration, and toward financial integration. The trilemma then dictates that either domestic monetary policy or exchange-rate stability must be sacrificed.

Many developing nations have attempted to gain control over this trilemma by building up huge volumes of foreign reserves.[6] The response to the trilemma then depends on the strength of reserves and of control over all the mechanisms of monetary policy, including banks' behavior in domestic markets. But this, in turn, brings us to another set of constraints that has not been previously recognized in the many elaborations and extensions of the Mundell–Fleming thesis.

In principle, every nation is free to choose bank regulations. Post-crisis policy interventions in developing nations have assumed as much: after both the Latin American and Asian financial crises, the IMF promoted "better regulation" as a universal antidote against future financial crises. The implication is that any nation, even in the global South, is free to shape financial regulations as it wishes; and if it does this badly, calamity can result. But the reality is different.

National authorities' regulations and enforcement about what banks can do is constrained by two factors. The first is whether this nation is in a regional compact, such as the EMU or NAFTA, for regional compacts typically impose uniformity and market-entry rules on participating nations' financial systems. A second key factor is whether foreign megabanks have significant shares of a given nation's banking market. If so, these megabanks' behavior is constrained primarily by the rules of the Basle system and these banks' own home-nations' banking authorities. While megabanks may comply with domestic rules about loan-making and financial-service provision, their overall strategies will be dictated elsewhere – and, of course, these large banks may attempt to attain exceptions to local rules on fair-competition grounds.

So this is another type of trilemma: a nation cannot simultaneously be in an integrated regional compact, have a large share of its market occupied by foreign megabanks, and freely make its own financial rules and regulations.

Further, this trilemma works one way for financial-center countries, and another way for developing nations. Financial-center nations can dictate the scope of action for their megabanks, insist on harmonization for foreign banks operating domestically, and police the remainder of their system as they please. Developing nations' regulatory options are constrained by the behavior permitted to the megabanks operating within their borders. Efforts to regulate more strictly will be met by threats of retaliation or departure. In effect, in nations outside of financial centers, compensation for risk must replace regulation of risk.

THE US'S FINANCIAL DILEMMA: REGULATING TWO DISPARATE BANKING SYSTEMS

If there is a financial trilemma affecting Mexico and other nations in Latin America, then the US has its own version. This dilemma arises because of regulatory and operational tensions between the megabank and community bank sub-sectors within the US financial structure, which are intertwined with US banking authorities' lender-of-last-resort function.[7]

The US entered the neoliberal era with a large banking population: some 14,434 commercial banks were insured by the Federal Deposit

Insurance Corporation (FDIC) as of December 1980. This large population included both state- and federally chartered banks, and thus two tiers of regulation; as such, it was prone to excessive risk-taking. With the election of the pro-market Reagan Administration, regulatory policy favored mergers as a means of achieving more banking efficiency (Dymski, 1999). And indeed, by September 2009, the US had 6,911 banks, a decline of 52% from the 1980 population. Large banks participated fully in this consolidation. For example, of the 24 largest bank holding companies (BHCs) in the US as of 1997, only 13 still existed in 2004; the remainder eliminated by non-assisted mergers (two with foreign-owned banks). By September 2011, only ten remained.

Furthermore, the very largest banks in the US banking hierarchy became larger even relative to other large banks: in December 1997, the average asset size of the three largest BHCs – Citibank, Bank of America, and Chase – equaled just over 300% of the asset size of the other banks included among the US's top 24 BHCs; in June 2008 – before investment banks and other non-banks were classified as bank holding companies – this figure for the (same) three largest BHCs had climbed to over 800%. This "gigantification" is due both to these largest BHCs moving more forcefully than smaller banks to take over small commercial banks (and their deposit bases), and to these institutions' expansion into investment banking, broker-dealer activity, and/or insurance.

This latter expansion, of course, combined with other competitive shifts, put these large BHCs into direct competition with large non-bank Wall Street firms. Of course, this competition eventually encompassed the bundling, holding, and sale of subprime paper and of collateralized debt obligation (CDOs). Once the subprime crisis hit home, US banking was suddenly transformed. For in 2008, three of the five largest Wall Street non-commercial-bank firms either failed or disappeared through merger (Lehman Brothers, Merrill Lynch, Bear Stearns); the other two were converted into BHCs. Consequently, as of December 2009, six megabanks – Bank of America, JPMorgan Chase, Citibank, Wells Fargo, Goldman Sachs, and Morgan Stanley – stood alone as the commanding heights of US banking.

The 2008 Troubled Asset Relief Program (TARP) program that preserved these megabanks' existence was fully consistent with the broader design of US banking policy. The US government provided subsidies for large banks to buy failed savings and loan associations after the 1980s thrift crisis, and then encouraged their transformation to megabanks through a series of financial deregulation acts. In effect, the emergence of the six largest US megabanks through the eventual intersection of Wall Street and super-sized commercial banks should be understood not as an accidental byproduct of the 2007–08 subprime crisis, but as the endpoint of a lengthy period of intentional policy choices regarding the activities and market scope of a reshaped, more efficient US banking industry. What was unintended was that these megabanks' final emergence should have required such huge public interventions to survive crises of their own making.

And what was perhaps also not intended was that the US, at the end of 30 years of a bank merger wave, would have two essentially distinct banking sectors. For paralleling the megabanking sector is a community-banking sector. Small banks dominate this sector, and over 9 of every 10 US banks have under $1 billion in assets.

The question immediately arises whether large and small banks in the US differ in important ways. Some contrasts can be drawn using balance-sheet data. One important contrast involves the source of revenue: banks under $1 billion in assets derive about three-quarters of their income from interest, whereas interest income and non-interest (fee-based) income have been approximately equal in larger banks.[8] In some other areas – such as non-performing loans as a share of all loans, and net profits per dollar of assets – small banks and other banks' performance is quite similar. Where a clear contrast emerges is in the extent of risk-taking related to off-balance-sheet activities. Banks below $1 billion in assets have virtually no derivatives exposure; and by contrast, the issuance of derivatives by banks above $1 billion in assets has climbed steadily, reaching nearly 2000% of assets, on average, by the end of the 2000s. Further, banks with under $1 billion in assets have engaged in virtually no loan securitization; by contrast, loan sales with recourse – which means that loan purchasers can seek compensation from issuers if the loans they have bought perform poorly – have climbed above 30% for larger banks.

The contrasts go still further. Smaller banks' business model depends on local economies – on local circuits of business activity, housing construction, and employment. By contrast, megabanks' business model depends on fee-based activity, securitization, and off-balance-sheet position taking in global finance circuits. So the profitability of local banks depends on maintaining the vitality of local economic spaces. The profitability of megabanks depends on identifying new targets for fee- or margin-generating activities.

This brings us to the US banking trilemma. US financial regulators are charged with maintaining the viability of a globally competitive megabanking sector, with maintaining a community-banking sector that responds to local economic needs; and of using their lender-of-last-resort capacity when necessary to stop crises that might destroy US financial structure. The problem is that extensive failure in one of these two banking sectors will lead to interventions that will undercut the viability of the other sector. The implication is that a portion of the banking needs of the US economy – defined as these are now – will go unmet.[9]

It was famously the megabanking sector with its extensive securitization activities that required a massive bailout; and it is this sector that has positioned itself as "too big to fail." So this leads to a mismatch between economic functionality and subsidy. For the part of the banking system that participates in local economic circulation, and that supports small businesses without other means of finance, is unprotected; the part of the banking system that is abstracted from local economy and provides few services to small businesses is instead the recipient of direct and indirect subsidies (respectively, TARP and the Federal Reserve's purchase at book value of large volumes of suspect commercial paper and securitized mortgages from 2009 onward). As stressed above, the result of this unbalanced use of subsidies and bailouts, and of the three-decade-long merger policy, is that an ever-larger share of banking activity – on and off balance sheet – is being conducted by the largest megabanks.

THREE FUTURES FOR BANKING IN THE AMERICAS

This chapter has pointed out a number of factors that threaten to create narrow boundaries for the future of financial structure in the Americas: the lack of imagination in experts' thinking about what banking is; asymmetric structures of power in global and national financial systems; and the failure to remember the lessons of history about the nature of effective financial regulation.

To see where the compounded impact of these factors might lead, we set out and briefly evaluate three different banking futures here. In one possible future, the US and European megabanks that dominate their home markets will compete fiercely for market share in emerging markets, including Latin America. Not all megabanks are the same; consider, for example, the differences in Citibank and Santander's experiences of the subprime crisis. Although with this said, offshore megabanks could conceivably attempt to carve out portions of Latin American markets.

Some national spaces within Latin America will see intense rivalry in many financial markets and product lines. Here, Mexico has led the way, with Brazil and Argentina close behind. These countries' consumer banking markets offer desirable targets because of the size and income and wealth of the population. For parallel reasons, other markets are less attractive. Unless a new regional compact opens up space for one-size-fits-all banking products, other nations will see less foreign-bank entry with fewer financial products.

So in this future, Latin America emerges as one site of a struggle for global megabank supremacy. This struggle might also encompass the future of the dollar in the global economy. A second future imagines Latin America as the site of an intensifying global competition for scarce resources (such as petroleum, water, and food) and hence for global income share. Then relatively resource-deprived countries will scour the globe even more intently than now to meet their requirements. Here China comes immediately to mind. In tandem with resource-seeking, Asian banks – perhaps led by Chinese banks – will aggressively enter Latin American markets, alongside the US and European banks already there.

If this future comes to pass, the focus of financial entry will be quite different than above. There, domestic economic units provided the impetus. Here, resource-seeking nations' banks would likely emphasize cross-border flows of capital and credit, not the establishment of Latin American branch networks. In this event, Latin America would become one hub of a global competition for power and hegemony.

A third future proceeds differently: it begins with the possibility of reconstructing banking and finance on a socially and economically functional basis. Banking in the Americas could be shaped to serve national and regional development needs, based on goals such as the equalization of wealth and opportunity. Policy-makers could then freely consider such questions as whether microcredit should be expanded, whether access to transactions accounts should be universalized, whether new consumer financing instruments are welfare-enhancing or exploitative, and whether a state development bank like Brazil's BNDES is needed to finance critically needed investment. The question then becomes whether the existing financial structure can achieve these goals; if not, changes in institutions or incentives are needed.

This way of thinking about finance is not well developed, for several reasons. First, it would require renewing the historically attuned developmentalist approach to finance; and as argued above, this would require rediscovering ways of thinking about the economic role of banking and finance that have been nearly lost since the 1960s. Second, it would require some modification of regional-compact rules that establish rights of market access for non-domestic financial firms.

These three potential futures may not be mutually exclusive. Elements of each might unfold, with points of tension where these views of banking collide. In the US, the social-accountability requirements rooted in the 1977 Community Reinvestment Act are certainly at odds with megabanks' "caveat emptor" approach to financial-service provision. In Brazil, the developmentalist agenda of BNDES coexists with the customer-market-expansion agenda of the nation's private (and semi-public) banks; the tension between the resource-extraction approach to finance and the developmentalist approach was illustrated in 2008 when China insisted that Brazil provide trade credit through BNDES for its own soy exports.

CONCLUSION

The 2007–08 global financial crisis provides a good opportunity for thinking anew about the economic functions and social impacts of banking and finance. If another world of banking and finance is possible, apart from the Wall Street-led system that broke down so spectacularly, what would that world look like? This chapter has briefly sketched out three possible futures for banking and finance in the Americas. One highlights a contest for consumer and business financial services markets, especially in the more populous or wealthy countries of the Americas. A second highlights the use of finance as an adjunct to a global struggle for resources, in which the Americas will invariably be involved. A third suggests a future that begins by renewing a broad-based discussion among all segments of society about the economic goals and social functions that financial institutions should meet.

But for any nation in the Americas, any effort at improving the functioning of banking by rethinking its purposes must acknowledge and respond to barriers to change. One such barrier identified here is a crisis of vision: a confusion among experts between how finance works in idealized abstract settings, and how real-world financial systems operate. The many crises of finance have provided stark reminders of the gap between the idealized and real worlds of financial flows. Despite all that has happened, many experts continue to assert that something like efficient financial markets will emerge if only regulators permit sufficient access to markets. Jane D'Arista's work stands as both a resource and an inspiration for those who seek to reestablish a historically informed, structurally consistent approach to banking structure and regulation at the heart of American policy-making.

This chapter has also identified two types of financial-regulation trilemmas that haunt the Americas. We have suggested that most American nations' ability to create rules that make banking systems more socially productive and economically functional is limited by the existence of regional economic compacts and by the presence in many domestic banking markets of large multinational banks. The US, in turn, faces a trilemma due to tensions between its Wall Street and community-based banking sectors and its regulators' lender-of-last-resort capacity. The US's Wall Street complex operates so very differently from its community banks that the regulations, subsidies, and guarantees needed for the success of the Wall Street complex are largely distinct from the regulatory atmosphere needed to encourage renewed vigor for US community banks.

The immensity of the challenge of creating truly functional financial systems in the face of the constraints described here may suggest that the exercise of imagining the third future may be useless. But including this third possible future here makes precisely the point that such a future can only take shape as a reality if those who wish for it give it the same force that has been given to analyses of financial system malfunction. What sequence of steps could bring us from the present state of financial system malfunction and non-responsiveness to a different future with socially responsive, economically functional finance? No matter how improbable it seems, this journey has to be thought before it can be walked.

NOTES

* This chapter draws from a paper published, in Spanish translation, in *Tres Crisis: Economía, Finanzas y Medio Ambiente*, edited by Eugenia Correa, Alicia Girón, Arturo Guillén and Antonina Ivanova (2011; Mexico D.F., Mexico: Miguel Àngel Porrúa). The author thanks Jane D'Arista, the editors of *Tres Crisis*, and participants in the 2009 conference of Red Globalización Financiera y Desarrollo Sustentable for insightful comments on preliminary versions of the ideas presented here.

1. Mason (2010) discusses US banks' bad loans; Enrich et al. (2009) discuss their failure to lend after the crisis. Business News Americas (2009) describes non-performing loans in Mexico, and Pineda (2009) covers lags in lending in Mexico's banking system.
2. This phenomenon, described below, is sometimes termed the Mundell–Fleming impossibility theorem or trilemma, as it was first elaborated in Mundell (1960) and Fleming (1962). Young and Darity (2004) provide an encyclopedic discussion of the historical context and trajectory of the Mundell–Fleming model.
3. For references to the literatures referred to here, see Dymski (2006).
4. In this respect, it is interesting to imagine Walter Wriston's famous phrase, "A country does not go bankrupt" (Wriston, 1982) having been written in 1882, not a century later. Eventually, the use of market criteria to judge national policy actions would be extended to every nation, even the United States.
5. This is the essential idea of the "second-generation model" of currency crises; see Dymski (2006).
6. Among the recent papers exploring this phenomenon are Aizenman et al. (2008) and Obstfeld et al. (2008).
7. The rationale for including the lender-of-last-resort function among the powers and duties of a financial regulatory authority is presented in Dymski (2009).
8. These data are taken from the author's calculations using data from the FDIC and from the federally maintained National Information Center.
9. Two comments are in order. First, in light of recent experience, it is easy to forget that the savings and loan crisis involved systemic failure in a portion of the community-banking sector, not in the megabanking sector. The German economy's *landesbanken* provide

a more recent example. Second, it is tempting to imagine a US economy that does not count the Wall Street complex among the sources of US national economic advantage. But to implement this would require a sea change in legislation that is hard to envision at the time of writing. Consequently, among the banking "needs" of the US economy – at least for now – are maintaining global competitiveness in megabanking.

REFERENCES

Acharya, Viral V., Thomas F. Cooley, Matthew Richardson, and Ingo Walter, 2011. *Regulating Wall Street: The Dodd–Frank Act and the New Architecture of Global Finance*. New York: Wiley Finance Series, John Wiley and Sons.

Ambrose, Soren, 2009. "IMF Reforms: Mere Tinkering or Change We Can Live With?", *Foreign Policy in Focus*, Washington, DC: Institute for Policy Studies, September 17.

Aizenman, Joshua, Menzie D. Chinn, and Hiro Ito, 2008. "Assessing the Emerging Global Financial Architecture: Measuring the Trilemma's Configurations over Time," NBER Working Paper No. 14533. Cambridge, MA: National Bureau of Economic Research, December.

Akyüz, Yilmaz, 2007. "Debt Sustainability in Emerging Markets: A Critical Appraisal," DESA Working Paper No. 61, United Nations Department of Economic and Social Affairs, November.

Business News Americas, 2009. "Mexican banks: Picking up the pieces as the crisis wanes," Financial Services Intelligence Services, October. Accessed at http://member.bnamericas.com on January 12, 2010.

Cavallo, Eduardo, and Alejandro Izquierdo, 2009. "Dealing with the Crisis: Lessons from Latin America," posted on Voxeu.org on 28 March. Accessed at http://www.voxeu.org/index.php?q=node/3358 on January 13, 2010.

Chortareas, Georgios E., Jesus G. Garza-Garcia, and Claudia Girardone, 2011. "Banking Sector Performance in Latin America: Market Power versus Efficiency," *Review of Development Economics*, **5** (2), 307–25.

Correa, Eugenia, and Gregorio Vidal, 2006. "Financial Deregulation and Capital Flows in Latin American Countries," in Philip Arestis, Jesus Ferreiro, and Felipe Serrano (eds), *Financial Developments in National and International Markets*. London: Palgrave Macmillan, pp. 165–75.

D'Arista, Jane W., 1994a. *The Evolution of U.S. Finance, Volume I: Federal Reserve Monetary Policy: 1915–1935*. Armonk, NY: M.E. Sharpe.

D'Arista, Jane W., 1994b. *The Evolution of U.S. Finance, Volume II: Restructuring Institutions and Markets*. Armonk, NY: M.E. Sharpe.

D'Arista, Jane W., and Stephany Griffith-Jones, 2001. "The Boom of Portfolio Flows to 'Emerging Markets' and its Regulatory Implications," in Stephany Griffith-Jones, Manuel F. Montes, and Anwar Nasution (eds), *Short-Term Capital Flows and Economic Crises*, New York: Oxford University Press, pp. 29–51.

de la Torre, Augusto, and Sergio L. Schmukler, 2007. *Emerging Capital Markets and Globalization: The Latin American Experience*. Washington, DC: The World Bank (co-published with Stanford Economics and Finance).

Dymski, Gary A., 1999. *The Bank Merger Wave: The Economic Causes and Social Consequences of Financial Consolidation in the United States*. Armonk, NY: M.E. Sharpe.

Dymski, Gary A., 2006. "Banking and Financial Crises," in Philip Arestis and Malcolm Sawyer (eds), *Handbook of Alternative Monetary Economics*, Cheltenham, UK and Northampton, MA, USA: Edward Elgar, pp. 385–402.
Dymski, Gary A., 2009. "Financial Risk and Governance in the Neoliberal Era," in Gordon L. Clark, Adam D. Dixon, and Ashby H.B. Monk (eds), *Managing Financial Risks: From Global to Local*, Oxford University Press, pp. 48–68.
Dymski, Gary A., 2011a. "On the Possible Replacement of the Efficient-Market Hypothesis: Social Efficiency as a "Thick" Approach to Financial Policy," in Philip Arestis and Malcolm Sawyer (eds), *New Economics as Mainstream Economics*, Basingstoke, UK: Palgrave Macmillan, pp. 77–115.
Dymski, Gary A., 2011b. "Genie out of the Bottle: The Evolution of Too-Big-to-Fail Policy and Banking Strategy in the US," mimeo, University of California, Riverside, June 15.
Eaton, Jonathan, Mark Gersovitz, and Joseph Stiglitz, 1986. "The Pure Theory of Country Risk," *European Economic Review*, **30**, 481–513.
Enrich, David, Michael R. Crittenden, and Maurice Tamman, 2009. "Bank Lending Keeps Dropping," *Wall Street Journal*, April 20, p. A1.
Fama, Eugene F., 1980. "Banking in the Theory of Finance," *Journal of Monetary Economics*, **6** (1), 39–57.
Fleming, J. Marcus, 1962. "Domestic Financial Policies under Fixed and under Floating Exchange Rates," *IMF Staff Papers*, **9**, 369–79.
Franko, Lawrence G., 2004. "U.S. Competitiveness in the Global Financial Services Industry," Working Paper 1001, Financial Services Forum, College of Management, University of Massachusetts Boston, October.
Gerschenkron, Alexander, 1962. *Economic Backwardness in Historical Perspective: A Book of Essays*. Cambridge, MA: Harvard University Press.
Kane, Edward J., 1989. *The S&L Insurance Mess: How Did It Happen?* Washington, DC: Urban Institute Press.
Mason, Joseph, 2010. "The Outlook for 2010: Bank Failures and Bank Losses Ahead," posted on the Roubini Global Economics website on January 12. Accessed at http://www.economonitor.com/blog/2010/01/the-outlook-for-2010-bank-failures-and-bank-losses-ahead/ on January 12, 2010.
Mundell, Robert, 1960. "The Monetary Dynamics of International Adjustment under Fixed and Flexible Exchange Rates," *Quarterly Journal of Economics*, **74**, 227–57.
Obstfeld, Maurice, Jay C. Shambaugh, and Alan M. Taylor, 2008. "Financial Stability, the Trilemma, and International Reserves," NBER Working Paper No. 14217. Cambridge, MA: National Bureau of Economic Research, August.
Pineda, Javier Guillermo Gomez, 2009. "Whither the Credit and Asset Price Cycle in Latin America?" posted on the Roubini Global Economics website on December 21. Accessed at http://www.roubini.com/latam-monitor/258156/ on January 12, 2010.
Roubini, Nouriel, 2001. "Debt Sustainability:How to Assess Whether a Country is Insolvent," mimeo, Stern School of Business, New York University, December 20.
Saunders, Anthony, and Ingo Walter, 1994. *Universal Banking in the United States: What Could We Gain? What Could We Lose?* New York: Oxford University Press.
Stiglitz, Joseph E., 2002. *Globalisation and Its Discontents*. New York: Norton.
Wriston, W., 1982. "Banking Against Disaster," *New York Times*, September 14.
Young, Warren, and William Darity Jr., 2004. "IS-LM-BP: An Inquest," *History of Political Economy*, **36** (Suppl. 1), 127–64.

9. Boulevard to broken dreams: the standards-surveillance-compliance system in the run-up to the Crash of 2008

Robert H. Wade[1]

> Milton Friedman's most important contribution lay in convincing people of the importance of allowing free markets to operate. (Lawrence Summers, 2006)[2]

> This historical legislation will better enable American companies to compete in the new economy. (Lawrence Summers, referring to the repeal of the Glass–Steagall Act, 1999)

> Macroeconomics has succeeded: its central problem of depression prevention has been solved. (Robert Lucas, doyen of modern macroeconomics and Nobel laureate, presidential lecture to American Economic Association, 2003)

> Taxing [financial] transactions [. . .] penalises an activity – trading – that has the useful social function of transferring assets to those with most demand for them. (*Financial Times*, editorial, 2012)[3]

> Self-regulation is to regulation as self-importance is to importance. (Willem Buiter)

INTRODUCTION

In 1997, just before the start of the East Asian/Latin American/Russian/ Long Term Capital Management (LTCM) crisis of the late 1990s, the value of financial transactions was about 15 times the world's annual gross product. Today, finance is booming: even in the hard times following the crash of 2008, the value is almost 70 times. The jump from 15 to 70 times in little more than a decade reflects the intense concentration of corporate power over the 2000s. A recent analysis identifies a cluster of 147 cross-owned firms accounting for a high share of the world's corporate revenues.

This global "super-cluster" is itself dominated by finance: *all* of the top 50 except one are financial firms.[4] Such concentration provides financial firms with the leverage to capture nation states and shape public policy in line with their preferences, creating a ratchet such that the power of finance over public policy, both national and international, cannot be much diminished, however much some politicians and activists try. Finance generates fortunes, fortunes generate influence, and influence generates more finance and more fortunes.

This essay goes back to the "beginning," to the years after the start of the East Asian crisis, and examines the new system of global financial regulation put in place – or attempted to be put in place – to guard against repeated multi-country crises. You might think, looking back from 2013, that nothing was done after 1997, because financial regulators in the West did rather little to reign in the build-up of debt in their own economies. In fact, however, the High Command of world finance (US Treasury, US Federal Reserve, G7/G8, Bank for International Settlements, International Monetary Fund [IMF], World Bank) decided in the late 1990s that the system of global financial regulation needed strengthening, urgently. After all, the convulsion was only the latest in a series of multi-country financial crises over the 1980s and 1990s, occurring much more frequently and severely than in the Bretton Woods period from 1945 to the early 1970s.

The key to the credit and property bubbles of the 2000s is that the High Command interpreted "strengthening" to mean the development of comprehensive and universal standards of best practice in such areas as data dissemination, bank supervision, corporate governance, and financial accounting, using organizations like the IMF, the Basel Committee on Banking Supervision, the Financial Stability Forum, the G20 of finance ministers, and a gamut of nonofficial bodies. Enforcement was to come largely by peer pressure and market reactions to information about compliance. Countries, banks and firms that complied more with the standards would gain better access to finance than those that complied less, was the assumption. The resulting system received no name, but I call it here the standards-surveillance-compliance (SSC) system. The failure of this brave new world system enabled private debt to skyrocket in many Western economies over the 2000s to 2008.

Earlier, through the 1980s and 1990s, the High Command had agreed on a single broad economic policy recipe for countries in general and developing countries in particular. This is the recipe known as the Washington Consensus, summarized in the commandment, "liberalize the market."[5] The commandment expressed: (a) the economic theory that free markets allocate goods, services, capital and labor efficiently, coupled with (b) the classical liberal norm that free markets give individuals freedom to follow their preferences, whereas government "intervention" entails bureaucrats, politicians and other elites imposing their preferences on those of private citizens – hence when government "intervention" is shrunk freedom expands. Internationally, governments should get out of the way of cross-border economic transactions between private actors, including both trade and investment. As Martin Wolf said in *Why Globalization Works*, "it cannot make sense to fragment the world economy more than it already is but rather make the world economy work as if it were the United States, or at least the European Union."[6] In other words, the world economy should be made into a free trade zone, a free production zone, and (with more qualifications) a free capital flow zone.

However, the shock of the Asian and other financial crises of the late 1990s, coming on top of the earlier ones, prompted a subtle shift in the consensus from "liberalize the market" to "standardize the market." Standardize meant to use public power, especially interstate organizations, to promote convergence in national political economies to a broadly Anglo-American political economy model. Convergence of regimes would create a level playing field; a level playing field would accelerate globalization; globalization would generate higher profits, higher growth in the world at large and especially in developing countries, and also lower poverty and income inequality in developing countries as the wages of the less skilled rose relative to those of the more skilled. What was there not to like?

The shift from "liberalize" to "standardize" is not just a tweaking of the Washington Consensus. While the new consensus continued to accept the theory that markets allocate resources efficiently, it emphasized more than before the need for *national and global political authorities* to reshape and standardize markets, as distinct from governments just getting out of the way. This amounted to turning classical liberalism on its head, because it gave normative sanction to a big *increase* in governmental and multilateral "intervention" to effect the standardization. The difference between "liberalize" and "standardize" is significant enough to be denoted as a shift from the Washington Consensus to what could be called the Intensified Washington Consensus.

The crafting of the standards and rules was done by an institutional complex including *developed* country governments and multilateral organizations like the IMF, and also by private international financial and accounting firms from developed countries and their industry associations and think tanks. The center of gravity, namely the Basel Committee on Banking Supervision, included representatives of the governments of ten European countries, the US, Canada, and Japan. *Developing* country entities had little involvement (prior to the upgrading of the G20 to heads of government level in late 2008). So the result reflected the collective preferences of developed country governments and firms.

Certainly, some more radical proposals for strengthening the international financial system, beyond "standardize," were advanced after the Asian crisis – including an array of new international financial organizations. But the more radical proposals would have seriously shrunk the freedom of Wall Street, the City and other financial centers, whose preferences began to prevail in governmental circles as it became clear that the crisis would not hit the West badly, contrary to initial fears. The more radical proposals did not leave the drawing board.

The SSC system described here is just one part of a larger complex of international regimes, backed by the authority of the leading Western states (often delegated upwards to interstate organizations), which helped to sluice opportunities and income towards (a) the financial sector, and (b) the top percentile of world income distribution. These international regimes complement the upward-redistributing domestic regimes of the leading Western states as well as most developing countries. But the role of state authority in this upward redistribution is obscured by the standard framing of "conservative" and "progressive" world views as "pro-market" and "pro-government." The standard framing is misleading, because it obscures the common conservative endorsement of government interventions which assist upward distribution and expand the scope for private profit making. The SSC system is part of this broad thrust of rule-making which has the effect – intended or not – of sluicing resources upwards.[7]

But stabilizing the financial system while enabling its expansion and soaring profitability were only two of the High Command's motives behind its response to the late 1990s crises. A third was the High Command's concern to open markets in the rest of the world and reconfigure domestic political economies so as to facilitate the operations of Western, especially Anglo-American firms – without much more than lip service to the idea of compromise with the national interests and preferences of developing countries (hence the lack of developing country representation in the standard setting bodies). This is a paradox of liberalism: in the name of liberalism, the Western side sought to build a comprehensive system of global economic standardization, surveillance and correction around one particular variety of capitalism, and to shrink the scope of national "policy space." It sought to do so through interstate organizations with democratic deficits so big they could almost be called democratic absences.

This chapter contributes to an understanding of the conditions which gave rise to the crash of 2008 by describing the evolution of the SSC system, the arguments used to justify it, and evidence of its effects. The crash represents a spectacular failure of the SSC system to produce counter-cyclical policy responses. But the ideological ideas underlying the system have remarkable Darwinian capacity to replicate themselves in the minds of successive generations of economists and politicians. The present danger is that the same ideas about "transparency," "good practice," "self-regulation," "rewards for success but not for failure" are even now being resurrected in governments' attempts to be seen to be "doing something" to reduce the risk of subsequent crises, while triangulating with the entrenched power of private financiers – on whom politicians and political parties depend for electoral finance, thanks to that stratospheric figure of global financial transactions at 70 times global output.

THE SHOCK OF THE ASIAN CRISIS

In the late 1990s the High Command of world finance was petrified that the biggest Western economies would be dragged down as the crisis ricocheted out of Asia and into Russia, Brazil and elsewhere. Paul Blustein, author of *The Chastening* (2001), gives a tick-tock account of how these several crises unfolded, and quotes chairman of the Federal Reserve, Alan Greenspan, in October 1998 saying to the National Association for Business Economics: "I have been looking at the American economy on a day-by-day basis for almost a half century, but I have never seen anything like this" ("this" meaning the disintegration of market confidence).

Blustein also quotes a bond market analyst telling his forecasting consultant, in mid October 1998, "I've never called you before, and I wouldn't do it, but I owe it to you to let you know, it's never been like this before out there." Stanley Fischer, deputy managing director of the IMF, told Blustein that when the Brazilian governor of the central bank told him, in January 1999, that Brazil would no longer make an iron-clad defence of its exchange rate, "I thought, this is it. We're going to lose Latin America, and then it will go back to Asia."[8]

The High Command's worries about the Asian crisis went far beyond the fact that it affected a sizable portion of the world's population in fast-growing countries. It seemed likely to discredit the hard-won consensus about the virtues of market liberalization, including the core proposition that the optimal degree of openness for developing countries was maximum openness. The crisis-affected countries had been garlanded as star pupils of the Washington Consensus – their economic success was attributed to their adherence and held up as proof of its general validity. This proof in turn affirmed the *duty* of the World Bank and IMF to give developing countries every encouragement to adopt it. Indeed, the Bank had crafted a formula called the Country Policy and Institutional Assessment (CPIA) formula, by which it scored countries on more than a dozen domains of policies and institutions. A country's score affected the Bank's country dialogue and its willingness to lend. The scoring criteria directly expressed the Washington Consensus; so to get the top score for "trade policy" a country had to have a virtually completely free trade regime, and to get the top score for "labor market institutions" the country had to have no "frictions" in the labor market, including collective bargaining.

Moreover, the crisis hit only a few years after the Mexican "peso crisis" of 1994, and Mexico too had been garlanded with praise by Washington. In the wake of the Mexican crisis academics and official agencies rushed to present proposals for safeguarding the world economy against a repeat, including better financial supervision at the international level, more transparency of financial markets, sensible macroeconomic policies and exchange rate regimes, and better monitoring of macroeconomic performance. But once the crisis was seen as confined to Mexico, complacency resumed. So the shock of the Asia crisis was compounded by the realization that nothing much had been done to strengthen the international financial system in the several years since the Mexican crisis.

NEW INTERNATIONAL FINANCIAL ARCHITECTURE

The frightening events of the late 1990s plunged policy circles into cognitive fog. Once beyond the panic stage, many leading economists rushed to offer up plans for a "new international financial architecture" (NIFA) – not merely new interior decoration, or even new plumbing, but new architecture to create a much stronger supranational authority in financial markets, intended as the boldest rethinking since the Bretton Woods conference of 1944.

The NIFA proposals included ambitious new global organizations such as a much larger IMF, a global financial regulator, a sovereign bankruptcy court, an international deposit insurance corporation, even a global central bank. They included the proposal for the IMF to be given greater authority to support standstills – postponement of foreign debt repayments and even controls on capital outflows, which amount to "bailing in" countries' private creditors – so as to give countries protection from creditor panics, analogous to the kind of protection companies get with bankruptcy laws. (You would think that the translation of the principle of corporate bankruptcy to the sovereign level would have been done long before.)

In the event, these proposals were stillborn. The IMF was not supersized, as some analysts wanted on grounds that the giant size of global financial markets required a big increase in the Fund's resources and staff so that, when crises erupt, it could provide enough hard currency for financial investors not to panic about a shortage of liquidity. On the other hand, nor was the IMF abolished, as prominent conservatives like former Secretary of State George Shultz wanted; nor even substantially cut, as wanted by the majority on a congressionally appointed panel led by conservative economist Allan Meltzer.

One of the more radical proposals to originate from the official sector – the Sovereign Debt Restructuring Mechanism (SDRM) proposed by Ann Krueger, number two at the IMF, which contained elements of a global bankruptcy procedure – was defeated by a combination of developed country states and private financial organizations at the Spring Meetings of the World Bank and IMF in March 2003. The SDRM would have involved full debt restructuring: changes in interest rates, reductions in amounts owed, and influence over private investments and contracts. It would have entailed a big jump in the authority of one or more international organizations over private financial markets.

However, it turned out that the necessary authority for the SDRM would require the Fund to change its Articles of Agreement. Fund members are extremely reluctant to change the Articles of Agreement, having changed them only three times between the IMF's founding in the 1940s and 1999. Also, major Western countries would have to pass laws recognizing the Fund's authority so that bondholders would be prevented from asserting claims in court. But such laws recognizing the Fund's authority would encounter storms of opposition, because they involve (a) authority to abrogate contracts (the covenants that govern borrowers' obligation to pay interest and principal on loans and bonds), and also (b) authority to block a country's own citizens, as well as foreigners, from moving their money abroad. The US Congress, in particular, would be sure to oppose tooth and nail.

The proposal for Contingent Credit Lines (CCL) was implemented, in that the IMF did create a facility that enabled the Fund to lend preemptively to help prevent a crisis, for the first time. However, countries had to volunteer to join the facility, and the IMF had to certify that the country had strong enough economic policies. In the event, no country signed up and even the IMF was unenthusiastic. From the country's side, signing up looked like a confession of fragility. From the IMF's side, ejecting a country that had acquired a new government not to the Fund's liking would send a bad signal to the markets, possibility precipitating a crisis.[9]

In short, there was little movement on any of the more radical NIFA proposals. The central reason was the unwillingness of participants in private financial markets to accept more international authority or constraints. They prefer to operate in a world where authority lies mainly with nation-states, where they can more readily game the political process with whatever combination of weak regulation and strong regulation generates the most profit.

Such movement towards strengthening the international financial system as occurred in the decade before 2008 was movement towards *strengthening developing countries' ability to sustain high integration into the world financial system* – on the implicit premise that the cause of the crises lay with developing countries' weak institutions and practices ("cronyism"), and not with the international system itself (such as the lack of sanction for regulation of capital flows, and the lack of discipline on countries running persistent payments surpluses and on the issuer of the international reserve currency, the US, running persistent deficits).

Accordingly, there was *real movement* in the area of global economic standardization: standards for good quality financial data ("transparency"), standards of best practice (including the Basel II capital requirements for international banks), and surveillance of national financial systems by multinational authorities, aimed especially at developing countries.

The central thrust of this effort was further to constrain policymaking and institutional arrangements in developing countries in order to ensure they fitted the preferences of international investors for full openness, arm's-length relations between firms, banks, financial markets, and government, and no government guarantees to banks that might give them an "unfair" competitive advantage. The arm-twisting spirit in which Western leaders tried to push this agenda is caught in a moment at the Annual Meetings of the World Bank and the Fund in Hong Kong, October 1997 (after the onset of the crisis in July). Lawrence Summers, US Deputy Treasury Secretary, was in a meeting when an aid whispered to him that the East Asian finance officials were meeting in another room, on their own. He leapt to his feet, rushed to the indicated room, threw open the door, bounded in, sat down in an empty seat, glared around the table, and said, "Now, where were we?"[10] Later, in 2000, a senior member of Summers' team explained the logic of the US government requiring the IMF to impose conditions on emergency loans to crisis-hit East Asian countries which went far beyond getting out of the crisis, but reflected long-standing US demands that East Asian countries open themselves to multinational corporations. "If we can't get them when they are down, we'll never get them", he explained (in an off-the-record conversation).

CONSTRUCTION OF THE SSC SYSTEM

In October 1998, with the crisis still in full flood, the G7 Finance Ministers and Central Bank Governors declared agreement on "the need for greater transparency" (repeating their declaration after the Mexican crisis) – meaning the provision of "accurate and timely" macroeconomic and financial supervisory data, including the reserve positions of central banks and levels of national public *and* private indebtedness.[11] World Bank economists supported this line of crisis prevention with the argument that the East Asian crisis was due in large measure to "lack of transparency" in financial data. (The Bank, as an ostensibly "apolitical" organization, could not endorse the prevailing "cronyism" theory, but "lack of transparency" was an apolitical approximation to it.) In the words of a World Bank paper published in 2001, "The findings suggest that these [crisis-affected] countries did not follow International Accounting Standards and that this likely triggered the financial crisis. Users of the accounting information were *misled* and were not able to take precautions in a timely fashion."[12]

The IMF argued in 2003 that the global "adoption of internationally recognized standards of good practices [would help] foster financial market stability and better risk assessment". Compliance with standards – said the IMF – would help a country "mitigate the impact of an external crisis by supporting continued access to external borrowing," and "help *prevent* crises" by reducing the cost of foreign capital and thereby help a government "remain solvent in cases it otherwise might not have remained solvent."[13]

Notice how the underlying theory of crisis protects the IMF and World Bank from blame. It implies that they did not act in advance to counter the build-up of crisis potential in Mexico and then in East Asia *because the Mexicans and East Asians misled them*. It eclipses an alternative theory, that they (and central bankers) were asleep at the wheel or seduced by the "This time is different" euphoria coming from Asia and international investors.

The initial concern to improve "transparency" grew into a broader concern to reorder economic activity around the world. The reordering had four main components: (1) standards of good information; (2) standards of best practices, including banking supervision, payments systems, corporate governance, and financial accounting; (3) systematic surveillance of economies in order to judge compliance with the standards; and (4) mechanisms for encouraging governments and firms to comply with the standards.[14]

The Financial Stability Forum (FSF) – established in April 1999 with the G7 finance ministers and central bankers at its core, plus those from four other industrial countries (or territories, in the case of Hong Kong), together with representatives from international financial organizations like the IMF, World Bank, and Bank for International Settlements (BIS), and representatives from private sector associations of financial firms – helped to develop standards in many areas, in the domains of banking supervision, risk management systems of banks, financial accounting, and corporate governance. The FSF was chaired by the general manager of the BIS. It included no representatives of developing countries.

The IMF was charged with developing Special Data Dissemination Standards (SDDS), mainly for macroeconomic data. The IMF was also to be the primary enforcer of many of the standards, through formal mechanisms of structural conditionality, contingent credit lines, and Article IV consultations.

However, these formal IMF-based enforcement mechanisms were not developed, for the same reason that the more radical of the NIFA proposals were not developed. Instead, the IMF – and the "transparency" thrust more generally – relied on indirect enforcement through the response of "financial markets" (aka the Electronic Herd). The IMF would make public the results of the surveillance, either publishing them itself or having the government publish them. (Even if the government restricted the public information, the unstated hope was that the network of experts who did the surveillance was leaky enough to ensure that anyone who wanted to see the real results could see them.) Financial markets would respond to the high-quality information appropriately; they would lend more funds at cheaper rates to governments that complied more fully with the standards, and less at higher rates to governments that complied less. Knowing this market-driven reward and punishment system, governments would strive for more compliance, and the international financial system would become more convergent around the Anglo-American model, and therefore more stable.

This was the theory behind the SSC system. With its justification the IMF (supplemented by the World Bank) in 1999 set about producing Reports on the Observance of Standards and Codes (ROSCs), and undertaking a Financial Sector Assessment Program (FSAP). Between 1999 and end 2006 the IMF produced 502 ROSCs and the World Bank 92, making a total of almost 600. A total of 130 countries had at least one ROSC. This was a big effort.

The ROSCs fed into the larger exercise of the FSAP, which had three main assessment components: (1) compliance with standards (based on the ROSC); (2) stability of the financial system; and (3) the financial sector's needed reforms. Operationally, the FSAP exercise may entail, for a large country, a sizable team of people from the IMF, the World Bank, and outside consultants, coming to a country and having sustained dialogue with financial authorities on critical matters such as, for example, payments systems, then feeding back their recommendations to the authorities.

At much the same time on a separate track, the Basel Committee on Banking Supervision, under the umbrella of BIS (the club of rich world central banks), was developing a new set of standards for banks' capital and for banking supervision. The impetus came from (a) bank regulators' feeling overwhelmed by financial innovations in the 1990s; (b) banks' development of new kinds of risk assessment models; and (c) the prevailing norm that "markets (as distinct from regulators) know best." Formulating the new set of standards came to be known as the Basel II process, because the original Basel rules, announced in 1988, had come to be seen as lagging far behind financial innovation. The first version of the Basel II proposals from the Basel Committee was published in 1999 after nearly a decade of leisurely negotiation, the Asian crisis having given it urgency. (The more-or-less final version was published in 2004.) The FSAP was meant to assess every financial system against Basel II principles, giving those principles more teeth than had they been strictly advisory.

A whole gamut of unofficial, private sector bodies was also busy formulating standards with global reach. They included the International Association of Insurance Supervisors, the International Accounting Standards Board (created in 2001), the International Organization of Securities Commissioners, the International Organization for Standardization, the International Federation of Stock Exchanges, and the Institute for International Finance. Global standards became the name of the game.

EFFECTS OF THE SSC SYSTEM

What were the effects of the drive for transparency, standards, surveillance, and correction? At first glance more transparency and common standards are as desirable as motherhood and apple pie. But things are not so simple.

On the plus side: The FSAP exercise produced useful results, according to insiders at the country end. The IMF's FSAP team typically concentrated on "supervising the (national) supervisors" – examining how the national financial supervisory system was working and making suggestions for improvement. Often its political role was to strengthen the hand of regulators against the government. The regulators could say to the government, "The IMF says X and Y must be done. If we don't comply, we will be subject to international criticism and market discipline." Indeed, quite a few governments overhauled their financial regulatory system ahead of an

FSAP exercise, especially when the government undertook in advance to publish the FSAP's findings. The UK Financial Services Authority (FSA), for example, was often asked to provide technical help to other governments in advance of an FSAP exercise.

On the other hand, the list of negatives is long: First, the FSAP and the ROSCs tended to be compiled with a checklist approach. As one involved World Bank insider put it:

> The problem with the FSAP is that the shareholders, primarily G7, burdened it with doing a huge amount of mindless assessments of compliance with a large number of standards. This prevented and/or distracted staff from looking at first-order issues. For example, in [an Eastern European country] two successive heads of the SEC were assassinated by "defenestration" from their office windows. Yet the FSAP concentrated on their compliance with IOSCO standards, even though with this degree of lawlessness, it is difficult to expect any securities market activity except for trade among insiders. Such silly exercises took resources away from consideration as to why some markets were missing or malfunctioning. The British, the French, Canadians, and Americans were the worst in their relentlessly checklist approach to doing assessments. If the Bank and Fund had been serious about this effort, they would have needed a number of new staff to implement it.[15]

In other words, the country assessments tended to lack focus, and to include much detail on so-called "structural" issues not closely related to what should be the focus, external stability. (Structural issues refer to institutional domains, such as social security systems or the energy sector, as distinct from macroeconomic policy issues to do with international reserves, external borrowing, and fiscal balances.)

Second, as Rachel Lomax, deputy governor of the Bank of England, said:

> The Fund does not devote enough time and effort to overseeing the system as a whole, through assessing global economic prospects and analysing international economic linkages and policy spillovers (so-called multilateral surveillance) [. . .] The Fund needs to be better focused on the big global issues, including financial issues and on the interactions between different regions and countries.[16]

Moreover, the IMF's Independent Evaluation Office found that the Fund's operational staff tended not even to *read* the global stability reports, let alone integrate findings into their bilateral work. Only 14% of senior staff said that the IMF's findings from its "multilateral surveillance" were discussed with national authorities.[17] Conversely, bilateral surveillance reports showed little discussion of policy spillovers even from systemically important countries like Germany and Russia, not to mention the US. The operational staff work in country silos.

Third, it seems that on the whole, financial market participants paid little attention to the data provided through "transparency" exercises – even though they would presumably no longer be "misled" (as they supposedly were before the Asian crisis). An independent evaluation of the IMF's FSAP concluded that "while many authorities identified the 'signalling role' to markets as one of their motivations for participating in the FSAP exercise, the impact of FSSAs [Financial Sector Stability Assessments] on the views of financial market participants appears *modest*."[18]

Again,

> Our interviews with a wide range of market participants indicate that most have limited knowledge of the contents of FSSAs, a conclusion reinforced by the results of the recent survey conducted in connection with the internal review of the standards and codes initiative. Use of FSSAs by credit rating agencies appears to be somewhat greater, but they have used them only selectively.[19]

Financial markets pay more attention to "traditional" macroeconomic indicators like inflation than to compliance with standards of good financial practice. Most studies of the link between compliance with standards and cost of foreign capital have found no significant impact of the former on the latter.

Yet as noted, the Fund's approach to enforcement of compliance with standards of best practice relied on indirect enforcement through financial markets rewarding high-compliance countries and punishing low-compliance policies. *If financial markets did not pay much attention to the data released from surveillance exercises, the compliance mechanism was hobbled.*

Fourth, to the extent that markets did pay attention to the information made available through transparency exercises the effects may have been to make financial markets less stable and more prone to crisis. Why? Because these developments, by homogenizing the data about economies and reducing the diversity of opinion on the near future, may have accentuated the tendency to *pro-cyclical herding behaviour* – bankers and investors buying what others were buying, selling what others were selling, owning what others were owning.

In short, the IMF's attempt to alter what the High Command took to be a major cause of the Asian financial crisis – to ensure that the users of accounting information would not again be "misled" – may have helped to strengthen financial supervision, through the FSAP process. On the other hand, it probably had rather little effect on behavior of financial market participants – because they did not notice much of the resulting information. Moreover, to the extent than their behavior was affected by the provision of more transparency, it may have been in a more pro-cyclical and destabilizing direction than the opposite.

The discussion has been about the impacts of IMF surveillance. What about the impact of the Basel II standards? Though agreed in outline in 1999, they were only finalized in 2004, and governments only started implementing them in 2007. Still, judged in terms of their potential effects as a key part of the SSC architecture erected after the late 1990s, we see that the Basel II rules would probably generate pro-cyclical tendencies and raise the volatility of borrowers' access to bank finance.

Avinash Persaud, former head of research at State Street Bank, argued that Basel II's move to widen the scope for banks' self-regulation, using more quantitative, market-sensitive risk-management practices, would reinforce herding behavior and market volatility in a vicious circle.[20] Two other analysts made the same point: "The application of models-based risk management may result in the creation of second-order dangers," which "raises questions about the recent move of financial regulators worldwide toward an integration of mathematical risk assessment tools in the regulatory framework."[21]

One reason is that the Basel II standards encouraged the more sophisticated and international banks – those based in developed countries – to adopt a single type of internal ratings-based (IRB) model. The IRB model relies on current asset prices, which tend to be pro-cyclical; and the model raises capital requirements at times of downturns when banks were less able to meet the requirements, adding to pro-cyclicality. Moreover, when banks use the same type of risk assessment model they tend to react similarly to similar signals, downgrading or upgrading clients en masse.

So Basel 2 standards, like IMF standards, would probably make market participants behave in ways that increase rather than decrease market volatility. But the impact of standards of best practice and their diffusion through regular surveillance is not limited to the behavior of market participants. There are also distributional impacts between countries.

EFFECTS ON DEVELOPING COUNTRIES' ACCESS TO FINANCE AND COMPETITIVENESS OF DEVELOPING COUNTRY BANKS[22]

Standards of best practice are rarely distributionally neutral: they usually benefit some participants more than others. The SSC system put in place in the decade after the late 1990s (including standards coming from the Basel Committee, the IMF, the FSF and the like, and surveillance in line with the standards) may have had at least two far-reaching distributional impacts, disadvantageous for developing countries and advantageous for developed countries, especially the Anglo-American kind.

First, Basel II, as compared to Basel I (or as compared to a "first best" solution), would shift competitive advantage even further towards developed country banks and against developing country banks, by raising the cost of finance to developing countries; and would likely hurt development prospects more broadly by making developing country access to finance more pro-cyclical. Why? Because Basel II requires banks with less sophisticated risk management systems – which tend to be based in developing countries – to carry relatively more supervisory capital than banks with more sophisticated systems. Therefore it raises their costs of lending relative to those with more sophisticated risk management systems, which tend to be based in developed countries. The latter are allowed to establish their credit risks and capital adequacy themselves ("self-regulate"), subject to the financial supervisor approving their model. Also, Basel II requires bigger differential risk weighting to lower-rated borrowers than Basel I, who are disproportionately in developing countries. And its standards insufficiently recognize risk diversification benefits of lending to clients in developing countries.

The Basel Committee's own quantitative impact study revealed a large variance in the amount of capital required for banks using the different Basel II-based risk assessment methodologies. For example, some banks using the advanced IRB approach – coming predominantly from developed countries – were expected to have big *reductions* in their capital requirements of the order of 30%. Banks using the simpler "foundational" approach – predominantly from developing countries – were expected to experience an *increase* in their capital requirements of over 38%.[23] The Basel II standards thus gave structural advantage to large developed country banks and structural disadvantage to developing country banks – and also to the regional, national, and local economies they are nested within.

The upshot is that developing countries under Basel II could face a higher cost of capital and a lower volume of lending than under Basel I, with more pro-cyclical volatility, and with their banks having less chance of establishing international operations and more likely to be taken over by developed country banks.[24]

THE PULL TOWARDS NORMS OF ANGLO-AMERICAN CAPITALISM

The second far-reaching distributional impact is the way that the standards and surveillance mechanisms framed a global "attractor" point, taking the Anglo-American or liberal market economy as the "normal" or "proper" kind of capitalism.[25] By the Anglo-American or liberal type we mean:

- short-term and arm's-length relations between banks, non-financial companies, and the state
- non-discretionary regulation which is delegated to "independent" agencies, like the FSA in the UK
- banks oriented to maximizing profits.

A contrasting type has been common in East Asia, based on longer-term and more "multiplex" relations between companies, financiers, and the state, discretionary regulation, and some banks invested with social purposes beyond profit maximizing (including development banks). I have argued elsewhere that this system, with its greater scope for longer-term, development-oriented finance, was an important factor in the very high rates of investment and diversification in capitalist East Asia over the 1950s to the 1980s, particularly because it enabled big firms to carry very high levels of debt to equity compared to counterparts operating in an Anglo-American type of capitalism. High debt/equity ratios supported high rates of investment within the national territory.[26]

As long as the East Asian system operates on the basis of long-term relationships, patient capital, and government guarantees, Anglo-American capital is at a disadvantage in these markets. On the other hand, US and UK financial firms believe they can beat all comers in an institutional context of arm's-length relations, stock markets, free capital flows across national borders, and new financial instruments. Therefore the Asian system must be changed towards theirs. For example, the US Senate passed a Foreign Operations Appropriation Bill in 1998 saying that *no US funds could be available to the IMF until the Treasury Secretary certified that all the G7 governments publicly agreed that they require the IMF to require of its borrowers: (a) liberal trade and foreign investment rules, and (b) elimination of "government directed lending on non-commercial terms or provision of market distorting subsidies to favored industries, enterprises, parties or institutions"* (that is, elimination of sectoral industrial policy).

When an East Asian economy adopts the High Command's standards of best practice its banks have to operate under much tighter prudential standards, and cannot support debt/equity ratios anywhere close to those they supported before. This puts pressure for change on the whole chain of savings, credit, and investment, and curbs the rate of productivity growth towards the world frontier.

The Basel Committee's rules illustrate the mechanism by which the SSC system pulls other economies towards the Anglo-American model. The rules have as their ostensible purpose the enforcement of a uniform level of prudence sufficient to make bank failure and contagion unlikely. The High Command – taking as "normal" the Anglo-American system of arm's-length relations between banks, firms and government, and banks oriented solely to maximizing profits – has defined the level of prudence in terms of value of the bank's assets, liabilities, and core capital. Hence the Basel Committee's rules of prudence translate into rules of capital adequacy. But in a national economy where banks receive government guarantees they have to mobilize less capital for their operations. This has been the case with Japanese banks, other East Asian banks, the German *lande* banks, and developing-country development banks. These are different kinds of banks than those assumed in the Basel rules. They are not devoted solely to maximizing profits for their shareholders. Their government guarantees allow them to support a cross-subsidizing mixture of public and private purposes, and to operate with a trading ethic that does not force them to drop unprofitable borrowers overnight. The High Command, however, considers that such banks have an unfair competitive advantage, and wants them to behave like "normal" banks, without government guarantees – which means giving up their mix of public and private purposes.

In other words, the justifiable rules of prudence become rules for forcing convergence of a key feature of political economies to the Anglo-American model, disguised as making a "level playing field" for all competitors.

Moreover, financial systems are sub-systems within a larger institutional complex. Changes in financial systems spill over into changes in related institutional areas, including corporate governance, product markets, labor markets, and further on into the welfare state and education. By making it more difficult for developing countries to reform their financial systems in the direction of the East Asian type the SSC system also makes it more difficult for developing countries to adopt other features of a "coordinated market economy", as distinct from a "liberal market economy."[27]

So to the extent to which the High Command is able to get its standards of best practice accepted as "normal" and non-compliance as "deviant," it imparts a "global warming" type of change in the international political economy away from coordinated market economies towards the liberal market economy of the Anglo-American type. Therefore the High Command's efforts at surveillance should not be understood as just a small add-on to previous efforts at market liberalization. The drive for transparency and standards involves not so much "removing the veil" as a project of homogenization around norms derived from good practice in the liberal market economy type of capitalism rather than from good practice in more coordinated forms of capitalism. It thereby reinforces and legitimizes the injection of the power of dominant states and multilateral organizations in order to intensify and stabilize financial liberalization. This is why the change is big enough to warrant the label Intensified Washington Consensus.[28]

THE PROCESS OF PUBLIC POLICY

How did this agenda of transparency, standards, and surveillance crystallize out? The G7 finance ministers and their deputies led the debate, in the spirit of Lawrence Summers' jubilant declaration as the US Congress passed legislation in 1999 to lift six decades of restrictions against banks combining commercial, insurance and investment services (repealing the 1933 Glass–Steagall Act): "This historical legislation will better enable American companies to compete in the new economy." The Basel Committee, which formulated the Basel rules, was a self-appointed group of supervisors and central bankers mostly from European countries – but centered on the US–UK axis. Most of the other bodies which did the further decision making and implementation, including the FSF and the Organisation for Economic Co-operation and Development (OECD), included virtually no developing country members. At the IMF and the World Bank, their executive boards, with 24 seats (until 2010), are dominated by the G7 states; seven executive directors from developed countries represent only their own country, and another seven, including such mighty powers as Belgium, the Netherlands, Spain, and Italy, represent 64 developing countries between them.

The big international developed country banks have an especially effective spokesperson for the industry in the form of the Institute for International Finance (IIF), based in Washington, DC, which does research and lobbying on their behalf. It pressed the Basel Committee on Banking Supervision to consult with "the industry" about improving the working of Basel I in the mid 1990s. Naturally the Basel Committee turned to it as its principal interlocutor. In formulating Basel II the Basel Committee relied even more on the IIF. But the IIF has the reputation of being the voice of the international developed-country banks, and of taking little notice of the preferences of less international banks, including most developing-country banks.[29]

In short, the process of formulating how to strengthen the global financial system after the Asian crisis was shaped by the preferences of the developed country states and developed country private financial actors, and very little by developing country states or their private financial actors.[30] At the heart of it was the US–Wall Street–UK–City axis.[31] Given that their financial systems would be assessed against the new standards and rules through the FSAP process, developing countries, in the words of Howard Davies (a prominent British central banker and supervisor), "are reasonably complaining that they are being assessed against principles and detailed rules when they have no role in determining them."[32]

That being said, it is misleading to say that the spread of Anglo-

American norms occurred only because of "supply" push, as distinct from demand pull. The mechanism of diffusion involved two steps: first, pressure from the IMF, the FSF, the G20 and the like, especially in the wake of the Asian crisis, for countries to adopt best-practice standards. These standards were derived from "Western" practice, and especially Anglo-American, as distinct from, say, Japanese, German, or Scandinavian. But they were fairly general, for the most part. At the second step, once governments began formally to adopt the standards, they turned to more specific regulations on the books in Western countries, especially to the regulations of Anglo-American countries; this was the demand pull.

PUSHBACK AND PRETEND COMPLIANCE

The story of the SSC system cannot stop here, however. The effects of the system on the ground cannot simply be inferred from the features of the system, because compliance, too, is a variable. Developing country compliance with the standards unsurprisingly often fell a long way short. In some countries and with respect to some standards a post-crisis surge of formal compliance was followed by regulatory forbearance and selective enforcement – hence pretend compliance and behavioral non-compliance.

For example, in the four crisis-affected countries of East Asia (Korea, Malaysia, Thailand, Indonesia), compliance as of 2006 varied across standards and across countries. In general, compliance with the Special Data Dissemination Standards for macroeconomic data was highest, for the costs of compliance do not bear on private firms, and the degree of compliance is relatively easily monitored. Next highest was banking supervision. Compliance with the standards of corporate governance and financial accounting was lowest, for these ones are most costly to the private sector and the most difficult to monitor. Malaysia had the highest overall compliance, then Korea, Thailand, and, at the bottom, Indonesia.[33]

CONCLUSION

In the decade following the Asian crisis the High Command of international finance continued to place the onus on developing countries to prevent crises, without allowing regulatory changes at the international level which would *constrain* private actors and mitigate the intensity of pressures from global financial liberalization. For example, it rejected capital account regulation (aka capital controls), even though surges of capital inflows are about the most reliable leading indicator of crises, as in the Latin American debt crisis of the 1980s, the East Asian/Latin American/Russian crises of the late 1990s, and the European crisis of the late 2000s. It also rejected mechanisms for reducing the severity of crisis such as the SDRM, and standstills more broadly. It approved rules for international banking (Basel II) which contained built-in handicaps on developing country banks. Moreover, by enabling self-regulation in combination with government guarantees to depositors, Basel II rules encouraged the owners and managers to take high risks on the assumption that they could appropriate outsized profits and pass losses onto taxpayers; as though the High Command had not heard of "moral hazard," or that "self-regulation is to regulation as self-importance is to importance."

Meanwhile, at the national level, the High Command gave little attention to tightening constraints on finance within Western countries. On the contrary, the US and UK governments, among others, rushed to deregulate their financial systems. The spirit of the times was caught at the press conference to welcome a new head of the US Office of Thrift Supervision in 2003. In front of a banner proclaiming "Cutting Red Tape," the new head appeared on the podium wielding a chain saw at a chest-high pile of banking regulations, flanked by the vice chair of the FDIC and by three banking lobbyists waving pruning shears, all smiling broadly into the camera, *all members of the same team*. The photo appeared in the Annual Report of the Federal Deposit Insurance Corporation.[34]

The irony, then, is that the High Command established what was meant to be a universal system of regulation after the late 1990s, but focused its attention mainly on developing countries, not on Western countries. One reason, of course, is that some developing countries were the locus of crisis in the late 1990s. Another is the belief that Western financial systems, thanks to their combination of competition and light-touch regulation, were stable; indeed, that the Anglo-American type of financial system should be the model for developing countries. And a third reason is that the High Command included only slight representation of developing countries, while it included strong representation of internationally active private financial firms based in developed countries. Private financial market participants in the West remained hostile to measures that went beyond standardization on an Anglo-American model of arm's-length, short-term capital markets. No surprise, then, that the international financial architecture continued to operate in a way that would have "externalized" serious costs onto developing economies had world macroeconomic conditions not appeared to be benign over the 2000s.

Looked at more broadly, the SSC system showed the following drawbacks:

1. It tended to treat each national economy as a unit and gave only slight attention to the world economy as a whole and to policy spillovers from "systemically important" economies onto others.
2. It may have raised the propensity of financial market participants to "herd," and thereby increase the volatility and pro-cyclicality of developing country access to finance.
3. It tended to give a structural advantage to developed-country banks and other financial organizations and a structural disadvantage to those based in developing countries, especially through the dramatic effect on the cost of their capital adequacy requirements.
4. It tended to further shrink developing country "policy space" even beyond that allowed by the Washington Consensus.
5. It tended further to narrow the notion of the national interest to promoting economic growth and increasing personal economic welfare, and to marginalize important developmentalist objectives such as constructing national unity, deepening national economic integration, and strengthening social cohesion. For these latter objectives, banks of the coordinated market economy type would have been more useful than those of the liberal market economy type. But Western investors (including those from Western coordinated market economies) prefer developing countries to adopt a regime of full openness and arm's-length, short-term relations between banks, firms, and government.

The SSC system was therefore deeply problematic from a liberal perspective. In the name of economic freedom – expanding market participants' freedom to move their finance where and how they wish – it curbed the liberal value of national choice of policy framework, by injecting a single model from above. And by nearly excluding developing countries from the standards-setting fora it curbed the liberal value of democratic participation, such that those who are subject to a decision should have some role in making it or at least in holding those who make it to account.

On the other hand, developing countries by no means complied with the regulatory push emanating from the High Command. They may have formally complied and advertised their formal compliance as though it was behavioral compliance. But domestic politics shape what happens between formal compliance and behavioral compliance. Inside the regulatory agencies and the regulated banks and firms "a varying combination of regulatory forebearance, administrative blockage and private sector non-compliance [can] flourish. The result [is] mock compliance: a combination of considerable formal compliance with international standards and behavioural departure from their prescriptions."[35]

The fact that the world economy then had a run of fast growth without crisis for about six years from 2001 to 2007, in contrast to the crisis-prone period from the 1980s through to the early 2000s, was due less to national or global regulatory changes than to generally benign world macroeconomic conditions, including fast growth in China and India and downwards pressure on prices of manufactured goods thanks to the China price. We now know, of course, that the benign macroeconomic conditions were largely illusory, based on a China–US interaction system that is inherently unstable. But at the time, plenty of economists told us that global imbalances between Asia and the West are benign and temporary.

Looking back from 2013 we see that some important institutional changes have been made since 2008, responding to defects in the SSC system. For one thing, the G20 council of finance ministers and central bankers established in 1999 was upgraded to the G20 council of heads of government in 2008, which soon declared itself to be the global steering committee (not just crisis committee) in economic and financial affairs. This marked a small but significant step in integrating the newly heavyweight developing countries into global governance. For another, the process of "G20ization" of global governance, already underway before 2008, has been accelerated, such that G20 member countries are now members of most of the international standards-setting and supervision bodies. For example, they are now all members of what was called the FSF, the expansion signaled by a change of name to Financial Stability Board. The Basel Committee has rushed out a new set of rules of bank regulation, Basel III, intended to force all lenders – particularly the largest – to build up buffers of equity, cash, and liquid assets to protect themselves against unexpected losses or another market crisis. Basel III has been hailed in some circles as "the single most important step towards preventing the next financial Armageddon."[36]

But compared to the needed scale of change these and other steps amount to a "mouse" (tripling a capital adequacy ratio of almost nothing still amounts to almost nothing). The upgrading of the G20 to heads of government level has provoked accusations that the G20 has mounted a "coup d'état by stealth," bypassing the United Nations and the legitimately constituted governing bodies of the World Bank and IMF. The Norwegian finance minister declared in 2010 that the G20 is "one of the greatest setbacks since World War II."[37] The well-known governor of a non-G20 central bank said to a mission from the Financial Stability Board as it arrived to inspect his bank's books, "On whose authority do you come? Go away," implying that the FSB has no legitimacy because its "parent," the G20, has no legitimacy.[38] The Nordic-Baltic Executive Director at the World Bank has been trying to stop the World Bank from serving as "secretariate" to the G20 for its development agenda, for the same reason. But there is no serious discussion in policy circles about reforming the G20 to place it on a firmer constitutional foundation.[39]

Moreover, the global financial industry has been mounting a full-on assault on the Basel III rules. As one observer noted, "The large banks are seeking to undo the relatively moderate progress that has been made on improving regulation thus far, using the very economic crisis they helped trigger as an excuse."[40] Bank lobbyists are having success in "divide and rule," persuading legislators and regulators in charge of implementing Basel III in each country that the rules must be watered down in order not to disadvantage their banks.

Given the gigantic size of financial transactions relative to the world's gross annual product, and the dense concentration of corporate financial power in the "super-cluster," the prospects are not good even for steps to "throw some sand in the wheels of our excessively efficient money markets," as James Tobin recommended long ago. The strong default assumption against sand in the wheels is caught in an editorial in the *Financial Times*, February 2012. It stipulates that any tax on a financial transaction penalizes a "useful social function" of transferring assets to those who want them (see the epigraphs) – ignoring what should be a basic lesson from the financial crisis of 2008 that not all trading is of social value.

Certainly there is plenty of talk and even some legislation about tightening up on the banks. The Dodd–Frank Act in the US aims to restrict commercial banks from proprietary trading, for example. The UK parliament has debated much the same issue of insulating commercial banks from all trading as a condition of them being protected by an official safety net of access to the central bank, deposit insurance and possible assistance in emergencies. The Basel II rules have been revised and somewhat tightened to make Basel III. And everyone now recognizes the desirability of a procedure for winding up insolvent international banks, arguably the most important challenge of regulatory reform.

Identifying what is desirable is easy enough, but translating it into legislation and rules which are both workable and free of damaging side effects is another matter. For example, the effort to separate commercial banks from investment ("casino") banking runs into the problem that commercial banks rely on selling securities to match short-term debt with long-term lending, and must hold some tranches of the securities for some period as inventory on their own books even if they act as pure intermediaries. It is then difficult to construct an incentive regime such that they stick to being pure intermediaries, given that the high profits accrue from strategic or speculative trading (which under the Volcker Rule would be reserved for investment banks). So far no solution for this conundrum has been found; and still less for the conundrum of winding up insolvent international banks.

In any case, the Dodd–Frank Act is so long and complex as to leave holes big enough for a coach and horses. And the Basel II rules run to more than 800 pages excluding notes and appendices.

What is worse, the focus on financial regulation eclipses bigger structural changes, such as re-framing big banks as utilities (akin to electricity, rail, water supply), even to the point of bringing some of them into public ownership as a source of discipline on the private banks. The focus on financial regulation also eclipses the big "outer wheel" of financial instability, namely, the international monetary system: its systematic mispricing of foreign exchange and inability to curb persistent large external payments surpluses and deficits, which have to be matched with equally large – precarious – internal financial structures. The US's external deficits have to be matched with US internal deficits by households, firms, or government. One of the useful effects of the Great Crash is its undermining of the faith that American capital markets can sustain ever-rising leverage without risk.

The New Dealers had it easy, in comparison. Today their descendants face a financial global super-cluster, which holds governments over a barrel. For the foreseeable future the ratio of financial transactions to world output will most likely remain above 50; income concentration will remain close to present levels; average wages will grow less than productivity; governments will be tempted to "solve" the problem of insufficient demand by allowing fast credit growth; and multi-country financial crises will therefore continue to roil the world at much the same frequency as the past 20 years – one every four to six years – each preceded by a chorus of "This time is different." And all this without even mentioning the restructuring required by tightening ecological constraints.

NOTES

1. In addition to the cited references I have drawn on discussions with Jane D'Arista, Jakob Vestergaard (Danish Institute of International Studies), Kevin Young (formerly of Government Department, LSE), Charles Goodhart (Financial Markets Group, LSE), Howard Davies (former head of the UK FSA and former director of LSE), Young Cho (PhD student, LSE). See further: R. Wade, 2000, "Wheels within wheels: rethinking the Asian crisis and the Asian model", in N. Polsby (ed), *Annual Review of Political Science 2000*, Annual Reviews, Palo Alto, CA, pp. 84–116; Wade, 2003, "What strategies are viable for developing countries today? The World Trade Organization and the shrinking of 'development space'", *Review of International Political Economy*, **10** (4), 621–44; Wade, 2006, "Choking the South", *New Left Review*, **38**, 115–27; Wade, 2008, "The first-world debt crisis of 2007–2010 in international perspective", *Challenge*,

51 (4), 23–54; Wade, 2009, "The global slump: deeper causes and harder lessons", *Challenge*, **52** (5), 5–24; Wade, 2009, "From global imbalances to global reorganizations", *Cambridge Journal of Economics*, **33** (4), 539–62.

2. L. Summers, "The great liberator", *New York Times*, 16 November 2006.
3. *Financial Times*, "Taxation fit for a *mesentente cordiale*", editorial, 15 February 2012.
4. A. Coghalan and D. MacKenzie, 2011, "Revealed – the capitalist network that runs the world", *New Scientist*, 19 October.
5. R. Wade, 2008, "The Washington Consensus", in W.A. Darity Jr. (ed.), *International Encyclopedia of the Social Sciences*, 2nd edition, volume 9, Macmillan Reference USA, Detroit, MI, pp. 38–40.
6. M. Wolf, 2004, *Why Globalization Works*, Yale University Press, New Haven, CT, p. 4.
7. R. Wade, 2014, " Growth, inequality, and poverty: evidence, arguments, and economists", in J. Ravenhill (ed.), *Global Political Economy*, 4th edition, Oxford University Press, Oxford; D. Baker, 2006, *The Conservative Nanny State*, Center for Economic and Policy Research, Washington, DC.
8. P. Blustein, 2001, *The Chastening: Inside the Crisis that Rocked the Global Financial System and Humbled the IMF*, Public Affairs, New York, pp. 349, 351, 357, respectively.
9. See IMF Fact Sheet dated July 2, 2000 entitled "Progress in strengthening the architecture of the international financial system" (http://www.imf.org/external/np/exr/facts/arcguide.htm). See also IMF, 2003, *Review of Contingent Credit Lines*, The International Monetary Fund, Washington, DC.
10. From a participant who requested anonymity. For Summers' interactive style, see the film *Inside Job*, directed by Charles Ferguson.
11. G7 Statement on the world economy, Declaration of G7 Finance Ministers and Central Bank Governors, London, October 30, 1998.
12. T. Vashwanath and D. Kaufman, 2001, "Towards transparency: new approaches and their application to financial markets", *The World Bank Research Observer*, **16** (1), 44, emphasis added.
13. IMF, 2003, *Review of Contingent Credit Lines*, Washington, DC, 26.
14. My argument on transparency and surveillance is indebted to Jakob Vestergaard, 2007, *Discipline in the Global Economy: Panopticism and the Post-Washington Consensus*, Copenhagen Business School, Copenhagen, Denmark.
15. Anonymous source, April 2007.
16. R. Lomax, 2006, "International monetary stability – can the IMF make a difference?", Lecture delivered at Somerset House, London, 1 November, p. 8.
17. Independent Evaluation Office of the IMF (IEO), 2006, "An evaluation of the IMF's multilateral surveillance", February, at www.imf.org/external/np/ieo/2006/ms/eng/pdf/report.pdf.
18. IEO, 2006, "Multilateral Surveillance", Evaluation Report, p. 13, emphasis added.
19. IEO, 2006, Report on the evaluation of the FSAP, p. 57. See also IMF, 2005, "The Standards and Codes Initiative—Is It Effective? And How Can It Be Improved?" The latter reports that the use of ROSCs by market participants is low, and has not increased in recent years (as indicated by responses to the question, "To what extent do you use ROSCs in your work?"). The most-used information was about compliance with Basel Core Principles and Data Dissemination; but even these scored only in the low 3s on a scale of 1 (not at all) to 5 (a very great deal).
20. A. Persaud, 2001, "The disturbing interactions between the madness of crowds and the risk management of banks in developing countries and the global financial system", in S. Griffith-Jones and A. Bhattacharaya (eds), *Developing Countries and the Global Financial System*, Commonwealth Secretariate, p. 61.
21. B. Holzer and Y. Millo, 2004, "From risks to second-order dangers in financial markets", CARR Discussion Paper, London School of Economics, p. 17.
22. I am indebted to Kevin Young for points made in this section; and to S. Claessens, G. Underhill and X. Zhang, 2008, "The political economy of Basel II: the costs for poor countries", *The World Economy*, **31**, 313–44.

23. Basel Committee on Banking Supervision, 2006, *Results of the Fifth Quantitative Impact Study*, Bank for International Settlements, Basel, 16 June, p. 2.
24. Claessens et al., 2003, p. 17.
25. Vestergaard, 2007.
26. Wade, 2004, *Governing the Market*, Princeton University Press, Princeton, NJ; Wade, 1998, "The Asian debt and development crisis of 1997–? Causes and consequences", *World Development*, **26** (8), 1535–53; Wade, 1998, "From 'miracle' to 'cronyism': explaining the Great Asian Slump", *Cambridge Journal of Economics*, **22** (6), 693–706; Wade and F. Veneroso, 1998, "Two views on Asia: The resources lie within", By Invitation, *The Economist*, 7–13 November. See also J. Zysman, 1983, *Governments, Markets, and Growth: Financial Systems and the Politics of Industrial Change*, Cornell University Press, Ithaca, NY.
27. P. Hall and D. Soskice, 2001, *Varieties of Capitalism: The Institutional Foundations of Comparative Advantage*, Oxford University Press, Oxford.
28. This is a central point of Vestergaard, 2007.
29. This, notwithstanding that about half of its membership comes from developing countries.
30. This point is central to Claessens et al., 2003.
31. The G20 grouping of developed and developing country finance ministers, formed in 1999 by the Clinton administration, has been less a forum of debate than an occasion for declarations of faith in free markets and the Washington Consensus. In meetings below ministerial level, representatives of Australia and Canada have led the cajoling of consensus, while representatives of major developing countries often sit mute. See Wade, 2011, "Emerging world order? From multipolarity to multilateralism in the G20, the IMF and the World Bank", *Politics and Society*, **39** (3), 347–78.
32. H. Davies, 2005, "A review of the review", *Financial Markets, Institutions and Instruments*, **14** (5), December, 247–52.
33. A. Walter, 2008, *Governing Finance: East Asia's Adoption of International Standards*, Cornell University Press, Ithaca, NY, Chapter 7.
34. Federal Deposit Insurance Corporation, 2003, "Cutting Red Tape", Annual Report, Washington, DC.
35. Walter, op. cit., Chapter 7.
36. B. Masters and T. Braithwaite, 2011, "Bankers versus Basel", *Financial Times*, 3 October, p. 11.
37. *Der Spiegel*, 2010, "Norway takes aim at G20: 'One of the greatest setbacks since World War II', interview with Jonas Gahr Støre", 22 June.
38. From the central bank governor, who requested anonymity.
39. J. Vestergaard and R. Wade, 2012, "Establishing a new Global Economic Council: governance reform at the G20, the IMF and the World Bank", *Global Policy*, **3** (3), 257–69; Wade, 2011, "Emerging world order? From multipolarity to multilateralism at the G20, the World Bank and the IMF", *Politics and Society*, **39** (3), 347–78.
40. Sony Kapoor, quoted in Masters and Braithwaite, op. cit.

PART IV

Global Finance

10. Would a North American monetary union protect Canada and Mexico against the ravages of "Dutch disease"? A post-financial crisis perspective

Robert A. Blecker and Mario Seccareccia*

INTRODUCTION

After the formation of the North American Free Trade Agreement (NAFTA) in 1994, enthusiasts of regional integration in North America turned their attention to "deeper" forms of integration, especially a customs union or monetary union.[1] Interest in proposals for deeper integration peaked around the turn of the new millennium, both north of the 49th parallel and south of the Rio Grande (Río Bravo). However, enthusiasm for deeper integration with the US has waned in both Canada and Mexico since the first decade of the twenty-first century for several reasons, including the post-9/11 US focus on national security, the failure of the US to adopt comprehensive immigration reform, the increase in drug-related violence along the US–Mexican border, and both Canada and Mexico's return to more bilateral approaches to their relations with the US. Also, the Eurozone crisis that broke out in 2010 provided a warning for smaller countries that adopting a single currency as part of a larger monetary union may not be a guarantee of economic stability or sustained prosperity. Nevertheless, proposals for further integration remain "in the air" and could easily be revived by future North American governments when the political climate changes.

One important trend that could potentially revive interest in a monetary union is the sharp rise in oil and other raw materials prices since the first decade of the twenty-first century. For both Canada and Mexico, this has meant large influxes of foreign exchange from energy exports (and, in Canada, other primary commodity exports); in Mexico, increased foreign exchange earnings from oil exports have been augmented by record levels of remittances from Mexican migrants working in the US. In both countries, the rising inflows of foreign exchange have contributed to high values of the national currencies that have inhibited the competitiveness of their manufacturing sectors—the very industries that earlier policy initiatives, including NAFTA, were intended to promote. In this context, some economists in Canada (and to a lesser extent in Mexico) have been arguing since the mid 2000s that their countries are suffering from "Dutch disease"—a term coined in the 1970s to describe the experience of the Netherlands during the 1960s when the discovery of North Sea gas pushed up the exchange rate.[2] The high value of the Dutch guilder at the time rendered Holland's manufacturing sector less competitive and resulted in a certain degree of de-industrialization.

This chapter seeks to investigate, first, whether Canada and Mexico are indeed suffering from Dutch disease, and second, whether a North American Monetary Union (NAMU) is a viable solution—or whether this "cure" might be worse than the disease. On the first point, the data we review below will show that both the Canadian dollar and Mexican peso reached uncompetitively high values during the past decade (roughly 2001–11), and that these currency overvaluations were associated with declines (either relative or absolute) in manufacturing output and employment in each country. The surge in real oil prices to levels that exceed those of the late 1970s (see Figure 10.1) makes the Dutch disease hypothesis a plausible explanation for these phenomena. Although oil prices temporarily sank during the worst of the financial crisis in late 2008 and early 2009, they have since recovered to relatively high levels. Since both the Canadian and Mexican currencies began to appreciate prior to the latest upsurge in oil prices, it is likely that other factors, particularly monetary policies, were important causes of the rising values of the two currencies prior to the financial crisis and the ensuing Great Recession, but high oil prices could still be a contributing factor in explaining those countries' high exchange rates.

Assuming that there is some truth to the Dutch disease diagnosis, the prescription of a NAMU has a fairly obvious logic: since the North American economy as a whole (which is dominated by the US) is not a major net exporter of oil, gas, and other primary commodities, a single North American currency would be unlikely to appreciate in response to a boom in energy and commodity prices. However, the potential gains for Canada and Mexico from eliminating exchange rate fluctuations driven by resource prices could be offset, depending on the exchange rate parities at which the Canadian dollar and Mexican peso would be converted to a new North American currency or (under some scenarios) to the US dollar, as well as the exchange rates that would then prevail between the North

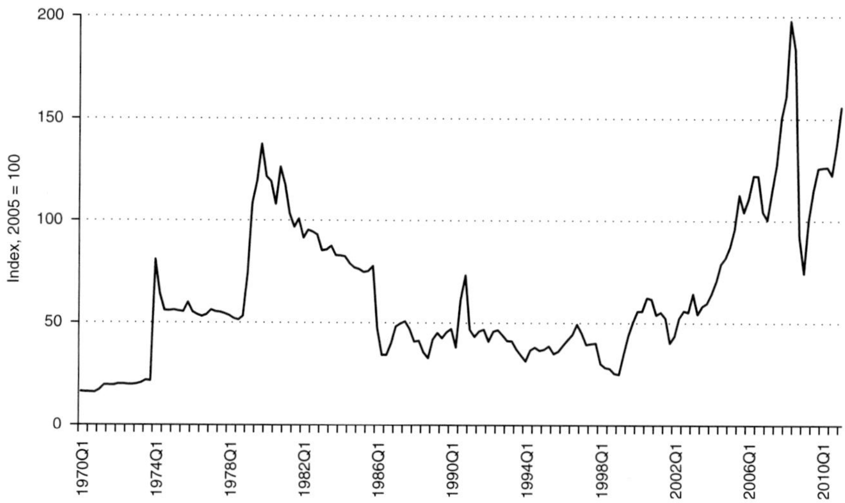

Note: This index of real oil prices was constructed by taking the ratio of the IMF's index of world petroleum prices (in US dollars) to the US producer price index for industrial commodities less fuels.

Sources: International Monetary Fund (IMF), International Financial Statistics; US Bureau of Labor Statistics, www.bls.gov; and authors' calculations.

Figure 10.1 Real oil price index, quarterly, 1970 Q1 to 2011 Q1

American currency and currencies in other global regions. Furthermore, creating a NAMU to combat Dutch disease would ignore an obvious alternative, which would be to adopt monetary and fiscal policies that would act to offset the pressure for exchange rate appreciation in response to a natural resource boom.

Also, based on the precedent of the European Economic and Monetary Union (EMU), the type of fiscal policies that the member countries would be allowed to pursue and the nature of the monetary policy that the regional central bank would follow are important determinants of how a monetary union would affect its member countries. Ironically, both Canada and Mexico currently (and independently) follow monetary and fiscal policies that are similar in spirit (if not in exact design) to those of the EMU: their monetary policies are focused mainly on controlling inflation,[3] while their fiscal policies are targeted on preventing large budget deficits or achieving surpluses (indeed, more successfully than some EMU members, such as Greece). How a NAMU would be regulated in this regard—what sort of monetary policy its central bank would follow, and what sorts of fiscal policies it would allow its member states—would therefore be a critical factor affecting whether the cure of monetary integration would be worse than the disease of an overly strong currency.

Although enthusiasm for a NAMU has waned at present, the proposals for creating one have engendered a significant amount of analysis and discussion that have, at least, clarified some of the likely parameters if a NAMU is ever formed. Unlike in the EMU, where the countries are more similar in size, the extreme asymmetries in North America—where Canada and Mexico's gross domestic products (GDPs) are, respectively, only about 11 and 7 percent of US GDP[4]—seem likely to ensure a subordinate role for these two countries in the formulation of monetary policy in a NAMU. Many observers have argued that the US would be unlikely to want to create a new, euro-like North American currency, and hence the formation of a NAMU would mean that Canada and Mexico would have to adopt the US dollar. This could be done unilaterally by each country, in which case it would be called "dollarization," but it could also be accomplished by expanding the US Federal Reserve System (Fed) to include Canada and Mexico. More specifically, some have argued that Mexico and Canada would essentially have to become mere Fed districts, similar to the existing 12 Fed regions in the US—with at most one seat on the Federal Open Market Committee (FOMC) for each country.[5]

Even if a new North American currency and North American Central Bank (NACB) were created, the profound asymmetries in North America make it likely that US interests would still have a preponderant role in setting monetary policies (Smith 2002). Needless to say, the prospect of such a diminished role for Canadians and Mexicans in setting their own monetary policies has diminished support for a NAMU in their respective countries; in effect, a NAMU that was politically acceptable in the US might not be politically acceptable in the other two countries. Nevertheless, the idea of taking monetary policy even further out of the hands of national political leaders could still be appealing to business interests and free-market ideologists in Canada and Mexico, not to mention politicians eager for a bold policy initiative, and therefore we proceed to analyze how a NAMU would or would not address the exchange rate and competitiveness problems of those two countries under today's circumstances.

CANADIAN PERSPECTIVES

Canadian interest in greater North American monetary integration since the 1990s seems to have followed the ebb and flow of the Canadian dollar *vis-à-vis* the US dollar. With the international value of the Canadian dollar hitting unprecedented lows and the proportion of trade with the

US peaking under NAFTA during the late 1990s and early 2000s, a growing number of academics, pundits, and politicians in Canada began to propose greater monetary integration with the US.[6] Interest in this proposal reached its peak just after the launch of the euro in 1999 when, among other things, a motion proposed by Canada's political opposition to study the possibility of a currency union in North America, especially along the lines of the EMU, was entertained and defeated in the federal House of Commons. However, several alternatives to the current floating rate have been proposed, including the adoption of a fixed exchange rate, the abandonment of Canada's national currency (US dollarization), and the formation of a NAMU with a new single currency.

Historically, interest in greater monetary integration appears to have been strongest in those sectors of the Canadian economy that are most heavily involved in foreign trade. Firms in the foreign sector often view the Canadian dollar as a "nuisance cost" largely because their revenues are in US funds but their costs are in Canadian dollars. A rising value of the Canadian dollar puts a squeeze on firms engaged in the export sector. Hence, industries with a certain degree of exchange rate exposure must engage in exchange rate risk-management strategies. Exchange rate hedging is commonplace, and companies can shield themselves over a short period by various currency options. These special administrative and transactions costs are faced only by business enterprises engaged in foreign trade, thereby making the latter more receptive to any proposal that would eliminate such costs.[7] Advocates of greater monetary integration have, therefore, traditionally emphasized the argument for the static efficiency gains from the reduction of transactions costs, relating not only to the elimination of exchange rate risk for business firms, but also to the elimination of the costs of converting currencies for the millions of Canadians who travel regularly to the US and Mexico for work or pleasure.

In addition to eliminating certain transaction costs, those partial to greater monetary integration have at times referred to at least one other important benefit of a NAMU that is often connected with the name of Robert Mundell, who argued that the regional configuration of a currency area is very important. Canada is characterized by a great diversity of industries across regions, such as manufacturing in Ontario (where growth depends on low energy costs) and oil in Alberta (where economic performance depends on high energy prices). A common external shock to these regions, such as a major jump in the international price of oil, naturally hurts Ontario manufacturers and benefits Alberta's oil producers. The existence of a floating exchange rate only compounds the negative effect on Ontario exporters, because Canada's exchange rate also faces upward pressure from the rising price of oil. In this case, Ontario manufacturing exporters would be better off with either a fixed exchange rate *vis-à-vis* the principal importer of Canada's exports—the US—or an outright monetary union. On the debatable assumption that Canada is not an optimal currency area (OCA) but, somehow, North America is, the abandonment of Canada's floating exchange rate in favor of greater monetary integration could be viewed as beneficial to Canadian manufacturing exports.[8]

Interestingly, with a falling nominal and real exchange rate during the pre-2002 period, it was the former argument over the need to eliminate the above-mentioned transactions costs for Canadian consumers and the exchange rate risk to exporting firms (much as the euro had been sold to the Europeans—see Emerson et al. 1992) that held sway. However, from about 2002 until just before the financial crisis that erupted in 2008, with rising international energy prices accompanied by a meteoric rise in the Canadian dollar, it was the Mundellian argument relating to OCAs that became fashionable among those partial to greater monetary integration. In the Canadian media, this has been associated with the debate over whether Canada has been afflicted by the Dutch disease. As a result, some have pointed to the floating Canadian dollar as the cause of a similar growing distress in Canada's manufacturing sector (see Rajasekaran 2008). Since this controversy over the role of Canada's exchange rate hinges on whether or not the Canadian dollar has become strongly sensitive to fluctuations in international oil prices, let us first discuss briefly the debate over the growing importance of energy in the determination of Canada's exchange rate.

Is the Canadian Dollar a Commodity Currency or a Petro-currency?

As displayed in Figure 10.2, the Canadian dollar was roughly at par with the US dollar in nominal terms at the end of the Bretton Woods era. Starting in the mid 1970s, the Canadian dollar went through two successive waves of depreciation until it hit bottom at the beginning of 2002. The first wave was associated with the oil price shocks of the 1970s followed by the major recession of the early 1980s. As the only one of the G-7 industrialized nations that is a major net exporter of primary products (with primary commodities constituting somewhat less than one-third of Canada's overall merchandise exports), Canada was hit badly not only by the oil price hikes that caused havoc in its industrial heartland, but also by the subsequent slump in primary commodity prices internationally, as industrial economies faced slower growth and descended into recession.

The situation reversed during the late 1980s, when the Bank of Canada tightened its monetary policy, thereby raising interest rates and the value of the Canadian dollar. However, following the 1990–91 recession and a

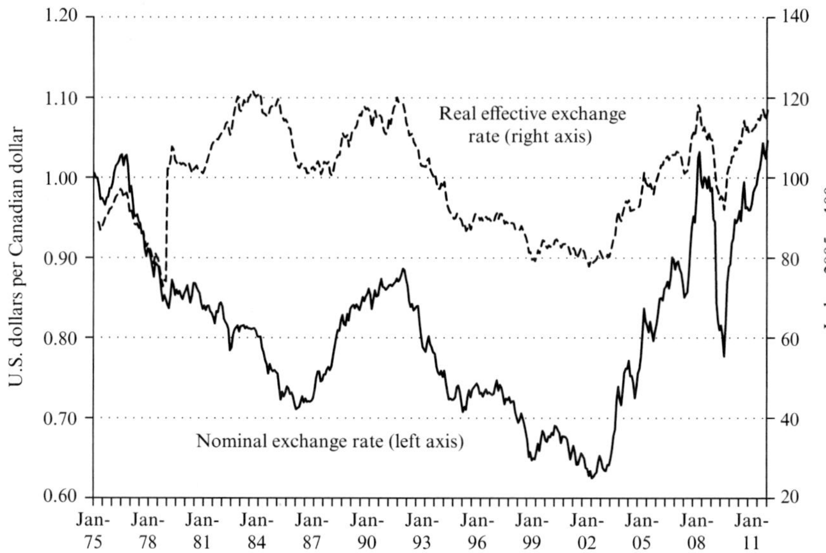

Note: The real effective exchange rate index is based on relative consumer prices and has missing values for a few months in 1975, 2003–06, and 2008.

Source: IMF, *International Financial Statistics*.

Figure 10.2 Canada's nominal and real exchange rates, monthly, January 1975 to July 2011

loosening of monetary policy, the Canadian dollar once again resumed its downward trend. The low primary commodity prices of the 1990s coupled with strong US economic growth during the Clinton era also contributed to a soaring US dollar *vis-à-vis* the anemic Canadian dollar, and the latter hit bottom only after the US economy slipped into recession, particularly in the winter of 2001–02. The initial recovery of the Canadian dollar in 2002–03 preceded the subsequent run-up in world oil prices, which began in the second half of 2004 (see Figure 10.1), and hence must be attributed to other factors (especially, low interest rates in the US that were not matched by Canadian interest rate cuts in 2002–03). The rapid increase in oil prices between late 2004 and early 2008 may have contributed to the further appreciation of the Canadian dollar during that period. Nevertheless, it is worth noting that the Canadian dollar has not appreciated much more than the euro relative to the US dollar during the 2002–11 period as a whole (except for a significant jump in the former during 2010–11), even though Canada is an oil exporter and the EMU as a whole is not. This suggests that one should not exaggerate the impact of oil or commodity prices relative to other factors such as monetary policy and market expectations in driving Canada's floating exchange rate. This point has also been made by Beine et al. (2009), who have argued that the Canada–US exchange rate has been affected more and more by factors affecting the denominator, namely the US dollar, thereby suggesting that some of the evidence in support of the Dutch disease may well be spurious.[9] For example, the Bank of Canada's failure to match the Fed's interest rate cuts in response to the US financial crisis in 2007–08, coupled with a loss of confidence in the US economy, also contributed to the Canadian dollar's surge at that time. Whatever the causes, by 2011 the Canadian dollar had returned to nominal parity with the US dollar and was near a record high value in real terms, after what proved to be a temporary decline immediately following the financial crisis in 2008–09.

The combined effects of interest rates and commodity prices are reflected in a well-established and often-cited econometric equation developed by researchers at the Bank of Canada to forecast the evolution of the Canada–US exchange rate (see Murray et al. 2003). According to the Bank of Canada equation, the Canada–US exchange rate depends on three key market "fundamentals": a primary commodity price index (excluding energy), an energy price index (mainly oil, natural gas, and electricity), and a measure of the Canada–US short-term interest rate differential (the difference in the Canada–US 90-day commercial paper rates). Estimates of this equation have always shown that an increase in (non-energy) international commodity prices and an increase in Canadian short-term interest rates *vis-à-vis* US rates lead to an appreciation of the Canadian dollar, as expected. However, the results concerning the role of energy prices in influencing Canada's exchange rate have varied over time. In the original estimates based mainly on the experience of the pre-1990s era, an increase in world energy prices, after controlling for the other variables, was found to lead to depreciation in the international value of the Canadian dollar (Murray et al. 2003). Hence, during the period when Canada had not yet become an important net exporter of energy, an increase in the international price of oil would have slowed down the world economy and would have reduced demand for Canadian exports, thereby putting downward pressure on Canada's exchange rate, as occurred during the late 1970s and early 1980s (Issa et al. 2006).

Since the 1990s, however, Canada has become a significant energy exporter in the context of the North American energy market, the development of which was first facilitated by the Canada–US Free Trade Agreement of 1989 and subsequently reinforced under NAFTA. Because of Canada's vast oil sands reserves (officially second only to Saudi Arabia's conventional reserves) and the new continental energy environment, when the price of oil goes up, this now pushes up the demand for Canadian dollars and therefore leads to an appreciation in the international value of Canada's currency—as is confirmed by estimates of the Bank of Canada exchange rate equation and other estimates in recent years (Bayoumi and Mühleisen 2006; Issa et al. 2006; Maier and DePratto 2008). Some have therefore suggested that, given the growing importance of energy exports, Canadian industry is now also ailing from Dutch disease—that is, a jump in the international price of oil puts upward pressure on the Canadian dollar and bleeds manufacturing exports. In light of this, it would seem that the continued, yet fluctuating, rise in Canada's "petrocurrency" accompanying the increasing price of oil in recent years spells continuing difficult times ahead for Canada's manufacturing sector. The Bank of Canada exchange rate equation suggests that looser monetary policy (a lowering of Canadian interest rates relative to US rates) could help to prevent this outcome, but such a policy response may be less possible since the financial crisis, when interest rates in both countries reached their lower bound.

The Dutch Disease in Canada

In the media, there are numerous examples that provide anecdotal evidence of serious problems faced by Canadian firms resulting from the high exchange rate. One striking example that made headlines over the past decade was the Canadian movie industry—"Hollywood North"—which grew rapidly under the protection of a low Canadian dollar but has now been seriously battered by its appreciation. However, the most strongly hit sector is manufacturing, which, in absolute terms, has seen significant net job losses since late 2002 and early 2003. Rising oil prices, the appreciating Canadian dollar and, in more recent years, a slump in the world economy have negatively affected the manufacturing sector.

As shown in Figure 10.3, despite the relatively high growth of the Canadian economy that, until 2007, had been spurred on by high consumer spending and rising commodity prices, the share of manufacturing employment in total Canadian employment declined sharply after a local peak in 2002–03. Figure 10.3 reveals that, over the last quarter-century, the manufacturing share of employment has not suffered such a dramatic decline since the deep recession of 1990–91. When looked at from the angle of real output, Figure 10.4 shows that the real output of the manufacturing sector peaked around 2000 after the high-tech crisis, and completely lost its previous momentum compared to the output of the Canadian business sector as a whole, which continued its upward climb, at least until the financial crisis and ensuing recession in 2008–09. After 2005, the output of the Canadian manufacturing sector fell significantly, mainly as

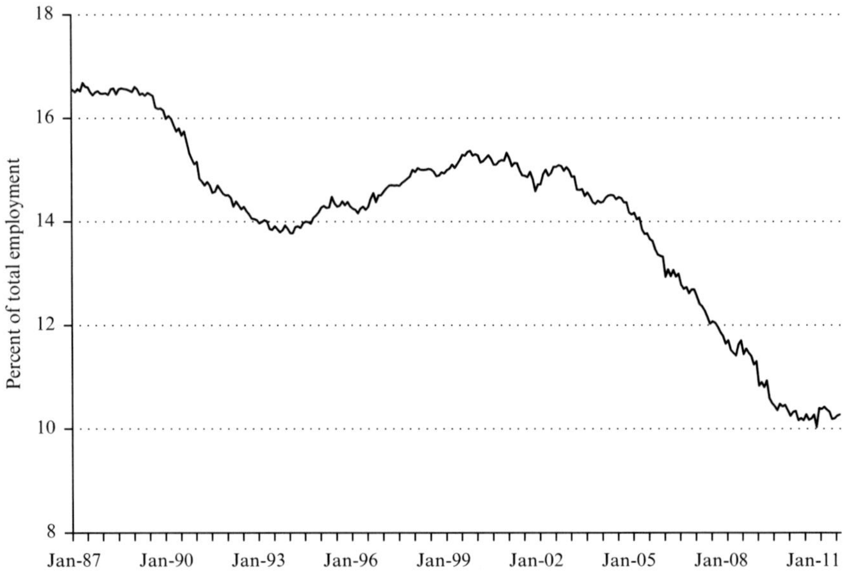

Sources: Statistics Canada, CANSIM II Series V13682073 and V13682079, and authors' calculations.

Figure 10.3 Manufacturing employment as a percentage of total employment in Canada, monthly, January 1987 to August 2011

a result of declining exports. Hence, while high oil prices favored western Canadian energy producers and led to a quadrupling of the share of oil exports in the value of total merchandise exports from about 5 percent in 1996 to approximately 20 percent in 2011 (with a temporary decline only immediately following the financial crisis), this growth occurred largely at the expense of manufacturing exports, which have declined as a share of the value of total exports.[10]

Thus, although there is growing evidence that Canada is experiencing some of the symptoms of Dutch disease, it is not clear to what extent the overvaluation of the Canadian dollar and the associated decline of the manufacturing sector should be attributed to oil prices versus other causes, particularly the strict inflation-targeting stance of monetary policy that has often held up Canadian interest rates relative to US rates. In terms of the evidence shown here, it appears that the decline in manufacturing employment did accelerate after 2004 when oil prices began to skyrocket (Figure 10.3), but manufacturing output began to stagnate earlier (Figure 10.4). Some researchers have raised questions as

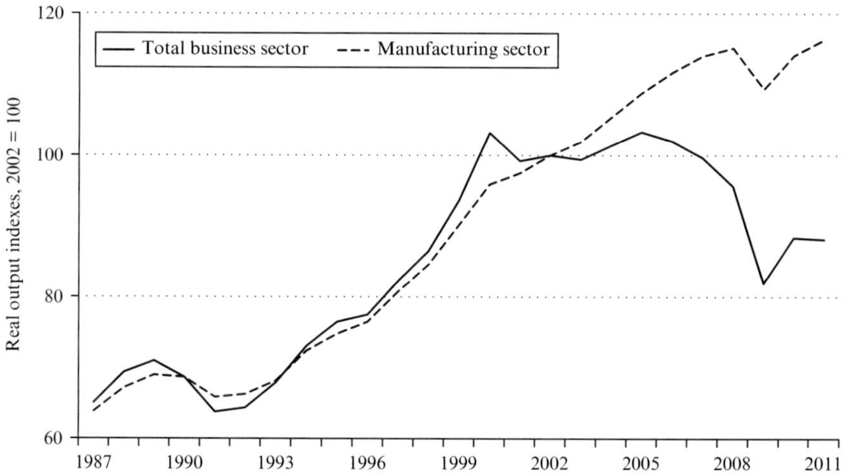

Note: Data for 2008 are for the first quarter.

Sources: Statistics Canada, CANSIM II Series V41707535, V41712932, V41881176, V41881185, and V41881886, and authors' calculations post-2007.

Figure 10.4 Real gross domestic product of total business and manufacturing sectors, Canada, annually, 1987–2011 (indexes, 2002 = 100)

to whether the boom in the oil sector could turn out to be a terrible curse for the Canadian economy (Bergevin 2006), while others have questioned altogether the significance of the Dutch disease diagnosis (Macdonald 2007; Beine et al. 2009). According to Macdonald (2007), much of the decline in Canadian manufacturing between 2003 and 2007, just prior to the financial crisis, was due to the so-called "China syndrome" as major emerging nations, notably China, were integrated into the global economy. Indeed, with the Chinese yuan essentially pegged to the US dollar until 2005 (and then appreciating very slowly until after the financial crisis), the Canadian dollar prices of Chinese imports were falling throughout most of the decade after 2002, thus accelerating the decline of the manufacturing sector in Canada.

Nevertheless, if the oil and commodity boom is indeed turning out to be a curse, then policy makers will surely want to find remedies to this problem. Policies such as limiting wage growth (to ensure that unit labor costs do not rise thereby further compounding the problem of declining competitiveness) or limiting public and private spending in an overheated economy (so as to curb inflationary pressures) have been proposed. But these measures are hardly more than what the Bank of Canada already does indirectly through its inflation-targeting monetary policy, which (as argued above) has tended merely to worsen the problem of an overvalued currency. A more interesting proposal, based on the Norwegian experience, is to constitute a separate petroleum fund financed by oil revenues upon which governments could rely so as to intervene and compensate sectors that are suffering as a result of the Dutch disease (Tremblay 2008). However, this could become a jurisdictional nightmare, not unlike the Canadian federal National Energy Policy of the early 1980s, because of the federal–provincial squabbling that would inevitably ensue.

An alternative and more straightforward solution to the problem of the ailing Canadian manufacturing sector would be to do away with the exchange rate—and the Canadian dollar—altogether. Needless to say, this is what would be preferred by all those partial to greater monetary integration (Courchene 2007, 2010; Grubel 2008). In principle, any one country in a currency union can be effectively insulated from Dutch disease, as long as the other member countries are not specialized in the same energy or commodity exports, and as long as the conversion to a single currency occurs at a competitive exchange rate. Could a monetary union therefore be the appropriate response to the alleged Dutch disease problem for Canada, or could it turn out to be worse than the disease itself? We shall discuss this question below, after we turn to an examination of these same issues in Mexico.

MEXICAN PERSPECTIVES

In Mexico, as in Canada, enthusiasm for a possible monetary union or dollarization policy has receded since it peaked around 2000. In the late 1990s, the initial success of NAFTA in stimulating trade and foreign direct investment (FDI) led some Mexican business interests to promote a monetary union as the next step in the country's regional integration.[11] At that point, memories of the 1994–95 "tequila" crisis were still fresh, and a monetary union was seen as a possible way of stabilizing the Mexican financial system and preventing another crisis. A monetary union was also seen as a means of ensuring price stability in a country where inflation had risen to a 35 percent annual rate in 1995 following the devaluation of the peso, and did not return to a single-digit rate until 2000 (when it was a still high 9.5 percent). Since the US dollar was strong at the time, inflation hawks were interested in linking Mexico's currency to a stronger one (or simply adopting the latter). Moreover, the launch of the euro in 1999 naturally led to interest in emulating Europe's monetary integration in Mexico as well as in Canada.

Some of the reasons why Mexicans subsequently lost interest in a NAMU are well known, and mostly (although not entirely) political.[12] After Mexican President Vicente Fox Quesada made it a priority of his administration (2000–06) to obtain better treatment of Mexican migrant workers in the US, he was effectively rebuffed by the George W. Bush administration, which (following the attacks of September 11, 2001) tightened security along the US–Mexican border and turned its attention to other foreign policy concerns such as the invasion of Iraq. In spite of the growing problem of millions of "illegal" or "undocumented" Mexican migrants living in the US, the US Congress never passed a comprehensive immigration reform bill, and instead in 2006 it passed a punitive law mandating tougher enforcement of border security and the construction of a 700-mile border fence. As the US made it harder for Mexican people and goods to cross the border, but not for drug cartels to bring money and weapons back into Mexico from the US, most Mexicans were in no mood to pursue wider integration efforts with the US.[13] Furthermore, for anyone who thought that Mexico should simply abandon an independent monetary policy and link the peso rigidly to the US dollar (for example, by establishing a currency board or unilaterally dollarizing), the Argentine crisis of 2002 provided a sharp lesson that such a policy was no sure route to financial stability.[14]

Macroeconomic Stabilization and Slow Growth in Mexico

The economic incentives for Mexico to seek a monetary union have also diminished since 2000. Given Mexico's history of recurrent financial and currency crises from the 1970s to the 1990s, the attraction of a monetary union derived mainly from the promise of greater macroeconomic and financial stability, rather than from the more conventional efficiency gains contemplated in the concept of an OCA or the reduced "nuisance costs" that were formerly seen as most important in Canada. However, in the decade preceding the crisis of 2008–09, the Mexican government was able to achieve macroeconomic stabilization via other means, thereby lessening interest in a monetary union or dollarization.

In 2000, the Banco de México set a goal of making the country's inflation rate converge with US inflation (then about 3 percent annually).[15] In combination with fiscal restraint eventually formalized in a balanced budget requirement, this inflation-targeting monetary policy led to exactly the sort of macroeconomic stabilization that advocates of a monetary union had promised. Consumer price inflation fell to just below 4 percent in each year from 2005–07; this was only slightly above the Canadian and US inflation rates, which were in the range of about 2 to 3 percent in those years (International Monetary Fund, 2011). Mexican inflation then ticked up to about 5 percent per year in 2008–09, before falling back to 4 percent in 2010. Although the Mexican economy suffered a mild recession in 2001, there was no repeat of a major financial crisis or currency collapse of the 1982–83 or 1994–95 variety. Of course, Mexico suffered greatly as a result of the Great Recession in 2008–09, but this crisis was external in origin, even if the impact was exacerbated by misguided policy responses as discussed below. In this environment of relative macro stability (at least, the absence of any domestically generated crises) and low inflation, the financial interests that might otherwise be supportive of creating a monetary union (or dollarizing) have had no immediate reason to do so.

Mexico's real exchange rate also stabilized to a remarkable degree during the past decade compared with previous years. As can be seen in Figure 10.5, the peso exhibited tremendous volatility from the mid 1970s to the 1990s, with repeated real appreciations and sharp crashes mirroring the boom–bust cycles in the Mexican economy. Since the early 2000s, however, the peso has fluctuated within much narrower bands than in the past, especially in bilateral terms with the US dollar (the wider fluctuations

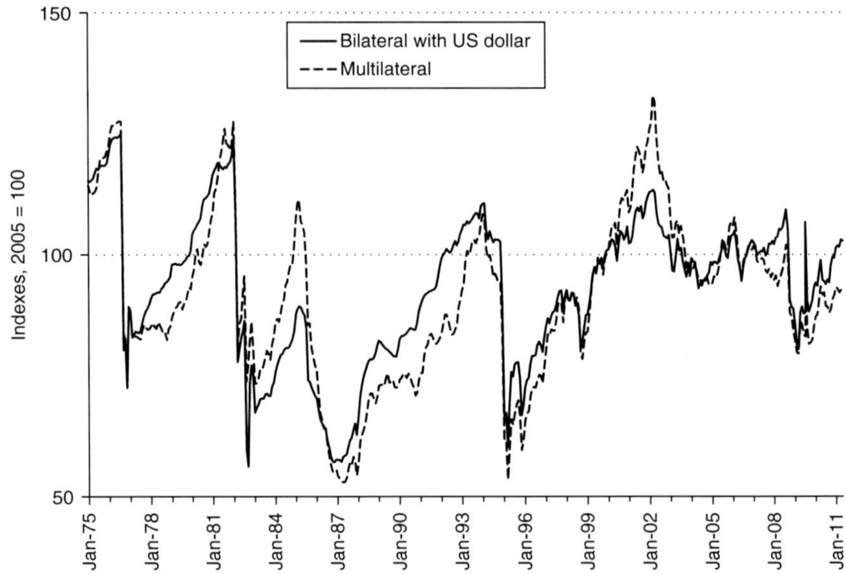

Sources: Banco de México, www.banxico.gob.mx; IMF, *International Financial Statistics*; and authors' calculations. The multilateral series was only available through April 2011.

Figure 10.5 Real value of the Mexican peso, monthly indexes, January 1970 to May 2011

in the multilateral exchange rate are mainly due to the dollar's fluctuations with other global currencies). After the peso fell briefly during the worst of the 2008–09 crisis, as of mid 2011 the peso had recovered to a level where its real value was close to the pre-crisis peak levels of 1993–94, and above its value in the late 1990s when Mexico enjoyed a brief export-led, post-NAFTA boom (or the late 1980s, when the first boom in manufactured exports occurred following Mexico's initial trade liberalization). Thus, as of 2011 the Mexican exchange rate was again at a level that could be considered overvalued, and as a result Mexico's export-led growth model has faltered (see Gallagher et al. 2008; Ibarra 2008; Blecker 2009).

Indeed, Mexico's macroeconomic stabilization has been achieved at a considerable cost in terms of both slow short-run growth and limited progress toward long-term development goals. After Mexico recovered from the debt crisis and opened its economy in the late 1980s, its growth rate averaged only 2.7 percent per year (from 1987 to 2010); starting with the year when NAFTA went into effect, the average growth rate for 1994 to 2010 was merely 2.5 percent.[16] And, during the first decade of the twenty-first century when inflation-targeting monetary policies were adopted and the peso again became chronically overvalued, Mexico's growth shrank to a paltry average annual rate of 1.7 percent from 2001 to 2010. This was very disappointing performance, considering that Mexico's growth rate averaged 6.4 percent per year during the three decades from 1951 to 1980 (Urquidi 2003).[17] It also pales by comparison with the growth of the developing countries in south and east Asia (including China and India), which averaged roughly 8 percent per year during each of those periods, as well as the growth of the east Asian "four tigers" (South Korea, Taiwan, Hong Kong, and Singapore), which averaged nearly 6 percent over the whole period 1987–2010, 5 percent for 1994–2010, and 4 percent for 2001–10.[18] In per capita terms, Mexico has not gained any ground relative to the US since it joined NAFTA in 1994, and has not recovered the ground it lost after the debt crisis of the early 1980s.[19] The migration of millions of undocumented Mexican workers to the US over the past decade, under difficult and dangerous conditions, speaks volumes about the lack of job opportunities at decent wages in Mexico, where real wages have stagnated since 1994 and have fallen further behind US levels.[20]

In addition to their negative impact on long-term growth and development, Mexico's supposedly stabilizing macroeconomic policies actually turned out to be destabilizing during the financial crisis and Great Recession of 2008–09. As noted earlier, this was the first time in the modern era that Mexico faced an economic crisis that was initiated mainly by external shocks, the origins of which could not be attributed to domestic macro policy failures (since Mexico did not have large budget deficits, high inflation rates, excessive international debt, or any of its other former maladies). Mexico was indeed hard hit by the combined effects of sharply fallen exports, dramatically decreased oil prices, and reduced migrant remittances, as well as the *sui generis* impact of the H1N1 flu epidemic in 2009. Nevertheless, Mexico's response to the crisis was crippled by the extremely rigid form of inflation targeting followed by the Banco de México (which kept raising interest rates throughout 2008, due to the slight up tick in inflation, while ignoring the likely impact of a severe US recession) combined with the balanced budget rule for fiscal policy (which led the government to adopt one of the smallest discretionary fiscal stimuli of any OECD member country, aside from highly indebted ones like Iceland and Greece that were forced to adopt severe austerity measures). As a result, Mexico had the largest decrease in GDP (−6.1 percent) of any country in Latin America in 2009, while GDP fell only by 2.6 percent in the US and 2.5 percent in Canada in the same year (IMF 2011).[21]

Paradoxically, then, Mexico has effectively accomplished some of both the promises and the pitfalls of an EMU-type monetary union, without actually joining one. Similar to the European countries that have joined the EMU, Mexico has achieved low inflation and price stability at the expense of inadequate job creation in its formal sector (there is relatively little open unemployment in Mexico, but a large number of workers are consigned to the informal sector at low incomes or else driven to emigrate), along with sluggish output growth, stagnant real earnings, and an overvalued currency. Mexico uses its monetary policy strictly to achieve price stability—more like the European Central Bank (ECB), and less like the US Fed or even the Bank of Canada, which demonstrated a relatively greater willingness to engage in countercyclical monetary policy during the financial crisis. Price stability (low inflation) has been accomplished at the cost of sacrificing long-term growth and exacerbating short-run cyclical responses to external shocks. Nevertheless, in the absence of a monetary union that would completely deprive it of an independent monetary policy, Mexico has the potential to change its policy framework, for example, by targeting a lower real value for the peso or using monetary policy to stimulate output and employment, if the political climate in the country should change.

Dutch Disease in Mexico?

Since a brief oil boom in the late 1970s—which ended abruptly in the debt crisis of 1982–86—Mexico has become increasingly specialized in manufactured exports, which reached a peak of about 85 percent of the total value of exports in the period 1998–2001.[22] Nevertheless, Mexico remains a significant oil exporter, and the importance of oil exports has revived along with the high prices of the past several years. The Dutch disease concept is therefore possibly relevant to Mexico, especially if it is widened to incorporate other sources of sudden windfalls of foreign exchange inflows that Mexico has experienced, such as the "hot money" financial inflows of the early 1990s and more recently, at least until the Great Recession, the upsurge in remittances from migrant workers in the US.

The same Bank of Canada research team that developed an econometric equation for Canada's real exchange rate also developed a parallel one for Mexico (see Murray et al. 2003). Primary commodity prices other than oil are not included in the Mexican equation, since Mexico is not a major exporter of other primary products. With data estimated through the late 1990s, the equation shows unambiguous evidence for a positive, long-run effect of oil prices on the real value of the peso. Presumably, the rise in oil prices since 2000 and the continued strength of the peso most of the time since then (along with the fall in both oil prices and the peso in 2008–09) would confirm the same positive relationship, if the data set were extended to include more recent years. Murray et al. (2003) did not include worker remittances in their exchange rate equation for Mexico, but because those have since become more important, one may surmise that inflows of foreign currencies (mostly US dollars) from migrant workers would have analogous effects to inflows of oil export revenue. However, Murray et al. (2003) found that interest rate differentials also affect the Mexican–US exchange rate, as they do the Canadian–US rate. Thus, monetary policy and oil prices both affect the value of the peso.

As noted above, prior to the 2008 crisis, the peso leveled off at a real exchange rate that inhibited Mexico's success in export-led growth focused on manufacturing.[23] As a result of the once-again overvalued peso, Mexico's non-oil export revenue grew more slowly and its FDI inflows stagnated in the early 2000s (Blecker and Esquivel 2010). Moreover, manufacturing employment—which Mexico had hoped would grow strongly, following the creation of NAFTA—has stagnated, if not actually declined, in recent years. According to data from Mexico's quinquennial Economic Census (shown by the vertical bars in Figure 10.6), total payroll employment in Mexican manufacturing grew from 2.5 million in 1988 to 3.8 million in 1998, following the country's liberalization of trade and the enactment of NAFTA, but then declined to 3.3 million in 2008. More detailed data show that most of the increases in manufacturing employment in the 1990s occurred in the export-oriented "maquiladora" assembly plants, but even maquiladora employment fell and then stagnated in 2000–06 (separate data for the maquiladora industries are not available after 2006). Comprehensive annual data, while only available since 2007, confirm that total Mexican manufacturing employment has stagnated: it fell sharply in the recession of 2009 and recovered only partially in 2010 and the first four months of 2011 (see Figure 10.6). The decline and stagnation in manufacturing employment during the past decade correspond precisely to the period when the peso became chronically overvalued, as shown in Figure 10.5.

To corroborate the evidence from the (admittedly incomplete) employment data, measures of manufacturing output as a percentage of GDP (using the overlapping real GDP series with 1993 and 2003 base years) are shown in Figure 10.7. The manufacturing share of GDP increased significantly in the late 1980s and again in the late 1990s, following Mexico's trade liberalization and the adoption of NAFTA (note also that the peso was temporarily lower in each of these periods). However, after the peso became overvalued again in the 2000s, this share declined back to about

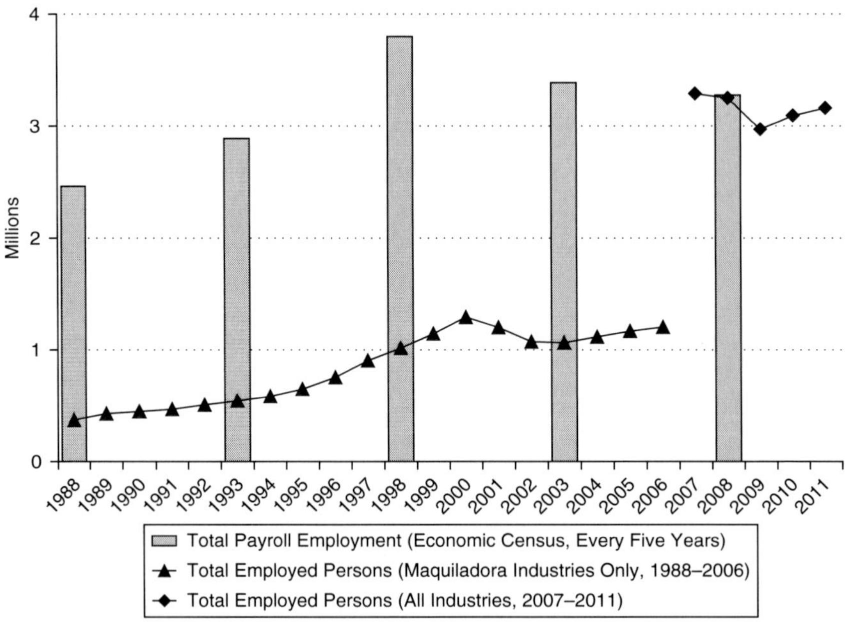

Notes: The Economic Census is conducted quinquennially. Separate data for maquiladora industries were discontinued after 2006; the new survey of total manufacturing employment began in 2007 (data for 2011 are for January–April only).

Sources: Censos Económicos, Encuesta Mensual de la Industria Manufacturera, and Industria Maquiladora de Exportación, all from Instituto Nacional de Economía, Geografía e Informática (INEGI), www.inegi.gob.mx.

Figure 10.6 Alternative measures of employment in Mexican manufacturing, 1988–2011

its pre-NAFTA level by 2010–11, even after recovering from a bigger dip during the recession in 2009.

Much as for the Canadian dollar, it remains to be seen to what extent the real appreciation of the Mexican peso can be attributed to higher oil prices, as is required for a Dutch disease diagnosis. Most of the rise in the peso occurred between about 1999 and 2002 (see Figure 10.5), before the boom in oil prices, which really didn't take off until late 2004. In fact, the peso exhibits remarkable stability during the years of the recent jump in oil prices, although this could be due in part to Banco de México purchases of foreign exchange reserves that have prevented the peso from rising more.[24] Furthermore, the stagnation of manufacturing employment and the decline in the manufacturing share of GDP both began several years before the biggest spikes in oil prices in 2007–08 and 2010–11. Thus, while Mexico exhibits some symptoms of the Dutch disease, the application of this diagnosis remains at best uncertain.

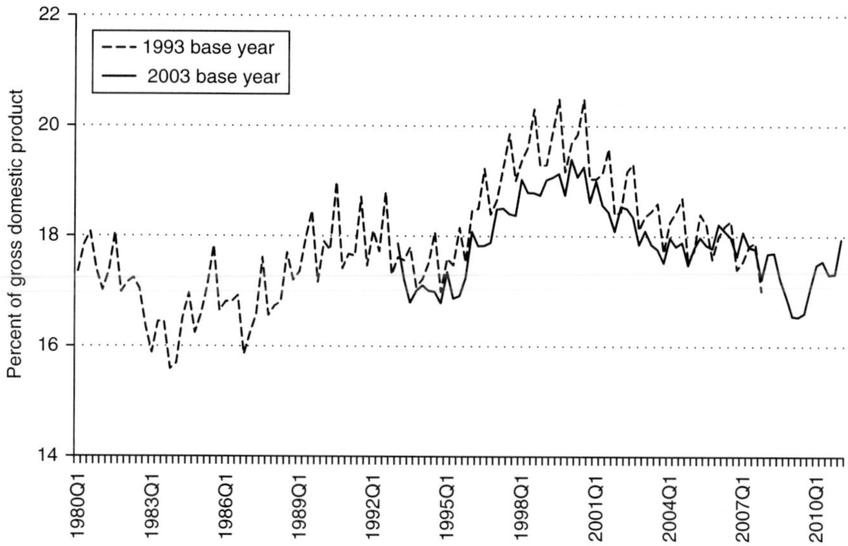

Note: Based on real GDP data at constant base year prices. The 1993 base year data were discontinued after 2007 and the 2003 base year data begin in 1993. Data for 2009–2011 are preliminary.

Sources: INEGI, Sistema de Cuentas Nacionales de México, www.inegi.gob.mx, and authors' calculations.

Figure 10.7 Manufacturing output as a percentage of gross domestic product in Mexico, quarterly, 1980 Q1 to 2011 Q1

WOULD A NAMU SOLVE THE DUTCH DISEASE PROBLEM FOR CANADA AND MEXICO?

It is of course true that creating a supranational North American currency comparable to the euro, such as the "amero" proposed by Grubel (1999)—or even the adoption of the US dollar by Canada and Mexico—would protect Canadian and Mexican industries from future increases in their countries' bilateral exchange rates with the US. However, adopting a single regional currency would not protect the industries of the member countries from future increases in the value of that currency relative to other national or regional currencies, such as the euro, British pound, and Japanese yen. For both Canada and Mexico, however, the US is by far their largest trading partner, so those fluctuations might not be as important for them as they would be for other countries that might want to link to the US dollar—as, for example, when Argentina adopted its fixed (1:1) peso–dollar exchange rate, in spite of having relatively little trade with the US.

In terms of avoiding Dutch disease, North America as a whole has a pattern of trade and migration flows that would probably dampen fluctuations in the value of a single regional currency related to energy prices and worker remittances.[25] If anything, the three NAFTA countries combined are probably net importers of energy products, since the US absorbs most of Canada and Mexico's oil and gas exports but still buys about two-thirds of its imported oil from other countries.[26] Since so much of the three countries' energy trade is intra-regional, global "oil shocks" would probably have much less impact on the exchange rate of a North American single currency (amero or dollar) with other global currencies than it presently has on the exchange rates of the Canadian dollar and Mexican peso.

By the same token, however, fixing the Canadian and Mexican exchange rates permanently to the US dollar (or to a new currency) would prevent those rates from depreciating in the event of unfavorable "shocks," including future declines in oil prices, albeit for a different reason, as it has also been the major problem faced by Greece, Spain, and other southern European countries during the Eurozone crisis of 2010–11. Unless a compensating regional fiscal transfer mechanism was put in place (an unlikely prospect), Canada and Mexico would suffer more severe adjustment costs when hit by those sorts of shocks. This is especially true because the US is a large net importer of oil and other commodities from non-NAFTA countries, and hence would benefit from such a supply shock that was detrimental to Canada and Mexico—in which case, the dollar (or amero) might actually go up in value, just when the latter two countries would need it to go down. Adjustment would then require a severe deflation in prices and incomes within each of those countries to absorb future negative oil price shocks, with potentially devastating effects on their manufacturing sectors. Thus, the loss of this important instrument of adjustment would mean that any future adverse shocks would have greater negative repercussions on incomes domestically in Canada and Mexico (see Bougrine and Seccareccia 2004).[27]

A further problem would arise if a NAMU was formed during a period in which both Canada and Mexico's manufacturing sectors were already suffering from overvalued currencies and depressed international demand. If the Canadian dollar and Mexican peso were converted to a North American currency (ameros or US dollars) at anything like the exchange rates of 2011, for example, this would merely lock-in a situation of currency overvaluation for Canada and Mexico. This would permanently institutionalize the negative effects of the overvaluation in both countries—or else it would require severe deflation to adjust to the fixed conversion rates, not unlike what happened when Britain pegged the pound to gold at an overvalued exchange rate after World War I, as famously described by Keynes (1925), or the "internal devaluation" (mostly via wage cuts) that southern European countries have had to face more recently.[28] Therefore, it would be a profound and tragic mistake to lock-in overvalued exchange rates in a NAMU in the name of preventing an epidemic of Dutch disease, especially if there is some likelihood that this disease may turn out to be perhaps less important than other shocks to either of these two economies.

Fiscal and Monetary Policies under a NAMU

There is, however, a further problem concerning whether an EMU-type arrangement would be a positive improvement over the current status quo of independent floating exchange rates for Canada and Mexico. As pointed out elsewhere (see Seccareccia and Lequain 2006), the establishment of the euro has been a historic monetary experiment that, some have argued, for the first time in centuries has given birth to a monetary system that formally separates money from the individual nation-state. The policy system that underlies the two main pillars of the EMU—the Maastricht Treaty (1992) and the Amsterdam Stability and Growth Pact (1997)—was put in place specifically to secure this separation. This has meant a loss of the two principal instruments of macroeconomic stabilization policy—monetary policy and, perhaps to a lesser, yet still very significant extent, discretionary fiscal policy—at the national level, even though the recent experience of Greece suggests that national governments can circumvent such restrictions until the financial markets catch up with them, with severe consequences on the servicing costs of their debt and their ability to refinance it over time.

According to the rules of the Treaty, fiscal policy is supposed to be severely constrained. Governments of EMU member states not only must fulfill the two fiscal requirements of keeping budget deficits within 3 percent of GDP and public debt-to-GDP ratios within a 60 percent of GDP ceiling, but also are required to target zero budget balances over the medium term. Supposedly, strong sanctions are imposed against those who do not meet these legal obligations, unless countries file cumbersome petitions for exceptions under the "severe recession" clause of the Treaty. Even before the Greek crisis in 2010, there had been some prominent short-term violations of the 3 percent rule. However, these were not always subject to the legally mandated penalties—which suggest that the legal framework for fiscal policy in the EMU is impractical and unrealistic, as the recent experience of many of the countries of southern Europe now confirms. Nevertheless, the Maastricht Treaty militates against the regular and accepted use of countercyclical fiscal policy, even if some countries follow its mandates more strictly than others. Indeed, as already noted by Seccareccia and Lequain (2006), until just prior to the Great Recession, the Maastricht Treaty and the Stability and Growth Pact actually forced discretionary fiscal policy to behave pro-cyclically.

With the relegating of activist fiscal policy exclusively to times of "severe" recession (as happened in 2008–09), the member states' control over the macroeconomy rests primarily on monetary policy conducted by the ECB—a supranational, independent institution over which the European Parliament has no direct power. The only policy innovation that was permitted under the Maastricht Treaty, but never implemented until the Greek crisis in 2010, was the intervention of the ECB in providing support for governments facing acute liquidity needs via the purchase of previously issued national government securities in the secondary bond market. The ECB has now been forced into the uncomfortable role of indirectly influencing fiscal policy via the back door, as a political arbiter of fiscal decisions made by national governments. However this situation is not politically tenable in the long term (Auerback 2010–11). Hence, if such an EMU structure were to be parachuted into the North American context, more active fiscal policy would no longer be possible in any one NAMU member, except during periods of severe crisis, and, even then, would depend on the capacity of a national government to raise sufficient funds in the financial markets. At the same time, with a "one size fits all" monetary policy within the NAMU, the NACB (or expanded Fed) would not cater sufficiently to Canada's or Mexico's regional needs, since the latter countries would, as noted earlier, probably hold only one seat each on the governing board of a NACB or an expanded FOMC.[29]

However, North America is not Europe, and the likely predominance of the US in a NAMU would create some special opportunities and challenges for the two smaller partners. In terms of monetary policy, because of its dual mandate of seeking to achieve high employment and low inflation, the Fed has shown itself to be more willing to adopt countercyclical interest rate cuts during recessions than the ECB, which only targets price stability. Indeed, following the financial crisis, the Fed has pegged interest rates at historically low levels and introduced less conventional policy measures, such as quantitative easing which, although not particularly successful, got the Fed to intervene directly in the bond market so as to reshape somewhat the yield curve. Even though the Fed is strictly concerned with US business cycle conditions at present, Canada and Mexico nevertheless benefit from the Fed's more flexible stance to the extent that their business cycles are positively correlated with US cycles.[30] If Mexico and Canada were to join a NAMU in which the central bank (NACB or expanded Fed) followed current Fed procedures, those countries would be subject to a less strict inflation-targeting monetary policy than they currently have today. Nevertheless, they would not give up inflation control, since the Fed—in spite of its lack of legally mandated inflation targets—effectively pursues a low inflation rate as part of its "dual mandate" to achieve both price stability and full employment.

It is unclear whether Canada and Mexico would have to agree to strict fiscal targets in a NAMU, similar to those that have been imposed on EMU members. On the one hand, the US is unlikely to want to tie its own hands by giving up the right to run large budget deficits or to have the Fed hold US government debt. Therefore, if Mexico and Canada were to be treated as co-equals with the US, they should not be subject to any fiscal restrictions as a condition of joining a NAMU or having a seat on the FOMC. On the other hand, insofar as Mexico and Canada might be treated as mere Fed districts, they could possibly be required to have balanced budgets or to meet certain arbitrary fiscal targets, more on the model of the US states, many of which cannot run budget deficits as the US federal government does. In this case, Canada and Mexico would face conditions similar to those of individual US states that would also be under financial market pressure to restrict deficit spending, much as is the case with national governments in the Eurozone. Hence, it is possible that an expanded North American Fed or NACB would not be allowed to hold Canadian or Mexican government debt, and that the Bank of Canada and Banco de México might similarly be prohibited from doing so (although the Banco de México does not currently hold any Mexican government debt anyway).

In some ways, Mexico would have an easy time adjusting to EMU-like fiscal restrictions today, because the Mexican government already operates a fiscal policy that targets the fiscal balance itself, and which is therefore largely procyclical rather than countercyclical (see Moreno-Brid and Ros 2009: Ch. 8; Esquivel 2010). Furthermore, the procyclical bias of Mexican fiscal policy is amplified by the reliance of the government on the national oil company Pemex for a substantial part of its tax revenue (see Puyana 2006). But for this very reason, a monetary union could lock-in a type of fiscal policy that Mexico would otherwise retain the option of changing in the future (for example, if the country were to focus more on infrastructure investments aimed at promoting long-run development, and stop targeting the fiscal balance itself).

Indeed, one should not discount the possibility that, at some future time, some interests in Mexico might seek a NAMU as a means of locking in the current monetary and fiscal policy regime. After all, one of the chief arguments in favor of NAFTA in the early 1990s was precisely that it would lock-in Mexico's liberalizing reforms of the late 1980s, especially the opening to foreign trade and investment, by preventing future Mexican governments from abandoning the country's commitment to liberalized trade and investment policies (Lustig 1998). A similar case could be made by proponents of the current macro policies, in the not-too-distant future, that Mexico should similarly lock-in its commitments to price stability and a balanced government budget by joining a monetary union that would force it to maintain those commitments in perpetuity—especially if there appeared to be a realistic prospect of a future left-wing government that might seek to change those policy priorities—as noted previously by Bowles and Moreno-Brid (2008: 137).

Canada also would not encounter any significant political or institutional barriers in abiding by EMU-style fiscal rules under present conditions. In the Canadian context, with the exception of the immediate post-financial crisis period, successive governments since the mid 1990s have been committed not only to balanced budgets, but also to targeting budget surpluses so as to achieve a pre-established, long-term decline in the ratio of federal debt to GDP, to which it recommitted itself at the G20 Toronto summit in June 2010. As shown elsewhere, these persistent federal surpluses have been achieved at the cost of destabilizing private household finances, thereby leading to ever declining personal saving rates and rising household indebtedness (Seccareccia 2005). In much the same way, on the monetary front, Canada's central bank has already achieved the EMU's commitment to price stability via its official inflation targeting and, much like the federal government's commitment to "sound finance" and fiscal surpluses, the Bank of Canada has been officially targeting a 2 percent inflation rate over the last the last two decades (see Seccareccia and Lavoie, 2010).

Nevertheless, there is some evidence for countercyclical fiscal policy in Canada, in spite of the high average level of the budget surplus that the Canadian government had achieved until the Great Recession. According to Seccareccia and Lequain (2006), primary (cyclically adjusted) fiscal balances respond negatively to the unemployment rate in both Canada and the US, unlike in the EMU where the authors find a perversely positive response. Therefore, if a NAMU imposed any restrictions on Canada's fiscal autonomy, it could lessen the ability of the Canadian government to adopt countercyclical fiscal policies attuned to short-run conditions in the Canadian economy (and it would also prevent Canada from rethinking its current commitment to long-run, average budget surpluses).

CONCLUSIONS

Both Canada and Mexico experienced currency appreciations in the first decade of the twenty-first century that stymied the growth of their manufacturing sectors and reduced manufacturing employment. Since oil prices have also risen rapidly in recent years, some observers (see Rajasekaran 2008, Courchene 2010, and Francis 2011 on the Canadian case) have leapt to the conclusion that these countries are suffering from Dutch disease, and that monetary integration with the US might be a solution. In the Mexican case, however, the currency appreciation largely preceded the rapid increase in oil prices (and there is some evidence of the central bank resisting further upward pressure on the peso by buying foreign exchange reserves), while in Canada the currency appreciation began earlier than the rise in oil prices and at most may have been aggravated by the latter. With the possible exception of the period immediately following the financial crisis, strict inflation-targeting monetary policies in both countries have led the monetary authorities to tolerate overvalued currencies to the detriment of real economic activity. Overall, currency overvaluation in these two countries seems to have resulted from a combination of monetary policy and commodity prices (and other sources of foreign exchange inflows, such as remittances), not commodity prices alone—and alternative monetary policies could have prevented some of the appreciation that has occurred (for example, by matching US interest rate cuts).

If, nonetheless, Canada and Mexico were to participate in a North American scheme for monetary integration, under any politically conceivable set of arrangements neither country would be likely to retain adequate instruments to implement national stabilization policies in response to foreign demand shocks or to pursue other, longer-run objectives (such as addressing Mexico's profound development needs). Even though a

NAMU could prevent future outbreaks of Dutch disease, it could also lock-in potentially overvalued exchange rates of the Canadian dollar and Mexican peso, while also creating a deeper problem of disarming national authorities from pursuing macroeconomic stabilization policies or long-term growth strategies. An example of this is the incapacity of European countries even before the euro crisis to address their problems of deindustrialization and mass unemployment through both macroeconomic and exchange rate policies. Despite Europe's problem of long-term unemployment, under the EMU's constraining framework no national government is able to pursue a rigorous pro-growth policy, and the Eurozone as a whole lacks the capacity to do this. Hence, greater monetary integration with the creation of currency blocs of either "peer groups" (as with the EMU) or "client states" (as with a NAMU) is not a viable solution to international currency problems, such as Dutch disease. What is needed is a more fundamental reform of the global payments system that would maintain intact the ability of national governments to pursue independent macroeconomic policies while still retaining their respective national currencies.[31] But such could only be achieved at a broader international level that the proliferation of regional currency blocs would preclude.

NOTES

* Earlier versions of this chapter were presented at the Congress of the Latin American Studies Association (LASA), Montreal, Quebec, Canada, September 2007, and "The Political Economy of Monetary Policy and Financial Regulation: A Conference in Honor of Jane D'Arista," Political Economy Research Institute (PERI), University of Massachusetts Amherst, Massachusetts, USA, May 2008. The authors would like to thank Ellen Meade, Juan Carlos Moreno-Brid, the LASA panelists, and the D'Arista conference participants for helpful comments on the earlier drafts. The usual caveats apply.

1. In theory, a group of countries should form a customs union—and a common market (with free mobility of labor as well as capital)—*before* forming a monetary union, as occurred in Europe (where the European Economic Community and its successor, the European Union, preceded the European Economic and Monetary Union). However, this has not stopped supporters of a monetary union in North America from proposing one before a customs union or common market could be formed in this continent.
2. In this chapter, "exchange rate" always refers to the value of the home country currency, unless otherwise stated.
3. Technically speaking, Canada and Mexico are considered to have "inflation-targeting" monetary policies, while the EMU has an apparently looser commitment to more vaguely defined "price stability," but we believe that in practice the ECB has effectively focused on the inflation rate as the main (de facto) target of its monetary policies. For a critical analysis of the inflation-targeting regime in Canada, see Seccareccia and Lavoie (2010).
4. Data are for 2010 from International Monetary Fund (IMF, 2011).
5. Smith (2002: 386–87, 394 n31) cites Bergsten (1999: 6) as making this argument. Smith (2002: 390) also cites Drummond et al. (2001) as arguing that "dollarization is the only

viable fixed exchange rate regime for Canada since a pegged rate is not sustainable and the US is not interested in a currency union." See, as well, Seccareccia (2006), and Kenen and Meade (2007: Ch 5) for a discussion of proposals to construct an augmented Fed including Canada and Mexico.

6. See Smith (2002) for a balanced but largely sympathetic discussion of proposals for greater monetary integration in North America from that time period. See Grubel (1999) for a specific proposal involving the creation of a new currency, the "amero," to be issued by a North American Central Bank. See also Kenen and Meade (2007: Ch. 5) for further discussion of Canadian support for North American monetary integration.
7. Estimates of the likely magnitude of Canadian savings in transactions costs from switching to a North American currency vary widely, but those savings are not likely to be large (and at most would be a one-time gain) that must be pitted against the cost of converting to a single currency. Grubel (1999: 9) provides some casual estimates in the range of 0.1 to 0.4 percent of GDP. See Seccareccia (2002, 2006) for a critical discussion of these estimates.
8. See Courchene (1999, 2007, and 2008) and Grubel (2008); see also Bayoumi and Eichengreen (1994), who argue to the contrary that North America is not an OCA. Indeed, as emphasized by McKinnon (2000), Mundell's (1961) original insight was to show that OCAs ought to be smaller rather than larger. Both Mundell (1961) and Bayoumi and Eichengreen (1994) argue that, based on OCA criteria, North America should be divided north/south instead of east/west in terms of optimal currency zones. Hence, OCA criteria traditionally do not favor a large North American currency area as some current supporters of greater monetary integration have argued.
9. See Beine et al. (2009). From their respective troughs in January and February 2002 through the last full month available at the time of this writing (June 2011), the Canadian dollar and the euro appreciated by very similar amounts (49 and 50 percent, respectively, measured by differences in natural logarithms). Data are from US Board of Governors of the Federal Reserve System, statistical release H.10, Foreign Exchange Rates, downloaded July 4, 2011, from http://www.federalreserve.gov/datadownload/default.htm.
10. See Statistics Canada, CANSIM II series V173905, V173931, and V173932 (data for 2008 are the average for January–May).
11. For example, Kenen and Meade (2007: Ch. 5) cite the Mexican Bankers Association as voicing support for a single currency in North America in 1999. Bowles and Moreno-Brid (2008: 130–31) cite the Centro de Estudios Económicos del Sector Privado and the Mexican Council of Businessmen (the latter of which is described as "the voice of the Mexican entrepreneurial elite") as supporting dollarization in 1998–99.
12. See Ibarra and Moreno-Brid (2001) and Bowles and Moreno-Brid (2008) for critical perspectives on Mexican proposals for monetary integration or dollarization circa 1989–2000; the latter also provide a retrospective on why the idea subsequently lost support in Mexico.
13. Mexico, like Canada, formally participated in the Bush administration's "Security and Prosperity Partnership" (SPP), since neither country could afford to say "no" to the US government. This initiative was then quietly dropped by President Barack Obama, who—while not keeping his campaign promise to renegotiate NAFTA—has shown no inclination to promote greater continental integration.
14. One could argue that Mexico is very different from Argentina and might be a more appropriate candidate for dollarization or fixing its currency to the US dollar, given the much greater commercial integration of Mexico with the US compared with Argentina. Nevertheless, the Argentine crisis effectively deflated the credibility of the fixed exchange rate cum currency board option for large Latin American nations.
15. According to Ramírez de la O (2004), the initial target date for this convergence was 2003—a date which he viewed as too ambitious, and which was not actually met. He argued presciently that this policy was likely to result in a real appreciation of the peso that would be detrimental to the country's long-run growth.

16. Calculated from data in IMF (2011).
17. For various perspectives on the slow growth of the Mexican economy in recent years, see Ibarra (2008), Blecker (2009), Moreno-Brid and Ros (2009), Hanson (2010), and Kehoe and Ruhl (2010), among others.
18. According to IMF (2011), the average growth rates for the "developing Asia" region were 7.8, 7.9, and 8.5 percent, respectively, during each of the periods indicated, and for the "newly industrialized East Asian countries" (four tigers) they were 5.9, 4.9, and 4.2 percent, respectively.
19. In the most recent year (2009) for which data were available on a purchasing power parity basis at the time of this writing, Mexico's real per capita GDP was 28 percent of the US level, the same as in 1994; this percentage had reached as high as 41 percent in 1982. Data from Heston et al. (2011).
20. See Hanson (2006) for evidence on the wage differentials and incentives that induce Mexicans to migrate to the US and estimates of the number of migrants.
21. Ros (2011) shows that Mexico and Canada suffered similar magnitudes of external shocks, yet Mexico's performance was significantly worse during the crisis. See also Esquivel (2010) on the procyclical nature of Mexico's monetary and fiscal policies and Blecker (2011) for further analysis of Mexico's crisis response.
22. Data are from World Bank, *World Development Indicators*, www.worldbank.org.
23. Galindo and Ros (2008) found evidence that the Banco de México followed an asymmetrical monetary policy that was biased toward peso appreciation, in the sense that the Banco generally tightened credit when the peso was falling but did not loosen credit when the peso was rising. But see the next note for possibly contrary evidence, which suggests that the Banco has attempted to limit the appreciation of the peso to some extent more recently.
24. Mexico's total foreign exchange reserves (excluding gold) nearly tripled from US$44.7 billion at year end 2001 to US$120.3 billion at year end 2010 (IMF 2011). One could question whether all of this reserve accumulation represented intentional currency market intervention, but the net impact must have been to hold the peso down somewhat in the face of pressures for it to rise even further than it actually did.
25. As already alluded to in note 8 above, Bayoumi and Eichengreen (1994) found that the effects of supply shocks vary not only between Canada, Mexico, and the US, but also across regions of each country, with resource-exporting regions in each country experiencing shocks that are more correlated on a north/south basis—that is to say, correlated with those of similar regions in the other countries than with other regions in their own country.
26. As of 2006, Canada and Mexico together accounted for 32 percent of US imports of crude oil (measured by quantity in barrels). See US Census Bureau (2007). This proportion did not change significantly over the next several years.
27. See also Murray et al. (2003), who emphasize the importance of the shock-absorbing role of the floating exchange rate in Canada, and who also note that Mexico's adherence to a fixed nominal exchange rate in the past contributed to its repeated economic crises.
28. Keynes (1925) attacked Winston Churchill's policy of returning Britain to the gold standard in 1925 and argued against the deflationary consequences of the British pound's return to its pre-war parity. One could also argue that Germany joined the EMU at an overvalued exchange rate for the Deutsche Mark in the 1990s, following German reunification, with adverse consequences for the German economy (we are indebted to Ellen Meade for suggesting this point).
29. For a discussion of the problems faced by policy makers when trying to implement a "one shoe fits all" monetary policy in a non-optimal currency area, see Palley (2003).
30. This positive correlation has existed between Canada and the US for several decades, but is a relatively recent phenomenon for Mexico and the US, and may be diminishing for Canada and the US. Although Canada's business cycles have been strongly synchronized with those of the US in the past, this has changed over the last two decades. For example, Canada suffered a more severe "Made in Canada" recession in 1990–91 with

only a milder counterpart in the US, while the latter went through a recession in 2001 when Canada experienced only slower growth but not an actual fall in output. To the extent that the US and Canada are now experiencing different shocks, of course, they represent less of a potential OCA than before. For Mexico, the correlation is strong and significant only since the formation of NAFTA and the end of the peso crisis (that is, since the late 1990s). See Chiquiar and Ramos-Francia (2004), Blecker (2009), Blecker and Esquivel (2010), Lederman (2005), and Mejía Reyes et al. (2006). Since both Canada and Mexico sell around 80 percent of their exports in the US market, however, any stabilization of the US economy is bound to help at least the export-oriented sectors of those two countries.

31. See D'Arista (1999, 2004) for suggestions along these lines.

REFERENCES

Auerback, M. (2010–11), "A 'United States of Europe' or full exit from the Euro", *International Journal of Political Economy*, **39** (4): 87–102.

Bayoumi, T. and B. Eichengreen (1994), "Monetary and exchange rate arrangements for NAFTA", *Journal of Development Economics*, **43** (1): 125–65.

Bayoumi, T. and M. Mühleisen (2006), "Energy, the exchange rate, and the economy: macroeconomic benefits of Canada's oil sands production", IMF Working Paper WP/06/70, March.

Beine, M., C.S. Bos, and S. Coulombe (2009), "Does the Canadian economy suffer from Dutch Disease?", Tinbergen Institute, Discussion Paper TI 2009–096/4, Amsterdam.

Bergevin, P. (2006), "Energy resources: boon or curse for the Canadian economy?", Canadian Library of Parliament Report PRB 05–86E, March 31.

Bergsten, C.F. (1999), *Dollarization in Emerging-Market Economies and Its Policy Implications for the United States*, Testimony to US Senate Subcommittee on International Trade and Finance, April 22.

Blecker, R.A. (2009), "External shocks, structural change, and economic growth in Mexico, 1979–2007", *World Development*, **37** (7): 1274–84.

Blecker, R.A. (2010), "Comercio, empleo y distribución: efectos de la integración regional y global", in N. Lustig (ed.), *Los Grandes Problemas de México*, vol. 9, *Crecimiento Económico y Equidad*, Mexico City: El Colegio de México.

Blecker, R.A. (2011), "Más allá de la crisis actual en México: Cómo fomentar más estabilidad a corto plazo y mayor crecimiento a largo plazo", in B.L. Avendaño Vargas, J.A. Vázquez Muñoz, and I. Perrotini Hernández (eds), *Estructura Económica y Estrategias de Crecimiento y el Desarrollo Económico para América Latina con Especial Énfasis para México*, Puebla, Mexico: Benemérita Universidad Autónoma de Puebla.

Blecker, R.A. and G. Esquivel (2010), "NAFTA, trade, and development", *CESifo Forum*, **2010** (4): 17–30.

Bougrine, H. and M. Seccareccia (2004), "Alternative exchange rate arrangements and effective demand: an important missing analysis in the debate over greater North American monetary integration", *Journal of Post Keynesian Economics*, **26** (4): 655–77.

Bowles, P. and J.C. Moreno-Brid (2008), "Mexico", in P. Bowles, *National Currencies and Globalization: Endangered Species?*, London: Routledge.

Chiquiar, D., and M. Ramos-Francia (2004), "Bilateral trade and business cycle synchronization: evidence from Mexico and US manufacturing industries", Banco de México Working Paper, October.

Courchene, T.J. (1999), "Towards a North American common currency: an optimal currency analysis", in T.J. Courchene (ed.), *Room to Manoeuvre? Globalization and Policy Convergence*, Kingston, Ontario: The John Deutsch Institute, Queen's University.

Courchene, T.J. (2007), "The Loonie and the FTA", *Policy Options*, October: 55–61.

Courchene, T.J. (2010), "Canada's floating exchange rate needs fixing", in H. Bougrine and M. Seccareccia (eds), *Introducing Macroeconomic Analysis: Issues, Questions and Competing Views*, Toronto: Emond Montgomery Publications Ltd.

D'Arista, J. (1999), "Reforming the privatized international monetary and financial architecture", in *Financial Markets and Society*, Philomont, Virginia: Financial Markets Center, November.

D'Arista, J. (2004), "The case for international monetary reform", *Journal of Post Keynesian Economics*, **26** (4): 557–72.

Drummond, D., M. Lévesque, and C. Alexander (2001), *The Penny Drops*, Toronto: TD Economics.

Emerson, M., D. Gros, A. Italianer, J. Pisani-Ferry, and H. Reichenbach (1992), *One Market, One Money: An Evaluation of the Potential Benefits and Costs of Forming an Economic and Monetary Union*, Oxford: Oxford University Press.

Esquivel, G. (2010), "De la inestabilidad macroeconómica al estancamiento estabilizador: el papel del diseño y conducción de la política económica", in N. Lustig (ed.), *Los Grandes Problemas de México*, vol. 9, *Crecimiento Económico y Equidad*, Mexico City: El Colegio de México.

Francis, D. (2011), "Canada's case of 'Dutch Disease'", *Financial Post*, April 16.

Galindo, L.M. and J. Ros (2008), "Alternatives to inflation targeting in Mexico", *International Review of Applied Economics*, **22** (1): 201–14.

Gallagher, K.P., J.C. Moreno-Brid, and R. Porzecanski (2008), "The dynamism of Mexican exports: lost in (Chinese) translation?", *World Development*, **36** (8): 1365–80.

Grubel, H.G. (1999), "The case for the amero: the economics and politics of a North American monetary union", *Critical Issues Bulletin*, Vancouver: Fraser Institute, September.

Grubel, H. (2008), "Fix the Loonie", *Financial Post*, January 18.

Hanson, G.H. (2006), "Illegal migration from Mexico to the United States", *Journal of Economic Literature*, **44** (4): 869–924.

Hanson, G.H. (2010), "Why isn't Mexico Rich?", *Journal of Economic Literature*, **48** (4): 987–1004.

Heston, A., R. Summers, and B. Aten (2011), *Penn World Table Version 7.0*, Center for International Comparisons of Production, Income and Prices at the University of Pennsylvania, May, http://pwt.econ.upenn.edu.

Ibarra, C. (2008), "Mexico's Slow-Growth Paradox", *CEPAL Review*, **95** (August): 83–102.

Ibarra, D. and J.C. Moreno-Brid (2001), "Currency boards and monetary unions: the road ahead or a cul de sac for Mexico's exchange rate policy?", in M. Puchet Anyul and L. Punzo (eds), *Mexico Beyond NAFTA: Perspectives for the European Debate*, London: Routledge.

International Monetary Fund (IMF) (2011), *World Economic Outlook Database*, April, http://www.imf.org/external/pubs/ft/weo/2011/01/weodata/index.aspx.

Issa, R., R. Lafrance, and J. Murray (2006), "The turning black tide: energy prices and the Canadian dollar", Working Paper 2006–29, Bank of Canada, August.
Kehoe, T. and K.J. Ruhl (2010), "Why Have Economic Reforms in Mexico not generated growth?", *Journal of Economic Literature*, **48** (4): 1005–27.
Kenen, P.B. and E.E. Meade (2007), *Regional Monetary Integration*, New York: Cambridge University Press.
Keynes, J.M. (1925), "The economic consequences of Mr. Churchill", in *Essays in Persuasion* (1931); reprinted in D. Moggridge (ed.), *The Collected Writings of John Maynard Keynes*, Vol. IX, London: Macmillan Press.
Lederman, D., W.F. Mahoney, and L. Servén (2005), *Lessons from NAFTA for Latin America and the Caribbean*, Washington, DC: World Bank, and Palo Alto, CA: Stanford University Press.
Lustig, N. (1998), *Mexico: The Remaking of an Economy*, 2nd edition, Washington, DC: Brookings Institution.
Macdonald, R. (2007), *Not Dutch Disease, It's China Syndrome*, Statistics Canada, Cat. No. 11–624-MIE – No. 017, August.
Maier, P., and B. DePratto (2008), "The Canadian dollar and commodity prices: Has the relationship changed over time?", Bank of Canada, Discussion Paper 2008–15, October.
McKinnon, R.I. (2000), "Mundell, the euro, and the world dollar standard", *Journal of Policy Modeling*, **22** (3): 311–24.
Mejía Reyes, P., E.E. Gutiérrez Alva and C.A. Farías Silva (2006), "La sincronización de los ciclos económicos de México y Estados Unidos", *Investigación Ecónomica*, **65**, October–December: 15–45.
Moreno-Brid, J.C., and J. Ros (2009), *Development and Growth in the Mexican Economy: A Historical Perspective*, Oxford: Oxford University Press.
Mundell, R.A. (1961), "The theory of optimal currency areas", *American Economic Review*, **51** (4): 657–65.
Murray, J., L. Schembri, and P. St-Amant (2003), "Revisiting the case for flexible exchange rates in North America", *North American Journal of Economics and Finance*, **14**: 207–40.
Palley, T. (2003), "Monetary policy in a non-optimal currency union: lessons for the European Central Bank", in L.-P. Rochon and M. Seccareccia (eds), *Dollarization: Lessons from Europe and the Americas*, London: Routledge.
Puyana, A. (2006), "Mexican oil policy and energy security within NAFTA", *International Journal of Political Economy*, **35** (2): 72–97.
Rajasekaran, V. (2008), *Implications of a High-Valued Canadian Dollar: Has the Canadian Economy Caught Dutch Disease?*, Toronto: Public Policy Forum (January).
Ramírez de la O, R. (2004), "Prospects for North American monetary cooperation in the next decade", in S. Weintraub (ed.), *NAFTA's Impact on North America: The First Decade*, Washington, DC: Center for Strategic and International Studies Press.
Ros, J. (2011), "The economic crisis of 2008–09 and development strategy: the Mexican case", in M. Haddad and B. Shepherd (eds), *Managing Openness: Trade and Outward-Oriented Growth after the Crisis*, Washington, DC: World Bank.
Seccareccia, M. (2002), *North American Monetary Integration: Should Canada Join the Dollarization Bandwagon?*, Ottawa: Canadian Centre for Policy Alternatives, November.
Seccareccia, M. (2005), "Growing household indebtedness and the plummeting

saving rate in Canada: an explanatory note", *Economic and Labour Relations Review*, **16** (1): 133–51.
Seccareccia, M. (2006), "Is the Canadian dollar destined to disappear? A critical perspective", in M. Vernengo (ed.), *Monetary Integration and Dollarization: No Panacea*, Cheltenham, UK and Northampton, MA, USA: Edward Elgar.
Seccareccia, M. and M. Lavoie (2010), "Inflation targeting in Canada: myth versus reality", in G. Fontana, J. McCombie, and M. Sawyer (eds), *Macroeconomics, Finance and Money: Essays in Honour of Philip Arestis*, London: Palgrave Macmillan.
Seccareccia, M. and M. Lequain (2006), "What can we learn from the EMU model? Lessons for Canada and Britain", *Current Politics and Economics of Europe*, **17** (2): 289–315.
Smith, C. (2002), "Dollarization and its alternatives: currency arrangements under NAFTA", in E.J. Chambers and P.H. Smith (eds), *NAFTA in the New Millennium*, La Jolla, CA: Center for US–Mexican Studies, University of California, San Diego, and Edmonton, Alberta: University of Alberta Press.
Tremblay, R. (2008), "La main invisible du marché . . . doit parfois être guidée", *Policy Options*, July/August: 14–16.
Urquidi, V.L. (2003), "Mexico's development challenges", in K. Middlebrook and E. Zepeda (eds), *Confronting Development: Assessing Mexico's Economic and Social Policy Challenges*, Stanford, CA: Stanford University Press.
US Census Bureau (2007), "U.S. International Trade in Goods and Services, December 2006", news release (February 13), FT900 Supplement, Exhibit 3.

11. Rethinking the economics of financial capital mobility and capital controls

Thomas Palley[1]

INTRODUCTION

The 1990s saw global implementation of the Washington Consensus, a key element of which was financial liberalization that included promotion of international financial capital mobility. This chapter re-examines the economics of international financial capital mobility and argues there are good economic reasons for restoring capital controls as a standard part of the policy arsenal.

The current moment constitutes an opportune time to re-engage this issue. The policy debate over capital controls has been closed for the past 25 years. Now, it is gradually being pried open for both political and economic reasons.[2]

At the political level there is increasing popular disenchantment with globalization. At the economic level, proponents of financial liberalization were humbled by the unexpectedness and severity of the East Asian financial crisis of 1997. That crisis has compelled even die-hard liberalizers to qualify talk of capital flow liberalization in terms of a) prior development of appropriate financial market institutions, and b) sequencing of reforms that start with domestic financial markets and only extend gradually to international opening.

Additionally, even the International Monetary Fund (IMF) (Kose et al., 2006) has been unable to find clear empirical support for the claim that capital mobility increases growth. Instead, where capital mobility is positively associated with growth, it is also associated with sound macroeconomic policies and benign macro conditions. Furthermore, countries that have grown fastest (China, the East Asian tigers, Chile, India) have all used controls. These findings have therefore created space for renewed debate about capital controls.

REFRAMING THINKING ABOUT CAPITAL CONTROLS

The contemporary view of capital controls is that if they are relevant, they are only relevant for developing countries. That view is prompted by the experience of the 1994 Mexican peso crisis and subsequent tequila effect that impacted Latin America; the 1997 East Asian financial crisis; the 1998 Russian ruble crisis; the 1999 Brazilian crisis; and the 2000 Brazilian and Argentine crises.

However, the issue of capital controls was previously viewed as extremely relevant for industrialized countries and was an important part of the European policy landscape in the 25 years after World War II. In 1982 capital mobility was at the center of the French franc crisis that prompted the Mitterrand government to abandon its Keynesian expansionary fiscal policies. Likewise, capital mobility was an issue in the sterling and Swedish krone crises of 1992. Most recently, capital mobility has been invoked to explain why long term U.S. interest rates did not increase during the period 2005–07 despite the Federal Reserve hiking short-term rates. The claim is that this was due to China recycling its trade surplus back to the U.S. as capital inflows, but that implies capital mobility remains a legitimate concern for developed countries.

Analytical discussion of capital mobility is often framed in terms of Krugman's (1999) construction of the "impossible trinity" that is shown in Figure 11.1. The argument is that there exists a fundamental inconsistency between the trinity of fixed exchange rates, sovereign monetary policy that sets domestic interest rates, and unfettered international capital mobility.

According to the impossible trinity a country can have any two of these three. If a country fixes its exchange rate and interest rate, it needs capital controls to block international arbitrage flows that would undermine the exchange and interest rate settings. If it fixes the exchange rate and has free capital flows, it loses control over the interest rate since monetary policy

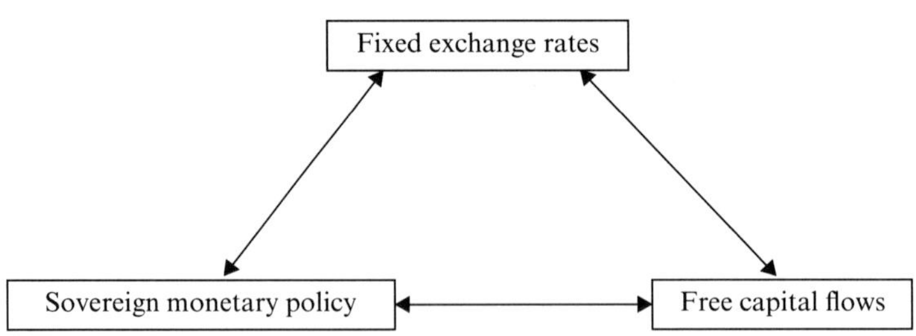

Figure 11.1 The impossible trinity

must be directed to maintaining the exchange rate. If it fixes the interest rate and has free capital flows, it loses control over the exchange rate, which is determined by capital flows.

Whereas the economic logic of the impossible trinity is correct, the framework engages in intellectual sleight of hand. The exchange rate and interest rate are critical "macro" prices, and a country is unlikely to prosper if it gets these prices wrong. That means there is every reason why policymakers should want to control these variables. However, there is no equivalent reason for wanting free capital flows. Yet, the impossible trinity presents all three as if they are of equal standing, and in doing so distorts perceptions and debate.

THE CASE FOR CAPITAL MOBILITY

The impossible trinity begs the question of why a country would want unrestricted capital mobility. There are two sets of arguments for capital mobility as shown in Figure 11.2. One set is rooted in neo-classical microeconomic theory and concerns the efficient allocation of resources. The second set is rooted in neoliberal political economy and concerns the need for constraints on government to promote good policy and freedom.

Neo-classical Economic Efficiency Arguments

The neo-classical microeconomic efficiency arguments concern both stocks and flows. On the stock side, the argument is that capital mobility improves portfolio investment outcomes. It does this by increasing the range of investment opportunities, thereby increasing returns available to savers and increasing possibilities for diversification. That increases the efficiency

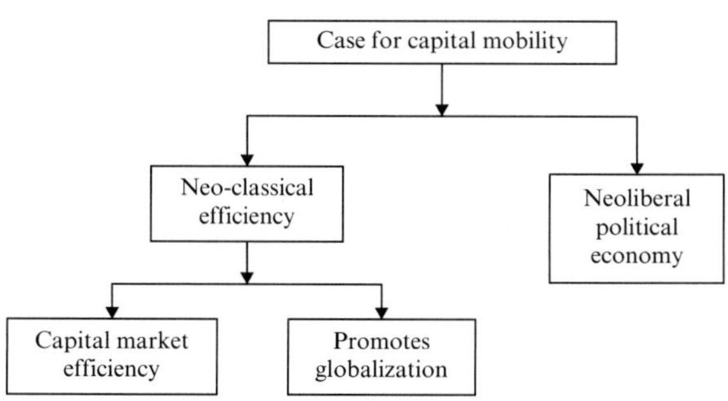

Figure 11.2 The case for capital mobility

of portfolios, which increases economic well-being – though this benefit goes largely to wealthy elites since wealth is highly concentrated.

The second and most important efficiency claim regarding capital mobility is that it increases national saving and investment, thereby enhancing capital accumulation and economic growth. This is a flow argument based on the loanable funds theory of interest rates, according to which the interest rate is determined by demand and supply in the loanable funds market.

Analytically, the effects of capital mobility can be described by the following simple model that adds trade and exchange rate considerations to the conventional classical model.[3] Prior to capital market opening outcomes in the loanable funds market are determined by the following six equations:

$$y = y^* \tag{11.1}$$

$$S = I \tag{11.2}$$

$$S = S(i, y, e) + [T - G] \quad S_i > 0, S_y > 0, S_e \gtrless 0 \tag{11.3}$$

$$I = I(i, y, e) \quad I_i < 0, Iy > 0, I_e < 0 \tag{11.4}$$

$$X(e, y^f) = M(i, y, e) \quad X_e < 0, Xyf > 0, M_e > 0, M_i < 0, My > 0 \tag{11.5}$$

$$e = p^f/p \tag{11.6}$$

Where y = output, y* = full employment (natural) output, S = real domestic saving, T = lump sum taxes, G = government spending, I = real domestic investment, X = exports, M = imports, i = interest rate, e = exchange rate (foreign currency per unit of domestic currency), p^f = foreign price level, and p = domestic price level.

Equation (11.1) determines the level of output, which is equal to the full employment or natural level of output. Equation (11.2) is the loanable funds market clearing condition. Equation (11.3) determines national saving, which consists of private and public sector saving. Equation (11.4) is the domestic investment function. Equation (11.5) is the trade balance condition, and (11.6) determines the exchange rate.[4]

The logic of the model is as follows. The level of output is equal to natural output, which is determined by the capital stock, labor supply, and the state of technology. The loanable funds market then determines the interest rate that equalizes saving and investment. Since there is no capital mobility, exports must equal imports. This is accomplished by price level adjustment that determines a real exchange rate consistent with trade balance.

After capital opening the loanable funds market is described by:

$$y = y^* \tag{11.7}$$

$$e = p^f/p \tag{11.8}$$

$$i = i^f \tag{11.9}$$

$$S = S(i^f, y, e) + [T - G] = S' \tag{11.10}$$

$$I = I(i^f, y, e) + X = I' \tag{11.11}$$

$$KM = I' - S' \tag{11.12}$$

where i^f = global interest rate, and KM = capital flow. If I' > S' there is a capital inflow, and if I' < S' there is a capital outflow. The logic is when I' > S' the economy is using more resources for investment and exports than it is saving, and this excess demand is provided via imports that are financed with capital inflows. The reverse holds for I' < S', in which case the country is running an export surplus and accumulating foreign capital.

The effect of capital mobility is to set the national interest rate equal to the global interest rate. Figure 11.3 shows the effect of capital opening on a developing economy. Such economies are viewed as being constrained by limited saving, but they have strong investment demand due to shortage of capital. The domestic interest rate (i^*) is above the global interest rate (i^f) because of strong investment demand owing to the country's relative scarcity of capital and saving. Capital mobility supposedly gives the economy access to the global saving pool with its lower interest rate. The result is capital inflows that increase investment, lower domestic saving,

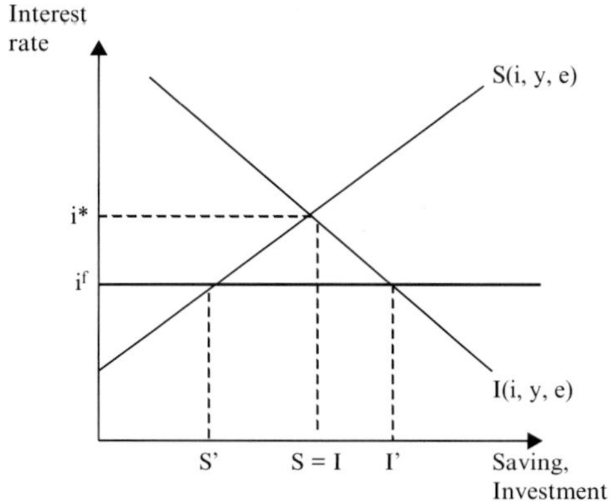

Figure 11.3 The effect of capital mobility on a developing country

and increase domestic consumption. This makes the country better off as capital opening accelerates capital accumulation while smoothing intertemporal consumption, enabling more consumption today that is repaid with the returns from increased investment.

Figure 11.4 shows the case of a developed economy that opens itself to capital mobility. This case is the symmetric opposite of a developing country. Now the global interest rate (i^f) is above the domestic interest rate (i^*) because the country is relatively capital abundant compared to the rest of the world. Consequently, there is a net capital outflow. Domestic investment falls but domestic saving rises. The logic is that the higher interest rate encourages more saving but discourages domestic investment. Instead, investment is directed offshore to developing countries where the marginal efficiency of investment is higher. The country is made better off because it can access higher returns by investing offshore. Interestingly, consumption falls due to increased saving, but consumption is higher in future periods due to increased income from higher returns on foreign investment.

The third and final neo-classical efficiency argument for capital mobility is an informal claim that it yields a host of collateral benefits. This seems to be an increasingly popular assertion in business media. The claim is that capital mobility fosters trade, foreign direct investment (FDI), technology transfer, global production chains, and financial development, and together this improves efficiency and growth. From a conventional neo-classical perspective these developments increase global productive efficiency through application of the principle of comparative advantage, thereby benefitting all countries.

However, this "collateral benefits" argument is challenged by lack of

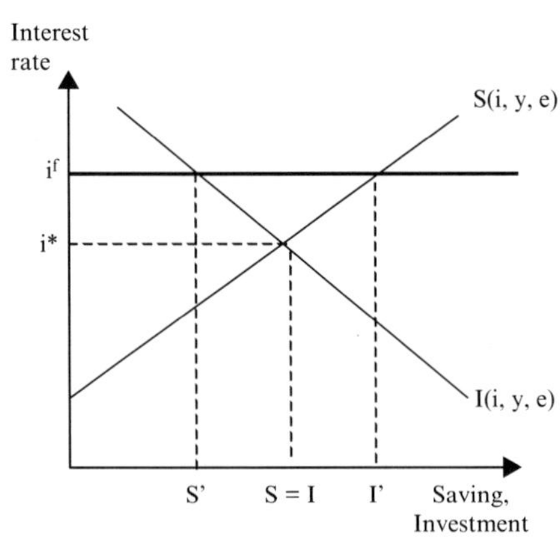

Figure 11.4 The effect of capital mobility on a developed country

empirical support regarding a robust positive association between financial liberalization and growth (Kose et al., 2006). Furthermore, the microeconomic basis of the collateral benefits argument is challenged by Gomory and Baumol (2000) and Palley (2008a), who argue that FDI and outsourcing can be good for companies but may be bad for national income and wages. Lastly, the argument ignores the fact that trade, financial development, FDI, and technology transfer also take place with capital controls, as evidenced by China.

The Neoliberal Political Economy Case for Capital Mobility

The neo-classical economic efficiency argument for capital mobility is complemented by neoliberal political economy arguments. One argument that has its origins in Tiebout's (1956) theory of local public goods is that capital mobility creates a competitive market discipline that improves the quality of governance and policy. The claim is capital will tend to exit countries with bad governance and flow toward countries with good governance. That in turn creates a "race to the top" between country governments as they compete to attract productive capital, resulting in better governance and more efficient markets that are free of government distortions.[5]

A second Hayekian-styled (Hayek, 1944) argument for capital mobility is that the freedom to move capital and property is an intrinsic element of personal freedom. Freedom of movement is an essential element of choice, and choice is the essence of freedom. That makes capital mobility both a means and an end. Capital mobility helps protect personal freedom by disciplining governments, and it is also an essential part of personal freedom. However, there is widespread recognition of the legitimacy of restrictions on people moving between national jurisdictions, so it is unclear why capital should be treated differently.

A third argument is that controls generate costly rent seeking (Krueger, 1974). Thus, even if there is a market failure that appears to warrant capital controls, such a policy solution may generate worse outcomes than doing nothing. This is because a) agents will expend valuable resources engaging in rent seeking activity that aims to circumvent controls by influencing government, and b) such rent-seeking activity may corrupt government and contribute to bad policy and governance.

A fourth pragmatic argument against capital controls is that they have limited effectiveness in the presence of sophisticated financial markets. Carvalho and Garcia (2006) report on the Brazilian experience with capital controls in the 1990s and report that they were only temporarily effective in deterring inflows, for a brief period of two to six months. They then hypothesize that this is because financial institutions performed sophisticated operations to avoid controls.

Balanced against this, several empirical studies find capital controls have statistically significant effects that go in the theoretically predicted direction. Gregorio et al. (2000) find that unremunerated reserve requirements on inflows tilt the composition of inflows toward longer maturity as predicted by theory (Palley, 2005). Edwards (2005) reports that countries with capital controls have smaller growth declines once a financial crisis begins. Lastly, Edwards and Rigobon (2005) report tightening of capital controls on inflows depreciates the exchange rate and capital controls also reduce the vulnerability of the nominal exchange rate to external shocks.

These findings of statistically significant effects from capital controls mean controls work even if there is avoidance and evasion. Moreover, the effect of controls would be strengthened by greater political commitment to capital controls, tougher enforcement of controls with larger penalties, and greater international cooperation regarding enforcement that would follow universal acceptance of capital controls as a legitimate policy tool.

THE CASE AGAINST CAPITAL MOBILITY

Balanced against the above neo-classical and neoliberal arguments *for* capital mobility are three different types of argument *against* capital mobility. These counter arguments are illustrated in Figure 11.5 and can be labeled: 1) the Keynesian macroeconomic efficiency argument; 2) the neo-Walrasian market failure argument; and 3) the neo-Marxian social structure of accumulation argument.

Figure 11.5 is important as it highlights the different theoretical perspectives in play. Today's intellectual climate is dominated by neo-classical economics. This climate allows neo-Walrasian market failure arguments to get a hearing but Keynesian and Marxian social structure of accumulation arguments are excluded. This exclusion prevents full presentation of the case against capital mobility and it highlights the policy significance of

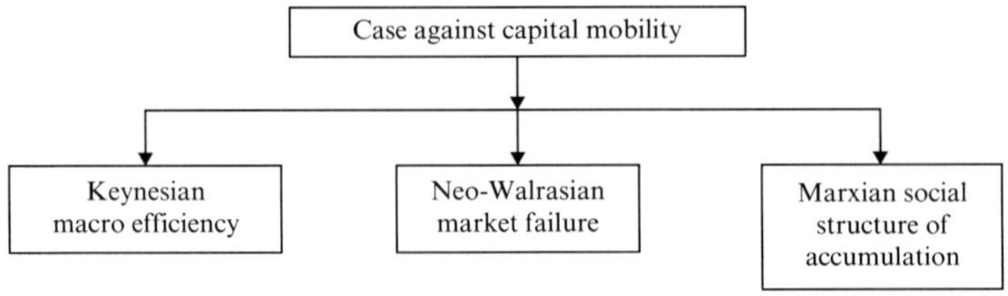

Figure 11.5 The case against capital mobility

macroeconomic theory. Put bluntly, theory matters for policy justification, and if theories are politically excluded, then that will distort the policy debate and policy choice. That is why intellectual openness and economic theory should be of concern to pragmatic politicians.

The Keynesian Macroeconomic Case against Capital Mobility

The Keynesian challenge to capital mobility rests on a fundamentally different theoretical construction of the determination of exchange rates, interest rates, saving, and investment. First, whereas the neo-classical model has the exchange rate determined by purchasing power parity (PPP), the Keynesian model treats the exchange rate as a financial price that is determined in the foreign exchange (FX) market. Second, interest rates are not determined in a fictional loanable funds market, but are instead determined in financial markets that can be significantly affected by the policies and actions of central banks. Third, saving and investment are determined in the goods market by the consumption and investment spending decisions of households and firms, and are equalized by output adjustment rather than interest rate adjustment.

Figure 11.6 shows the determination of saving, investment, and net exports in the Keynesian model. Output adjusts in response to excess (or deficient) aggregate demand (AD), and this adjustment process continues until output and AD are equalized. At that point leakages out of the flow of circular income (saving) equal injections into the circular flow (investment, government budget deficit, and net exports).

This Keynesian process of equilibrium output determination is described by the following equations:

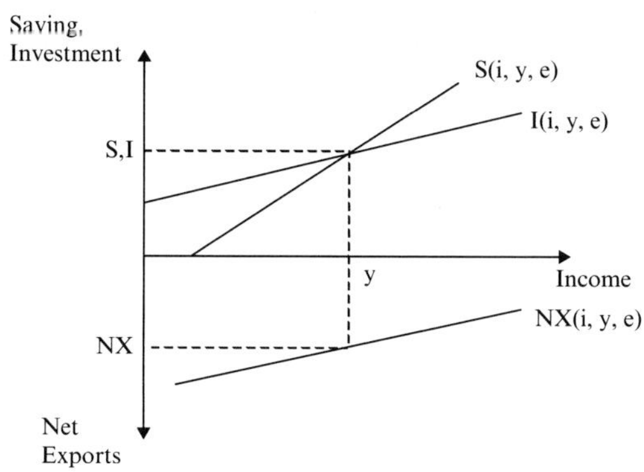

Figure 11.6 Determination of saving, investment, and net exports in the Keynesian model

$$y = AD \tag{11.13}$$
$$y = C(i, y, e) + S(i, y, e) + T$$

$$C_i < 0, Cy > 0, C_e \gtrless 0, Si > 0, S_y > 0, S_e \gtrless 0 \tag{11.14}$$

$$AD = C(i, y, e) + I(i, y, e) + G + NX(i, y, e) \tag{11.15}$$

$$I_i < 0, Iy > 0, I_e < 0, NXi \gtrless 0, NX_y < 0, NX_e < 0 \tag{11.16}$$

Where y = income (output), AD = aggregate demand, C = consumption, S = saving, T = lump-sum tax payments, I = investment spending, G = government spending, and NX = net exports (exports minus imports). Combining equations (10) – (12) and re-arranging, then yields

$$S(i, y, e) = I(i, y, e) + [G - T] + NX(i, y, e) \tag{11.17}$$

Goods market equilibrium requires that demand leakages (S) equal demand injections (I + [G – T] + NX). Given the equilibrium level of income determined in goods markets, there is an associated level of net exports.

The exchange rate, which affects leakages and injections into the circular flow of income, is determined in the foreign exchange market by the interplay of demand and supply for different currencies. The demand for home country currency is principally determined by foreigners who need currency to pay for their purchases of the home country's exports and by foreigner desires to purchase assets in the home country. The supply of home country currency is principally determined by home country residents who sell their currency to buy foreign currency to pay for imports and to purchase foreign country assets.

Figure 11.7 shows the determination of the exchange rates in the Keynesian model with floating exchange rates. Figure 11.8 shows the determination of exchange rates in the Keynesian model with fixed rates. In the latter case any discrepancy between demand and supply at the fixed exchange rate is covered by central bank intervention, and that intervention shows up as the official settlement balance (OSB).

The Keynesian case against capital mobility rests on the argument that it can cause macroeconomic problems, including unemployment and inflation. In a regime of fixed exchange rates capital inflows compel official intervention to prevent appreciation, which can give rise to undesirable monetary expansion that can cause generalized and asset price inflation. Conversely, capital outflows compel intervention to protect the exchange rate, and that runs the risk of running out of reserves and tempting speculative attacks on the exchange rate.

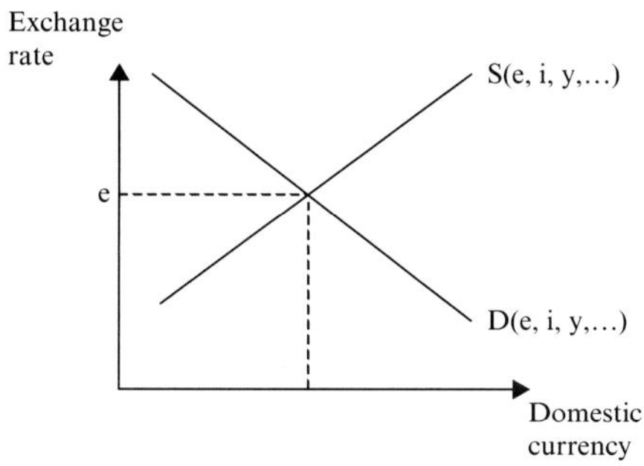

Figure 11.7 Determination of exchange rates in the Keynesian model with floating rates

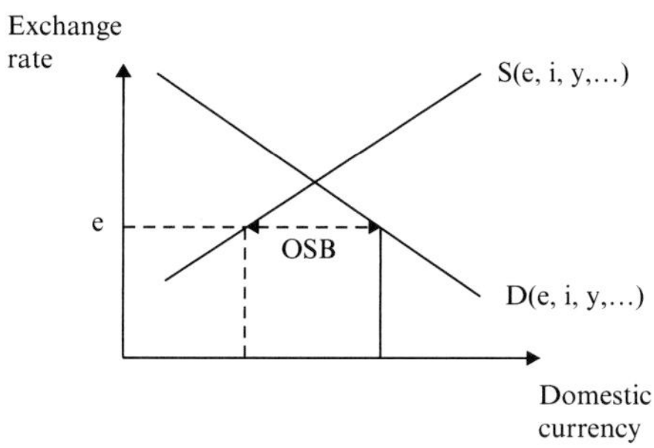

Figure 11.8 Determination of exchange rates in the Keynesian model with fixed rates

For Keynes (1942), a deeper problem was that a country might need low interest rates for full employment, yet capital outflows might compel the monetary authority to push the domestic interest rate above that consistent with full employment to protect the exchange rate. This "Keynes Problem" is illustrated in Figure 11.9. The right hand panel shows the interest rate (i^y) needed to secure full employment output (y^T) in the goods market, while the left hand panel shows the interest rate (i^e) needed to maintain the fixed exchange rate (e^T) given full employment output and foreign interest rates (i^f).

Conventional classical macroeconomics dismisses this Keynes problem on the grounds that price deflation will ensure full employment. However, it is now clear that price deflation can be destabilizing and can actually aggravate the problem of inadequate AD and unemployment (Tobin 1975, 1980; Palley, 2008b, 2008c).

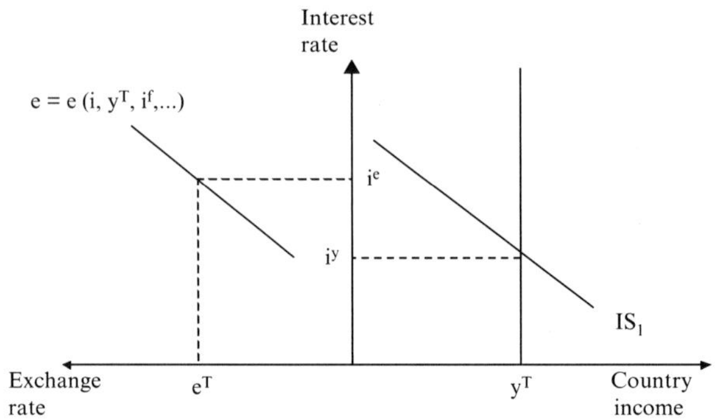

Figure 11.9 The Keynes problem

With flexible exchange rates, capital openness can lead to large inflows that appreciate the exchange rate, causing a contraction of investment spending and net exports. That in turn reduces output and employment, as shown in Figure 11.10.[6] This problem is amplified in a globalized world in which capital flows are larger and in which economies more sensitive to exchange rates owing to an increase in the share of exports and imports in GDP.

Moreover, there can be additional problems when one country opens its capital markets while others do not. In this event, the country with capital controls can pursue strategic "beggar my neighbor" policies that frustrate market exchange rate adjustment mechanisms, making it better off at the expense of the open country. A recent example of this is China, which fixed its exchange rate *vis-à-vis* the U.S. dollar at an undervalued rate, and capital controls enabled it to maintain that rate despite an enormous trade surplus.

A last problem with open capital markets concerns the impact of capital inflows on internal balance. For example, during the recent (2001–07) U.S. economic expansion capital inflows hampered long-term interest rates from rising and frustrated the Federal Reserve's attempt to raise the general level of interest rates. This contributed to an unbalanced expansion marked by a boom in the non-traded (NT) goods sector (housing) and a slump in the traded (T) goods sector (manufacturing).

This internal balance problem is illustrated in Figure 11.11. The top right-hand panel shows non-traded sector employment as a negative function of the interest rate. The bottom left-hand panel shows traded sector employment as a positive function of the exchange rate defined as domestic currency per unit of foreign currency. The top left-hand panel then relates the exchange rate to the domestic interest rate. The problem results when a surge in capital inflows ($X_0 < X_1$) shifts the exchange rate function

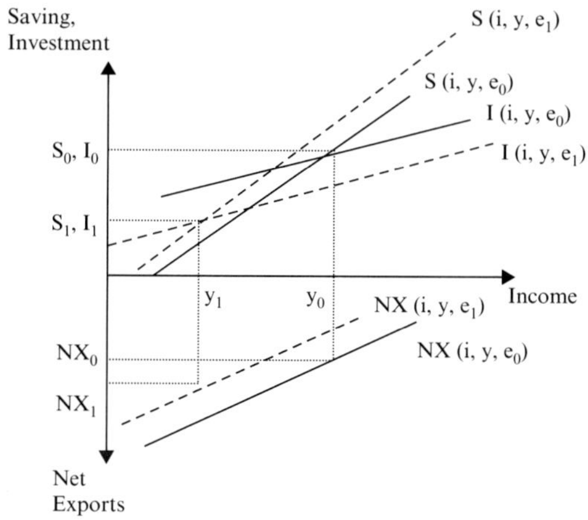

Figure 11.10 Effect of capital inflows in the Keynesian model with exchange rate ($e_0<e_1$)

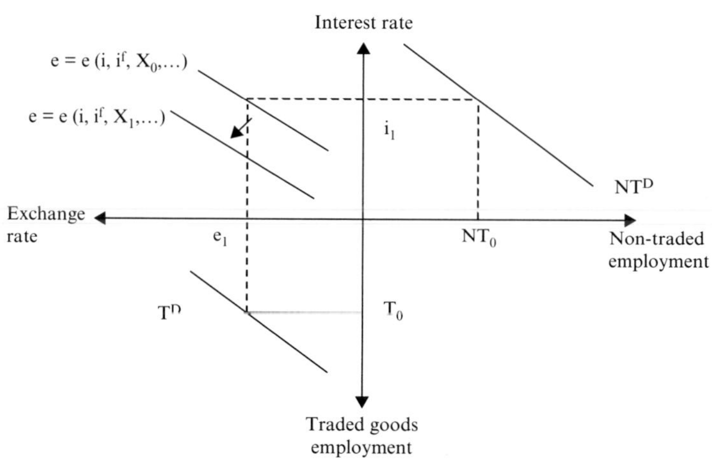

Figure 11.11 The Greenspan problem ($X_0 < X_1$)

left, causing an appreciation of the exchange rate and a decline in the interest rate. This spurs a boom in the NT sector and a slump in the T sector.

Moreover, this shift can be cumulative so that an appreciating exchange rate and rising asset prices caused by falling interest rates causes further capital inflows that further shift the exchange rate function.[7] Policymakers aiming for balance in the NT and T goods sector would like to target the interest rate on the NT sector and the exchange rate on the T goods sector. Capital mobility frustrates this.

To summarize, whereas the classical macroeconomic model predicts unambiguously good outcomes from capital mobility, the Keynesian model is less sanguine. In the classical model capital mobility impacts economic outcomes via the loanable funds market, improving the global allocation of saving. In effect, the classical model is a corn model in which corn stocks (saving) get reallocated (invested) to countries where corn grows faster, thereby producing more corn for all. Moreover, there can be no employment impacts as the economy is assumed to be at full employment.

The Keynesian model views the loanable funds market as a fiction. Instead, capital flows affect the foreign exchange market, giving rise to exchange rate effects that can have significant adverse consequences on employment and output.

That raises the question of when capital mobility is a good thing in the Keynesian model. The short answer is when a country suffers from a shortage of foreign money (that is, there is a foreign exchange supply gap). For instance, a developing country may want to import capital goods but is running a trade deficit and will not benefit from exchange rate depreciation owing to adverse terms of trade effects and higher imported inflation. In this case the country may be better off by borrowing abroad.

The important feature is the underlying problem capital mobility addresses is not a shortage of domestic saving as claimed by loanable funds theory, but rather a shortage of foreign exchange to purchase foreign-produced goods. The Washington Consensus talks of international capital mobility as analogous to domestic capital mobility, thereby framing international financial opening as analogous to domestic financial deregulation. From a Keynesian perspective that analogy is wrong and international financial capital mobility is about filling foreign exchange gaps rather than improving financial intermediation and the allocation of capital.

The Neo-Walrasian Case against Capital Mobility

A Keynesian perspective emphasizes macroeconomic problems arising from capital mobility. A neo-Walrasian perspective emphasizes microeconomic market failure problems that result in allocative inefficiencies, the solution to which are capital controls.

One source of micro inefficiency is noise traders (De Long et al., 1990) who generate excessive exchange rate volatility and exchange rate mispricing. That volatility and mispricing distorts trade and foreign investment decisions, giving rise to microeconomic inefficiencies.[8]

Capital mobility can also amplify endemic proclivities to runs and financial panics by encouraging speculative short-term "hot money" flows. When these flows reverse, financial disruption that causes real economic damage can be triggered. This type of problem is likely to be particularly acute in developing economies. First, they tend to experience inflows that are large relative to the system. Second, they tend to have weaker regulatory and institutional frameworks that make them more vulnerable to financial market disruptions. Third, exchange rate depreciations resulting from sudden reversals are especially destabilizing in developing countries as they tend to be international debtors with foreign currency denominated debt, making them prone to exchange rate induced debt crises.

The problem of exchange rate instability is illustrated in Figure 11.12, which shows how the foreign exchange market can have multiple equilibria. Capital flows can cause significant local volatility around each equilibrium and can also cause large jumps between equilibria.

The problem of hot money flows is discussed in Palley (2005), who presents a model in which there are two types of investors – short-term speculators and long-term patient investors. In such a situation Chilean-style temporary reserve requirements on capital inflows can act as a screening mechanism that discourages inflows from short-term speculators. That is because the cost of temporary reserve requirements is small for patient investors who plan to stay a long while, but it is very high for speculators who plan on a quick round trip in and out of a currency.

A similar logic holds for the Tobin tax (Palley, 1999) where a small exchange transactions tax is of little consequence to importers and exporters but it is highly significant to noise traders speculating on minute fractional movements of exchange rates. Consequently, a Tobin tax also has the properties of a screening mechanism.

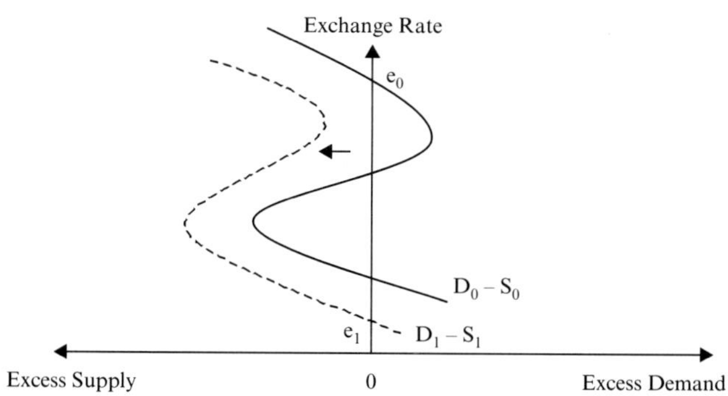

Figure 11.12 The problem of exchange rate instability

The neo-Walrasian critique rests on imperfections in capital markets – be they due to the existence of speculators who create noise and impose negative externalities on others or due to imperfect or asymmetric information among market participants. This market imperfections approach is consistent with both Classical and Keynesian macroeconomics, and neo-Walrasian considerations can be included in either type of model.

However, the impact is larger when neo-Walrasian concerns are introduced into classical macro models. This is because they move the classical model's equilibrium away from the first best, enabling the classical model to generate the type of sub-optimal outcomes Keynesians are concerned with. Contrastingly, adding neo-Walrasian concerns to the Keynesian model merely adds another reason (albeit with a different economic logic) why the economy will be away from the first best position and why policy intervention is needed.

The Neo-Marxian Social Structure of Accumulation Case against Capital Mobility

Capital mobility gives financial capital the right of international exit. The neo-Marxian social structures of accumulation (SSA) approach emphasizes how that right confers on capital the power to discipline governments, affect policy, and transform the structure of economy (Crotty and Epstein, 1996). This power affects both developed and developing economies.

The classic example of this power in action is the French franc crisis of 1982–83. The crisis compelled the Socialist Party government of President Mitterand in France to do a policy U-turn and abandon its Keynesian policies aimed at reflating the French economy. In hindsight, that U-turn signaled a permanent movement away from explicitly Keynesian policies in Europe. Thereafter, European policymakers shifted their attention to creating a common European currency, a project that has imposed a permanent deflationary policy bias because of its emphasis on fiscal austerity and very low inflation in order to build so-called "monetary credibility" for the new European currency.

The debate about the constraining effect of capital mobility on "policy space" (Grabel, 2000; Palley, 2001b; Bradford, 2005) partially captures some of the issues raised by the SSA critique. Thus, different international arrangements and rules affect the space available for countries to pursue economic policies of their choosing. This is because institutional arrangements and rules affect the costs and benefits of alternative policies.

The pressures that capital mobility places on policy space and choice can again be understood through the Tiebout (1956) local public goods model. Whereas neoliberals view capital mobility as promoting a dynamic competition between governments that produces a race to the top in governance and policy, SSA theory sees it as creating a race to the bottom. According to SSA logic, firms use the threat of exit to erode standards that are socially desirable. Moreover, that can result in a prisoner's dilemma situation in which unrestricted competition between firms produces an "uncooperative" equilibrium that leaves firms worse off. This is exemplified by competition over labor standards (Palley, 2004). From this perspective, capital controls can be viewed as a device for preventing undesirable competition and ensuring the superior "cooperative" equilibrium.

However, the SSA critique runs deeper than the policy space debate. Thus, the power given to capital by capital mobility not only affects surface policies, it may also dull the aspiration to and feasibility of social democracy. This impact seems to be particularly evident in Brazil, where it can be argued that globalization has tamed the left (Palley, 2006). Thus, in Brazil under President Lula, poverty alleviation programs appear to have replaced an earlier vision of social democracy that would tackle deep, lasting social and economic inequalities.

ABANDONING THE IMPOSSIBLE TRINITY

The impossible trinity focuses on the inconsistency between sovereign monetary policy, fixed exchange rates, and free capital flows. That framing has promoted today's policy configuration, which consists of sovereign monetary policy, free capital flows, and floating exchange rates.

The problem with the impossible trinity is that it misrepresents the policy choice, making it look as if the current configuration is an optimal policy combination when it is not. In this regard, there are two types of misrepresentation. The first is to make it look as if sovereign monetary policy, control over the exchange rate, and free capital flows are of equal policy importance, when they are not. The second is that the impossible trinity presents an incomplete policy menu that leaves much off the table. This omission includes: a) coordinated monetary policy across countries; b) managed exchange rates between countries; and c) managed capital flows.

The impossible trinity emerged out of the work of Milton Friedman (1953) and Robert Mundell (1961a, b). That work is infused with the laissez-faire predispositions of those authors, and as such the impossible trinity frame traps policy debate by obscuring other possibilities. That suggests it is time to time to abandon the impossible trinity frame.

Figure 11.13 shows the evolution of international financial policy over the decades, shifting from a gold standard regime of fixed exchange rates

		Exchange Rates	
		Fixed	Flexible
Capital Controls	Yes	1950–60s	1970s
	No	Gold standard 1920–30s	1980–2000s

Figure 11.13 The evolution of policy regimes

with capital mobility to the current regime of flexible exchange rates with capital mobility. The decade of the 1970s was pivotal. The pressures of that decade were used to ram through a program of deregulation and laissez-faire in all spheres of policy, including international economic policy. As a result, policymakers too easily surrendered the benefits of capital controls.

At this stage there is need to create a new policy agenda of managed exchange rates and managed capital flows. That agenda can be thought of as aiming to capture the advantages of both fixed and flexible exchange rates and both free and controlled capital flows. The impossible trinity should be replaced by a possible trinity of coordinated monetary policy, managed exchange rates, and managed capital flows.

This possible trinity is shown in Figure 11.14, and its elements are mutually supportive rather than antagonistic. Of course, the possible trinity raises difficult issues of international political economy regarding what a regime of co-operative monetary policy and managed exchange rates looks like and how it is achieved.

Countries can significantly go it alone on capital controls, though the effectiveness of controls depends on the degree of international cooperation regarding enforcement. However, co-operative monetary policy and managed exchange rates are intrinsically joint efforts. Co-operative monetary policy requires countries collaborate on issues of interest rate setting and inflation management. Likewise, managed exchange rates require countries to agree on rules for managing the exchange rate. Those rules involve criteria for establishing the target exchange rate, as well as rules governing the process of exchange rate intervention. Palley (2003, pp. 77–9) discusses these rules of exchange rate management, placing particular emphasis on the need for the country whose currency is appreciating to conduct exchange rate interventions. That assignment prevents the possibility of the intervening central bank running out of foreign currency reserves and being beaten by a concerted attack by speculators.[9]

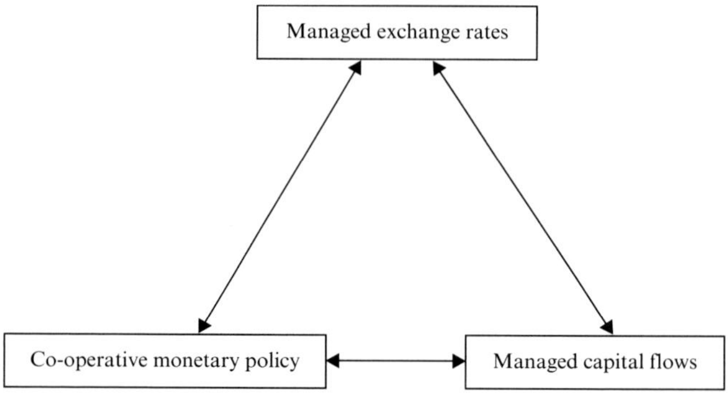

Figure 11.14 The possible trinity

CONCLUSION: THE POLITICS AND SOCIOLOGY OF POLICY ADVICE

Capital mobility has become today's economic orthodoxy, yet the pure economic case for capital mobility is amazingly flimsy. Instead, there are strong grounds for believing capital controls can contribute significantly to economic stability and create important space for autonomous national economic policy. That capital mobility dominates the policy agenda so completely is indicative of the ideological dimension of the debate.

Whether controls are well or poorly used depends on the quality of governance. Neoliberals tend to automatically assume they will be used badly and make that assumption a centerpiece of opposition against capital controls. However, a combination of democratic transparent accountable government, a professionalized civil service, and strong civil society can ensure that capital controls are used well. The neoliberal concern with regulatory capture is real, but the answer should be promotion of effective governance rather than abandonment of this important policy tool.

Finally, sociology matters. Official policy discussion regarding capital controls and exchange rate regimes has been led by institutions such as the IMF, the World Bank, the Organization for Economic Cooperation and Development (OECD), and the Bank for International Settlements (BIS). These organizations are peopled by high-paid international bureaucrats drawn from around the world, who own global investment portfolios, and have homes and family in more than one country. A strictly neo-classical standpoint suggests these bureaucrats have a strong private interest in capital mobility, which likely taints the advice these institutions provide. That potential sociological contamination provides additional grounds for fresh public debate over capital controls.

NOTES

1. Published in *Brazilian Journal of Political Economy*, 29 (July–September 2009), 15–34.
2. Brazil is a country where there is support among many academic economists for capital controls and controls are viewed as a legitimate policy tool by sections of the political and policymaking community. This is illustrated by several recent articles on the issue of capital controls – see Carvalho and Siesu (2004), Oreiro et al. (2004), Oreiro (2004) and Ferrari Filho et al. (2005). The challenge is to extend this intellectual openness to other countries, the International Monetary Fund (IMF), the Bank for International Settlement (BIS), the World Bank, and the multilateral regional development banks.
3. The full closed economy classical macro model without trade and exchange rates is described in Sargent (1979, Chapter 1).
4. Throughout the chapter the exchange rate e is denoted as foreign currency per unit of home currency. That means a higher value of e corresponds to exchange rate appreciation, and a lower value corresponds to depreciation.
5. This type of argument can be thought of as a dynamic version of Tiebout's (1956) theory of local public expenditure whereby agents self-select and choose to live in jurisdictions supplying their desired level of public goods. Capital mobility creates competition among jurisdictions to attract productive citizens, leading to improvements in governance that increase economic efficiency and make all better off. Race to the bottom logic works in the opposite direction with jurisdictions cutting standards to gain a competitive cost advantage.
6. Figure 11.10 shows aggregate saving as increasing in response to an exchange rate appreciation ($Se > 0$). However, in principle aggregate saving could fall as the sign of Se is theoretically ambiguous.
7. This pattern has similarities with the East Asian financial crisis of 1997. In East Asia, capital inflows drove pro-cyclical destabilizing movements in financial markets. Thus, inflows drove interest rates down and increased asset prices, giving rise to strong financial accelerator effects that amplified the boom in the NT sector. Meanwhile, appreciating exchange rates undermined the T goods sector, contributing to a deteriorating trade outlook.
8. The issue of microeconomic inefficiency in the foreign exchange market due to speculation is examined in Palley (2001a) as part of a discussion of the Tobin tax.
9. Cooperative monetary policy is essential to cooperative managed exchange rate policy. Countries will not agree to defend the exchange rate of another country if they believe the weaker country is engaged in monetary mismanagement.

REFERENCES

Bradford, C.I., Jr., 2005. "Prioritizing Economic Growth: Enhancing Macroeconomic Policy Choice," G-24 Discussion Paper No. 37, April.

Carvalho, B.S. and M. Garcia, 2006. "Ineffective Controls on Capital Flows under Sophisticated Financial Markets: Brazil in the Nineties," NBER Working Paper No. 12283, June.

Carvalho, F.C and J. Sicsu, 2004. "Controvérsias recentes sobre controles de capitais," *Brazilian Journal of Political Economy*, **24** (2) (April–June).

Crotty, J. and G. Epstein, 2004. "In Defence of Capital Controls", in L. Panitch, C. Leys, A. Zuege and M Konigs (eds), *The Globalization Decade: A Critical Reader*, London: The Merlin Press, pp. 80–110.

De Long, J.B., A. Shleifer, L.H. Summers and R.J. Waldman, 1990. "Noise Trader Risk in Financial Markets," *Journal of Political Economy*, **98**, 703–38.

Edwards, S., 2005. "Capital Controls, Sudden Stops and Current Account Reserves," NBER Working Paper No. 11170, March.
Edwards, S. and R. Rigobon, 2005. "Capital Controls, Exchange Rate Volatility and External Vulnerability," NBER Working Paper No. 11434, June.
Ferrari Filho, F., F. Jayme Jr, G.T. Lima, J.L. Oreiro, and L.F. Paula, 2005. "Uma avaliação crítica da proposta de conversibilidade plena do Real," *Brazilian Journal of Political Economy*, **25** (1) (January–March).
Friedman, M., 1953. "The Case for Flexible Exchange Rates," in *Essays in Positive Economics*, Chicago: Chicago University Press.
Gomory, R.E. and W.J. Baumol, 2000. *Global Trade and Conflicting National Interest*, Cambridge, MA: MIT Press.
Grabel, I., 2000. "The Political Economy of 'Policy Credibility': the New-Classical Macroeconomics and the remaking of Emerging Economies," *Cambridge Journal of Economics*, **24**, 1–19.
Gregorio, J., S. Edwards and R. Valdes, 2000. "Controls on Capital Flows: Do They Work?" NBER Working Paper No. 7645, April.
Hayek, F., 1944. *The Road to Serfdom*, Chicago: University of Chicago Press.
Keynes, J.M., 1942. Letter to R.F. Harrod, 19 April.
Kose, M.A., E. Prasad, K. Rogoff and S. Wei, 2006. "Financial Globalization: A Reappraisal," IMF Working Paper WP/06/189, August.
Krueger, A.O., 1974. "The Political Economy of Rent-Seeking Society," *American Economic Review*, **64** (June), 291–303.
Krugman, P., 1999. "O Canada: A Neglected Nation Gets its Nobel," *Slate Magazine*, October 19.
Mundell, R.A., 1961a. "Capital Mobility and Stabilization Policy under Fixed and Flexible Exchange Rates," *Canadian Journal of Economics and Political Science*, **29** (November), 475–85.
Mundell, R.A., 1961b. "Flexible Exchange Rates and Employment Policy," *Canadian Journal of Economics and Political Science*, **27** (November), 509–17.
Oreiro, J.L., 2004. "Autonomia de política econômica, fragilidade externa e equilíbrio do balanço de pagamentos: a teoria econômica dos controles de capitais," *Economia & Sociedade*, **13** (2) (July–December).
Oreiro, J.L, L.F. Paula and G.J. Silva, G.J., 2004. "Por uma moeda parcialmente conversível: uma crítica a Arida e Bacha," *Brazilian Journal of Political Economy*, **24** (2) (April–June).
Palley, T.I., 1999. "Speculation and Tobin Taxes: Why Sand in the Wheels can Increase Economic Efficiency," *Journal of Economics*, **69**, 113–26.
Palley, T.I., 2001a. "Destabilizing Speculation and the Case for an International Currency Transactions Tax," *Challenge* (May/June), 70–89.
Palley, T.I., 2001b. "Escaping the "Policy Credibility" Trap: Reshaping the Debate Over the International Financial Architecture," *Problemas del Desarrollo*, **32** (July/September), 111–24.
Palley, T.I., 2003. "The Economics of Exchange Rates and the Dollarization Debate: The Case Against Extremes," *International Journal of Political Economy*, **33** (Spring), 61–82.
Palley, T.I., 2004. "The Economic Case for International Labor Standards," *Cambridge Journal of Economics*, **28** (January), 21–36.
Palley, T.I., 2005. "Chilean Unremunerated Reserve Requirement Capital Controls as a Screening Mechanism," *Investigacion Economica*, **LXIV** (January/March), 33–52.

Palley, T.I., 2006. "Globalization Tames the Left in Brazil," *YaleGlobal*, September 5.
Palley, T.I., 2008a. "The Economics of Outsourcing: How Should Policy Respond?", *Review of Social Economy*, **66** (3), 279–95.
Palley, T.I., 2008b. "The Macroeconomics of Aggregate Demand and the Price Level," *Investigacion Economica*, **LXVII** (263) (January–March), 49–66.
Palley, T.I., 2008c. "Keynesian Models of Deflation and Depression Revisited," *Journal of Economic Behavior and Organization*, **68** (October), 167–77.
Sargent, T.J., 1979. *Macroeconomic Theory*, New York: Academic Press.
Tiebout, C.M., 1956. "A Pure Theory of Local Public Expenditure," *Journal of Political Economy*, **64** (October), 416–24.
Tobin, J., 1975. "Keynesian Models of Recession and Depression,"*American Economic Review*, **65**, 195–202.
Tobin, J., 1980. *Asset Accumulation and Economic Activity*, Chicago: Chicago University Press.

12. Global economic volatility and slap-dash repairs to the international financial architecture

Patrick Bond

INTRODUCTION

The Third World debt emerged as an acute crisis in 1982 and has never ceased its harm, but the debt crisis is merely a *symptom* of deeper global financial imbalances. Much has happened since that time, including dubious debt relief programs two decades later (which actually increased low-income Africa's annual repayments from 2006–11!) and amplified uneven development between regions of the South. Hence, we have to spend some time at the outset establishing context dating back several decades. Only then can we properly proceed to consideration of global reform proposals to assess their feasibility, with particular emphasis on Jane D'Arista's Keynesian proposals, and then onwards to an alternative strategy – 'bottom up' – with the same aims as D'Arista but based upon different readings of the balance of forces and hence of the impetus for genuine reform, which in my view will continue to emerge at the *national* not international scale.

The crisis that is today still undermining the shaky international financial architecture – in 2012 most obviously manifest in Portugal, Ireland, Italy, Greece and Spain (PIIGS) and in 2013 moving to the 'Fragile Five' middle-income economies of South Africa, India, Turkey, Brazil and Indonesia – is profound, by all accounts. Consider this frightened view from the mainstream economics tradition of the International Monetary Fund (IMF, 2009):

> The global economy has entered a period of unprecedented turmoil, with the prospect of a prolonged economic downturn, heightened financial volatility, and social instability. *Weakly coordinated macroeconomic policies among major world economies, deficient financial regulation, and insufficient commitment to financial stability* as a public good have each contributed to the current global economic conditions. The world needs a multilateral institution at the center

> of the world economy to *help anchor global financial stability*. Achieving that aim depends on *the monitoring of risks, coordinated policy responses, and agreed norms and standards to which all countries subscribe*. To be effective, the institution requires a strong and respected voice, human and financial resources appropriate to its mission, and it must be accountable to its members. It must also work closely with other international organizations and standard setters, and provide a focal point for discussions on crisis management and the macroeconomics of financial regulation. The International Monetary Fund is well placed to be this institution, but it needs *a re-energized multilateral mandate* to reflect the evolution of the world economy and *to increase its legitimacy* and effectiveness in addressing today's global challenges. *Few of the conditions outlined above are currently being met*. (Emphasis added)

This mainstream view diagnoses the global financial crisis only in terms of 'weakly coordinated macroeconomic policies' and deficient regulation. Then, in seeking a solution, the mainstream perspective advocates a larger role for the IMF in rather limited terms: monitoring risk, coordinating policy and establishing norms and standards. These are functions it has already, yet the IMF was notable for its failure to predict and monitor the nature of the crisis (which continues into new terrains of financial destruction including the bonds of Greece, Ireland, Portugal, Spain and Italy), much less to identify the appropriate norms and standards or to support a coherent counter-cyclical policy.

After all, during the crisis, much of the South – especially Africa – was given rehashed IMF pro-cyclical policy advice, and in the wake of the worst manifestations, the IMF has returned to relatively unchanged neoliberal austerity demands for its new set of European borrowers. The only genuinely new factor in the IMF's repertoire is its flush accounts, for in 2008 the Fund was losing large amounts of capital, borrowers and staff. The revival of neoliberalism was possible because the IMF did indeed receive a 're-energized multilateral mandate' in April 2009. It took the form of a vast funding increase of around a trillion dollars, and in November 2010, decisions were taken to adjust its voting power (by 6 percent) and shift two board positions (from Europe to emerging markets) so that IMF Managing Director Dominique Strauss-Kahn could claim a new 'legitimacy'. In May 2011 he lost this, of course, and French Finance Minister Christine Lagarde's 'election' to an office that apparently has a 'Europeans Only' sign on it confirms what some South Africans (who remember this sign well) term 'global apartheid'. By late 2012, when the Brazil-Russia-India-China-South Africa (BRICS) bloc had donated another $75 billion to the IMF's recapitalization, anger at the lack of voice for Africans rose to unprecedented levels, because making room for the BRICS meant a lower share for Africa, and the two European board seats remained unmoved. For not rocking the boat, China was rewarded with assimilation incentives:

the deputy IMF managing director is Zhu Min and the new head of the International Finance Corporation is Jin-Yong Cai.

Even if a profound critique can be offered of 'false-flag' IMF Keynesianism, it cannot be denied that in search of legitimacy, the IMF's neoliberal economic managers have permitted increased national sovereignty in relation to capital flows. The opportunities to impose both inward and outward exchange controls increased after the 1980s–90s liberalization experience did enormous damage, especially in the 1994–95, 1997–98 and 2008–09 crises, as well as at present. The main opposition to the kind of international financial architecture that would permit currency controls, as an example, comes from financiers themselves, as well as their most enthusiastic advocates, professional economists.

An important component in the debate over the new international financial architecture is the foundational ideology of those economists. The revival of neoliberalism, notwithstanding the ongoing financial meltdown, reflects their residual credibility. The leaders of this profession came to occupy a greater power within academia and society since the 1980s because of their claims to having developed 'an all-encompassing, intellectually elegant approach that also gave economists a chance to show off their mathematical prowess', according to Krugman (2009). A few economists 'questioned the belief that financial markets can be trusted and pointed to the long history of financial crises that had devastating economic consequences. But they were swimming against the tide, unable to make much headway against a pervasive and, in retrospect, foolish complacency.' Added Galbraith (2009),

> Leading active members of today's economics profession [. . .] have formed themselves into a kind of Politburo for correct economic thinking [. . .] They oppose the most basic, decent and sensible reforms, while offering placebos instead. They are always surprised when something untoward (like a recession) actually occurs. And when finally they sense that some position cannot be sustained, they do not reexamine their ideas. They do not consider the possibility of a flaw in logic or theory. Rather, they simply change the subject. No one loses face, in this club, for having been wrong.

The financial markets offered some of the greatest instances of flawed economic reasoning based on the 'efficient markets hypothesis' and a general commitment to liberalization. One high-profile economist, Columbia University's Jagdish Baghwati, argues for trade liberalization but not financial capital liberalization (Baghwati, 1998). But most have resisted the necessary move towards reregulation of capital accounts on grounds of incorrect economic thinking. In contrast, the greatest economist of the 20th century, John Maynard Keynes, had a much deeper understanding of intrinsic contradictions within capitalism, and as a result, he opposed the neoliberal (then called 'Treasury View') commitment to a footloose flow of capital because, according to him, such a policy:

> assumes that it is right and desirable to have an equalisation of interest rates in all parts of the world. In my view the whole management of the domestic economy depends upon being free to have the appropriate interest rate without reference to the rates prevailing in the rest of the world. Capital controls is a corollary to this. (Keynes, 1980, p. 149)

Keeping in mind the need for capital controls, Keynes advocated an International Currency Union as the name for an international financial architecture to be negotiated at Bretton Woods, New Hampshire in 1944. However, in the arrangement that was arrived at, and that lasted until 1971, Keynes failed to persuade the dominant US negotiators of the need for a more expansive strategy based on penalizing countries with persistent trade surpluses. His defeat at the Bretton Woods and 1946 Savannah conferences reportedly left Keynes despondent, and he soon died of a heart attack.[1] Keynes's most forceful statement of the merits of inward-oriented development in a context of *socio-political* globalization is as follows, from the 1933 *Yale Review*:

> I sympathise with those who would minimise, rather than with those who would maximise, economic entanglement among nations. Ideas, knowledge, science, hospitality, travel – these are the things which should of their nature be international. But let goods be homespun whenever it is reasonably and conveniently possible and, above all, let finance be primarily national. (Keynes, 1933, p. 769)

Given the pre-Keynesian context of both the economics discipline and economic policy-makers, it is important to view international financial turmoil historically, and to establish the roots and patterns associated with financial crises and the rise and collapse of financial architectures.

REPETITIVE GLOBAL CRISES

A financial crisis typically consummates a period of irrational speculation, in the wake of monetary/credit expansion during a structural stagnation (or even decline) in underlying economic growth rates, at the peak of a crisis of overaccumulation.[2] Starting with the 1720 South Sea Company bubble, panics occurred in financial, commodity or property markets in 1763, 1772, 1793, 1797, 1799 and 1810. Such panics reflected relatively immature markets, underdeveloped institutions, the uneven expansion of financial systems, the gullibility of investors, and systemic vulnerability to emotion. Wars and geopolitical conflict were often catalysts. In this earlier era, both the Bank of England and City of Amsterdam performed lender-of-last-resort functions. As capitalism matured, however, the tendency to generate period financial crises did not wane but instead became more acute. There were episodes of stagnation, speculation and crashes from 1815–48, 1873–96, 1917–48, and 1974–present (the exact beginnings and endings are subject to dispute), featuring international financial influences.

Such periodic cycles (or 'long waves') suggest that a crescendo of financial turbulence may contribute to economic catharsis and renewed capital accumulation. Yet discrete crashes are sometimes insufficient to restore conditions for recovery, generating instead 'payment-freeze', which in turn makes commerce or investment very difficult to finance in subsequent years. Past cycles were interrupted by severe financial panics – 1873, 1882, 1890, 1893; 1920, 1929, 1931; and various 1980s–90s crises – which did not immediately rejuvenate growth. Instead, it was only much more dramatic economic devaluations that laid the basis for a revival of accumulation. Within the long-wave of accumulation, there are even more obvious 'Kuznets cycles' of 15 years to three decades long, witnessed in particular by labour migration patterns (to the extent states permit) and investment in buildings, infrastructure and other facets of the built environment. Ultimately, as in the 1929–45 period, massive devaluations of both financial and real capital – 'creative destruction' as Joseph Schumpeter would say (even if war is very uncreative) – are typically required to remove excess capacity, invoke technological innovation, and thus begin a new round of accumulation (Harvey, 1982).

Before reaching the stage of system-wide devaluation, partial devaluations occur, and increasingly, financiers gain the power to direct the austerity process, even when financial markets are in chaos. Financial panics have caused enormous economic, social and ecological harm, often to firms, workers or entire societies, which were innocent of speculation. As contemporary speculator George Soros put it, financial markets 'move in a herd-like fashion in both directions. The excess always begins with over-expansion, and the correction is always associated with pain' (Soros, 1997). The Bretton Woods Institutions and US government will often bail out investors and institutions instead of assisting the victims of finance. Their propensities to impose austerity and enforce extractive-oriented export-led economic strategies are typically justified as necessary for debt repayment.

Hence the asymmetric liability (or 'moral hazard') for the enormous costs associated with recent and ongoing financial meltdowns is one important reason for the challenge to 'Washington Consensus' economic policy. However, given the adverse power relationships and context of deeper economic crisis, elite reforms to the international financial system have failed to address imbalanced power; indeed, most mainstream reform proposals amplify banker power. Before exploring why, it is useful to locate the development of globalized finance within an understanding of economic crisis.

INTERNATIONAL FINANCIAL ARCHITECTURE AND ACCUMULATION CRISES SINCE THE EARLY 1970S

Moving to the next step, we can verify the rise and fall of finance during the course of accumulation cycles, especially at the global scale, and hence the ways that the international financial architecture was constructed under stress. During four periods – the late 1820s, 1870s, 1930s and 1980s – at least one third of all national states fell into effective default on their external debt following an unsustainable upswing of borrowing. With the exception of the 1980s (in which there was a significant lag), the onset of global debt crisis was the precursor for the onset of decades-long downswings in the Kondratieff cycles, also known as 'long waves' of accumulation followed by crisis. The reason for sustained financial speculation (instead of a full-fledged global crash), was the *bailout* role of the international financial architecture, in which the IMF and World Bank provided debt 'restructuring' instead of permitting the kinds of national defaults that had been required to systemically clear away financial deadwood in earlier epochs, a topic to which we will return.

Drawing on the world-systems perspective pioneered by Immanuel Wallerstein, Christian Suter explains the 'global debt cycle' by way of stages in the long wave, beginning with technological innovation and utilizing international product cycle theory. At the upswing of a Kondratieff cycle, as basic technological innovations are introduced in a labor-intensive and unstandardized manner, both the demand for and supply of external financing are typically low, and in any case the residue of financial crisis in the previous long-cycle does not permit rapid expansion of credit or other financial assets into high-risk investments. As innovations gradually spread, however, peripheral geographical areas become more tightly integrated into the world economy, supported by international financial networks. However, as the power of innovation-led growth subsides, and as the consumer markets of the advanced capitalist countries become saturated, profit rates decline in the core. This pushes waves of financial capital into peripheral areas, where instead of achieving balanced accumulation and growth, low returns on investment plus a variety of other political and economic constraints inexorably lead to sovereign default. In sum, at the global scale there is a three-stage process characterized by, as Suter (1992, p. 41) puts it, 'first, intense core capital exports and corresponding booms in credit raising activity of peripheries; second, the occurrence of debt service incapacity among peripheral countries; and third, the negotiation of debt settlement agreements between debtors and creditors'.

One of the reasons that debt crises took the form they did was the failure of monetary systems to retain the integrity required to halt excessive credit creation. The weak anchoring of international financial integration, followed by a demooring that signified financial autonomy, can be understood in part through considering the prevailing international financial architecture. Columbia University monetary specialist Robert Mundell set out a chronology for the international financial architecture over two centuries, with distinct periods entailing combinations of monetary bases. Simplifying Mundell (2000), in modern economic history, five core strategies were used at various times:

1. Gold Standard (pre-1932)
2. Anchored $ Standard (1944–71)
3. Flexible Exchange Rates (1973–85)
4. Managed Exchange Rates (1985–99)
5. Dollar and Euro (1999–present).

The chaotic architecture's wobbly add-ons permitted severe slippage right down to the foundations, especially with respect to financial regulation and currency valuation, and especially as banks and other financial institutions internationalized their activities in recent decades. The current period of excessive financial integration began in 1971. It is therefore instructive to review how the Bretton Woods system broke down at the outset of a general rise in financial turbulence, and how over the subsequent four decades the monetary and financial systems reacted, leaving us with the desperate need for a new international financial architecture. Over the last four decades, a series of speculative bubbles and panics ensued, reflecting uncontrolled financial turbulence. To some extent these were offset by bailouts, but they generally destroyed more than 15 percent of the value of financial assets at stake within a short period of time: the dollar crash (1970s), gold and silver turbulence (1970s–80s), Third World debt crisis (1980s), US farmland collapse (1980s), energy finance shocks (mid 1980s), crashes of international stock (1987) and property (1991–93) markets, the long fall (from 1973–2002) in non-petroleum commodity prices and related securities, and after the dot.com crash of 2000–01, vast new devaluations of real estate, commodities, financial institutions and exposed sovereign securities in Europe (2007–12). Emerging markets offered spectacular examples of financial panic, including Mexico (1995), South Africa (1996, 1998 and 2001), Southeast Asia (1997–98), South Korea (1998), Russia (1998), Brazil and Ecuador (early 1999), Argentina (2001–02) and Turkey (2001–03). Trouble moved north, as far as Iceland (2008), Ireland (2009), Greece (2010), Spain (2011) and Cyprus (2013), and then southwards to the Fragile Five (including three BRICS, as Goldman Sachs' James O'Neill downgraded that concept in search of new pickings in the MINTs of Mexico, Indonesia, Nigeria and Turkey, which contain the two other Fragile Fives, thus confirming O'Neill's penchant for sovereign-finance flipping). Other examples of investment gambles gone sour included derivatives speculation, exotic stock market positions, and bad bets on currency, commodity and interest rate options, futures and swaps, with specific victims covering enormous losses.

Chronologically, we can see how the following thirteen moments of fragility reflect systemic global financial volatility. Because international policymakers generally reacted with increasing commitments to fiscal bailouts, the problems were merely displaced to more extreme levels, as we have recently seen in Europe and the Fragile Five:

- In 1973, the Bretton Woods agreement on Western countries' fixed exchange rates – by which from 1944–71, an ounce of gold was valued at US$35 and served to anchor other major currencies – disintegrated when the US unilaterally ended its payment obligations, representing a default of approximately $80 billion, leading the price of gold to rise to $850/ounce within a decade, and at the same time, several Arab countries led the formation of the Organization of the Petroleum Exporting Countries (OPEC), which raised the price of petroleum dramatically and in the process transferred and centralized inflows from world oil consumers to their New York bank accounts ('petrodollars').
- From 1973, 'los Chicago Boys' of Milton Friedman – the young Chilean bureaucrats with doctorates in economics from the University of Chicago – began to reshape Chile in the wake of Augusto Pinochet's coup against the democratically elected Salvador Allende, representing the birth pangs of neoliberalism.
- In 1976, the IMF signaled its growing power by forcing austerity on Britain at a point where the ruling Labour Party was desperate for a loan, even prior to Margaret Thatcher's ascent to power in 1979.
- In 1979 the US Federal Reserve addressed the dollar's decline and US inflation by dramatically raising interest rates, in turn catalyzing a severe recession and the Third World debt crisis, especially in

Mexico and Poland in 1982, Argentina in 1984, South Africa in 1985 and Brazil in 1987 (in the latter case leading to a default that lasted only six months due to intense pressure on the Sarney government to repay).

- At the same time, the World Bank shifted from project funding to the imposition of structural adjustment and sectoral adjustment (supported by the IMF and the 'Paris Club' cartel of donors), in order to assure surpluses would be drawn for the purpose of debt repayment, and in the name of making countries more competitive and efficient.
- The overvaluation of the US dollar thanks to the Fed's high real interest rates was addressed by formal agreements between five leading governments that devalued the dollar in 1985 (Louvre Accord), but with a 51 percent fall against the yen, led to a 1987 revaluation (Plaza Accord).
- Once the Japanese economy overheated during the late 1980s, a stock market crash of 40 percent and a serious real estate downturn followed from 1990, and indeed not even negative real interest rates could shake Japan from a long-term series of recessions.
- During the late 1980s and early 1990s, Washington adopted a series of financial crisis-management techniques – such as the US Treasury's Baker and Brady Plans – so as to write off (with tax breaks) part of the $1.3 trillion in potentially dangerous Third World debt due to the New York, London, Frankfurt, Zurich and Tokyo banks which were exposed in Latin America, Asia, Africa and Eastern Europe (although notwithstanding the socialization of the banks' losses, debt relief was denied the borrowers).
- In late 1987, crashes in the New York and Chicago financial markets (unprecedented since 1929) were immediately averted with a promise of unlimited liquidity by Alan Greenspan's Federal Reserve, a philosophy which in turn allowed the bailout of the Savings and Loan industry and various large commercial banks (including Citibank) in the late 1980s notwithstanding a recession and serious real estate crash during the early 1990s.
- Likewise in 1998, when a New York hedge fund – Long Term Capital Management (LTCM; founded by Nobel Prize-winning financial economists) – was losing billions in bad investments in Russia, the New York Fed arranged a bailout, on grounds the world's financial system was potentially at risk.
- Starting with Mexico in late 1994, the US Treasury's management of the mid and late 1990s 'emerging markets' crises again imposed austerity on the Third World while offering further bailouts for investment bankers exposed in various regions and countries – Eastern

Europe (1996), Thailand (1997), Indonesia (1997), Malaysia (1997), Korea (1998), Russia (1998), South Africa (1998, 2001), Brazil (1999), Turkey (2001) and Argentina (2001) – whose hard currency reserves were suddenly emptied by runs, followed by the Fragile Five's misfortunes of mid-2013 when slower Federal Reserve money-printing ('tapering' of the 'Quantitative Easing' strategy from $85 billion/month) led to crashes of more than a third of their currency values.

- In addition to a vastly overinflated US economy (with record trade, capital and budget deficits) whose various excesses have occasionally unraveled – as with the dot.com stock market (2000) and real estate (2007) bubbles – the two largest Asian societies, China and India, picked up the slack in global materials and consumer demand during the 2000s, but not without extreme stresses and contradictions that in coming years threaten world finances, geopolitical arrangements and environmental sustainability.
- The 2007–09 crash was catalyzed by the US real estate market's collapse due to excessive securitization and unrepayable consumer debt, but the overextension of financial gambling in commodities, shares and many other forms of fictitious (paper) capital was exposed by the collapse in their prices of half or more in the last six months of 2008, before the bailout gifts to financiers kicked in and reflated some of the burst bubbles.

UNDERLYING FACTORS

Powerful underlying forces are the main reason for such extreme financialization. Recall that the world's per capita annual gross domestic product (GDP) increase fell from 3.6 percent during the 1960s, to 2.1 percent during the 1970s, to 1.3 percent during the 1980s, to 1.1 percent during the 1990s, followed by a rise to 2.5 percent for the first half of the 2000s, but then a crash in absolute terms at the end of the 2000s, according to the World Bank. To be sure, the bundle of goods measured over time has changed (high-technology products enjoyed today were not available in the last century). Yet overall, GDP measures are notorious overestimates, especially since environmental degradation became more extreme from the mid 1970s, when a 'genuine progress indicator' went into deficit.

Related debates unfold over what is mainly a symptom of economic crisis: declines in the corporate rate of profit during the 1970s–90s, emanating from the United States. At first glance, the after-tax US corporate profit rate appeared to recover from 1984, nearly reaching 1960s–70s highs (although it must be said that tax rates were much lower in the recent period). On other hand, interest payments remained at record high levels throughout the 1980s–90s. By subtracting real (inflation-adjusted) interest expenses we have a better sense of net revenue available to the firm for future investment and accumulation, which remained far lower than earlier periods. Furthermore, we can trace, with the help of Duménil and Lévy (2004), the ways that US corporations responded to declining manufacturing-sector accumulation. Manufacturing revenues were responsible for roughly half of total (before-tax) corporate profits during the quarter-century post-war 'Golden Age', but fell to below 20 percent by the early 2000s. In contrast, profits were soon much stronger in the financial sector (rising from the 10–20 percent range during the 1950s–60s, to above 30 percent by 2000) and in corporations' global operations (rising from 4–8 percent to above 20 percent by 2000). Duménil and Lévy (2004) show that since the 1979 'Volcker Shock' (dramatic interest rate increases imposed by Paul Volcker) changed the interest/profit calculus, there have been more revenues accruing to capital based in finance than in the non-financial sector, to the extent that financiers doubled their asset base in relation to non-financiers during the 1980s–90s.

Many such trends continued into the 2000s, with low investment rates (especially after the dot.com software bubble burst), high debt loads and even bankruptcy threats to what were once some of the US's most powerful auto companies. Hence the restoration of profits for capital in general disguised the difficulty of extraction of surplus value, leaving most accumulation hollow, based increasingly upon financial and commercial activity rather than production. Although productivity increased and wage levels fell, profitability was mainly found outside the production process, especially in finance. Nevertheless, with much lower interest rates, low inflation and relatively low unemployment, resulting in steady GDP, a rising stock market and recovery from earlier outbreaks of currency volatility, it appeared to many investors that the US economy could continue along this trajectory.

This naivety changed immediately in 2008, as the world economy began what initially appeared to be an even worse decline than in 1929–30, in terms of crashed industrial output, trade, and stock market valuation. Commodity prices crashed by record amounts, and world GDP, industrial production and foreign direct investment (FDI) levels plummeted. The extreme devaluations required several major interventions: very rapid increases in government debt, dramatic declines in interest rates, and a vast inflow of new liquidity from the US Federal Reserve ('quantitative easing' on two occasions), which raised global money supply after a break associated with the 2008 crash.

Volatility associated with ongoing financial processes and minimalist intrastate regulation is addressed later, but Harvey's (1982) analyses of spatio-temporal 'fixes' (not resolutions) and of systems of 'accumulation by dispossession' are also appealing as theoretical tools. They help explain why economic crisis doesn't automatically generate the sorts of payments-system breakdowns and mass unemployment problems witnessed during the main previous conjuncture of overaccumulation, the Great Depression. Several obvious variables – the rise in US debt in comparison to the production of goods in the US economy, the rise of financial sector debt (in relation to other sectors), the rise of profits attributable to financial (not productive) activity, underinvestment and rising inventories – were all quite extreme during the 2000s, which allowed the system to continue displacing the overaccumulated capital into the financial circuit, achieving a 'temporal fix' (buy now, and pay later on credit).

Is there a framework that explains these events? Based on Harvey's broader theory of historical-geographical materialism, four core arguments emerge about the way financial volatility relates to social power and global macroeconomic management:

1. First, the durable late 20th century condition of overaccumulation of capital – as witnessed in huge gluts in many markets, declining increases in per capita GDP growth, and falling corporate profit rates – was displaced and mitigated ('shifted and stalled' geographically and temporally) at the cost of much more severe tensions and potential market volatility in months and years ahead.
2. Second, the temporary dampening of crisis conditions through increased credit and financial market activity has resulted in the expansion of 'fictitious capital' – i.e., paper representations of capital for the sake of facilitating financial asset trading, especially in real estate but other speculative markets involving derivatives – far beyond the ability of production to meet the paper values.
3. Third, geographical shifts in production and finance continue to generate economic volatility and regional geopolitical tensions, contributing to unevenness in currencies and markets as well as pressure to 'combine' market and non-market spheres of society and nature in search of restored profitability.
4. Fourth, capital uses power associated with the two stalling and shifting (temporal and spatial displacement) tools above to draw additional surpluses from non-market spheres (environmental commons, women's unpaid labor, indigenous economies), via extra-economic kinds of coercions ranging from bio-piracy and privatization to deepened reliance on unpaid women's labor for household

reproduction in an ever-expanding process of long-distance labor migration.

This background gives a better sense of why damage from termites, from sinking foundations, from periodic earthquakes and from uncontained financial fires have not only left the international financial architecture on the verge of collapse, but have also wrecked national economies because of their excessive reliance upon international financial flows. There are even more severe challenges just ahead, however, and the existing architecture is not likely to withstand the rising structural pressures that will undermine and potentially even collapse international finance.

VOLATILE GLOBAL FINANCIAL ARCHITECTURE

One of the strongest statements about why the current international financial architecture is fundamentally unsound came from Akyüz (2010):

- There are no effective rules and regulations to bring inherently unstable international financial market and capital flows under control.
- There is no multilateral discipline over misguided monetary, financial and exchange rate policies in systemically important countries despite their strong adverse international spillovers.
- National and international policy makers are preoccupied primarily with resolving crises by supporting those who are responsible for these crises, rather than introducing institutional arrangements to reduce the likelihood of their recurrence. Through such interventions, they are creating more problems than they are solving, and indeed sowing the seeds for future difficulties.

The problems associated with fixing finance with further financialization – especially Quantitative Easing – became increasingly evident since, especially in the European debt market and Fragile Five. There are several specific challenges that emerged as a result of the 1970s destruction of the Bretton Woods architecture, and especially since the financial meltdown of 2008, which any new international financial architecture would have to tackle: currency imbalances and volatility; fiscal deficits and the limits to neo-Keynesianism; US monetary policy; global and local real estate speculation; European national sovereign debt; US state/municipal debt; and various forms of unrepayable consumer debt in many parts of the world (e.g. US student loans).

The underlying problem, however, remains an imbalance in the real economy. 'As I have been saying repeatedly', insisted Wallerstein (2011), 'we are not in a recession but in a depression.' In these circumstances, 'politicians look for quick fixes. They call for "austerity," which means cutting pensions and education and child care even further.' Wallerstein warns, 'The governments of Russia, India, and South Africa are all facing rumbling discontent from large parts of their populations who seemed to have escaped the benefits of presumed economic growth.' He predicts continuing 'sharp rises in the prices of energy, food, and water, and thus a struggle for these basic goods, a struggle that could turn deadly'. In mid-2013, for example, higher public transport costs created extreme pressure in Brazil, leading to millions of protesters; in India later that year, the New Delhi municipal government was tossed out by voters who favoured a surprise newcomer, a populist party 'of the working man'; and in South Africa in 2013, the number of violent protests (amongst 12,400 total demonstrations) soared to 1882, according to the Police Minister, largely as a result of non-delivery or the soaring prices of electricity and water.

Likewise, in many European countries, riots and political protests continue to confront austerity policies, not just in the PIIGS. The unrest was also intense in Britain – with its revitalized student movement unwilling to accept the extreme Tory–Liberal tuition hikes – and France due to retirees' resistance to longer working lives.

Other troubling economic weaknesses are finally being noticed within the alleged world 'recovery'. US real estate continues to rot, even though the Federal Reserve Board chair Ben Bernanke had in 2008–09 bought over $1 trillion worth of mortgage-backed securities from banks that would have gone belly-up otherwise. In 2010, it was finally revealed that between March 2008 and May 2009, Bernanke not only pumped in $3 trillion into the US economy as emergency liquidity, but also secretly lent $9 trillion to bail out 18 financial institutions deemed 'too big to fail'. Citigroup, Merrill Lynch and Morgan Stanley were at such risk that they approached Bernanke for cheap loans on more than 100 occasions. Goldman Sachs went 84 times. It is not only the US taxpayer and all holders of dollars who lose in the process. The independent socialist US Senator Bernie Sanders (2010) remarks that ordinary homeowners are victims: 'Banks are foreclosing on untold numbers of families who have never missed a payment, because rushing to foreclosure generates lucrative fees for the banks, whatever the costs to families and investors'.

There are also other sources of financial turmoil awaiting, including major disruptions to large banks and mortgage companies that acted illegally in the recent wave of millions of home foreclosures, millions more foreclosures that could sink the property market further, more 'flash crash' financial markets incidents (as in May 2010 when the Dow Jones Index crashed 700 points within minutes), and much higher energy and especially oil prices (Bottari, 2011). These kinds of factors suggest the urgent need to shore up the international financial architecture, especially so as to protect low-income countries' economies from adverse exposure to monetary, fiscal and other macroeconomic tsunamis or earthquakes whose Ground Zeros will continue to be the US and Europe. A variety of options are on the table, including from the existing institutions, but these appear inadequate to the task at hand.

ONGOING ARCHITECTURAL DECAY

As in any such system-threating situation, the choices for reconstructing a new architecture include mere interior design, some exterior rehabilitation, full remodeling and demolition followed by rebuilding. So far, because of insufficient political will, no substantive work (aside from repainting) has begun, so the existing architecture[3] continues to decay, punctuated by extreme shocks that weaken the global system. As has often been remarked upon, the same arsonists who set the financial fires remain at the heads of international banks, national governments (especially the US) and multilateral institutions (especially the Bretton Woods Institutions). To ask the arsonists for a new, fireproof architecture, is to ask the fox to guard the henhouse.

To illustrate the limitations of those who hold power at present, a typical mainstream perspective on fixing the architecture would stress the following: transparency, crisis prevention, flexible exchange rates and ongoing capital mobility. Since the 1995 Mexican currency crash, the IMF has permitted a slight deviation from orthodoxy in the form of capital controls on incoming flows of funds (for example, the 'speedbump' on portfolio inflows so as to keep them in a given financial market for a minimum period). But the general regime of neoliberal financial deregulation and pro-cyclical macroeconomic policy remains.

For example, protection for US consumers from predatory finance was promised in legislation sponsored by Senator Christopher Dodd and Representative Barney Frank in 2010, but ultimately amounted to a slap-dash paint job on the existing architecture. As Jane D'Arista (2011, 1) remarked, although the Dodd–Frank Act at least began to 'deal with the interconnectedness of financial institutions', it 'failed in identifying and addressing structural faults in the global system' because of its 'reaffirmation of pro-cyclical capital requirements as the primary tool in the post-crisis regulatory framework'. Aside from the 2008–09 failure of several major US institutions and the purchase of their downgraded assets by newly centralized private financiers in the wake of US government bailouts of investors, none of the needed rehabilitations were made. There was no restructuring of the financial architecture comparable to Washington's early 1930s banking legislation which separated credit from investment and which maintained strict geographical controls limiting banks to operations within a single US state.

Many of the multilateral functions broke down fairly conclusively in 2008–09, when some of the world's largest financial institutions failed as a result. It may be possible to offer a kind of interior design strategy to relegitimize the architecture, as was attempted for the IMF. But all other indications suggest that elite managers have reached the limits of crisis management, both in terms of their analytical ability and their vision for architectural reform.

CONVENTIONAL ANALYSIS AND STRATEGIES FOR ARCHITECTURAL REPAIR

Although the roots are decades old, the most proximate cause of the ongoing international financial crisis can be traced to weak United States financial institutions. The 2008 crash of a variety of the main investments banks, the two main home mortgage guarantors, the largest insurance company, the largest-ever bank to collapse and the Dow Jones itself (which on 29 September 2008 had the biggest-ever fall in share prices) was superficially explained by mainstream commentators. Many mention deregulation, corruption, greed, feckless borrowing by debt-addicted consumers, or a combination. Stiglitz (2008) adds 'ideology, special-interest pressure, populist politics, and sheer incompetence'.

Populist posturing aside, it is more instructive to consider the view from the financial power center, in Washington. Three leading IMF economists – Olivier Blanchard et al. (2009) – typify what is wrong with the existing managers of global finance. The authors addressed what they understood as the deficiencies in 'regulation, macroeconomic policy and the global architecture for stability'. The causes were 'optimism bred by a long period of high growth, low real interest rates and volatility, and policy failures in financial regulation [. . .] macroeconomic policies [. . .] and global architecture, where a fragmented surveillance system compounded the inability to see growing vulnerabilities and links'. The lessons the three drew are 'that flawed incentives and interconnections in modern financial systems can have huge macroeconomic consequences', especially in relation to reform of the global financial architecture: 'The fragmentation into silos of expertise needs to be overcome and senior policy makers engaged in promoting global stability, including via early warning exercises. The case for cooperation is pressing in financial regulation, especially the resolution of cross-border banks.'

In other words, what the IMF economists are calling for is merely continuing occupation of the current architecture, with no major changes aside from more sophisticated residents who can utilize existing maintenance systems more effectively. Instead of seeing the financial crisis and collapsing architecture as indicative of broader financial power and long-term crisis, the IMF economists view the 2008–09 financial meltdown as the logical outcome of the *success* of the neoliberal project. Where the economists view market failure as a function of 'optimism bred by a long period of high growth, low real interest rates and volatility' during the 2000s, the reality is that the long era of *low* growth in the productive economy of the 1980s–90s was accompanied by *high* interest rates (the 1979 Volcker Shock and sustained positive levels far above the negative real rates of prior years) and then by volatility borne of the resulting political power shift that by the 2000s had so thoroughly deregulated global finance.

A genuinely new architecture focusing on reregulation (not a 'more flexible perimeter' of regulation) and national-scale protection from financial vulnerability would be required to accomplish the anti-cyclical policy the three IMF economists acknowledge is necessary. There is no way to carry off this kind of task within the existing system given the adverse power relations and the lack of institutional controls over footloose finance. In sum, the earlier Bretton Woods architecture was torn down during the 1970s; the possibilities for national regulation of finance were limited in the 1980s–90s by deregulation (the US was most notorious during the Clinton administration); the liberalization of financial markets was stressed as a condition for loans by multilateral creditors and for membership in the Organisation for Economic Co-operation and Development (OECD); and the capital controls which had earlier established firewalls between national economies and global financial markets were torn down nearly completely. Very little of the prior architecture – which had hosted a higher-growth, more balanced and financially far less volatile world economy prior to the 1970s – remained and thus the IMF economists' call for 'better' regulation within the context of the deregulated system is incongruous.

POST-WASHINGTON CONSENSUS REFORM PROPOSALS

Since the mid 1990s, when the emerging markets crises began in Mexico, the void of reason on economics has been so great that even moderate reform efforts in both disciplinary terms (as noted in the first section of this chapter) and public policy have been foiled. There have been two main sources of advocacy for international financial architecture reform within the United Nations system, but neither the UN Conference on Trade and Development (UNCTAD) nor the Commission of Experts of the President of the United Nations General Assembly on Reforms of the International Monetary and Financial System (known as the Stiglitz Commission) mustered sufficient clout to achieve their objectives. Nor were the objectives sufficient to address the foundational problems.

As UNCTAD (2010) argued:

> The crisis dynamics reflect failures in national and international financial deregulation, persistent global imbalances, absence of an international monetary system and deep inconsistencies among global trading, financial and monetary policies. Market fundamentalist laissez-faire of the last 20 years has dramatically failed the test. Financial deregulation created the build-up of huge risky positions whose unwinding has pushed the global economy into a debt deflation that can only be countered by government debt inflation.

In other words, it is merely neoliberal public policy that is to blame, and hence:

> this systemic failure can only be remedied through comprehensive reform and reregulation with a vigorous role by Governments working in unison. Contrary to traditional views, Governments are well positioned to judge price movements in those markets that are driven by financial speculation and should not hesitate to intervene whenever major disequilibria loom. (Ibid.)

But as for details, UNCTAD provided quite meek notions of reregulation. With regard to the 'speculative bubbles' in commodity markets, for example:

> Regulators need access to more comprehensive trading data in order to be able to understand what is moving prices and intervene if certain trades look problematic, while key loopholes in regulation need to be closed to ensure that positions on currently unregulated over-the-counter markets do not lead to 'excessive speculation'. (Ibid.)

Similarly: 'The absence of a cooperative international system to manage exchange rate fluctuations has facilitated rampant currency speculation and increased the global imbalances.' Yet UNCTAD merely desires that 'developing countries should not be subject to a "crisis rating" by the same financial markets which have created their trouble'. And while arguing that 'multilateral or even global exchange rate arrangements are urgently needed to maintain global stability, to avoid the collapse of the international trading system and to pre-empt pro-cyclical policies by crisis-stricken countries', this is a vague call with no strategic orientation for achieving a new international financial architecture.

The same reversion to orthodoxy was witnessed in Joseph Stiglitz's January 2009 report on 'Recommendations for Immediate Action' (United Nations, 2009). The Stiglitz Commission's brief statement consisted of a call to correct market imperfections (for which Stiglitz won the 2001 Nobel Prize) added to national Keynesianism. The gaps in the report were striking, especially because Stiglitz had once called for the replacement – not relegitimization/recapitalization – of the IMF. His report failed to mention ongoing IMF austerity conditions. He failed to get the commission to explicitly support capital/exchange controls. There were no suggestions for converting bank bailout nationalizations into genuine public utilities. The Jubilee movement's advocacy of debt cancellation, odious debt repudiation and reparations was not mentioned. There were no detailed strategies to address ecological debt and the financing implications of climate crisis (i.e., who should pay for what the UN acknowledges is massive 'loss and damage'), or even unregulated hot money centers – a revived financial transactions tax strategy later applied in Europe. There was no attempt at commodity price regulation. Instead, Stiglitz's commission endorsed the tired Doha Agenda of the World Trade Organisation. The hard work of insulating national economies from international financial volatility was simply not advanced by Stiglitz's group.

A few weeks later, Stiglitz's Commission proposed a UN Global Economic Council (with 20–25 members) with similar status to the UN Security Council, a potential codification of the G20. On the other hand, the Commission also proposed a new currency and reserve system that would suffer relatively less veto power from the wealthy countries, plus a 1 percent GDP levy to redistribute from North to South (United Nations, 2009). However, none of these very minor reforms had any scope for being passed given the adverse power relations.

CHALLENGES BEYOND THE SCOPE OF THE EXISTING ARCHITECTURE

The limits to reform of the existing architecture became obvious in 2007–10, as numerous financial markets and institutions collapsed. These limits will become even more obvious in coming years notwithstanding the alleged global recovery. The most important challenges in the world economy cannot be addressed using the strategies available within existing institutions, because those in charge have neither the analytical capacity nor political will to properly address them:

- The need to raise global effective demand (albeit in an environmentally more sustainable way), given that the IMF and World Bank have permitted only a momentary Keynesianism and remain committed to the Washington Consensus austerity and liberalization agendas.
- The need to transcend systemic false optimism about the state of the world economy, as revealed not only in repeated wishful thinking by economic forecasters, but also in G7 and G20 finance ministers' communiqués.
- The need to re-empower the politically most democratic multilateral institution, the UN, whose assessments of international financial architecture reforms (from Monterrey in 2002 to the 2009 Stiglitz Commission) failed to persuade those with real power to make the recommended changes.
- The need to address weaknesses in the banking standards of the Bank for International Settlements, whose emphasis on capital adequacy has been repeatedly unveiled as inadequate especially in view of derivatives market growth.
- The need to upgrade regional financial and monetary strategies, especially Asian and Latin American efforts to intervene in extremely uneven economic relationships.
- The need to redress geopolitical power imbalances in international finance and global financial and monetary governance, given the mainly cosmetic shifts accomplished through the G20.
- The need to systematize bilateral deal-making, including the Chinese government's currency swaps with various national authorities in other emerging markets, so as to avoid dollar-dependency.
- The need, at the national level, to permit appropriate sovereign defaults and generate effective resolution ('workout') mechanisms (as recently pioneered by Argentina and Ecuador), which have not yet reached the critical mass of the 'debtors' cartel' advocated by courageous leaders of some states (Julius Nyerere in Tanzania and Fidel Castro in Cuba in the early 1980s, for example).

To these ends, a dramatically different approach will be needed. To address the challenges listed above, a new architecture with a pro-South bias is required, so that the persistent crises can be addressed with appropriate national insulation, while new institutions (such as the Bank of the South) emerge to replace the outgoing neoliberal institutions. Remaking the global architecture requires reversing current tendencies towards extractive-oriented, export-led growth in which uneven development is amplified by deregulated, free-flowing finance.

The most appropriate global combination to rebuild this architecture was identified by Keynes in the 1930s, but his defeat in the initial 1944–46 Bretton Woods System negotiations meant his proposals for an International Currency Union and a 'Bancor' international currency were not implemented. However, because of relatively deglobalized finance and economics during the 1930s, national exchange controls were common, and short of an ambitious attempt to build an appropriate international financial architecture, could be easily restored. In addition, other controls – for example, a financial transactions tax – can be applied at national level, along with the kinds of banking regulations and even nationalizations and mandates for banks to serve as public utilities. A variety of strategies and tactics will be necessary to restore the proper economic balance between the financial and the real economies, as well as between the economy and the environment. These are all considered in turn.

Keynes worried about the inappropriate international financial architecture from the early 1920s' Versailles austerity for Germany, through the 1930s when he wrote *The General Theory*, until his death in 1946. The 'Treasury View' – or what we now consider 'neoliberalism' and the 'Washington Consensus' – was fixated on orthodox strategies. Instead, very new and creative approaches would be needed to establish the basis for balanced economic development, he argued. In particular, he insisted, countries which export too much for the world economy's good should be compelled to spend – not hoard – the resulting foreign currency reserves, so as to then raise the value of their own currency, hence re-establishing equilibrium between economies and preventing untenable mismatches of trade and financial relations. In 1941, Keynes (1980, pp. 42–66) proposed an International Currency Union, led by an International Clearing Bank, based on:

> a general and collective responsibility, applying to all countries alike, that a country finding itself in a creditor position *against the rest of the world as a whole* should enter into an obligation to dispose of this credit balance and not to allow it meanwhile to exercise a contractionist pressure against the world economy and, by repercussion, against the economy of the creditor country itself. (Original emphasis)

Accomplishing this coordination is possible, so long as every country (and its central bank) has

> unqualified control over the capital transactions of its residents both outward and inward (subject to the obligations of a Surplus Bank), and it shall be

> entitled to call on the collaboration of other member banks to prevent unlicensed movements [. . .] The object, and it is a vital object, is to have a means of distinguishing (a) between movements of floating funds and genuine new investment for developing the world's resources; and (b) between movements, which will help to maintain equilibrium, from surplus countries, to deficiency countries and speculative movements or flights out of deficiency countries or from one surplus country to another. There is no country which can, in future, safely allow the flight of funds for political reasons or to evade domestic taxation or in anticipation of the owner turning refugee. Equally, there is no country that can safely receive fugitive funds which cannot safely be used for fixed investment and might turn it into a deficiency country against its will and contrary to the real facts.[4]

This would be the ideal-type of international financial architecture for countries to achieve greater self-sufficiency and lower their dependence upon environmentally and socially destructive export-led growth strategies. Since the late 1990s, Keynes's ideas have been periodically revived. Eatwell and Taylor (1998) advocated the establishment of a World Financial Authority. Davidson (1997) proposed an international clearing union providing for capital controls and Akyüz (1995) made similar calls. Other far-sighted US economists – James Galbraith, William Darity and Dean Baker – suggested a new international public bank and regulatory framework. The ideas of perhaps the most visionary and experienced of these reformers, Jane D'Arista, are worth special attention.

DEBATING D'ARISTA'S REFORMS

To conclude, we must face up to a formidable reality: the current balance of forces is terribly adverse, with the financial fraction of capital in control at both global and most national scales. If we seek world financial regulation, the basic barrier is that too many neoconservatives and neoliberals populate the multilateral institutions. In areas ranging from democratization of the international financial institutions and UN Security Council, to climate change, to international aid and trade, efforts made to establish cooperative relations and promote reforms across North and South have utterly failed.

The hope for global economic reform *top-down*, seems myopic. Instead, what kinds of examples can we find, *bottom-up*, that correspond to the pressures of global financial volatility, and social resistance? And how might we move from the practice of national strategies to counter world vulnerability, to a more coherent international financial architecture built on a stable footing? To answer, consider a few of Jane D'Arista's contributions to the debate.

Beginning with universal values, D'Arista (2009a) testified to Congress that her objectives in promoting far-reaching changes to the financial regulatory architecture were to 'moderate the growth of financial institutions, control excessive credit expansion and prevent the recurrence of the economic tragedy we have experienced as a result of the failure of our financial system'. Many of the needed changes she advocated were well within the purview of US legislators and regulators, so some of her most effective commentaries are against the slap-dash cosmetic changes to Washington's architectural remodeling, such as the authorities' failure to address one of the root problems, securitization.

What about the global-scale reforms required? In 1999, in the wake of the East Asian, Russian and Brazilian meltdowns, and prescient about coming crises, D'Arista proposed the rearrangement and re-empowerment of global financial regulatory institutions, to penalize exporters and mitigate processes of worsening uneven financial development between countries. As she put it (D'Arista, 2000):

> A revision of Keynes's proposed structure is necessary because payments imbalances are no longer settled by transactions through central banks but through private financial institutions. An international clearing agency that would meet current needs and conditions would have to include a mechanism for clearing private cross-border payments as well as create a reserve system that would reinstate transactions among central banks as the primary channel for settling balance of payments surpluses and deficits.

The rehabilitation of Keynes's global-scale financial governance proposal is critical, but such an agency's work would not be effective if there were not also reforms to address other symptoms of the crisis (which are highlighted in italics to suggest their profound importance) (ibid.):

- a public international investment fund for emerging markets. Structured as a closed-end mutual fund, this investment vehicle would address the problems that have emerged with the extraordinary growth in cross-border securities investment transactions in the 1990s. The proposal advocates a role for the public sector in managing those problems so that private portfolio investment – now the dominant channel for flows into emerging markets – can promote steady, sustainable growth *rather than the boom and bust cycles that so far have been its primary contribution.*
- a new allocation of special drawing rights (SDRs), the international reserve asset issued by the International Monetary Fund (IMF). Issuing a new round of SDRs would provide substantial short-term relief from the *debt burdens that aggravate imbalances in nations'*

access to international liquidity and perpetuate policies favoring lower wages, fiscal and monetary austerity and deflation.

- an alternative to the privatized, dollar-based international monetary system that is a root cause of global instability and market failure. This proposal would create an international transactions and payments system managed by a public international agency in which cross-border monetary exchanges can be made in each country's own currency. This critical feature would help governments and central banks conduct effective economic policies, including countercyclical initiatives, at a national level. Equally important, it would allow all countries – *not just a privileged few* – to service external debt with wealth generated in their domestic markets. Thus it would help end t*he unsustainable paradigm of export-led growth that now governs the global economy.*

These are absolutely visionary reforms that address some of the most debilitating symptoms of the world economic crisis, to be sure. Most importantly, they are so logical that notwithstanding a terribly adverse balance of international forces, these reforms are beginning to take root in even rather inhospitable climes, mostly at national scales.

For example, the idea of a public fund to mediate emerging market relations with world finance – a $100 billion Contingent Reserve Arrangement – finds a hint of resonance in discussions underway in early 2012 within the BRICS bloc, which at their New Delhi summit mooted a $50 billion New Development Bank as an alternative to the Bretton Woods Institutions. Although the two new institutions failed to emerge as promised at 2013 summits in Durban and St Petersburg, it was likely that the July 2014 Fortaleza heads of state summit would include their launch. If so designed, such a bank could potentially serve as such a fund, and if the Brazilians (with weak capital controls and a large development bank) or Chinese (with strong capital controls and a very uneven banking system) were to combine strengths, there are already clear institutional examples of how emerging markets can keep speculative finance at bay. But rigorous anti-inward-capital controls would be needed as well, for this to be the vehicle of choice for institutional investors seeking to diversify, a point we return to shortly. In addition, as recommended by Nicolas Stern and Joseph Stiglitz in a commissioned paper, a BRICS Bank could serve as a countervailing force to the Bretton Woods Institutions' unfair power relations, orientation to austerity and penchant for fossil fuel financing – if, that is, the BRICS leaders were interested in challenging global finance. All indications, however, were the opposite: assimilation is preferred (in South African parlance, 'shining – not breaking – the chains of global apartheid').

The increased allocation of SDRs was achieved at the London G20 meeting in April 2009 alongside the IMF's tripling of lending resources, to the tune of $250 billion. Many countries took immediate advantage of the new monies in their IMF accounts and helped to boost world effective demand at a point the crisis could have become much worse. Already at that stage, indications of a downward spiral far worse than the Great Depression were periodically announced by Eichengreen and O'Rourke (2009).

The crisis was deferred by Federal Reserve quantitative easing and the SDR allocations. But unfortunately, even slightly left-of-centre leadership of the IMF (for Strauss-Kahn also promoted Keynesian ideology in the midst of world crisis) did (and could) not lead to substantive changes in the IMF's normal pro-cyclical, neoliberal approach. This problem remained evident in loan and advisory activity in low-income countries throughout the 2008–09 stage of the crisis, as well as in the PIIGS after 2009 and three North African countries in 2010 when IMF fingerprints were found on the austerity policies that contributed to the Arab uprising of 2011. Strauss-Kahn's replacement Lagarde was even more dogmatically a proponent of the Washington Consensus, as she demonstrated in late 2011 in Nigeria by insisting on removal of retail petroleum subsidies, causing Occupy Nigeria rioting and nearly leading to the fall of government in the most populous African country. Indeed the continual recapitalization of the IMF has the opposite logic to that D'Arista proposes: it makes this ideological inclination even worse.

An ideological reversal of the IMF is, indeed, what D'Arista (2009b, p. 651) seemed to assume when advocating:

> issues of SDRs in exchange for the government debt of countries undertaking infrastructure projects and programmes related to health and education could make a real contribution. The IMF would not only act as a buyer for that debt on reasonable terms but would release the foreign exchange reserves needed to fund the programmes by substituting SDRs as backing for domestic credit expansion.

Of course in reality, the SDRs flowed from IMF coffers to national elites who often used it not to benefit their societies, but to further entrench neoliberal policies, or to postpone these momentarily by maintaining existing spending programs even without revenue. There are no publicized cases in which the SDR bonanza was genuinely directed to health, education or appropriate infrastructure.

As for managing global transactions and payments in an extremely volatile and uneven world financial system, D'Arista (2009b) addressed a variation on such a global fund, resurrecting the idea – originally mooted by economists A.G. Hart, Nicholas Kaldor and Jan Tinbergen in 1964 – of a commodity-linked fund with the aims, D'Arista reminds, of 'adapting the world monetary structure to changes in world production and trade and contributing to the stabilisation of prices and trade in primary products'. But she acknowledged that an International Commodity Fund (ICF) worked only based upon:

> the assumption of a continuation of the Bretton Woods agreements for settling payments balances between countries through their central banks and maintaining capital controls. Unless these conditions were reinstated, their proposal that only central banks could hold the reserve unit issued by the ICF would limit its use in settling payments imbalances. (Ibid., pp. 645–6)

In short, the resurrection of capital controls is a prerequisite for global financial governance of this sort. Is there a global substitute for national capital controls? As one component for disincentivizing cross-border financial flows in the spirit of Keynes, the idea of International Transaction Taxes has been posed regularly, even gaining the occasional support of governments and parliaments such as France and Canada. Whether for 'throwing sand in the wheels' of a speeding financial system, or raising funds for climate mitigation and adaptation (as suggested by the UN's Stiglitz Commission; United Nations, 2009), there are potential applications of the 'Tobin Tax' now gaining increased credibility amongst more serious global reformers. Nobel Prize laureate James Tobin had suggested a 0.05–0.50 percent tax on cross-border financial transactions between major countries (Tobin, 1978; see also Eichengreen et al., 1995; Felix, 1995).

There are important logistical updates for the implementation of financial transaction taxes that help the idea withstand criticism. For example, environmental economist Hazel Henderson (1996) also advocated the prevention of currency 'bear raids' by taxing electronic funds transfers (and requiring a transparent transaction reporting system). To concerns that money would flee the major countries for off-shore centers (Bahama, Jersey, Guernsey, the Cayman Islands, Panama, and so on), Tobin Tax advocates insist that any funds flowing to or from such sites could be penalized by concerted G8 action (BIS, 1990). To concerns (expressed by Stiglitz and others) that the rise of derivatives trade and other financial innovations would make a Tobin Tax difficult to apply (Garber and Taylor, 1995; Garber, 1998), advocates suggest taxing profits *or* losses (through a 'contract for differences' payment mechanism) realized as a result of movements of the exchange rate relative to the notional principal amounts traded. In sum, logistical hurdles can be overcome. Establishing the European Union's common currency was, after all, a far more difficult technical exercise, yet was accomplished with few problems because there was sufficient political will at the time, and it is encouraging that in 2013, the EU appeared to be making progress to implementing a nominal financial transactions tax.

However, aside from the EU and minimal progress in discussing a tax within the G20 (sabotaged by Washington), the only substantive step in this direction, has been the renewed interest in capital controls, especially because of the hot money financial portfolio flows that have been moving into emerging markets since 2009. Thanks largely to Keynes (arguing in 1944 against the American negotiating team at Bretton Woods), the IMF Articles of Agreement still allow member countries to 'exercise such controls as are necessary to regulate international capital movements' (Henderson, 1996)

As recently as 1990, 35 countries retained capital controls. But from the early 1990s, the US Treasury Department led a formidable attack on this provision, and not only forced South Korea's financial doors open as a condition for it joining the rich nations club known as the OECD, but even attempted to change the IMF Articles of Agreement to ensure that all member states agreed to full financial liberalization. After the 1997–98 Asian crisis, this became more difficult, but the leading financial system, in the US, proceeded throughout the late 1990s and 2000s – under both Clinton and Bush administration rule – to deregulate to the point that a burst financial bubble in one market (low-income housing) could spread like wildfire to the rest of the system, as happened in 2007–08. As a result especially of hot money flows in late 2010, a new round of capital controls was initiated, mainly to keep footloose portfolio finance out rather than lock in existing finance. These included new actions against speculative inflows by governments in Brazil, Thailand, Taiwan, China, South Korea and Indonesia. To illustrate, Thailand placed a 15 percent tax on short-term inflows into its bond market, South Korea and Taiwan limited assets accessible to foreign capital, and the 50-member UN Economic and Social Commission for Asia and the Pacific endorsed capital controls just prior to the 2010 G20 meeting in Seoul.

Still, intent on foiling a global, regional or national-scale restructuring of the international financial architecture, the US government continued to disapprove of these controls. As a result, a group of reform economists (including Stiglitz, Dani Rodrik and James Galbraith) wrote an open letter in November 2010 arguing that: 'Authoritative research recently published by the National Bureau of Economic Research, the IMF and elsewhere has found that limits on the inflow of short-term capital into developing nations can stem the development of dangerous asset bubbles and currency appreciations and generally grant nations more autonomy in monetary policy-making.' The economists warned, under the banner of Third World Resurgence (2011), however, that:

> many US free trade agreements and bilateral investment treaties contain provisions that strictly limit the ability of our trading partners to deploy capital controls. The 'capital transfers' provisions of such agreements require governments to permit all transfers relating to a covered investment to be made 'freely and without delay into and out of its territory'. Under these agreements, private foreign investors have the power to effectively sue governments in international tribunals over alleged violations of these provisions.

The vital need to control both incoming and outgoing capital is especially obvious when it comes to broader-based economic democracy. In his book *Capitalism's Achilles Heel*, Raymond Baker (2005) documents 'falsified pricing, haven and secrecy structures and the illicit movement of trillions of dollars out of developing and transitional economies [. . .] Laundered proceeds of drug trafficking, racketeering, corruption and terrorism tag along with other forms of dirty money to which the US and Europe extend a welcoming hand'. Adds John Christensen of the Tax Justice Network, nearly one third of the value of the annual production in sub-Saharan Africa was taken offshore during the late 1990s. Across the world, eight million 'high net-worth individuals' have insulated $11.5 trillion in assets in offshore-financial centers (Campbell, 2005).

In sum, extreme levels of financial turmoil and capital flight highlight the extent to which exchange control liberalization had occurred in the Third World. Ironically, IMF researchers – including the then chief economist, Kenneth Rogoff – finally admitted in 2003 that there was severe damage done through more than two decades of financial liberalization. Rogoff and his colleagues (Prasad et al. 2003) admitted 'sobering' findings, namely 'evidence that some countries may have experienced greater consumption volatility as a result [. . .] Recent crises in some more financially integrated countries suggest that financial integration may in fact have increased volatility.' These conclusions are also conceded by the World Bank, which promoted financial liberalization with a vengeance during the 1980s–90s (World Bank, 2005, pp. 32–3).

Aside from capital controls, the final mode of national protection against the failure of the international financial architecture is unilateral debt restructuring, including default. Prior to 2001 when Latin Americans became more active, the most important sovereign defaults were Russia's in August 1998, Brazil's of 1987 and South Africa's of 1985. A few small countries with rogue regimes or completely bare treasuries also fall into regular default, including Zimbabwe. Others like Nigeria occasionally suffer poor foreign exchange management and miss payments, notwithstanding large oil-related inflows. To deal with these rare cases, which were largely a function of emergency inability to pay, UNCTAD suggested extending to the international scale some form of national bankruptcy procedure (along the lines of the US Bankruptcy Code Chapters 9 and 11).[5]

These national strategies are most crucial, notwithstanding the need, ultimately, for global financial regulations. Keynes (1980, p. 149) argued from the bottom up in his attempt to reconstruct an international financial architecture using national capital controls in the post-war era. The most important change in IMF thinking in the wake of ongoing systemic crises appears to be its endorsement of inward-oriented exchange controls, although as noted from the Malaysian experience, it is just as vital to regulate outward flows, a step the IMF appears unwilling to take even in 2014 when so much evidence has accumulated about world financial volatility.

CONCLUSION

To conclude, the ways that we analyze the deep-seated contradictions in the world economy, and the ways we understand the prospects for ongoing inter-imperial rivalry amongst leading countries, should help inform us about the scale politics most appropriate for advocacy. Although fully respecting D'Arista's contribution to the debates, the bulk of this chapter attempted to locate the financial crisis in underlying tendencies towards the overaccumulation of capital, which are displaced through time and space via financial markets. In contrast, D'Arista and Griffith-Jones (2010, p. 1) argued that the 2008–09 crisis is the result, simply, of 'inherent flaws in the way financial markets operate – such as their tendency to boom–bust behaviour and insufficient, incomplete and sometimes inappropriate regulation'.

Given that minimalist approach, the most basic solutions are thus to be found in both regulatory fiddling – 'varying regulatory requirements for reserves, loan to asset value ratios, capital, provisioning against losses, etc. according to the phase of the economic cycle' – and improved institutional strategies, of the sort discussed in these last pages. As to why the present world ruling elite is unable to remodel the architecture so that these regulatory changes and institutions can fit the needs of the times, D'Arista concludes by criticizing the monetarist, neoliberal ideology that guides them:

> Their current focus on stimulus programmes and financial regulation suggests that the G20 may attempt to solve the crisis without addressing the monetary aspect that is exacerbating the problem. If so, one must hope that other governmental and non-governmental groups will exert pressure to take up the discussion at a level that can realise the needed reforms. (D'Arista, 2009b, p. 251)

The contrasting argument I have tried to undergird with (Marxian) insights – into the core contradictions of capitalism and their manifestations in financial crisis symptoms (in the first half of this chapter) – leads to a different approach. Instead of expecting world elites to understand D'Arista's contributions and to manage financial reform accordingly, it is worth recalling the *realpolitiks* of global malgovernance. Not since the 1987 Montreal Protocol aimed at slowing the ozone hole's growth has global governance been able to properly solve global-scale problems with a global state solution (the ban on CFCs in that case). What we should learn from the ongoing failure of global financial governance is not just how a durable ideology and shortsightedness foil reform aimed at weakening financial capital's enormous powers. For as everyone now recognizes, 'even the most practical man of affairs is usually in the thrall of the ideas of some long-dead economist' (Ferguson, 2009).

The deeper lesson I propose is that during a capitalist crisis with financiers still retaining hegemony, still receiving bailouts at will and still defining global-scale policy-making, the scale of analysis required for reforms of the far-reaching nature D'Arista proposes, is not world-scale or even intra-G20, but instead national. This, perhaps, is where she may ultimately agree, cognizant of the lack of progress made in even modest international reforms. D'Arista and Ertürk (2010, p. 6) argued along similar lines, that 'new policies are needed that will pursue the following three objectives: one, the reassertion of public control over the credit-creation process; two, being prepared in case the dollar tanks; and, three, ensuring the resumption of the recycling of trade surpluses before contraction begins to destroy them'. The last of these three suggestions appears impossible given pro-cyclical and residual speculative processes in global financial and monetary mismanagement, but if the dollar crashes and if rising demands for reflation in Southern Europe, the Third World and even the US are impossible to ignore, it will be exceptionally important for D'Arista's insights on national economic policies – especially, macroeconomic and financial-regulatory – to be more widely communicated.

As a result, it makes more sense to identify nationally based sociopolitical movements – of which Occupy was briefly both most important for changing the ideological conversation and most relevant to Wall Street and Treasury/Fed reformers in D'Arista's position – which might push harder for capital controls on both inwards and outward flows. (From where I write, South Africa, this role is played by the National Union of Metalworkers of South Africa, whereas in the US, the most vocal economists promoting capital controls have been those associated with the Triplecrisis blog).[6] As argued above, this strategy is a prerequisite for what ultimately might need to be an updated Keynes-style international clearing agency. Until that stage, when capitalism has been replaced as the world's main mode of production by a more rational system, we can only hope that some state elites will heed the advice Jane D'Arista can so eloquently provide about how to save the system from its most visible contradictions.

NOTES

1. According to Caufield (1997, p. 47): 'Keynes had argued so bitterly at Savannah with US Treasury Secretary Fred Vinson and was so distressed by the course on which the Bank seemed to be set that his friends blamed the meeting for the heart attack he suffered on the train back to Washington, and for a second, a month later, which killed him at the age of 63.'
2. The notion of overaccumulation comes from Marx's *Das Kapital* and refers to a situation in which excessive investment has occurred and hence goods cannot be brought to market profitably, leaving capital to pile up in sectoral bottlenecks or speculative outlets without being put back into new productive investment. Other symptoms include unused plant and equipment; huge gluts of unsold commodities; an unusually large number of unemployed workers; and the inordinate rise of financial markets.
3. In addition to the Bank for International Settlements (BIS) in Basel and each country's central bank and finance ministry, there is a dizzying array of institutions involved in the international architecture, as it now stands:

   - intergovernmental fora representing the leading economic powers (especially the G7 finance ministers and G8 heads of state, and their expansion into the G20 group of major economies),
   - international financial institutions charged with the surveillance of different aspects of domestic and international financial systems (IMF, World Bank, OECD),
   - sector-specific international groupings of regulators and supervisors,
   - committees of central bank experts concerned with market infrastructure and functioning, and
   - a cross-sectoral international grouping – the Financial Stability Forum – in which national authorities, international financial institutions, sector-specific international groupings of regulators and supervisors as well as the committees of central bank experts are represented.

4. Keynes continued by setting out six 'essential general principles':

   (i) All remittances must be canalised through central banks and the resulting balances cleared by them through the International Clearing Bank.
   (ii) No remittances in respect of the outstanding capital of existing or future assets owned by nonresidents shall be made except under licence of both the central banks concerned.
   (iii) The ownership of such assets may be freely shifted between non-residents, and non-residents may exchange one investment for another within a country.
   (iv) The net current income of such assets may be freely remitted together with an annual amortisation of capital not exceeding (say) 5 percent.
   (v) The offer of investments or assets to non-residents to be newly acquired by them shall require the approval of both the central banks concerned.
   (vi) Floating and liquid funds, apart from those required to finance current trade through bills and acceptances and in connection with current banking business approved by the central bank concerned (much as in this country under present conditions) shall only be lent and borrowed between central banks.

5. UNCTAD (1998) proposed the establishment of an independent panel to determine when a country under attack by speculators can be permitted to impose exchange or capital controls (including debt standstills), consistent with the IMF's article VIII, section 2(b).
6. See especially the posts by Kevin Gallagher at http://triplecrisis.com/tag/capital-controls.

REFERENCES

Akyüz, Y. (1995), 'Taming international finance', in J. Michie and J.G. Smith (eds), *Managing the Global Economy*, Oxford: Oxford University Press.

Akyüz, Y. (2010), 'South Centre paper argues that the G20 agenda misses some of the key issues for reform of the international monetary system', Geneva, South Centre, http://www.southcentre.org/index.php?option=com_content&view=article&id=1407:sb51&catid=144:south-bulletin-individual-articles&Itemid=287&lang=fr.

Baker, R. (2005), *Capitalism's Achilles Heel*, London: Wiley.

Barr, C. (2010), 'Goldman says Fed faces $4 trillion hole', CNN Money, 25 October, http://finance.fortune.cnn.com/2010/10/25/goldman-says-fed-faces-4-trillion-hole/.

BIS (1990), 'The Lamfalussy Report: Report of the Committee on Interbank Netting Schemes of the Central Banks of the Group of Ten Countries', Basle, Bank for International Settlements.

Blanchard, O., J. Caruana and R. Moghadam (2009), 'Initial lessons of the crisis', Research, Monetary and Capital Markets, and Strategy, Policy, and Review Departments, International Monetary Fund, Washington, http://www.imf.org/external/np/pp/eng/2009/020609.pdf.

Bottari, M. (2011), 'Full catastrophe banking in 2011', Bankster, http://www.banksterusa.org/content/full-catastrophe-banking-2011.

Campbell, D. (2005), 'Where they hide the cash', *Guardian*, 5 December.

Caufield, C. (1997), *Masters of Illusion: The World Bank and the Poverty of Nations*, London: Macmillan.

D'Arista, J. (2000), 'Reforming the privatized international monetary and financial architecture', *Challenge*, **43**(3), 44–82.

D'Arista, J. (2009a), 'Statement of Jane D'Arista representing Americans for financial reform', US House of Representatives Committee on Financial Services Hearting on Systemic Regulation, Washington, DC, 29 October, pp. 6–7.

D'Arista, J. (2009b), 'The evolving international monetary system', *Cambridge Journal of Economics*, **33**, 633–52.

D'Arista, J. and K. Ertürk (2010), 'The monetary explanation of the crisis and the ongoing threat to the global economy', *Challenge*, March–April, http://www.challengemagazine.com/extra/005_029.pdf.

D'Arista, J. and S. Griffith-Jones (2010), 'Agenda and criteria for financial regulatory reform', Forum on Debt and Development, Amsterdam, http://www.fondad.org/uploaded/D%20Arista%20-%20Griffith-Jones/DArista-Griffith-Jones%20on%20Financial%20regulatory%20reform.pdf.

Davidson, P. (1997), 'Are grains of sand in the wheels of international finance sufficient to do the job when boulders are often required?', *The Economic Journal*, **107**.

Duménil, G. and D. Lévy, (2004), *Capital Resurgent: Roots of the Neoliberal Revolution*, Cambridge, MA: Harvard University Press.

Eatwell, J. and L. Taylor (1998), 'International capital markets and the future of economic policy', CEPA Working Paper Series III, Working Paper 9, New School for Social Research, New York, September.
Eichengreen, B. and K. O'Rourke (2009), 'A tale of two depressions', Vox-EU, http://www.voxeu.org/index.php?q=node/3421.
Eichengreen, B., J. Tobin and C. Wyplosz (1995), 'Two cases for sand in the wheels of international finance', *Economic Journal*, **105**.
Felix, D. (1995), 'Financial globalization vs. free trade: the case for the Tobin Tax', Geneva, United Nations Conference on Trade and Development Discussion Paper 108.
Ferguson, N. (2009), 'History lesson for economists in thrall to Keynes', *The Financial Times*, http://www.ft.com/intl/cms/s/0/a635d12c-4c7c-11de-a6c5–00144feabdc0.html.
Galbraith, J. (2009), 'Who are these economists, anyway?', *Thought and Action*, **85**, Fall.
Garber, P. (1998), 'Derivatives in international capital flow', National Bureau of Economic Research Working Paper No. 6623, New York.
Garber, P. and M. Taylor (1995), 'Sand in the wheels of foreign exchange markets: a sceptical note', *The Economic Journal*, **105**.
Harvey, D. (1982), *The Limits to Capital*, Chicago: University of Chicago Press.
Henderson, H. (1996), *Building a Win-Win World*, San Francisco: Berrett-Koehler.
IMF (2009), 'Final Report', International Monetary Fund Committee on Governance Reform, March, Washington DC: IMF, http://www.imf.org/external/np/omd/2009/govref/032409.pdf.
Keynes, J.M. (1933), 'National self-sufficiency', *Yale Review*, **22**(4), 755–69.
Keynes, J.M. (1980), *The Collected Writings of John Maynard Keynes, Vol. XXV, Activities 1940–44: Shaping the Post-War World: The Clearing Union*, London and Cambridge: Macmillan and Cambridge University Press.
Krugman, P. (2009), 'How did economists get it so wrong?', *New York Times Magazine*, 6 September.
Mundell, R. (2000), 'A reconsideration of the twentieth century', *American Economic Review*, **90**(3), 327–40.
Sanders, B. (2010), 'A real jaw dropper at the Fed', 3 December, Huffington Post, http://www.huffingtonpost.com/rep-bernie-sanders/a-real-jaw-dropper-at-the_b_791091.html.
Soros, G. (1997), 'Avoiding a breakdown', *Financial Times*, 31 December.
Stiglitz, J. (2008), 'Reversal of fortune', The Atlantic Monthly, October, http://www.vanityfair.com/politics/features/2008/11/stiglitz200811.
Suter, C. (1992), *Debt Cycles in the World Economy*, Boulder, CO: Westview Press.
Third World Resurgence (2011), 'Leading economists urge US to allow use of capital controls', *Third World Resurgence*, 245–6, January/February, 27, http://www.twnside.org.sg/title2/resurgence/2011/245–246/cover06.htm.
Tobin, J. (1978), 'A proposal for international monetary reform', *The Eastern Economic Journal*, **4**, July/October.
United Nations (2009) 'Final Report', Commission of Experts of the President of the UN General Assembly on Reforms of the International Monetary and Financial System, New York, http://www.un.org/ga/econcrisissummit/docs/FinalReport_CoE.pdf.
UNCTAD (1998), *Trade and Development Report*, Geneva: United Nations Conference on Trade and Development.

UNCTAD (2010), 'The global economic crisis', Geneva, United Nations Conference on Trade and Development, http://www.unctad.org/en/docs/gds20091_en.pdf.
Wallerstein, I. (2011), 'End of the recession? Who's kidding whom?', Braudel Centre Commentary 296, http://www2.binghamton.edu/fbc/archive/296en.htm.
World Bank (2005), 'Meeting the challenge of Africa's development: a World Bank Group action plan', Africa Region, Washington, DC, 7 September.

PART V

Theoretical Considerations

13. Liquidity, leverage, and financial instability

Lance Taylor[1]

INTRODUCTION

The financial events beginning in 2007–08 underlined points that Jane D'Arista has always emphasized – that the behavior of the financial system is strongly influenced by its structure, that the structure can change in unexpected ways, and that the nature of regulation has a big effect on the direction and stability or instability of the changes.

Such ideas are pursued herein, drawing on historical experience in the industrialized countries and more or less contemporary shifts in the developing economies. Emphasis is placed on the expanding role of liquidity as the nature of finance has evolved over time and space. More liquidity has historically been associated with greater leverage, and this linkage was a key factor underlying the crisis in the industrialized world. Its destabilizing effects were exacerbated by the pro-cyclical character of contemporary approaches to financial regulation. Possible remedies are suggested at the end of the chapter.

There is no strict progression of financial development, and initial conditions matter. But, broadly speaking, new financial structures can be seen as emerging in a sequence of stages. It is instructive to trace through five of them (with an acknowledgement of a sixth of uncertain chronology for developing countries at least), and consider how each particular structure constrains macroeconomic policy maneuver. Table 13.1 provides the accounting details.

NATIONAL FINANCIAL ACCOUNTS

The underlying concepts are a blend of flows of funds accounting principles and more traditional approaches. The main distinction lies in the treatment of "equity" or "net worth." When consolidated economy-wide, the net worth of the business sector has to be the value of its assets less

Table 13.1 Illustrative balance sheets ("T-accounts")

Private	Banks	Finance
$P_K K$ L_P	L H	$P_V V_F$ L_F
H_P eL_P^*	B_B QS	QS_F eL_F^*
B_P $P_V V$	eR^*	Z Z
$P_C C$ M	M_B	Ω_F
Ω_F Ω_P		
Government	**Rest of the World**	
Γ B	eL eR	
eL_G^*	$P_V V^*$ $e\Omega^*$	
	B^*	

Total wealth: $P_K K + P_C C + \Gamma = \Omega_P + e\Omega_R^*$
Net foreign assets: $-e\Omega_R^* = e(R^* - L_P^* - L_G^* - P_V V^* - B^*)$
Bank loan balance: $L_P + L_F - L = 0$
Government bond balance: $B_P + B_B + B^* - B = 0$
Foreign loan balance: $e(L_P^* + L_G^*) - eL = 0$
Equity balance: $P_V(V_F + V^*) - P_V V = 0$

liabilities. According to the flows of funds, the liabilities include debt *plus* the market value of the sector's outstanding shares. The conventional alternative is to *define* equity as the value of assets minus debt. In the late 1990s US during the stock market boom, business net worth was negative by the former definition and equal to zero by the latter (as it always is). Net worth according to the US flows of funds was positive as of mid 2008.

Table 13.1 defines five types of agents or sectors: private non-financial actors, the government, the consolidated banking system, a non-bank financial sector, and the rest of the world.[2] The entries represent values of *stocks* of financial claims. They change in two ways. One is through *flow* accumulation or decumulation over time of the stocks in response to net lending or borrowing by different actors. The other mechanism applies to outstanding shares and foreign loans, which have explicit asset prices (a price index for equity and the exchange rate respectively), so their values can jump "instantaneously" due to capital gains or losses.

STAGE I FINANCE

The simplest financial structure, Stage I, still applies to a significant number of developing countries today. Normally (one historically significant sort of "abnormality" is considered below), the only private assets are the value of tangible capital $P_K K$ with K as the existing stock at historical or replacement cost and P_K as its asset price. "Money" (broadly construed) H is the sole liability of the banking system.[3] There is no significant market in bonds, so private holdings of government securities (B_P) are negligible. On the liability side, private business may borrow L_P from the banks but loans from abroad eL_P^* and the value of equity outstanding $P_V V$ are negligible or effectively non-traded.

The system's assets are loans L (at this stage only L_P to the private sector), bonds B_B which the government has in one way or another placed with the banks, and international reserves of the central bank eR^*, with R^* as the value of reserves in foreign currency and e as the exchange rate (units of local currency per unit of foreign currency). Bank assets add up to determine the money supply H. The government's total borrowing, which at this stage is only from the banking system, is $B = B_B$. The corresponding asset is the "full faith and credit" of the state, Γ.

Liquidity is often interpreted as a measure of the financial flexibility of an individual actor, group of actors, or the financial system as whole. It constitutes "wherewithal" – the resources readily available for purposes of capital formation or financial transactions. For the private sector in Stage I, liquidity takes the form of one asset, namely money. Nothing else is at hand.[4]

The accounting framework just sketched puts strict limitations on policy options. First, it is the preferred arena for the International Monetary Fund's (IMF) venerable version of open economy monetarism. Suppose that money demand is described by the equation of exchange $HV = PX$ with P as the price level, X as output, and V as an institutionally determined "velocity" of circulation of money, which in the most simple frameworks is assumed to be constant. If X is set by "full employment" and P comes from an inflation forecast or target, then money demand must follow.

If loans L_P to the private sector are set by needs of production, the sum of bank loans to the government and international reserves is determined from the consolidated banking system's balance sheet: $B_B + eR^* = H - L_P$. If reserves are targeted to increase as the current account improves, then government debt B_B must fall via a larger fiscal surplus. This is the basis of the "twin" fiscal/foreign deficits, which have been at the heart of IMF financial programming for more than half a century.

Along with twin deficit hawks worldwide, the IMF implicitly assumes that causality runs from the fiscal to foreign deficit, but it can easily go the other way as appeared to be the case in Russia and the Middle East when oil prices shot up post-2000. Furthermore, these particular twins are not frequently observed in the data. Parallel movements of external financing and private net borrowing flows are a more frequent phenomenon (Rada von Arnim and Taylor, 2008).

Secondly, Stage I accounts support the basic closed economy monetarist inflation model, set out by the Swedish economist Knut Wicksell in the late 19th century and propagandized worldwide by Milton Friedman and disciples as recently as the 1970s and 1980s. The logic is that a higher fiscal deficit gets "monetized" (because the government cannot easily place debt obligations except with the banks). The resulting increase in H forces P to go up, as determined by the equation of exchange written in the form $P = HV/X$.

Because liquidity in many economies now comprises a spectrum of financial assets and liabilities far wider than simple money, financial programming and monetarist inflation models are anachronistic. Inflation in Zimbabwe, which took off in the mid 2000s, can be interpreted along monetarist lines (including money creation mostly in the form of cash) but this is not a common phenomenon today.

Finally, it is worth noting that even in simple Stage I finance (and certainly in the more complicated systems discussed below), financial manias can appear in "abnormal" circumstances. Unfortunately, such situations have arisen pretty regularly for the last 400 years.[5]

One familiar scenario is based on government assets $P_G G$ (with an asset price P_G), which have been privatized and sold through a dealer to the public.[6] If the dealer happens to have a captive bank at his disposal, he can lend money to himself and cronies to bid up the share place leading to a capital gain (or ongoing inflation) at rate π: the asset price rises to $(1 + \pi)P_G$. Other actors may then start borrowing from the captive and other banks to try to buy shares, setting off a boom that ends inevitably in a crash.

Premier examples were the Mississippi and South Sea crises early in the 18th century, in which John Law's Banque Générale in Paris and the Swordblade Bank in London issued the loans. With international complications discussed below, the Chilean crisis of 1982–83 followed the same pattern around companies privatized by Pinochet's Chicago Boys. These examples illustrate a recurring theme in financial instability. Capital gains are financed by liquidity in the form of *liabilities* assumed by financial actors to buy the appreciating assets. Manifold possibilities along these lines exist in more complicated financial systems.

STAGE II FINANCE

Assuming that a financial mania is not underway, the key element in Stage II is a domestic market in (at least short term) government debt. It may have been created by careful husbandry on the part of the central bank. The banking system and the public now have fairly substantial holdings of government bonds (B_B and B_p, respectively). In outline form, Keynes in the 1930s thought in terms of this sort of financial system, with the significant extension of having markets in corporate debt instruments as well.

Primary liquidity in Stage II is still money. Keynesian ideas about liquidity preference come into play, with the interest rate mediating portfolio choices between more liquid money and less liquid bonds (with government bonds being more liquid than corporates, which are subject to interest rate spreads associated with both liquidity and solvency risks). As far as the private sector is concerned, the liquidity spectrum still spans a collection of assets, with specific holdings responding to returns and costs.

If a corporate bond market exists, it can be of significant support to capital formation. But even without one, Stage II governments can issue bonds to fund national development banks specialized in production-oriented loans. Such institutions have been very important in developing countries; they played a significant post-war reconstruction role in advanced economies as well.

Finally, Keynes analyzed financial instability in terms of sharp shifts in liquidity preference. Mixed with overborrowing (high leverage), they provide the foundation for Minsky's "financial instability hypothesis" (Minsky, 1975). Although Keynes was certainly aware of possibilities for financial instability involving asset bubbles, they do not figure prominently in either the *Treatise on Money* or the *General Theory*. Certainly post-1929 he was analyzing a period in which use of liabilities as liquidity to acquire assets (allegedly) subject to capital gains was not an immediate threat.

STAGE III FINANCE

In Stage III, foreign financial capital comes into play. The economy gets access to *hard currency* foreign loans (eL_p^* to the private sector and e L_G to the government, expressed in *domestic* prices). Many countries and regions have gone through such a transition – Austria and Germany around 1930 when bank deposits from foreigners were used to acquire domestic assets leading into the Credit-Anstalt crash, Western Europe when capital markets were liberalized in the 1970s, and emerging markets subsequently.

External liabilities now become a form of liquidity, which can be used to acquire assets at home. Local actors such as the government may or may not be able to issue liabilities aboard denominated in domestic currency (such as government borrowing B^* in Table 13.1). If they cannot, the limitation is quaintly called "original sin" in the academic literature. But Stage III sinners in good standing with their creditors are welcome to borrow in foreign currency terms.

Of course that favorable situation may or may not last. The presence of foreign liabilities in portfolios immediately exposes their holders to exchange risk due to currency misalignment or mismatch. If their assets and expected net revenues are denominated in domestic currency but their liabilities are denominated in foreign currency, then an increase in the exchange rate e generates both capital and income losses. The higher rate cuts directly into net worth and jacks up the cost of debt service. The threat to balance sheets is greater if (as has often been the case) there is a maturity mismatch involving short-term foreign liabilities and long-term domestic assets.

These dangers are especially grave for actors such as firms producing non-traded goods and the government itself insofar as their main sources of income are set in local currency. Although some assets of exporters (for example, the real estate that they own and their deposits in the domestic financial system) may be denominated in local currency and be subject to the same problems, they could be more than offset by the larger domestic value of their current and expected net income in foreign currency.

Money and credit expansion due to reserve increases during phases of booming capital inflows has become a persistent problem in emerging market economies.[7] If there is a market in domestic bonds, the central bank can in principle sterilize the reserve increases by selling part of its stock B_B in exchange for money in an open market operation, although at the risk of driving up interest rates which may then bring in still more foreign capital.

Two other options for sterilization exist: reducing the public sector debt by running a budget surplus, or accumulating the domestic money generated by the additional international reserves as deposit reserves of commercial banks. These options are the only ones available if there is no well-developed domestic debt market (that is, we are closer to Stage I in terms of domestic financing). But a long sequence of currency crises shows that such interventions may be of limited effectiveness.

STAGE IV FINANCE

Use of liabilities as a source of liquidity expands greatly in Stage IV. A local market for equity issued by the private sector can provide the trampoline. Historically, the emergence of significant stock markets dates from the 1990s in many developing countries (with privatization of state enterprises often providing the impetus) and is fairly recent even in non-Anglo Saxon industrialized economies.

In Table 13.1, the value of private sector shares outstanding is $P_V V$ with P_V as a price index and V a measure of outstanding volume.[8] In a wonderful 17th century Dutch word, a Stage IV economy can enter into *windhandel* or "wind trade" based on the use of liabilities (and derivatives built around them) as sources of liquidity. This possibility is reflected in the table's "finance" sector which holds shares $P_V V_F$ financed by borrowing from banks and abroad (ignore the QS_F term from the moment). The sector's equity or net worth is Ω_F, held by the private sector as an asset.

Within the financial sector, there are offsetting asset and liability entries Z. Individual financial actors such as broker-dealers, Fannie Mae and Freddie Mac (in the US at least), and hedge funds can borrow from one another but for their "leveraged" subsystem as a whole many of these transactions will be mutually offsetting.[9] By increasing transactions such as Z, financial institutions can add to cash flow as they build up asset/equity or leverage ratios $\lambda_F = \frac{P_V V_F + Z}{\Omega_F}$. The liabilities $L_F + Z + eL_F^*$ underlying total assets $P_V V_F + Z$ can support imposing structures of leverage and liquidity.[10]

So long as P_V continues to rise, for example, then growing intra-financial sector claims make it possible to mobilize large sums of money to buy stock. Of course P_V can also fall, precipitating a collapse. As discussed in more detail below, "appetite for risk" during a boom becomes "flight to quality" in a crash marked by "deleveraging" or a contraction of liquidity in the form of liabilities and a retreat to assets such as government bonds and even money. Pro-cyclical regulatory rules can easily make the situation worse.

The financial sector can also be dependent on the rest of the world. If local operators borrow heavily from abroad (eL_F^* in Table 13.1) and invest at home ample possibilities arise for currency and maturity misalignments in national balance sheets of the sort that led to the succession of emerging market financial crises in the 1990s. The common pattern was for the domestic financial system to run up short-term foreign currency liabilities to acquire long-term assets valued in domestic currency with a (more or less) fixed exchange rate. An ultimate devaluation obliterated these positions.

Diversified finance as in Stage IV also creates opportunities. Somewhat surprisingly, firms in rapidly growing developing economies have relied on selling new shares for a significant portion of their investment finance (Singh, 1995; Staritz, 2008), certainly not the practice in many advanced economies where share buybacks predominate.

Active stock markets also allow entrepreneurs to cash in on their innovations via initial public offerings (IPOs) of shares, a significant incentive for technological advance.

STAGE V FINANCE

Stage V finance – not yet significant in most developing economies – adds the contemporary twist of asset securitization. In just one of many possible examples, suppose that besides productive capital the private sector holds a tangible asset C with price P_C (the obvious example is residential housing). It borrows M_P (for "mortgages") from banks, using $P_C C$ as collateral. The banks in turn bundle the mortgages into a security S with price Q, which is sold to financial actors. Such maneuvers make it possible to borrow large sums of money and pump up leverage by increasing claims on the non-financial sector.

But there are also problems. How to evaluate collateral for securitized loans is one of them. Aside from ample opportunities for fraud, one key point in recent US experience is that the housing collateral for "subprime" mortgages was itself subject to capital gains and losses, and that the ability of the borrowers to be able to meet their payment obligations was open to question (without, needless to say, any prior provision being made on the part of the lenders during the upswing for the loan losses they are likely to incur during the succeeding downswing).[11] In practice a capital gain on the primary asset (housing) led directly to a jump in the asset price Q which stimulated balance sheet expansion.

Secondly, complex securities were rarely marketed, and were given a hypothetical "marked-to-market" valuation Q based on mathematical models duly ratified by the ratings agencies. It was a wonderful source of liquidity until the bottom fell out of the subprime market. Then a crisis hit, with deleveraging and shrinkage of liquidity from liability to asset form.

As of 2012, the industrialized economies are still sorting out the consequences of deleveraging Stage V. Public regulation of both bank and non-bank financial operations can help reduce the likelihood of booms and crashes. Safety nets can be constructed. However, when liquidity takes the form of liabilities which can be used to pay for profit-seeking in financial markets (not to mention fees for the people who "guide" investors), sources of potential volatility will always appear, even in constricted early stage financial systems.

FINANCIAL REGULATION

The crisis was exacerbated – very much along D'Arista's critical line – by contemporary approaches to regulation such as the internationally accepted Basel I and II. They focused on commercial bank capital Ω_{comm}, held as an asset by the private sector. Even post-crisis, the Basel methodology sets targets for how much capital financial firms must hold as backing for assets.[12] Basically, when a bank gets into trouble it has to reduce its leverage (or ratio of assets to capital) by disposing of assets or building up equity. Cutting shareholder dividends and/or selling new stock are the usual mechanisms for the latter. Examples were rife in the rich economies after 2007–08.

Basel II rested on three "pillars," with the first being that a bank should maintain capital levels adequate to guarantee that if there is an adverse shock to its assets there will be only a small probability of a loss greater than a given target. The "assets" in question could be the market-to-market value of the bank's holdings over a given time horizon. Pillar One emphasized that such calculations should be based on the bank's internal risk weighting models as influenced by information provided by the ratings agencies.

We have already noted some of the difficulties implicit in the use of complicated mathematical models of asset valuation. An additional consideration is that going into the crisis all financial institutions were using models based on the same theory (the basics involving comparisons of returns and risks described by hypothetically *known* probability distributions go back to Markowitz, 1952) and estimated using the same historical data. There was already a lot of homogeneity built into their market perceptions. Worse still, the models presupposed that financial actors can always trade at stable "market-determined" prices. This assumption fails if all the players are thinking more or less the same thing about markets and then change their minds in the same direction – not everybody can attempt to buy or sell at the same time without causing prices to move!

Such herd behavior was exacerbated by Basel Pillar Three calling for market discipline enforced by greater disclosure of banks' financial status and their internal risk management procedures. Market discipline and an emphasis on internal risk management were not the most effective means to confront *systemic* risk – an externality not encompassed by internal procedures and not accounted for by the market. Supervision, the second Pillar, could not deal directly with systemic risk, either.

The major financial actors generally operated on the basis of "value at risk" or V as estimated by their models. Value at risk is linked to the equity capital Ω that the firm must hold to stay solvent with high probability (Adrian and Shin, 2007). Firms presumably adjust their balance sheets to target a ratio of economic capital to V, say

$$\Omega = \theta V.$$

Their leverage then becomes

$$\lambda = \frac{A}{\Omega} = \left(\frac{1}{\theta}\right)\left(\frac{A}{V}\right). \tag{13.1}$$

These are all *static* relationships, supported by models with probability distributions on V estimated from existing data at a point in time. The dangers they create result from their impacts on the *dynamic* behavior of financial firms.

The heart of the matter is that leverage responds *inversely* to asset price increases. In highly simplified form, a firm's balance sheet can be written as

$$A = D + \Omega$$

with A as assets and D as debt.

Suppose that there is a capital gain on a firm's assets. If debt stays constant for the moment, equity Ω will rise by an equal *absolute* amount. Because $\Omega \ll A$ for financial firms, the *proportional* increase in Ω markedly exceeds that in A. Hence leverage or $\lambda = \frac{A}{\Omega}$ goes down sharply. The firm has a strong incentive to increase debt to buy additional assets to build up leverage, engaging in *windhandel* to profit from increased cash flow while still respecting pre-set limits on risk. In the subprime mortgage adventure, firms were typically borrowing short-term to acquire long-term assets in anticipation of capital gains – back to the Mississippi and South Sea Companies of 400 years ago!

So what happens if asset prices go down? Leverage jumps up, and from equation (13.1) above, $\frac{V}{A}$ increases for a given θ. With greater value at risk relative to assets, Basel rules obligate the firm to reduce leverage by disposing of assets or building up equity. If firms are largely similar and react in much the same way to an adverse shock, the resulting fire sale of assets can lead to dramatic price reductions and a liquidity conflagration as in 2007–08.

BETTER REGULATION

So how could the financial system be run more effectively, in particular for developing countries? A combination of capital controls, prudential regulations affecting cross-border flows, and long-term state-backed funds could be appropriate.

As emphasized above, one area of concern is foreign currency borrowing by non-financial firms (or such borrowing by financial firms to acquire liabilities issued in domestic currency by firms producing non-traded goods). Various restrictions can be imagined but perhaps the simplest is prohibiting foreign borrowing by non-financial firms without foreign currency revenues (on-lending to them from financial firms would have to be monitored as well). Complementary price-based penalties on borrowing short-run for purposes not related to capital formation could be constructed.

Non-financial firms highlight the macroeconomic implications of prudential regulation. Traditionally, microeconomic risk management has been directed toward reducing "non-systemic" risk depending on the characteristics of individual borrowers, basically through segmentation and diversification. As we have seen, "systemic" risk can arise when individual financial firms do not internalize collective hazards resulting from economic policy changes or pro-cyclical private sector behavior during the business cycle, particularly during boom periods.

The situation is made worse by the pro-cyclicality of traditional regulatory tools, including Basel standards. To add to the discussion of pro-cyclical leverage above, it is helpful to work through an example involving loan-loss provisions, which tend to be tied to current delinquencies or short-term expectations about them. In an upswing, delinquencies are low and lack of provision can encourage risk-taking. In a crisis, a jump in delinquencies squeezes financial institutions' capital, possibly triggering a credit squeeze as the use of liabilities for liquidity contracts. Needless to say, such problems can be especially severe in developing countries just entering into the wonder worlds of Stage IV and V finance.

Most banks and other financial institutions tend to make provisions for when loans are supposed to come due. The insurance industry, however, makes provisions when a policy is issued. The analog for banks would be to build up provisions when loans are *disbursed* rather than when repayments (or, rather the lack of repayments) are *expected*. This sort of action counters the financial cycle, because it amounts to a pro-cyclical increase in the bank's own funds, or capital.

Under this system, provisions build up during an upswing and can be accumulated in a fund (along with special back-up for non-performing assets or borrowers under stress). The fund can be drawn down in a slump to cover loan losses. This system would be only cycle-neutral, but that is a still a considerable advance over current practices. At present, it appears to have been adopted only in Spain.

More directly counter-cyclical regulation would also be desirable. Objective criteria for intervention could include excessive growth of credit relative to a benchmark, bias in lending toward sectors subject to systemic risk, and (again) growth in foreign currency loans to sectors producing non-traded goods. Indeed, all currency mismatches on balance sheets as well as in expected income and payment flows are hazardous and should be subject to provisions or regulation.

Beyond the desirability of pro-cyclical provisioning, questions of general financial structure are important (Alexander et al., 2008). The 2007–08 crisis has three immediate implications. First, leading into the crisis, there had been increasingly broad acceptance of mark-to-market pricing of assets. If no relevant market happened to be at hand (as was the case for complex instruments such as collateralized debt obligations) then prices had to be constructed using models, with the consequences described above. For institutions in trouble, "regulatory forbearance" in the sense of not imposing mark-to-market in a downswing might have been more appropriate.[13] The drawback is that regulation which pursues counter-cyclical policy in a downswing and does nothing in an upswing does not encourage prudential private sector behavior.

Secondly, diversity in financial markets is stabilizing but often lacking in developing countries. The events of 2007–08 largely took place among risk *traders* who were borrowing short-term to get trading liquidity to sweep in capital gains on long-term assets. The infamous quotation by Chuck Prince, the subsequently ousted chief of Citigroup – "When the music stops, in terms of liquidity, things will be complicated. But as long as the music is playing, you've got to get up and dance. We're still dancing" – brilliantly captured the mood in July 2007.

What was left unsaid is that the financial world is populated not just by traders like Mr. Prince who assume that if they cannot fund their assets they will be able to sell them immediately at prevailing prices, but also by risk *absorbers* such as insurance companies and pension funds. They have long-term liabilities and relatively assured cash flow from premiums and contributions, and can use these resources to spread market and liquidity risks across time. In industrialized countries banks *formerly* played such a role but abandoned it when they turned to asset securitization. To a large extent, insurance companies and pension funds still do it.

Such entities, unfortunately, are not common in developing countries. Promoting institutional change toward a financial Stage VI in which issuers of long-term liabilities can acquire relatively long-term assets to hold to maturity would help stabilize the system. The state would probably have to take the lead. Broadly speaking, there are four classes of government-sponsored asset-holders, which can play a stabilizing role:

1. Central banks use their holdings of government bonds and foreign reserves to (among other tasks) maintain short-term macroeconomic stability.

2. Development banks issue debt, often to the government, to finance long-term physical capital formation.
3. Stabilization funds build up hard currency resources offshore which can be used to support domestic activity should export prices fall. Their track records have in practice been mixed.
4. Sovereign wealth funds may be financed by profits of state-owned enterprises exporting natural resources and/or by high savings flows of domestic residents intermediated via the banking system. As of mid 2008 they held around $3.5 trillion in assets – a non-trivial sum.

Both stabilization and wealth funds can in principle act as risk absorbers, both domestically and at the international level. Insofar as they do not fulfill the former role, taking *very* slow steps in the direction of securitization in developing countries would seem the prudent course to follow.

Finally, if securitization does become important, it will require changes in both central banks and ministries of finance. Central bankers can no longer just act as *lenders* of last resort to institutions in trouble but rather must be *buyers* of last resort willing to purchase assets no longer backed by adequate capital, restructure them, and (ideally) sell them at some appropriate future time. The costs to the treasury could be very high indeed.

Prudential regulation has become much more difficult, and in the best of times it did not always work. It involves discretionary interventions (both quantitative and price based), which may be subject to abuse. Information lacunae are rife and ever changing. But as Jane D'Arista has always emphasized, an unregulated financial system is prone to crisis. It can truly turn into a weapon of mass destruction.

NOTES

1. Research supported by the Centre for Financial Analysis and Policy, Judge Business School, University of Cambridge. Comments by John Eatwell, Tarik Mouakil, José Antonio Ocampo, and Codrina Rada von Arnim are gratefully acknowledged.
2. A natural extension would be to split the private sector into households and business. To simplify the exposition, it is not pursued here. Working with a sector that consolidates the central and commercial banks is traditional in IMF financial programming exercises and much of macroeconomics.
3. As is often the case in macroeconomic modeling, bank equity held as an asset by the private sector is omitted from Table 13.1. It is introduced and discussed in connection with financial regulation.
4. To hold down the number of symbols in the balance sheets, government liabilities to the private sector in the form of coin and currency are omitted from the present discussion. They were key components of the rich countries' financial systems well into the 19th century and remain important in many developing economies today.
5. Kindleberger (2002) is the classic narrative.
6. The "assets" might be claims on hypothetical future revenue streams (the South Sea and

Mississippi cases discussed below) or equity of former state enterprises (the standard case in late 20th century developing country events).

7. If the exchange rate e is constant, foreign assets $e\Omega_R^* = P_V V^* + B^* + e(L^* - R^*)$ can only change gradually over time via a surplus or deficit on current account. Hence a jump in foreign lending L^* must be met by an equal increase in reserves R^* which can stimulate money and credit expansion through the usual channels.
8. For the private non-financial sector, Table 13.1 follows the accounting convention of the flow of funds by treating equity outstanding as a "liability" and allowing non-zero net worth. To illustrate a point made earlier, in flow of funds terms Google has highly negative net worth because its stock market valuation vastly exceeds its tangible capital and financial assets. On a balance sheet set up to follow accountants' conventions, Google like all other corporations would have zero net worth.
9. In available US flows of funds data they do not offset completely – leveraged financial institutions typically have negative *net* positions in fed funds and security repurchase (repo) agreements. *Gross* repo asset and liability positions are not reported.
10. In the US at the end of 2007, leverage for households was around 1.2, for commercial banks it was about 10, and for investment banks it was over 30!
11. In US usage, subprime mortgages are not of sufficient quality to be bought and securitized by the government sponsored enterprises Fannie Mae and Freddie Mac. Their securitization was undertaken by the private financial sector.
12. There is an enormous literature on the Basel standards. Alexander et al. (2008) is a helpful review with a big influence on the following discussion.
13. One famous example involved major US banks at the outset of the Latin American debt crisis. Many were technically bankrupt because the market value of their Latin American assets was close to zero. Regulators turned a blind eye, allowing the banks to carry the assets on their balance sheets at their value at maturity. There was no doubt, however, that the banks would ultimately have to adjust.

REFERENCES

Adrian, Tobias, and Hyun Song Shin (2008) "Liquidity and Leverage," http://www.princeton.edu/~hsshin/www/LiquidityLeverage.pdf.

Alexander, Kern, John Eatwell, Avinash Persaud, and Robert Reoch (2008) *Financial Supervision and Crisis Management in the EU*, Strasbourg, France: European Parliament.

Kindleberger, Charles P. (2002) *Manias, Panics, and Crashes: A History of Financial Crises* (4th edition), New York: John Wiley and Sons.

Markowitz, Harry M. (1952) "Portfolio Selection," *Journal of Finance*, **7**: 77–91.

Minsky, Hyman P. (1975) *John Maynard Keynes*, New York: Columbia University Press.

Rada von Arnim, Codrina, and Lance Taylor (2008) "Growth Rates, Economic Structure, Energy Use, and Sources of Demand," in Philip Arestis and John Eatwell (eds), *Issues in Economic Development and Globalization: Essays in Honour of Ajit Singh*, London: Palgrave Macmillan.

Singh, Ajit (1995) "Corporate Financial Patterns in Industrializing Economies: A Comparative International Study," Washington, DC: International Finance Corporation Technical Paper 2.

Staritz, Cornelia (2008) "Financial Structure, Investment, and Economic Development: A Flow of Funds Analysis for Emerging Countries," Unpublished PhD dissertation, New York: New School for Social Research.

14. The decline of traditional banking and endogenous money

Korkut Ertürk and Gökçer Özgür

INTRODUCTION

As inflation rose in the 1970s monetarist economists argued that it was solely a monetary phenomenon and thus could simply be contained if the central bank curtailed the money supply. Post Keynesian economists challenged this view by correctly arguing that the central bank could not possibly control the money supply the way monetarist economists alleged. While the central bank had considerable discretion in setting the policy interest rate it had next to none over the money supply, which they argued lagged overall bank credit. The loans commercial banks issued to meet the credit demand from businesses returned to the banking system in the form new deposits, a process which the central bank was powerless to check unless it put at risk the very integrity of the payments system. Thus, Post Keynesians argued, the influence of the central bank over the economy rested not on its ability to control the money supply as such but instead in its ability to set interest rates that impacted businesses' willingness to borrow. For some this also meant that interest rates were mainly impervious to market forces. Others thought that the point was overdone, for they recognized that the central bank policy influenced banks' ability and willingness to make loans as well and emphasized the role of financial innovations and market forces in the determination of interest rates.

Both sides, however, took it for granted that the money creation process was based on firms' demand for commercial and industrial loans (that is, traditional banking). But, the trouble is that traditional banking has been on the wane ever since banking deregulation, if not earlier. Whether and to what extent banks' importance in overall credit mechanism decreased can be a little bit of a semantic issue, but what is exceedingly clear is that the share of commercial and industrial loans (traditional banking) in the overall credit supply has drastically declined over the last three decades. While traditional banking contracted, nonbank sources of credit experienced an explosive increase. It is no exaggeration to say that the very landscape of financial intermediation has been totally transformed in the last couple of decades, as credit became increasingly market driven rather than bank driven.

The question is what this means for the money supply process, and whether the traditional conception of money creation Post Keynesian economists take for granted needs to be revisited. Oddly enough, the issue received little attention within the endogenous money tradition which remains stubbornly locked in the long-running debate between the so-called "accommodationists" and "structuralists," now arguing what the debate was about (Lavoie, 2006; Dow, 2006). In our view, the argument for revisiting the money supply process rests on (i) the fundamental changes that have taken place in bank behavior – gone are the days when bank supply of credit passively responded to demand driven by the "state of trade" – and (ii) the finding that broad money supply can no longer be linked empirically to total bank credit in the period after 1995.[1]

In the era before financial liberalization, the link between total bank credit and money supply could not have been broken. Broad money was for all intents and purposes synonymous with total bank deposits, which was mainly one and the same with total consolidated bank liabilities. When banks extended credit on the asset side of their balance sheet, there had to be a corresponding increase on the liability side in the form of new deposits and thus in broad money as well. If portfolio choice shifted away from deposits, agents could not possibly run down their total size by moving out of them into other instruments in the aggregate. The only change would be in the relative reward of holding them which would vary until they would all be held voluntarily – that is, whatever their aggregate magnitude after adjusting for any deposits extinguished by loan repayments, if any, in the interim. Size of broad money balances was invariant to agent portfolio choice.

However, in the age of financial liberalization, it appears that broad money ceased to be invariant to shifts in portfolio choice, altering the money supply process. In a nutshell, the source of the broken link between bank credit and broad money was that not all bank loans returned as deposits, whether in banks or nonbanks, as they could now end up in non-deposit liabilities without a corresponding draw down on the asset side in banks' balance sheets. Moreover, loans could also be extinguished by asset securitization, swapping them for liquid funds in banks' balance sheets without any change on the liability side.

In this chapter we discuss how the money supply process was altered by the transformation of the credit creation mechanism brought about by financial deregulation. We begin with an overview of the decline in traditional banking along with the concomitant rise of nonbank sources of credit within the overall supply of credit; and continue with a discussion of the effect successive waves of financial deregulation had on banking since the early 1980s. We then take up the question of how these changes altered the money supply process and end with a few concluding remarks.

DECREASING IMPORTANCE OF TRADITIONAL BANKING

Figure 14.1 shows the share of total bank loans in the overall borrowing by the nonfarm, nonfinancial corporate sector. One can see a clear cyclical pattern as well as a declining trend since the 1980s. During this latter period, firms increasingly utilized a variety of debt instruments other

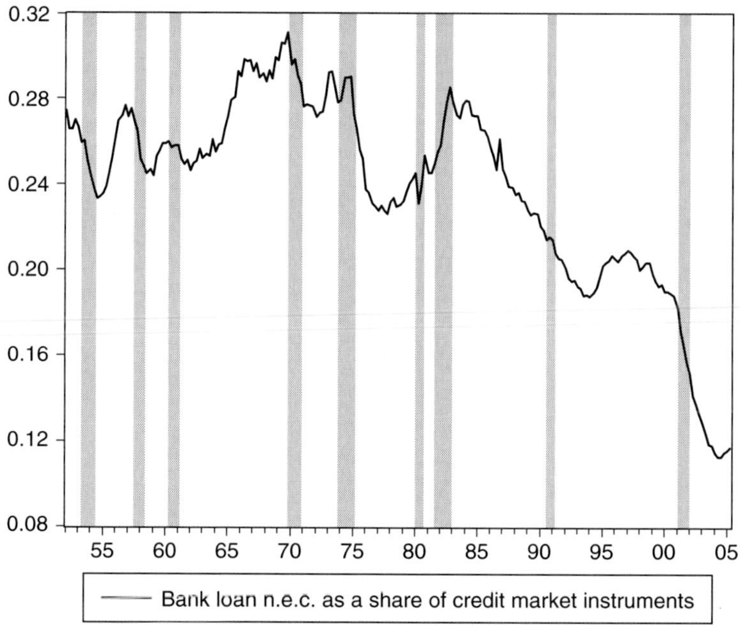

Notes: Shaded areas reflect economic recessions.

Source: Estimated from Table L.102, Flow of Funds Accounts.

Figure 14.1 Bank loans not elsewhere classified (n.e.c.) as a share of credit market instruments of the nonfarm, nonfinancial corporate sector

than bank loans, causing their relative importance to decline in relation to nonbank short-term borrowing and mortgages.

Throughout this period, depository institutions' relative size within the financial sector shrank (Table 14.1). The decreasing trend began with rising inflation in the 1960s and 1970s (Edwards and Mishkin, 1995; Samolyk, 2004) and gained impetus with the Employee Retirement Income Security Act (ERISA) of 1974, which had the effect of shifting household savings from commercial banks toward pension funds and mutual funds. This was the beginning of an "asymmetrical increase in borrowing through capital markets" (D'Arista, 2002: 3) as bonds and commercial paper became the assets of choice for institutional investors like pension funds. Subsequently, direct finance in corporate borrowing through credit market instruments started to increase at the expense of bank borrowing as well.

Table 14.1 Percent share of assets by financial sector (%)*

	1960	1970	1980	1985	1990	1995	2000	2005:2
Depository Institutions[1]	54.65	54.41	51.96	44.18	36.08	27.78	22.83	24.22
Insurance Companies[2]	22.38	17.38	14.34	12.77	13.94	13.39	11.23	11.64
Private Pensions	6.44	8.56	11.38	14.30	12.03	13.79	12.23	9.38
Public Pensions[3]	5.32	6.07	6.06	6.69	7.92	8.92	8.68	7.62
Mutual Funds[4]	3.68	3.66	3.24	5.79	8.54	13.04	17.95	16.42
GSEs and Agency- and GSE-backed Mortgage Pools	1.86	3.55	6.86	8.07	11.08	11.79	12.52	13.59
Nonbank Lenders[5]	4.58	4.89	4.73	4.24	4.41	3.37	3.29	3.12
Security Brokers and Dealers	1.05	1.12	1.01	1.82	1.94	2.71	3.43	4.37
Others[6]	0.03	0.37	0.43	2.13	4.05	5.21	7.84	9.63

Notes:

* All numbers are year-end results except 2005 which is second quarter.
1. Includes commercial banks, saving institutions, and credit unions.
2. Includes life-insurance companies and other insurance companies.
3. Includes state and local government employee retirement funds, and federal government retirement funds.
4. Includes money market mutual funds, mutual funds, and closed-end and exchange-traded funds.
5. Includes finance companies and mortgage companies.
6. Includes asset-backed securities issuers, real estate investment trusts and funding corporations.

Source: Estimated from Tables L.109 through L.131 of Flow of Funds Accounts.

Depository institutions could never recover the ground they lost in market share during the period. To support their profits they branched out into new activities, such as real estate loans, off-balance sheet activities, and lending for corporate takeovers and leveraged buyouts, among others. Table 14.2 gives an idea how banks' asset compositions were transformed through these changes. The single most important telltale sign of this repositioning is the increasing share of noninterest income in banks' total revenue, which exceeded 50 percent within a little more than a decade, while barely 20 percent in the early 1990s (Figure 14.2).

The 1988 Basel Capital Accord played a very important role in quickening the pace of decline in traditional banking (Basset and Zakrajsek, 2003). In an attempt to reduce banks' exposure to risk, Basel I stipulated minimum capital requirements for banks, which varied by type of lending assessed by its assigned level of risk. For example, the risk of a mortgage was weighted at half that of a commercial and industrial loan (Emmons et al., 2005: 13). Similarly, retail lending such as credit card debt also had a lower risk weight than commercial and industrial loans. Thus, given their level of assets, and holding all else constant, commercial banks could meet their capital requirements by simply varying the composition of their lending – by reducing the share of commercial and industrial loans in favor of other types of lending.[2]

Table 14.2 Percent share of selected assets in bank credit

	Treasury securities	Agency- and GSE-backed securities	Municipal securities	Corporate and foreign bonds	Open market paper	Bank loans n.e.c.	Mortgages	Consumer credit
1952	45.85	1.23	7.11	1.87	0.41	23.11	11.02	7.57
1960	29.11	0.85	9.07	0.80	0.43	29.36	15.01	13.00
1970	12.52	2.51	14.52	0.44	0.87	34.75	17.04	15.02
1980	8.19	4.55	11.60	0.83	1.07	35.50	21.21	15.61
1985	10.81	4.41	9.53	1.30	0.51	34.80	21.90	15.01
1990	6.71	9.43	4.88	3.22	0.36	30.09	29.71	13.98
1995	9.07	12.78	2.81	2.97	0.13	25.54	30.45	13.54
2000	4.47	14.68	2.29	4.16	0.03	28.86	31.66	10.40
2005	1.80	16.01	2.08	8.98	0.00	19.25	38.42	9.86

Source: Estimated from Table L.109, Flow of Funds Accounts.

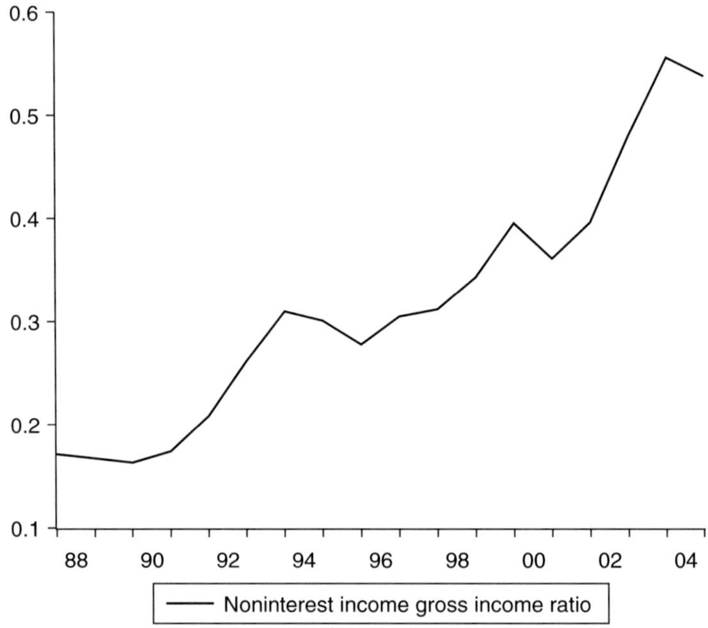

Source: Estimated from the data appendices of *Federal Reserve Bulletins*, years 1996 through 2004.

Figure 14.2 Noninterest income to gross income ratio of commercial banks

FINANCIAL DEREGULATION AND TRANSFORMATION OF BANKING

The first wave of financial deregulation goes back to Depository Institutions Deregulation and Monetary Control Act (1980), which abolished interest rate ceilings for most of the deposit accounts and introduced negotiable orders of withdrawal (NOWs) accounts (Teles and Zhou, 1995: 50). Later, Garn–St. Germain Depository Institutions Act (1982) introduced money market deposit accounts (MMDAs) so that depository institutions could compete with money market mutual funds (Teles and Zhou, 1995: 50). The second wave of deregulation started in the early 1990s when the Fed abolished reserve requirements for time deposit accounts and reduced them for checkable deposits in 1992. More importantly, the introduction of retail sweep accounts in 1994 reduced depository institutions' need for reserve requirements significantly, enabling them to meet their reserve requirements with their vault cash (Bennet and Peristani, 2002: 2).

Retail sweep accounts were different from the former business-oriented sweep accounts. The latter involved business transaction deposits that were turned into overnight repurchase agreements or money market mutual funds where profits had to be shared with customers (Anderson, 2002), making them relatively costly and thus limiting their scope. But, in the former, transaction accounts could be moved into money market deposit accounts under saving accounts, which had no reserve requirements without having to engage in money market transactions on behalf of customers. The result was an explosive increase in retail sweep accounts and in M1 (Federal Reserve Bank of St. Louis) as depository institutions could now reduce their reserve requirements drastically by shifting funds back and forth between transaction deposits and saving accounts during a business day (Figure 14.3). Thus, there was no longer "a binding constraint on banks' holdings of assets that qualify as reserves" (Bennett and Peristiani, 2002: 1–2).

Until the 1960s, the liabilities of depository institutions remained quite simple, consisting of mainly checking deposits, saving accounts, and time

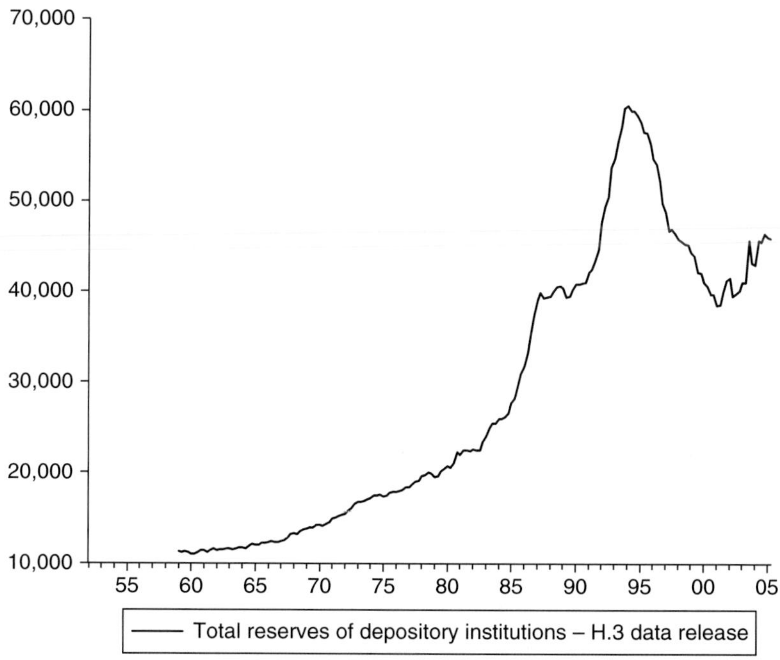

Source: H.3 data release of the Federal Reserve.

Figure 14.3 Total reserves of depository institutions

deposits, and thus liability management was limited. The emergence of certificates of deposits, however, changed all this. Commercial banks could now attract funds for a limited time period whenever a profit opportunity or a maturity (time) mismatch between their assets and liabilities emerged. The federal funds markets and repurchases, and credit market instruments such as bonds and commercial papers, were also increasingly used for similar purposes, enabling depository institutions to control the maturity of their liabilities similar to their assets.

Because of competition from money market mutual funds and mutual funds, the share of core deposits in depository institutions liabilities declined significantly (Nelson and Owen, 1997: 469–70), forcing banks to engage in liability management, relying increasingly on managed liabilities. Moreover, core deposits were increasingly interest-insensitive. This alone required that, especially, the largest banks rely on managed liabilities during periods of rapid asset growth. "Thus, even though core deposits on average are less expensive than managed liabilities, the latter may still be the more profitable means for banks to finance rapid growth in assets, with reliance on those liabilities declining when asset growth is weak" (English and Nelson, 1998: 397).

Since their emergence in the 1960s, managed liabilities as a trend have increased much faster than core liabilities (Figure 14.4). Core liabilities were relatively stable until then, but fell steeply in the 1990s as managed liabilities increased rapidly in the latter part of the decade following an initial short-lived dip. Initially, the biggest source of funds, total deposits held in depository institutions, lagged behind the expansion of lending by far during the rapid asset growth of the late 1990s.

Another important facet of financial deregulation was, of course, asset securitization. Though not new, it was eased by the shift of bank lending towards loans collateralized by real estate, which was in turn spurred by Basel I. Banks began to make mortgages only to offload them onto off-balance sheet entities – often called "securitized investment vehicles" (VICs) – generating their income not from holding assets with an interest rate spread but originating and moving them for a fee just like a broker would. The vehicle, in turn, issued liabilities and used the proceeds to buy the assets (mostly mortgages) the banks did not want to keep on their balance sheets. Using these as collateral to issue more liabilities of its own, it grouped these assets into different batches, called "tranches," to generate some desired earning stream and risk combination. The liabilities issued against the "senior" tranche received the lion's share of income at lowest risk and were given the investment grade by the rating agencies on account of being "overcollateralized," making them palatable to institutional investors. Whatever income was left over from the senior tranche went to the

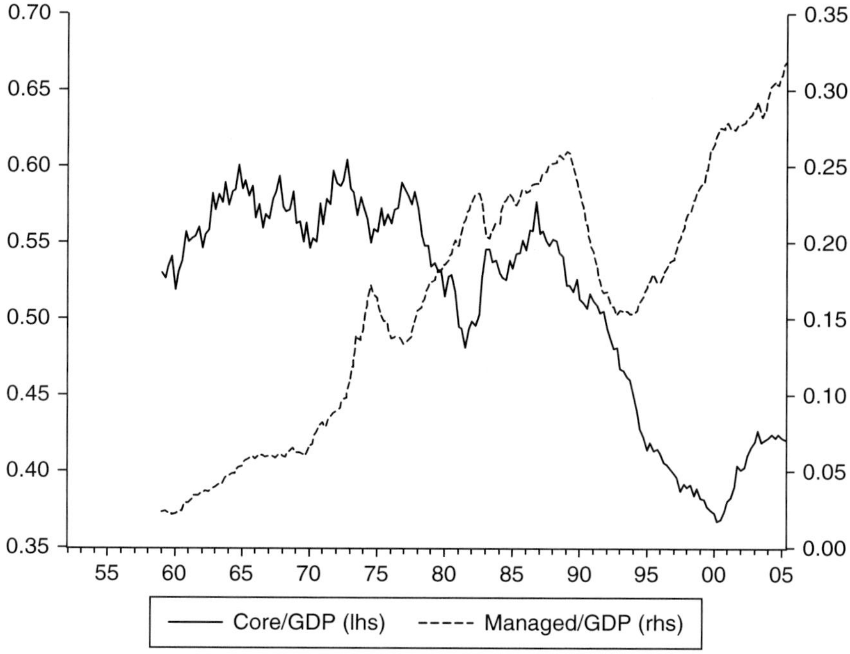

Source: L.109, L.114 and L.115 tables of Flow of Funds Accounts.

Figure 14.4 Core deposits and managed liabilities of depository institutions

residual tranche, which received a lower grade. The liabilities issued against them were sold to those with lower levels of risk aversion such as the hedge funds. Over time, residual tranches would themselves be regrouped to generate their own "overcollateralized" senior tranche, and be insured – either implicitly by the sponsoring banks by means of some buyback guarantee or explicitly by some credit default swap written by the monolines or some other financial institution – to increase their attractiveness to investors (Engdahl, 2008; Kregel, 2007). Thus, with asset securitization banks could sidestep the (only remaining) constraint posed to their credit supply by their capital base as well. When they lacked enough capital to put loans on their balance sheet, they could now create off-balance sheet vehicles to carry them anyway. A legal fig leaf obscured the connection between the VICs and the banks that set them up (Kregel, 2007).[3]

As the last vestiges of the old Glass–Steagall Act were removed by the Gramm–Leach–Bliley Act in 1999, the distinction between commercial and investment banks had completely disappeared for all intents and purposes. The cumulative effect of two decades of deregulation on "bank" behavior was drastic. The new bank conglomerates – *Financial Holding Companies* they were now called – had little affinity with the commercial banks of the bygone era of regulation. Most importantly for the discussion here, they were loan pushers on a massive scale, quite unlike the passive credit suppliers envisioned in the endogenous theory. The organizing principle behind structured finance, that the credit risk of any group of assets could be compensated by overcollateralization of the collateralized obligation itself, was run like a Ponzi scheme with the full complicity of these megabanks. Seemingly palatable collateralized debt obligation (CDOs) could be issued ad infinitum from increasingly riskier assets as long as a larger pool of even riskier assets could be found to collateralize them. As a result, new layers of intermediation emerged, expanded and multiplied, where self-fulfilling asset price expectations were the key driving force. As long as home prices kept rising, capital gain expectations made it easier to sell mortgages to increasingly higher-risk households and the credit increase that resulted from it fueled demand and thus the increase in home prices. The explosive increase in credit was not at all demand driven.

THE MONEY SUPPLY PROCESS

The time trend of total bank credit, deposits and broad money is shown in Figure 14.5. Note that the three variables do not move together, especially after 1995. In fact, when we just look at bank credit and deposits we see that the series diverge as early as the late 1970s. In fact, three distinct phases can be identified when these two series diverge in this graph.[4] First, they become divergent for about half a decade from late 1970s till the early 1980s; second, bank deposits move in tandem for about a decade though at a much lower level than total bank credit; and, third, the two series diverge again after the early 1990s with the gap between them increasing. On the other hand, total deposits and broad money diverge mainly after 1995, with the exception of the early 1980s.

In our view, the growing prevalence of *nonbank* deposits in the form of mutual money market funds and asset securitization are the main culprits for these divergent patterns. Prior to financial liberalization, the connection between total bank credit and broad money supply was simple enough: new bank deposits were created when banks made loans and extinguished when loans were paid back. In banks' consolidated balance sheet, total liabilities mainly comprised deposits and basically equaled broad money. However, in the age of financial liberalization not all deposits bank loans created returned as deposits, whether in banks or nonbanks,

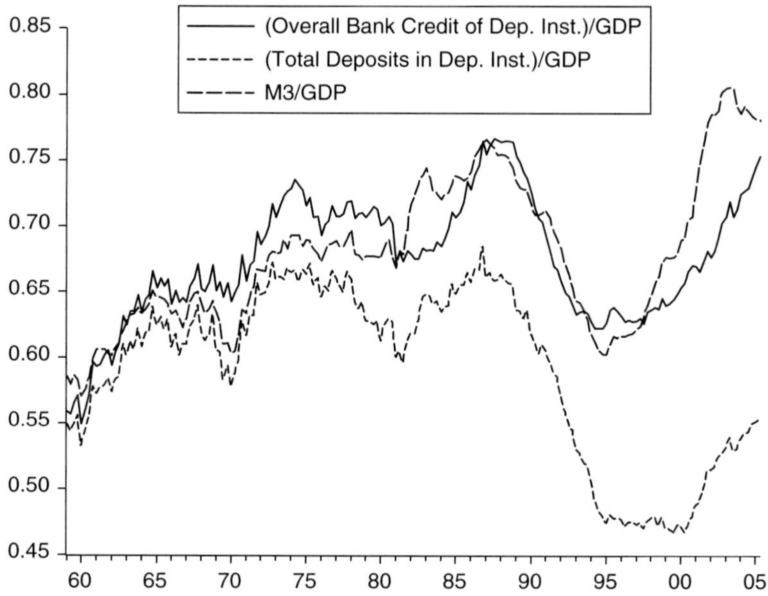

Sources: US Federal Reserve System H.8 Release and L.109, L.114 and L.115 tables of Flow of Funds Accounts.

Figure 14.5 Bank credit, deposits, and M3

as deposits could now be swapped for banks' nondeposit liabilities without a corresponding draw down on the asset side. Moreover, loans could also be extinguished by asset securitization, swapping them for liquid funds in banks' balance sheets without any change on the liability side.

The growing importance of liability management since the early 1970s and banks' reduced dependence on core deposits was discussed earlier. In fact, the emergence and increased use of certificates of deposits, federal funds and credit market instruments meant that following an extension of credit the balancing increase in banks' balance sheets could now be in nondeposit liabilities.

In addition, the proliferation of market funds (nonbank deposits) also meant that some of the proceeds of bank loans returned as deposits to nonbanks. Nonbank deposits such as mutual money market accounts are a part of M3 but they are not bank liabilities.

Looking at Figure 14.6, we see that the share of market funds in M3 spiked sharply in the late 1970s until the early 1980s and remained roughly around 10 percent throughout the latter part of that decade. There was another spike in the second part of the 1990s, pushing their share to almost

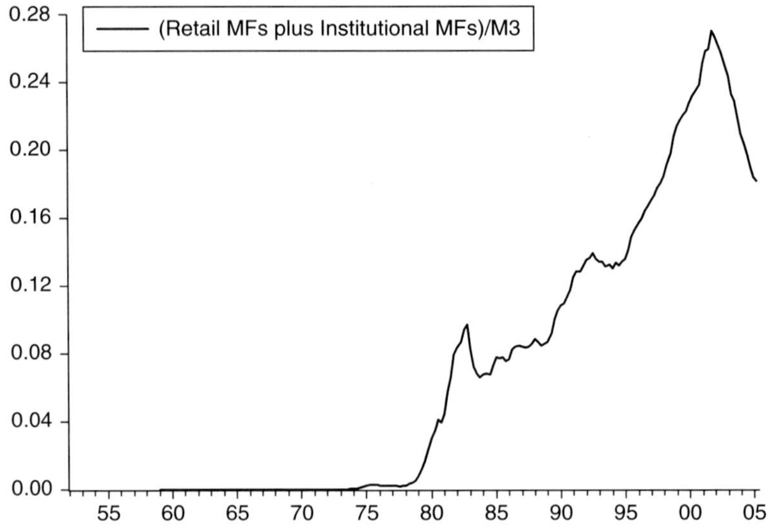

Source: Federal Reserve Bank of St. Louis, FRED 2 Data Release.

Figure 14.6 Nonbank deposits in M3

30 percent by 2002. Note that the trend line of bank deposits diverged from that of bank credit (as well as M3) during periods of rapid change in the share of *nonbank* deposits in M3. This happened during both the late 1970s and early 1980s and again after the early 1990s as well.

The increased prevalence of nonbank deposits however does not explain why broad money, comprising both bank and nonbank deposits, also became divergent from total bank credit after 1995. Note that the trend line of M3 in Figure 14.5 is steeper than that of total bank credit after 1995 and turns negative in the early 2000s while the latter continues to rise. Why did broad money grow much faster than total bank credit after 1995? The leakage into nondeposit bank liabilities cannot be an explanation since such a leakage would imply that for a given increase in bank credit the resultant increase in broad money is less, the exact opposite of what needs to be explained.[5]

A more likely explanation seems to be asset securitization. Note that the stylized effect of asset securitization is to swap loans with liquid funds in banks' balance sheets without any change on the liability side. This implies that banks can repeatedly issue new loans by the same funds that are recycled through securitization, while a new set of liabilities – some of which are a part of broad money – are issued against the same set of loans passed onto the nondepository institutions by these institutions.

The total sum of all deposit liabilities (bank and nonbank deposits) can then rise faster than total bank credit that remains in banks' balance sheets as long as agents' portfolio choices between deposit liabilities and other liabilities remain unchanged. That can possibly explain why M3 appears to have grown much faster than total bank credit in the 1990s. On the other hand, the trend reversal in M3 in the early 2000s appears to have been caused by the precipitous contraction in the share of nonbank deposits after 2002 (Figure 14.6) which in turn was the result of a marked shift in agent portfolio choice away money market funds as recovery began to take hold.

In summary, the ability of agents to *swap* deposit liabilities and nondeposit liabilities, and the explosive increase in asset securitization, has been responsible for the divergent patterns of total bank credit, total deposits and broad money. The shifts between total (bank plus nonbank) deposits into other debt instruments appears to have been as significant as shifts between bank and nonbank deposits. An important implication of all this is that broad money ceased to be invariant with respect to shifts in agent portfolio choice.

CONCLUSION

The central proposition behind an endogenous supply of money is the notion that the driving force of the money creation process is the nonfinancial business sector's demand for credit. Though the theory lends itself to different interpretations, the basic idea is straightforward: Loans that banks extend to firms return to them in the form of new deposits, causing the money supply to expand as the central bank has little realistic alternative to satisfying the needs of banks for increased reserves in the aggregate during this process – that is, if financial innovation has not in the meantime already rendered additional reserves redundant.

While we believe that the central insight of endogenous money, that credit creation causes monetary growth, makes much better sense that than the other way around, the theory might be in need of a major reformulation that can address two important shortcomings in its conventional form. First, financial deregulation has fundamentally transformed bank behavior as it drastically altered what a bank is. Thus, it is hardly persuasive to depict credit creation as a passive, solely demand-driven process. Secondly, at the level of empirical analysis it can no longer be taken for granted that total bank credit "statistically" causes broad money. It appears that asset securitization and portfolio choice can no longer be ignored in understanding how the money supply process works.

NOTES

1. Elsewhere (Özgür and Ertürk, 2012), we present detailed econometric evidence that shows that the relation between bank credit and broad money has ceased to be statistically significant in this period.
2. Another issue with the Basel Accord was that all commercial loans – regardless of their borrowers – have the same level of riskiness. As quoted in Cornford, this led to a situation in which "a loan to General Electric and the overdraft run up by the newsagent on the corner have identical capital charges" (Matten, 2000: 90; quoted in Cornford, 2005: 5). Thus, a from a bank's point of view, it may be more profitable to make a loan to a riskier borrower if all commercial borrowers have the same risk requirements.
3. The Gramm–Leach–Bliley Bank Reform Act, enacted in 1999, expanded the scope of capital market activities allowed for commercial banks, permitting them to own subsidiaries that could engage in the type of financial activities they could not.
4. For a detailed statistical analysis of these divergent patterns, see Özgür and Ertürk (2012).
5. Though, it is likely that the leakage to nondeposit liabilities can shed light on the trend reversal in M3 in the early 2000s.

REFERENCES

Anderson, R.G. (2002). "Federal Reserve Board Data on OCD Sweep Account Programs," http://research.stlouisfed.org/aggreg/swdata.html.

Basset, W.F., and E. Zakrajsek (2000). "Profits and Balance Sheet Developments at U.S. Commercial Banks in 1999," *Federal Reserve Bulletin*, March: 367–95.

Bennett, P., and S. Peristani (2002). "Are U.S. Reserve Requirements Still Binding?" *FRBNY Economic Policy Review*, (May): 1–16.

Cornford, A. (2005). "Basel II: The Revised Framework of June 2004," *UNCTAD Discussion Paper 178*.

D'Arista, J. (2002). "Rebuilding the Transmission System for Monetary Policy," *Financial Markets and Society*, November: 1–28.

Dow, S.C. (2006). "Endogenous Money: Structuralist," in P. Arestis and M. Sawyer (eds), *A Handbook of Alternative Monetary Economics*, Cheltenham, UK and Northampton, MA, USA: Edward Elgar, pp. 17–34.

Edwards, F.R. and F.S. Mishkin (1995). "The Decline of Traditional Banking: Implications for Financial Stability and Regulatory Policy," *Federal Reserve Bank of New York Economic Policy Review*, **1** (2): 27–45.

English, W.B., and W.R. Nelson (1998). "Profits and Balance Sheet Developments at U.S. Commercial Banks in 1997," *Federal Reserve Bulletin*, June: 391–419.

Engdahl, W. (2008). "Financial Crisis: Asset Securitization – The Last Tango," posted at Global Research Centre for Research on Globalization, www.globalresearch.ca, February 8.

Emmons, W.R., V. Lskavyan, and T.J. Yeager (2005). "Basel II Will Trickle Down to Community Bankers, Consumers," *The Regional Economist*, April: 12–13.

Kregel, J. (2007). "The Natural Instability of Financial Markets," *The Levy Economics Institute Working Paper 523*.

Lavoie, M. (2006). "Endogenous Money: Accommodationist," in in P. Arestis and M. Sawyer (eds), *A Handbook of Alternative Monetary Economics*, Cheltenham, UK and Northampton, MA, USA: Edward Elgar, pp. 17–34.

Nelson, W.R., and A.L. Owen (1997). "Profits and Balance Sheet Developments at U.S. Commercial Banks in 1996," *Federal Reserve Bulletin*, June: 465–89.
Özgür, G., and K. Ertürk (2013). "Endogenous Money in the Age of Financial Liberalization," Forthcoming in *Review of Political Economy*, **25** (2): 327–47.
Samolyk, K. (2004). "The Future of Banking in America," *FDIC Banking Review*, **16** (2): 29–65.
Teles, P. and R. Zhou (2005). "A Stable Money Demand: Looking for the Right Monetary Aggregate," *Federal Reserve Bank of Chicago Economic Perspectives*, Quarter 1: 50–63.

15. A new measure of liquidity premium*

Perry Mehrling and Daniel H. Neilson

1 INTRODUCTION

In his *Treatise on Money*, Keynes proposed what later generations have known as his theory of "normal backwardation" to explain the relationship between spot and forward prices in organized markets for basic commodities.

> If supply and demand are balanced, the spot price must exceed the forward price by the amount which the producer is ready to sacrifice in order to 'hedge' himself, i.e. to avoid the risk of price fluctuations during his production period. Thus in normal conditions the spot price exceeds the forward price, i.e. there is a backwardation. (Keynes, 1930, II, p. 143)

The speculator who provides the hedge by buying forward expects to profit by selling spot at the maturity of the forward contract, and Keynes suggests that such profit runs typically about 10 per cent per annum, or even higher for less organized markets.

In his *Value and Capital*, Hicks extended the theory of normal backwardation to the money market.

> It appears that the forward market for loans (like the forward market for commodities) may be expected to have a constitutional weakness on one side, a weakness which offers an opportunity for speculation. . . . The forward short rate will thus exceed the expected short rate by a risk-premium which corresponds exactly to the 'normal backwardation' of the commodity markets. (Hicks, 1939, pp. 146–7)

Hicks makes clear that this money-market premium is the general form of the phenomenon, and can be expected to be embedded in the risk premium for any specific commodity.

The Keynes–Hicks theory of the forward premium has been controversial, most importantly because it seems to be in contradiction to the requirements of informationally efficient markets which suggest that forward prices should tend to be equal to expected future spot prices (Samuelson, 1965), at least when properly adjusted for exposure to systematic risk. The result has been a continuing empirical debate, with no conclusive result even up to the present, mainly because of the degree of freedom inevitably involved in measuring expectations of future spot prices. In the following pages, we propose and implement an alternative approach that relies entirely on observable data—the difference between forwards and futures—and documents the existence of a risk premium in the short-term dollar money market, arguably the most liquid market in the world. Our data, it must be emphasized, end before August 2007 and the subsequent credit crisis that has produced unprecedented spreads even in the most liquid markets, even a year later as we are preparing this chapter for press. We provide evidence of a risk premium even in more normal times.

2 THE KEYNES–HICKS THEORY: A MODERN RESTATEMENT

The economy is chock full of natural forward positions. An American company orders a Swiss machine for delivery in three months, payable in Swiss Francs. This order involves a natural forward exchange position, the ultimate value of which depends on the spot exchange rate between dollars and Swiss Francs three months from now. The same company plans to finance its purchase by issuing dollar-denominated 90-day commercial paper three months from now. This plan involves a natural forward interest-rate position, the ultimate value of which depends on the spot rate of interest three months from now. If over the course of the next three months the exchange value of the dollar falls or the spot rate of interest rises, the company will lose on its natural forward positions, possibly so much so that the planned purchase no longer seems a wise business decision.

To avoid such potential losses, the company would like to hedge its natural forward positions. Ideally, it would like to find a counterparty that has exactly the opposite forward positions, which is to say a company with natural forward positions that will lose value if the exchange value of the dollar rises or the spot rate of interest falls. The coincidence, however, is unlikely. The ideal counterparty must be expecting to receive Swiss Francs and planning to invest those Francs in a 90-day dollar-denominated instrument, and it must also be planning to make those transactions on exactly the same date and at exactly the same scale. Even if such a company were to exist, and even were the inevitable counterparty risk to prove tolerable, the cost of finding the company and then arranging a one-off bilateral deal is likely prohibitive.

Historically, the banking system arose to solve problems like this.[1] For a fee, a bank sells Swiss Francs forward to the American company and so eliminates the exchange-rate risk. For another fee, it arranges a loan commitment that locks in the interest rate the company will pay. Now the company's natural forward positions have become the bank's formal forward contracts, and the company's problem of finding an ideal counterparty has become the bank's problem, but with some important differences. First, the bank has numerous clients with diverse payment needs, and some of those payment needs may offset, which means that the very same forward positions may pose less risk to the bank than they do to the company. More important, by dividing the company's natural forward positions into two separate forward contracts, the bank can search for separate counterparties for each, perhaps even multiple counterparties for each contract.

We conceptualize the bank's search for offset as beginning in the forward market with its regular banking counterparties, all of whom are trying to hedge their own net forward positions. Because the counterparties are familiar, counterparty risk in this market is controlled merely by limiting exposure to any one counterparty. But, just as the bank's own forward positions are unlikely to offset exactly, so too in interbank trading the bank will in general have to be prepared to enter into offsetting forward contracts that don't match its needs exactly. If a counterparty bank offers Swiss Francs at an attractive price but for a delivery date one week later than the bank has agreed with its client, it might be best to take the offer and plan to fill the gap by borrowing the Francs spot for a week, so accepting a week's worth of exchange-rate risk, which is a lot better than three months. If a counterparty offers dollars to the right maturity date at an attractive rate, but for an issue date that is three days late, it might be best to take the offer and plan to fill the gap by borrowing dollars for three days, again trading a large interest-rate risk exposure for a small one. In practice, forward trading organizes itself around a collection of standard dates, and it costs more to issue a forward that deviates from these standard dates.

The banking system's search for offset continues on the futures exchange where futures contracts are even more standardized than forwards, in terms of issue date, tenor, and also contract size. Unlike the forward market, futures counterparties are anonymous so margin requirements and mark-to-market accounting are used to ensure performance. (In effect, the futures exchange takes on the task of managing the line of credit available to each exchange participant.) Because of the standardization, hedging forwards with futures is inevitably imperfect, but the advantage is liquidity, since the greater standardization brings deeper market participation, including speculators who have no natural forward position to offset, but rather are willing to take whichever side of the contract offers an attractive risk–return profile. Ultimately any imbalance in the natural forward positions emerging from the real economy will be shifted to speculators on the futures exchange, as much as possible.

Taken as a whole, it is clear that the banking system works to pool offsetting risks to the extent possible, and then to move whatever risk is left over onto the balance sheet of the agents most willing to bear it. In our stylized model, part of the residual risk stays on the bank balance sheet because client needs do not match standard forward or futures dates. The rest is shifted onto the balance sheet of speculators who take up the slack in the futures market. The important point is that, the more complete the offset in the forward market, the better terms banks can offer to their clients. The less complete the offset, the more reliance on speculators, and the higher the cost that banks will pass on as compensation for residual risk bearing.

It is important to emphasize this point. In taking on the natural forward positions of their clients, the banking system inevitably winds up shouldering some residual risk. How much risk is partly a matter of technology and institutional structure—wider networks and more efficient communication may help to achieve more complete offset—but it is also partly a matter of the pattern of natural forward positions emerging from the real economy. If the time pattern of planned future payments across the economy matched exactly, there would be no residual risk and hence no compensation for bearing it. Residual risk comes from the fact that planned future payments do not match. Although bearing such risk involves exposure to exchange-rate and interest-rate risk, the price of that risk will depend crucially on the degree of mismatch in the pattern of natural forward positions. This residual risk is thus best understood as liquidity risk, and the price is best understood as a liquidity premium. Banks can be expected to charge for bearing that risk, and the price can be expected to vary over time, depending on the degree of payment offset achieved as well as on anything else that affects the cost of bearing that risk.

Table 15.1 shows a stylized diagram of the origin of residual liquidity risk that has guided our research and that provides the analytical framework for the empirical exercise that follows. It shows how the risk involved in myriad natural forward positions gets passed on to the banking system where it is netted out and the residual moved around using standard forward and futures contracts. Presumably the full premium for bearing liquidity risk is included in the price that the bank offers to its client for a non-standard forward. But the difference between the non-standard forward and the standard forward might also include some liquidity premium, to the extent that the cash flow patterns

Table 15.1 The origin and price of residual liquidity risk

	Client	Bank	Banking System	Exchange	Economic Theory
Contract	Natural Forward	Non-standard Forward	Standard Forward	Standard Futures	Ideal Futures
Interest rate			$f_0(N, T)$	$h_0(N, T)$	$El(N, T)$
Exchange rate			$G_0(T)$	$\mathbf{G}_0(T)$	$ES(T)$

Note: Our notation is discussed in Appendix 15A.

diverge and so leave the bank holding residual risk. For the same reason, we might expect there to be some liquidity premium in the difference between the standard forward and the standard futures contract, even when the dates are the same, because the latter but not the former is marked to market. We might even expect to find some liquidity premium in the difference between the market price of the standard futures contract and the theoretical ideal valuation of that contract (unobservable in the real world) that takes into account only the price risk of the underlying exchange rate or interest rate, and hence is an unbiased forecast of the future spot rate.

This last point requires further elaboration. Modern financial theory traces risk premia to systemic risk exposure, but largely abstracts from liquidity risk as a type of systemic risk exposure (Black, 1976; Cox et al., 1981). When this theory is taken to the data, it is quite clear that there exist time-varying risk premia in the pricing of both exchange-rate and interest-rate futures; the empirical failure of uncovered interest parity for exchange rates and of the expectations hypothesis of the term structure for interest rates are two of the most dependable findings in the literature (Burnside et al., 2006; Piazzesi and Swanson, 2006). The problem is that standard financial theory provides little help in understanding why these premia exist—the usual sources of systematic risk seem too small to explain it (Grinblatt and Jegadeesh, 1996, p. 1512; Tuckman, 2002, p. 354). One remaining possibility, however, is that these premia reflect a source of risk that is not included in the standard theory, namely liquidity risk. Large mismatches in the pattern of natural forward positions can be expected to put pressure on futures markets that will distort prices away from their theoretical ideal.

The rest of this chapter is best understood as an attempt to measure the liquidity premium in asset prices by using the difference between standard forward and standard futures prices, in both exchange-rate and interest-rate contracts, as a proxy. The main reason for this choice is data availability. We can obtain high-quality data for both (implied) forward and futures contracts, and line up the dates of each exactly. Standard theory attributes any difference between the prices of these two contracts to (1) reinvestment risk involved in the mark-to-market feature of futures and (2) differential counterparty risk involved in forwards relative to futures. Neither of these seem to amount to much quantitatively in the markets we study. We propose instead to interpret any difference as a liquidity premium.[2]

We choose to focus our empirical study on the short-term Eurodollar market (and Euroyen, and Euribor) for two reasons. First, these markets are the deepest and most liquid interbank borrowing markets; if we are able to measure a liquidity premium in them, we can be sure of finding one elsewhere. Second, these markets are in practice where the banks involved in the payments system are most likely to turn for funding or to place short-term funds.

3 MEASUREMENT

3.1 Liquidity Premium: Interest Rates

To measure empirically the price of liquidity risk embodied in the difference between forward and futures prices in interest rates, we proceed as follows. The forward interest rate comparable to the quoted futures "price" is the forward-interest parity rate $f_t(N, T)$.[3] This expresses the interest rate available at time t for a deposit from time N to time T, expressed in annual terms.[4]

The futures price $F_t(N, T)$ should be thought of as an index showing the change in the contract's value (and thus of variation-margin payments), and not as a price *per se*. $F_t(N, T)$ can be converted to a futures yield index $h_t(N, T)$ by the linear transformation

$$h_t(N, T) = 1 - \frac{F_t(N, T)}{100}. \tag{15.2}$$

The yield index $h_t(N,T)$ is in units comparable to the interest rate, expressed in annual terms in line with market convention, on a \$1 million deposit from time N to time T.

The price of liquidity risk in interest rates we define to be the difference between these two rates, namely

$$D_t^{\text{ir}}(N, T) = f_t(N, T) - h_t(N, T). \tag{15.3}$$

The calculation of $D_t^{ir}(N, T)$ depends on the measurement of $l(t, N)$ and $l(t, T)$. LIBOR is available for $N - t, L - t \in \{30, 60, \ldots, 360\}$.[5] The calculation also depends on the measurement of $F_t(N, T)$, where $T = N + 90$ by the design of the contract. Futures contracts are spaced so that one T occurs each month.[6] As a result of these constraints, we are able to compute a series of $D_t^{ir}(N, T)$ only for $N - t \in \{30, 60, 90, 120, 180\}$, with N the maturity date of a futures contract, and with corresponding $T = N + 90$, the notional end date of the futures loan. These calculations result in a set of $D_t^{ir}(N, T)$. Descriptive statistics concerning the series are presented in Table 15.2. The series are plotted in Figure 15.1 by the corresponding date N, that is, observations in different series corresponding to the same futures maturity day are vertically aligned.

Several observations concerning Table 15.2 are warranted. First, the average value of the series is greater than zero in all cases, in agreement with our theory. The large spike in the data visible in the second half of 1999 appears to be attributable to a slow adjustment in the Eurodollar futures market to the Fed's beginning a series of rate increases at that time. $\rho_{\text{fed funds}}$ shows the correlation of D^{ir} with the federal funds effective rate, another measure of the price of liquidity. This correlation is not large, nor is it of consistent sign across the maturities we consider. This suggests that our measure of liquidity premium captures a price not already implicit in the cost of overnight funds.

One of the strengths of our approach is in the care with which we constructed the series of D^{ir} and the series D^{fx} discussed below. The matching process just described involves careful tracking of futures expiration dates and of implied forward maturities. An alternative approach, taken by Grinblatt and Jegadeesh (1996), is to interpolate forward data between available maturities to find forwards to match futures with any number of days remaining.[7] We have not adopted this approach here, though it could be an avenue for further research.

Table 15.2 Liquidity-risk premium D^{ir}, descriptive statistics

	30	60	90	120	180
N	157	156	165	115	118
Mean	2.384	2.885	2.565	2.630	2.435
Standard deviation	5.389	6.384	7.636	6.034	6.225
$\rho_{\text{fed funds}}$	0.091	0.029	−0.038	−0.132	0.013

Note: $\rho_{\text{fed funds}}$ represents the correlation coefficient of the series with the federal funds effective rate.

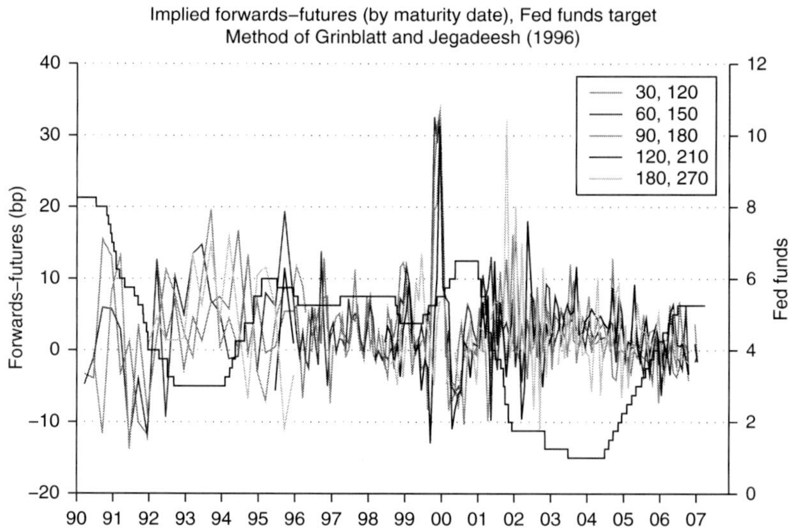

Note: $D_t^{\mathrm{it}}(N, T)$, $(N - t, T - N) \in \{(30, 120), (60, 150)\ (90, 180), (120, 210), (180, 270)\}$.

Figure 15.1 Liquidity-risk premium (interest rates) on left-hand scale; federal funds target rate on right-hand scale

3.2 Liquidity Premium: Foreign Exchange

To measure the price of liquidity risk implied by the prices of foreign-exchange futures and forwards, we proceed as follows. Denote by $G_t(N)$ the exchange rate implied by covered-interest parity, expressed as a quantity of dollars per unit of foreign currency.[8] Following the conceptual argument made in Section 2, we define the liquidity-risk premium to be the difference between the forward exchange rate and the futures exchange rate. We compute this difference as a dollar payoff, the return in dollars to buying one unit of foreign currency at the futures exchange rate $\mathbf{G}_t(T)$ and selling one unit of foreign currency at the forward exchange rate $G_t(N)$. The difference is therefore

$$D_t^{\mathrm{fx}}(N) = G_t(N) - \mathbf{G}_t(N). \tag{15.5}$$

As with interest rates above, data for $l(t, N)$ and $l^*(t, N)$ is available every day for $N - t \in \{30, 60, \ldots, 360\}$, while data for $\mathbf{G}_t(N)$ is available only for a limited set of fixed N.[9] Therefore our series includes dates t on which $\mathbf{G}_t(N)$ was available such that $N - t$ was equal to 30, 60, or 90. Because of the quarterly schedule of foreign-exchange futures, these

Table 15.3 Liquidity-risk premium D^{cc}, descriptive statistics

	EUR			JPY		
	30	60	90	30	60	90
N	32	32	31	69	68	68
Mean	0.00039	0.00011	−0.00013	−0.00000	−0.00000	−0.00000
Standard deviation	0.00101	0.00133	0.00119	0.00001	0.00002	0.00001
$\rho_{\text{fed funds}}$	−0.188	−0.036	−0.233	0.214	−0.015	0.003

Note: $\rho_{\text{fed funds}}$ represents the correlation coefficient of the series with the federal funds effective rate.

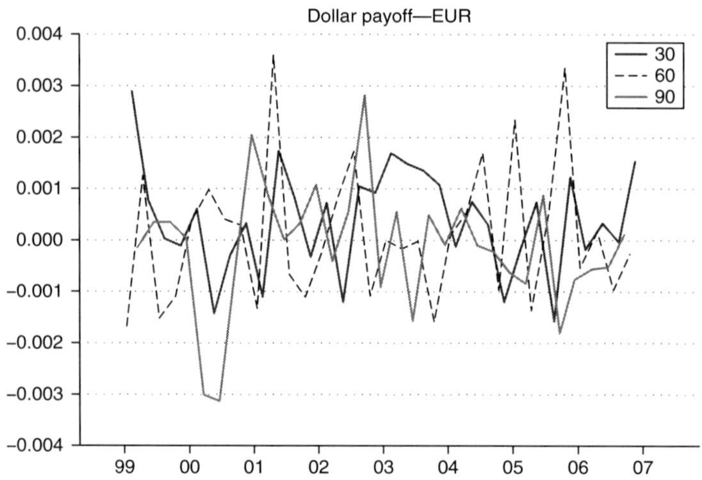

Note: $D_t^{fx}(t + \Delta N)$, $\Delta N \in \{30, 60, 90\}$.

Figure 15.2 Liquidity-risk premium (foreign exchange), euros

series are themselves quarterly. The series constructed in this manner are described in Table 15.3. The series, for various values of $N - t$, are shown in Figure 15.2 for euros, and in Figure 15.3 for yen.

Table 15.3 presents the same descriptive statistics for the D^{fx} as did Table 15.2 for D^{ir}. On average D^{fx} takes on very small value. The close match between foreign-exchange forwards and futures indicated by this fact suggests that the liquidity premium argued for in Section 2 may not in practice appear between forwards and futures, as it seems to with interest-rates contracts. This possibility is discussed at greater length below in

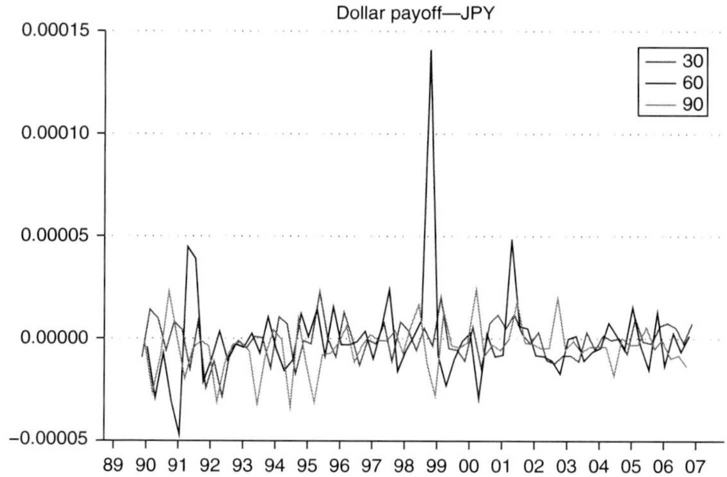

Note: $D_t^{fx}(t + \Delta N)$, $\Delta N \in \{30, 60, 90\}$.

Figure 15.3 Liquidity-risk premium (foreign exchange), Japanese yen

Section 5.5. The scarcity of foreign-exchange futures contracts, which are listed quarterly, and our effort to match forwards and futures, limit the number of observations of D^{fx} that we are able to use.

4 EH AND UIP INTERPRETATION

Two asset-pricing anomalies lie at the very center of monetary economics.[10] The first one has to do with the relationship between interest rates over different time horizons. The expectations hypothesis of the term structure (EH), although eminently plausible on theoretical grounds, simply fails empirically.[11] Long-term interest rates are on average greater than the subsequent sequence of short-term rates can explain. Put another way, the forward interest rates implied by the term structure are upwardly biased forecasts of realized future spot interest rates. In formal terms, $f_0(N, T) > El(N, T)$, where $f_0(N, T)$ is the forward rate at time 0 for the period from time N to T, $l(N, T)$ is the analogous spot rate that will be realized at time N, and E denotes expectations at time 0.

The interest-rate anomaly means that you should be able to make money by borrowing short and lending long, or (which is essentially equivalent) by taking a long position in an interest-rate forward contract.[12] There is risk in this "EH speculation." If the spot interest rate rises above the forward rate, you'll face a capital loss on your long position, or have to sell the proceeds of your forward contract in the spot market for less than you contracted to pay. But the spot rate may also fall below the forward rate, giving you a capital gain and allowing you to sell your forward deliverable for more than you paid. One way to understand the EH asset-pricing anomaly is that the probability that the EH speculation makes money is greater than the probability that it loses money. There is risk, but on average the speculation is profitable.

No one really knows why this is so. Empirically there is clearly a risk premium in the term structure, and it also seems that that risk premium varies over time, but it is not so clear why this should be so. The banking perspective adopted in this chapter suggests that forward rates get pushed around by an imbalance in the natural forward positions emerging from the natural economy, because that imbalance gets passed on to the banking system (broadly construed) which insists on being compensated for bearing it. If forward rates are pushed above expected spot rates, one reason might be that there are more people who want to lock in future borrowing rates than want to lock in future lending rates.

Table 15.4, panel (a) provides a stylized example of the balance-sheet relationships that would tend to push forward rates above expected spot. In the natural economy there are some people with natural short forward exposures who want to cover by acquiring a long forward hedge. That hedge is shown in the first row of the table as an on-balance-sheet transaction with T-month lending and N-month borrowing. There are other people with natural long forward exposures who want to cover by acquir-

Table 15.4 The possible origin of the EH (a) and UIP (b) anomalies

(a)		Economy		Banking system	
		Assets	Liabilities	Assets	Liabilities
Long forward	50	T-month dep.	N-month dep.		
Short forward	100	N-month dep.	T-month dep.		
Net short	50	N-month dep.	T-month dep.	T-month dep.	N-month dep.

(b)		Economy		Banking system	
		Assets	Liabilities	Assets	Liabilities
Long dollar	50	l deposit	l^* deposit		
Short dollar	100	l^* deposit	l deposit		
Net short	50	l^* deposit	l deposit	l deposit	l^* deposit

ing a short forward hedge, shown in the second row. These positions offset to some extent, and the banking system only has to bear the net, shown in the table as a net short hedge on the third row that forces the banking system to hold a net long forward position. Such an imbalance would mean that the short forward positions have to pay speculators a premium. The difference $f_0(N, T) - El(N, T)$ is a time-varying risk premium, and the relevant risk is liquidity risk.

Unfortunately we do not observe $El(N, T)$, so we cannot observe the risk premium directly. However, the banking perspective adopted in this chapter suggests further that that premium can be divided into two pieces, the difference between the forwards $f_0(N, T)$ and futures $h_0(N, T)$, and the difference between futures $h_0(N, T)$ and the expected spot rate $El(N,T)$. The latter is still unobservable, but the former we can see in market prices. Under the hypothesis that the two pieces of the premium move together, we can use the former as a measure of the overall liquidity premium.

Thus the measurement exercise in Section 3 can be interpreted as measuring a time-varying liquidity premium. If this measure in fact captures the liquidity premium, it follows that it should help us to forecast future spot rates. This will be the exercise in the next section, Section 5.

The second anomaly has to do with the relationship between interest rates in different currencies. Uncovered interest parity (UIP), another eminently plausible idea on theoretical grounds, fails even more resoundingly on empirical grounds. Currencies for which the nominal rate of interest is high not only fail to depreciate sufficiently against currencies for which the rate of interest is low, but they even tend to appreciate.[13] The difference between *ex post* realized returns from investing in different currencies is thus even greater than the difference between *ex ante* quoted returns. Put another way, the forward exchange rate implied by the pattern of interest rates is a biased forecast of the realized future spot exchange rate. In formal terms, when $G(T) > S(0)$ (i.e. $l^* < 1$) we also have $G(T) > ES(T)$ where G is the forward exchange rate and S is the analogous spot exchange rate that will be realized at time T (both expressed in dollars per unit of the foreign currency).

The exchange rate anomaly means that you should be able to make money by borrowing in the low-interest-rate currency and lending in the high interest rate currency, or (which is essentially equivalent) by buying the high-interest-rate currency forward.[14] There is risk involved in this "UIP speculation." The exchange value of the long currency position may fall by more than the interest differential, or the value of the forward contract may fall sufficiently to leave you with a net loss. But the exchange value may move the other way too, and the UIP anomaly consists in the empirical fact that it does so more often than not, so that the UIP speculation tends to make money on average.

No one really knows why this is so either. Empirically there is clearly a risk premium, and it also seems that that risk premium varies over time, but it is not so clear why this should be so. The banking perspective adopted in this chapter suggests that forward rates get pushed around by an imbalance in the natural forward positions emerging from the natural economy, because that imbalance gets passed on to the banking system (broadly construed) which insists on being compensated for bearing it. The UIP anomaly is that currencies with high rates of interest (equivalently, currencies that sell at a forward premium) tend to have their forward exchange rates pushed above expected spot exchange rates. The banking perspective suggests that this happens because there are more people who want to lock in the rate at which they can sell the high-interest-rate currency than there are people on the other side who want to lock in the rate at which they can buy the high-interest-rate currency.

Table 15.4, panel (b) provides a stylized example of the balance-sheet relationships that would tend to push the forward exchange rates of high-interest currencies above expected spot exchange rates. In the natural economy there are some people with natural short forward exposures who want to cover by acquiring a long forward hedge, shown in the first row of the table as an on-balance sheet transaction with borrowing in the foreign (low interest) currency and lending in the dollar (high interest) currency. There are other people with natural long forward exposures who want to cover by acquiring a short forward hedge, shown in the second row. These positions offset to some extent, so the banking system only has to bear the net, shown in the table as a net short hedge on the third row. Such an imbalance would mean that the short forward positions have to pay speculators a premium. The difference $G(T) - ES(T)$ is a time-varying risk premium, and the relevant risk is liquidity risk.

Unfortunately we do not observe $ES(T)$, so we cannot observe the risk premium directly. However, the banking perspective adopted in this chapter suggests that that premium can be divided into two pieces, the difference between the forwards $G(T)$ and futures $G(T)$, and the difference between futures $G(T)$ and the expected spot rate $ES(T)$. The latter is still unobservable, but the former we can see in market prices. Under the hypothesis that these two pieces of the premium move together, we can use the former as a measure of the overall liquidity premium.

5 TIME-VARYING RISK PREMIA

This interpretation of the EH and UIP anomalies as arising from the fundamental liquidity problem of banking suggests a natural empirical test: does our measure of the price of liquidity risk, derived from the prices of instruments with different patterns of cash flows, help explain observed deviations from the EH and UIP null hypotheses? If so, these terms will be significant when added to the standard regressions used to test these hypotheses.

5.1 Verification of the Failure of EH

The expectations hypothesis of interest rates states that forward interest rates should be equal in expectation to subsequent realized spot rates, that is:

$$f_0(N, T) = \mathrm{E}_0\, l(N, T). \tag{15.6}$$

This equality has been rejected in different forms by the literature (Fama and Bliss, 1987; Campbell and Shiller, 1991; Piazzesi and Swanson, 2006). Empirical tests are based on regressions of realized spot rates on past forward rates. Following Piazzesi and Swanson (2006), we tested the expectations hypothesis for spot and forward interest rates in our data. The simple version of the test we employed involves regression of the forecast error on a constant. The estimated constant will be equal to the mean of the forecast error, and so EH is rejected if the constant is different

Table 15.5 $10000(f_0(N, T)d(N, T) - l(N, T)d(N, T)) = \alpha + \varepsilon$

	30	60	90	120	180
30	7.401	7.483	10.588	13.724	13.125
	(0.294)	(0.439)	(0.562)	(0.717)	(1.177)
60	10.483	12.089	14.087	16.603	15.798
	(0.311)	(0.356)	(0.529)	(0.704)	(1.176)
90	14.218	15.341	13.193	15.093	22.187
	(0.267)	(0.359)	(0.570)	(0.755)	(1.116)
120	17.380	15.833	15.863	17.955	22.663
	(0.287)	(0.421)	(0.553)	(0.761)	(1.187)
180	19.758	20.702	27.116	24.527	30.993
	(0.347)	(0.408)	(0.575)	(0.781)	(1.064)

Notes: Row headings are $T - N$, column headings are N. Under the EH null, $\alpha = 0$. Interest rates are in basis points.

from zero. Table 15.5 reports the results of EH regressions of the form $10000(f_0(N, T)d(N, T) - l(N, T)d(N, T)) = \alpha + \varepsilon$, for various values of N and T. $f_0(N,T)$ is the forward interest rate for delivery at N and maturity at T. $l(N,T)$ is the spot interest rate available at (and observed at) N for maturity at T. Values are de-annualized and interest rates are in basis points. Results vary with both N and T, but in all cases we reject EH. The estimates for α are consistent with those found in the literature.

5.2 EH Regression with Liquidity-risk Premium

To test the significance of our measure of liquidity risk, derived from price differences between interest-rate futures and forwards, in explaining the observed deviation of interest rates from the EH null, we repeated the regression of Section 5.1 with the liquidity-risk premium D^{ir} as an additional term.

Because D^{ir} represents the forward rate less the futures rate, we expect its coefficient to be positive when we estimate the model. From the discussion in Section 4, if more people want to lock in forward borrowing rates than want to lock in forward lending rates (that is, if the real economy is net short forwards), the banking system is forced to hold a net long position and charges a premium for doing so. This premium, according to the view presented in Section 2, should be observable in D^{ir}. Thus to the extent that implied forward rates are greater than futures rates, forward rates will deviate more from the EH null. Equivalently, we expect $\beta > 0$ in the regressions below.

The results appear in Table 15.6. This table should be compared with the third row of Table 15.5, presented as Table 15.7 for easier comparison.

Table 15.6 shows that β, the coefficient on the liquidity premium D^{ir}, is statistically significant and of the expected sign, indicating that D^{ir} helps to explain deviations of interest rates from the EH null. β is statistically

Table 15.6 EH regression with liquidity risk: $10000(f_0(N, T)d(N, T) - l(N, T)d(N, T)) = \alpha + \beta D^{ir} + \varepsilon$

	30	60	90	120	180
α	10.330	10.628	14.889	11.918	16.152
	(1.506)	(2.115)	(3.422)	(5.315)	(8.376)
β	0.609	0.796	0.251	1.106	2.323
	(0.252)	(0.299)	(0.480)	(0.801)	(1.253)
N	152	152	149	113	118

Notes: Column headings are N. $T - N = 90$. Under the EH null, $\alpha = 0$. Interest rates are in basis points.

Table 15.7 *EH regression without liquidity risk, equivalent to third row of Table 15.5:* $10000(f_0(N, T)d(N, T) - l(N, T)d(N,T)) = \alpha + \varepsilon$

	30	60	90	120	180
α	14.218	15.341	13.193	15.093	22.187
	(0.267)	(0.359)	(0.570)	(0.755)	(1.116)
N	6,101	6,101	7,500	4,212	5,519

Notes: Column headings are N. $T - N = 90$ for comparison with Table 15.6: Under the EH null, $\alpha = 0$. Interest rates are in basis points.

significant at the 5 per cent confidence level for $N = 30$ and $N = 60$, and at the 10 per cent level for $N = 180$. This is despite the paucity of observations in these regressions, which is due to our insistence on having a clean match between forwards and futures in constructing D^{ir}.

A second effect is that, with the addition of D^{ir}, α decreases in all cases except $T = 90$. This indicates that the addition of our measure of liquidity-risk premium reduces the average deviation of the observed rates from the EH null. We conclude that liquidity-risk premium aids in resolving this asset-pricing anomaly.

5.3 Verification of the Failure of Uncovered Interest Parity (UIP)

Uncovered interest parity is the hypothesis that forward exchange rates are an unbiased predictor of future spot exchange rates. Tests of UIP take the form of regressions of the realized appreciation or depreciation on the past forward premium or discount and a constant. UIP is rejected if the estimated constant is different from zero or the coefficient on the past forward premium or discount is different from one. Table 15.8 shows the results of UIP regressions using the specification of Burnside et al. (2006) on our data. $S'(N)$ is the spot exchange rate available at time N in $\frac{\text{foreign currency}}{\text{dollars}}$ (we deviate from the convention used elsewhere in this chapter to conform to the notation used by Burnside et al. (2006)). $G'_N(N + 1)$ is the forward exchange rate available at time N for settlement at time $N + 1$. The unit of time is taken to be 30, 60, and 90 days. Consistent with the literature, we reject UIP. Moreover, as is usual, we find that currencies at a forward premium tend to *appreciate* and *vice versa*, exactly opposite to the claim of UIP.

Table 15.8 *UIP regression:*

$$\frac{S'(N+1) - S'(N)}{S'(N)} = \alpha + \beta\frac{G'_N(N+1) - S'(N)}{S'(N)} + \varepsilon$$

	JPY 30	JPY 60	JPY 90	EUR 30	EUR 60	EUR 90
α	−0.006	−0.011	−0.019	−0.003	−0.007	−0.010
	(0.003)	(0.007)	(0.010)	(0.003)	(0.005)	(0.010)
β	−0.772	−1.533	−2.406	−1.652	−3.172	−5.070
	(0.358)	(0.783)	(1.052)	(0.690)	(1.300)	(2.328)
N	209	104	69	97	48	32
R^2	0.022	0.036	0.072	0.057	0.115	0.137

Notes: Under the UIP null, $\alpha = 0$ and $\beta = 1$.

5.4 UIP Regression with Liquidity-risk Premium

To test the significance of our measure of liquidity risk, derived from price differences between FX futures and forward exchange rates implied by CIP, in explaining observed deviations from UIP, we repeated the regression of Section 5.3 with the liquidity-risk premium as an additional term.

Because D^{fx} represents the forward price less the futures price, we expect its coefficient to be positive when we estimate the model. From the discussion in Section 4, if more people want to lock in the price at which they can sell the high-interest-rate currency than want to lock in the price at which they can buy it, the banking system will be forced to hold a net long forward position in the high interest-rate currency and will charge a liquidity-risk premium for doing so. This premium should be observable in D^{fx}. To the extent that forward exchange rates are greater than futures rates, forward rates will deviate more from the UIP null. From the argument in Section 4, we expect $D^{fx} > 0$ to imply that $GN > ES(N + 1)$. In the regressions we use the reciprocal exchange-rate convention, so we this is equivalent to G'_N < ES9(N + 1). Thus we expect $\gamma > 0$ in the regressions.

The results appear in Table 15.9. Table 15.8 is reprinted as Table 15.10 for comparison.

Note that g is not significantly different from zero in any case. This is certainly due in part to paucity of observations, a consequence of the matching procedure between forwards and futures and the fact that foreign-exchange futures trade only quarterly. Note, however, that the estimates for *b*, which should be 1 under the UIP null, move toward the

Table 15.9 UIP regression with liquidity risk:

$$\frac{S'(N+1) - S'(N)}{S'(N)} = \alpha + \beta\frac{G'_N(N+1) - S'(N)}{S'(N)} + \gamma D_N^{fx} + \varepsilon$$

	JPY 30	JPY 60	JPY 90	EUR 30	EUR 60	EUR 90
α	0.003	−0.005	−0.014	−0.005	−0.006	−0.010
	(0.007)	(0.009)	(0.012)	(0.006)	(0.008)	(0.009)
β	0.184	−1.110	−2.080	−1.580	−4.009	−3.639
	(0.780)	(1.008)	(1.245)	(1.286)	(1.946)	(2.373)
γ	244.582	−92.134	235.148	7.076	4.292	−9.552
	(472.556)	(251.784)	(611.969)	(4.988)	(5.713)	(7.783)
N	69	68	68	32	32	31
R^2	0.004	0.019	0.047	0.093	0.140	0.172

Table 15.10 UIP regression:

$$\frac{S'(N+1) - S'(N)}{S'(N)} = \alpha + \beta\frac{G'_N(N+1) - S'(N)}{S'(N)} + \varepsilon$$

	JPY 30	JPY 60	JPY 90	EUR 30	EUR 60	EUR 90
α	−0.006	−0.011	−0.019	−0.003	−0.007	−0.010
	(0.003)	(0.007)	(0.010)	(0.003)	(0.005)	(0.010)
β	−0.772	−1.533	−2.406	−1.652	−3.172	−5.070
	(0.358)	(0.783)	(1.052)	(0.690)	(1.300)	(2.328)
N	209	104	69	97	48	32
R^2	0.022	0.036	0.072	0.057	0.115	0.137

Notes: Under the UIP null, $\alpha = 0$ and $\beta = 1$.

theoretical value when D^{fx} is added as an explanatory variable. While this evidence cannot be considered conclusive, it does suggest that the liquidity-premium argument we presented in Sections 2 and 4 may offer part of an explanation for the anomaly.

5.5 Observations

Our desire to limit ourselves as far as possible to observable prices reflecting actual trading opportunities available to market participants creates some limitations for these regressions. In particular, and as discussed above, since futures contracts trade with fixed maturity dates, and since Eurocurrency deposits (and hence our implied forwards) trade every day but with fixed terms, the number of observations we are able to use is limited to the number of days on which the maturity of the futures contract matches the maturity of the implied forwards. This occurs only once each quarter for each maturity for FX futures, which are listed quarterly, and only once each month for the interest-rate futures, which are listed monthly. For this reason, the EH regressions are limited to about 150 observations, while the UIP regressions are limited to about 70 observations for dollar–yen and about 30 for dollar–euro (owing to the longer series of yen FX futures).

One could increase the number of observations in these regressions by interpolation, for example by creating an entire term structure from the observed Eurodollar deposit rates. While this would allow comparison between futures and forwards on more days, we have avoided such measures because they add a layer of interpretation between our conclusions and the data, which largely reflects real trading opportunities available to market participants.

Our measure of liquidity risk helps to explain the failure of the expectations hypothesis of interest rates (EH). In explaining deviations of exchange rates from uncovered interest parity (UIP), though we see the average deviation decrease, the coefficient on the liquidity-risk premium itself is not statistically significant in our regressions. This fact may be due to the way in which banks internally manage credit risk with their foreign-exchange clients. If forward foreign-exchange transactions are internally marked to market, which would be a reasonable risk-management step to take in the highly volatile FX market, then the theoretical difference we have identified between forwards and futures would not be present. In terms of Table 15.1, there would be no liquidity difference between standard forwards and standard futures, so we should expect the liquidity premium to be priced elsewhere. This could be in instruments that do not appear in Table 15.1, such as currency swaps, or in *ad hoc* arrangements made directly between banks and their clients. That we do find the liquidity-risk premium to have explanatory power for interest rates suggests that liquidity risk has indeed been priced into the spot interest rates from which we derive our implied forward rates.

6 CONCLUSION

We have sought in this chapter to understand a fundamental payments problem, namely the mismatch between banking clients' natural forward positions arising from their business in the real economy. Banks act to address this mismatch by offsetting different clients' cash flows against one another. When this is impossible, banks can go to the forward and futures markets to try to achieve more complete offset there. The liquidity and depth of these markets comes at the cost of decreased flexibility in terms of contract dates, maturities and face values, so banks may still find it impossible to offset all cash flows. Since different means of offset differ in their detailed cash-flow characteristics, we can interpret their price differences as reflecting the price of the underlying liquidity risk which they help to offset.

Our work could be extended by interpolation of the interest-rate or futures-price series that enter in our analysis in order to obtain a more continuous data set, as is done by Grinblatt and Jegadeesh (1996). This would allow comparison of futures and forward prices on many more days than is possible without interpolation.

Another avenue for future research is suggested by the observation made at the end of Section 5.5—an extension to other interest-rate and exchange-rate instruments. The analysis undertaken here is a measurement of the price of liquidity risk deriving from instruments having different cash flows. The interest-rate and foreign-exchange markets have numerous instruments other than those we have studied here, each with its own specification of cash flows. In particular, interest-rate and currency swaps come to mind, and informal evidence suggests that these have come to hold much of the liquidity in these markets in recent years. A logical continuation of the analysis undertaken here, then, is to fully understand the institutional arrangements of those instruments (especially along the lines of Appendix Tables 15A.2 and 15A.3) and to measure the price of liquidity risk there. This could be viewed as adding columns to our Table 15.1, and work in this direction is undertaken by Johannes and Sundaresan (2007). With private data, one could also move left in those tables, to understand the price banks charge for the internal bearing of risk. Relation of these further measures of liquidity risk to macroeconomic problems would support our larger research aim of understanding the role of the banking system in monetary and macroeconomics.

NOTES

* The authors wish to thank participants in the Columbia Business School Finance Free Lunch, the Columbia Business School Macro Lunch, and the Festschrift in honor of Jane D'Arista for their comments. Errors are our own.

1. For concreteness the following discussion focuses on forward and futures contracts, but the reader will observe that the argument extends to exchange swaps and forward rate agreements, as well as more exotic instruments. Similarly, the activity of the stylized banking system that we are discussing does not map directly on to the activities of a specific category of financial institutions, but is rather meant to highlight a specific dimension of the monetary and financial system as a whole.
2. The closest paper to ours in the literature is Johannes and Sundaresan (2007). They

find that, empirically, swaps are priced as if they were between a portfolio of forwards and a portfolio of futures, and the price varies within that range depending on market conditions.

3. That is,

$$f_t(N,t) = \left(\frac{1 + l(t,T)d(t,T)}{1 + l(t,N)d(t,N)} - 1\right)\frac{1}{d(N,T)}. \tag{15.1}$$

4. The notation used throughout the chapter is discussed in Appendix 15A.
5. We used daily British Bankers' Association fixings of spot US dollar LIBOR. Implied forward interest rates were computed from these spot rates using equation (15.7). All data for this study were acquired using Bloomberg.
6. Eurodollar (ED) futures trade primarily on the Chicago Mercantile Exchange (CME). CME ED contracts are listed for ten years on the March quarterly schedule, with the four nearest-month contracts available as fill-ins. Thus, at the beginning of January 2008, quarterly contracts were available to December 2017, and January 2008, February 2008, April 2008, and May 2008 are the four serial contracts.
7. For dates when no interpolation is necessary, our procedure is exactly the same as that of Grinblatt and Jegadeesh. In line with standard theory, they expect $h_t(N, T) > f_t(N, T)$ (futures rate > implied forward rate), so they report $h_t(N, T) - f_t(N, T)$ and document convergence to near zero as markets become more efficient (see Appendix 15B.1). We however expect $f_t(N, T) > h_t(N, T)$ and so report $f_t(N, T) - h_t(N, T)$.
8. That is,

$$G_t(N) = S(t)\frac{1 + l(t,N)d(t,N)}{1 + l^*(t,N)d(t,N)}. \tag{15.4}$$

9. FX futures, and in particular USD/EUR and USD/JPY futures, trade on the CME. Both products are on a quarterly schedule, and neither has serial month contracts.
10. See for example Blinder (2004, pp. 74, 82).
11. See Piazzesi and Swanson (2006) for documentation and references.
12. The asserted equivalence follows from forward interest parity (see equation (15.7)). Throughout this Chapter we assume that this relationship holds identically.
13. See Burnside et al. (2006) for documentation and references.
14. The asserted equivalence follows from covered interest parity (see equation (15.10)). Throughout this chapter we assume that this relationship holds identically. Observe from this formula that $l^* > l$ implies $G(T) < S(0)$, and vice versa.

REFERENCES

Black, Fischer (1976), 'The pricing of commodity contracts', *Journal of Financial Economics*, **3**(1–2), 167–79.

Blinder, Alan S. (2004), *The Quiet Revolution: Central Banking Goes Modern*, Arthur M. Okun Memorial Lecture Series, New Haven: Yale University Press.

Burnside, Craig, Martin Eichenbaum, Isaac Kleshchelski, and Sergio Rebelo (2006), 'The returns to currency speculation', Working Paper 12489, NBER, November. Available at http://www.nber.org/papers/w12489.

Campbell, John Y. and Robert J. Shiller. Yield spreads and interest rate movements: a bird's eye view. *The Review of Economic Studies*, **58**(3), 495–514, May 1991.

Chance, Don M. (2006), 'A hedging deficiency in eurodollar futures', *Journal of Futures Markets*, **26**(2), 189–207.

Cox, John C., Jonathan E. Ingersoll Jr and Stephen A. Ross (1981), 'The relation

between forward prices and futures prices', *Journal of Financial Economics*, **9**(4), 321–46.
Fama, Eugene F. and Robert R. Bliss (1987), 'The information in long-maturity forward rates', *The American Economic Review*, **77**(4), 680–92.
Grinblatt, Mark and Narasimhan Jegadeesh (1996), 'Relative pricing of eurodollar futures and forward contracts', *The Journal of Finance*, **51**(4), 1499–1522.
Hicks, John R. (1939), *Value and Capital: An Inquiry into Some Fundamental Principles of Economic Theory*, Oxford: Oxford University Press.
Johannes, Michael and Suresh Sundaresan (2007), 'The impact of collateralization on swap rates', *Journal of Finance*, **62**(1), 383–410.
Keynes, John Maynard (1930), *A Treatise on Money. Volume II: The Applied Theory of Money*, London: Macmillan.
Piazzesi, Monika and Eric Swanson (2006), 'Futures prices as risk-adjusted forecasts of monetary policy', Working Paper 10547, NBER. Available at http://faculty.chicagogsb.edu/ monika.piazzesi/research/.
Samuelson, Paul A. (1965), 'Proof that properly anticipated prices fluctuate randomly', *Industrial Management Review*, **6**(2), 41–9.
Stigum, Marcia and Anthony Crescenzi (2007), *Stigum's Money Market*, 4th edn, New York: McGraw-Hill.
Sundaresan, Suresh (1991), 'Futures prices on yields, forward prices, and implied forward prices from term structure', *The Journal of Financial and Quantitative Analysis*, **26**(3), 409–24.
Tuckman, Bruce (2002), 'Eurodollar and Fed funds futures', in *Fixed Income Securities*, 2nd edn, Wiley, Chapter 17.

APPENDIX 15A: NOTATION

Principles of notation:

- All interest rates are lowercase letters; all prices (including exchange rates) are uppercase.
- Numbers inside parentheses are dates. As a consequence, interest rates have two dates inside, exchange rates have one.
- Variables correspond to quoted numbers when possible.
- Subscripts are avoided when possible.
- Exchange rates are dollars per unit foreign currency, which reflects the asymmetry in currency pairs.

$F_t(N, T)$	quoted interest-rate futures price at t on a notional deposit from N to T
$h_t(N, T)$	implied futures rate, i.e.) $1 - \frac{F_t(N,T)}{100}$
$l(t, T)$	quoted $T - t$-day spot LIBOR at time t
$d(N, T)$	de-annualization factor for a deposit from N to T, i.e. $\frac{T - N}{360}$
$f_0(N, T)$	annualized implied forward rate at time 0, i.e. $\left(\frac{1 + l(0,T)d(0,T)}{1 + l(0,N)d(0,N)} - 1\right)\left(\frac{1}{d(N,T)}\right)$
$S(t)$	spot exchange rate (dollars per unit foreign)
$G_0(N)$	implied forward exchange rate at time 0 for delivery at N i.e. $S(0)\frac{1 + l(0,N)d(0,N)}{1 + l^*(0,N)d(0,N)}$
$\mathbf{G}_t(N)$	quoted FX futures price at time t maturing at N
$l^*(t, T)$	quoted $T - t$-day spot foreign-currency LIBOR at time t.

APPENDIX 15B: PATTERNS OF CASH FLOWS

The payments problem solved by the banking system is to align mismatched patterns of cash flows stemming from natural positions in the real economy. To study the premium charged for the bearing of liquidity risk in providing this service, we study forward and futures contracts in interest rates and foreign exchange. The design of each of these contracts creates a specific pattern of cash flows. The use of this limited set of standardized contracts allows banks to achieve more complete offset of payments, but it remains unlikely that the offset will be perfect.

Forward contracts are traded in over-the-counter markets and are standardized in tenor, but are available in any size and can begin on any day. Futures contracts are traded on an exchange and are standardized in size and maturity date. The purchase of any of these contracts is equivalent to the purchase of the particular pattern of cash flows determined by the contract design, the purchase price, and the uncertain subsequent path of interest or exchange rates. Previous papers that have studied price differences between futures and forwards have mainly been interested in testing the efficiency of asset pricing in these markets, which they take to be a matter of convergence between futures and forwards (for example, Grinblatt and Jegadeesh, 1996; Sundaresan, 1991). Because of this motivation, these papers have not generally been clear about the precise pattern of cash flows in question. Our story is entirely about that time pattern, so we must be much clearer.

15B.1 Interest-rate Forwards and Futures

Table 15A.1 summarizes four interest-rate instruments along two of the dimensions which distinguish them. The instruments, of which two are hypothetical, are discussed in detail below. The left column shows contracts which settle to yield, including the actual Eurodollar futures contract and the hypothetical Eurodollar forward. The right column shows contracts which settle to price, including the hypothetical price-based futures and the actual implied forward. The top row shows contracts which are marked to market, that is, futures contracts, and the bottom row shows contracts that are not marked to market, that is, forward contracts. The consequence of each of these terms for patterns of cash flows is elaborated in this section.

Table 15A.2 outlines the cash flows that can be obtained by purchasing various interest-rate contracts. All are shown from the point of view of the long side of the trade (that is, the side which profits from a subsequent decline in interest rates) and with a loan of $1 in mind. Consistent with market convention, interest rates are expressed in annual terms, which means that an adjustment factor is required to compute actual interest payments when the maturity is different from one year. This de-annualization factor we denote $d(N, T)$.

Table 15A.1 Comparison of interest-rate contract feature

	Settles to yield	Settles to price
Marked to market	Traded futures	Price-based futures
Not marked to market	Eurodollar forward	Implied forward

Table 15A.2 Timing of cash flows for Eurodollar futures and forwards

	Time					
Instrument	0	$0< t < N$	N	T	obsv'd[α]	at
Implied forward	0	0	-1	$1 + f_0(N,T)d(N,T)$	S	0
Traded futures	0	$(F_t(N,T) - F_{t-1}(N,T))\frac{d(N,T)}{100}$	$((100 - l(N,T)) - F_{N-1}(N,T))\frac{d(N,T)}{100}$	0	Q	N
Refinanced forward	0	0	$-1 + \frac{(1 + f_0(N,T)d(N,T))}{(1 + l(N,T)d(N,T))}$	0	S	N
Eurodollar forward	0	0	$(h_0(N,T) - l(N,T))d(N,T)$	0	NE	N
Price-based futures	0	$\frac{1}{1 + \left(1 - \frac{J_t(N,T)}{100}\right)d(N,T)} - \frac{1}{1 + \left(1 - \frac{J_{t-1}(N,T)}{1}\right.}$	$\frac{1}{1 + l(N,T)d(N,T)} - \frac{1}{1 + \left(1 - \frac{J_{N-1}(N,T)}{100}\right)d(N,T)}$	0	NE	N

Note: [α] S: synthetic; NE: non-existent; Q: quoted.

The first row of Table 15A.2 shows the forward loan implied by spot LIBOR, the instrument in the lower-right corner of Table 15A.1. A suitable combination of long and short Eurodollar deposits allows the lender to fix at time 0 the rate on a loan from time N to time T. This nets a cash flow of 0 at time 0, -1 at time N and the return of the 1 plus interest at time T. The interest earned on this forward loan can be expressed in terms of the relevant spot rates, *viz*.

$$f_0(N, T) = \left(\frac{1 + l(0, T)d(0, T)}{1 + l(0, N)d(0, N)} - 1\right)\frac{1}{d(N, T)}. \tag{15.7}$$

This formula follows from forward interest parity, a pure arbitrage condition with strong empirical support. We think of the other contracts as variations on this pure forward.

The second contract we consider is the standardized interest-rate futures contract, found in the upper-left corner of Table 15A.1, typified by Eurodollar futures traded on the Merc and elsewhere. A key difference between futures and forwards is the mark-to-market feature of the former. Market participants are required to hold margin accounts at the exchange, and at the close of each trading day, the value of each contract is determined and payments flow from the losers to the winners. This reduces counterparty risk both for the investors and for the exchange (which is legally the counterparty to each trade) by limiting the degree to which any participant can be out of the money. Because money can be withdrawn from variation-margin accounts when the balance is sufficient, and must be deposited into them when insufficient, this process has cash-flow implications for the holders of futures positions. These are quantified in the second row of Table 15A.2. On each day until settlement, $0 < t < N$, the long side receives a payment reflecting the change in futures price, $(F_t(N,T) - F_{t-1}(N,T))\frac{d(N,T)}{100}$ (or makes such a payment if this quantity is negative, i.e. if the futures price has fallen). On the final day, time N, the contract settles to prevailing LIBOR and the final payment is made. In Table 15A.2, we omit the cash flows due to investing or financing margin payments. These are small relative to the amounts we consider, for example financing \$25 for 90 days at 5.25% costs $\$25 \times 0.0525 \times \frac{90}{360} = \$0.33$. The de-annualization factor $d(N, T)$ is always $\frac{90}{360} = 0.25$ for ED futures. The choice of contract terms has the consequence that a rise of 0.01 in $F_t(N, T)$ (that is, a one-basis-point drop in the implied interest rate) represents an increase in value for the long side of the futures contract of

$$\frac{0.01}{100} \times \$1{,}000{,}000 \times 0.25 = \$25. \tag{15.8}$$

The futures contract is cash-settled, meaning that although the final settlement depends on the spot interest rate for a deposit maturing at time $T = N + 90$, no money changes hands after time N. This is in contrast to the forward contract, where money flows in one direction at time N and in the other at time T. To create a synthetic Eurodollar investment that would address this incompatibility by moving all cash flows to time N, consider the addition to the implied forward of a third leg, which borrows at time N an amount requiring the payment of exactly $(1 + f_0(N, T)d(N, T))$ at time T. At time N, the available rate on such a loan is $T - N$-day spot LIBOR, $l(N, T)$, so the amount to be borrowed is

$$\frac{1 + f_0(N,T)d(N,T)}{1 + l(N,T)d(N,T)}. \tag{15.9}$$

At time T, the proceeds from the original long leg yield the amount needed to pay off this loan. We call the composite position a "refinanced" forward, and it is included as the third row of Table 15A.2. Note that, while the cash flows of the implied forward are fully determined at time 0, refinancing the forward at time N makes cash flows dependent on $l(N, T)$, which is unknown until N. Since this position does not differ from the basic implied forward in either mark-to-market or settlement features, it occupies the same cell of Table 15A.1. The refinanced forward is analogous to the forward contract in Treasury bills, which settles at time N with delivery of the T-bill itself. Even so it is not the forward version of the traded Eurodollar futures contract.

Beyond the cash-settlement distinction just described, two mismatches in cash flows between the implied Eurodollar forward and the Eurodollar futures contract remain. First, the futures is marked to market, so that cash changes hands every day until time N. This is the difference that is the focus of standard finance theory. Second, the futures settles to yield while the forward settles to price. The forward settles to price because the Eurodollar deposit pays add-on interest. The futures settles to yield because it was modeled after the T-bill futures contract (Chance, 2006; Stigum and Crescenzi, 2007). We can understand these mismatches by considering two hypothetical contracts which would address them in turn. These would occupy the lower-left and upper-right corners of Table 15A.1.

The hypothetical security that Sundaresan (1991) calls a "Eurodollar forward" lies in the lower left corner of Table 15A.1. Like the refinanced forward, the Eurodollar forward yields all its cash flows at time N. In addition to this, it settles to yield in a manner analogous to Eurodollar futures (and distinct from actual Eurodollar deposits). Using the terms of the foregoing discussion of patterns of cash flow, the Eurodollar forward yields the same net cash flows as a Eurodollar futures contract purchased at the same price, but without the mark-to-market feature of the futures contract on days $0 < t < N$.

To complete Table 15A.1, an alternative futures contract could be imagined. Retaining the mark-to-market feature, this would settle to price (that is, to $\frac{100}{1 + l(N,T)d(N,T)}$), rather than to yield (that is, to $100 - l(N, T)$), providing, on day N, exactly the amount needed to buy a Eurodollar deposit from time N to time T paying \$100 at time T. This would have the result that, unlike the existing Eurodollar futures contract, a one-basis-point move in the price would entail a variation-margin payment that varied with the price. This mismatch is discussed in detail by Chance (2006). The final row of Table 15A.2 shows such an instrument, which we refer to as a "price-based futures" and whose price we denote $J_t(N, T)$.

Standard theory says that the yield on traded futures should be greater than the yield on the implied forward, for two reasons—the mark-to-market effect and convexity.

Reinvestment risk depends on the covariance between the futures price and the rate of interest. In the case of interest-rate futures, the covariance leads us to expect futures to be priced below forwards, which is to say the futures rate should be greater than the implied forward rate (Tuckman, 2002, pp. 350–54). At short horizons, however, this effect is negligible (Grinblatt and Jegadeesh, 1996, p. 1512; Tuckman, 2002, p. 354), and we will assume that it is exactly zero. Because our theory suggests that the futures rate should be *less* than the forward rate, this assumption biases us against finding the effect in empirical data.

15B.2 Foreign-exchange Forwards and Futures

Table 15A.3 shows the pattern of cash flows of two contracts in the foreign-exchange markets. Consistent with market practice, we think of foreign currency as a speculative asset. As such, all exchange rates are expressed as prices of that asset, that is, in the $\frac{\text{dollars}}{\text{unit of foreign currency}}$. Thus, an appreciation of the asset is represented by an increase in the exchange rate.

Table 15A.3 shows both the domestic- and foreign-currency flows of a forward and a futures contract in FX. The implied forward, shown in the first row, is achievable through use of the spot exchange market and a suitable foreign-currency Euro deposit. The forward exchange rate shown, $G_0(N)$, is the rate implied by covered interest parity (CIP), namely

$$G_0(N) = S(0)\frac{1 + l(0, N)d(0, N)}{1 + l^*(0, N)d(0, N)}. \tag{15.10}$$

Table 15A.3 Timing of cash flows for foreign-exchange forwards and futures

Instrument		Time				
		0	$0 < t < N$	N	obsv'd[α]	at
Implied	\$	0	0	$-F0(N)$	S	0
forward	f.c.	0	0	1	S	0
Futures	\$	0	$\mathbf{G}_t(N) - \mathbf{G}_{t-1}(N)$	$-\mathbf{G}_{N-1}(N)$	Q	N
	f.c.	0	0	1	Q	N

Note: [α] S: synthetic; Q: quoted.

That CIP holds is strongly supported empirically. Note that all parameters of the forward transaction are known at time 0.

The second row of Table 15A.3 shows the cash flows entailed by the FX futures contract. The mark-to-market process works in a manner similar to that described for interest-rate futures above. In contrast to those contracts, however, "physical" delivery of the underlying commodity is possible in foreign exchange and is the normal practice if the futures contract is held until maturity. At settlement, the long side receives a quantity of foreign currency corresponding to one unit of domestic currency. By summing all of the domestic-currency payments made over the life of the contract, it can be seen that the long side has paid $\mathbf{G}_0(N)$ for this, that is, the futures exchange rate prevailing when the contract was purchased. As with interest-rate futures above, in Table 15A.3 we ignore cash flows due to the financing or reinvestment of variation-margin payments, since these are small relative to the other sums at issue. Note that all variation-margin payments are made in the domestic currency, consistent with the notion that the foreign currency functions as a speculative asset.

16. The last refuge of scoundrels: Keynes–Minsky perspectives on the uses and abuses of the "liquidity defense"[1]

James Crotty and Gerald A. Epstein

INTRODUCTION: THE LIQUIDITY DEFENSE IN THE BATTLE FOR FINANCIAL REFORM

The role played by investment banks in creating the conditions that led to the global financial crisis that broke out in 2007 is well chronicled.[2] These banks took excessive risks and used excessive leverage to support their immensely profitable proprietary trading; they were a major source of credit to other financial institutions, such as hedge funds, that were also major speculators; and they created, perfected and distributed the innovations in financial products at the center of the financial collapse.[3] The proprietary character of the banks' trading was often hidden within the banks' inventories, in their role as market-makers who buy and sell securities to help create and sustain "liquid" security markets. It was thus easy to disguise holdings of securities purchased with the intention to sell at some future date for the bank's profit – proprietary trading – as securities being kept in inventory for the bank's market-making activity.

To prevent the recurrence of excessive risk-taking with excessive leverage in institutions that are considered too big to fail and therefore potential wards of the state in a serious financial crisis, the U.S. government enacted the Volcker Rule, intended to prohibit proprietary trading as part of the Dodd–Frank financial reform legislation. Not surprisingly, the politically powerful giant investment banks and banking conglomerates that dominate the industry and had successfully lobbied on behalf of radical financial market deregulation for decades have fought tooth and nail against the effective implementation of the Volcker Rule.[4] They have waged an expensive campaign, using armies of lobbyists, generous contributions, their influence in the media and the promise of high-paying jobs in finance to legislators after they leave the government, to convince Congress and the President to eviscerate the Rule.

Jane D'Arista has played a key role in working with the Americans for Financial Reform (AFR) and SAFER (Experts for Stable, Accountable, Fair and Efficient Financial Reform) in fighting against these lobbyists. Her knowledge of financial and monetary history and grasp of the real operations of financial institutions and financial regulations helped to counter the arguments of these bankers and their allies. Yet, with many millions of dollars to spend, these forces of finance sent wave after wave of assaults against reforms such as the Volcker Rule.

In pleading their case, the banks have, above all else, mounted the "liquidity defense": essentially they claim that any regulation that reduces "liquidity" necessarily harms financial customers and the overall economy. Analytically, their liquidity defense is divided into two inter-connected arguments. First, the banks claim that the Rule, by limiting their proprietary trading, would make it difficult if not impossible for them to perform the crucial function of providing "*liquidity*" to the nation's securities markets. Here liquidity is defined as the ability of investors to buy and sell securities quickly at a very low transaction cost.[5] Without adequate liquidity, markets could not operate efficiently, these investment bankers claim. Investors would not be able to transact quickly when they needed or wanted to, and they might have to eventually accept a price that was well below what their securities were worth, or below the "appropriate price."[6] In turn, if investors came to believe that they would be punished when they sold securities by being forced to wait to sell and/or accept a substantial capital loss, they would be less willing to buy the securities that fund investment in capital goods, research and development, and business and residential construction, and make it possible for corporations and individuals to insure against excessive risk. This would, they argue, raise the costs to investors wishing to borrow money, slow economic and productivity growth, and reduce the efficiency of resource allocation.

The second argument is that the Rule would interfere with the crucial role of "*price discovery*" played by investment banks, hedge funds and other aggressive traders. It turns out that this argument is difficult to sustain within standard neoclassical financial theory, but these opponents of the Rule are unphased. Canonical models of neoclassical financial market theory assume that prices in financial security markets are always optimal equilibrium prices that properly reflect the true risk-return characteristics of securities. In such a world, it is hard to see why *discovery* would be required. However, when talking about the real world, these economists insist that financial market equilibrium prices must be discovered through the dynamic interaction of bulls and bears in liquid markets. They argue that investment banks accelerate the discovery process through informed proprietary trading by acting as market-makers. Financial market lobbyists insist that the Rule would seriously impede the price-discovery process, causing markets to generate the "wrong" prices much of the time.

These banker criticisms of the Volcker Rule on the grounds that they will reduce "liquidity" and "price discovery" are simply among many examples of the common response by the banking lobby and supportive economists to virtually any attempt to impose stricter financial regulation. The same arguments have been used against attempts to regulate derivatives, increase capital and liquidity requirements, regulate "naked" credit default swaps, limit commodity speculation, regulate high-frequency trading, or impose a financial transactions tax (Duffie, 2010). All of these policies are met with a chorus of opposition based on the claim that these regulations will limit market liquidity, raise costs for customers trying to access credit or hedge risk, and inhibit "price discovery." In short, the "liquidity defense" is the go-to weapon for defenders of the status quo in financial regulation and has been remarkably successful as they are repeated uncritically by much of the financial press, and rationalized by analysts from "think tanks" and academia alike (such as Duffie, 2012; Oliver Wyman, 2012).

In this chapter, we argue that the "liquidity defense" is theoretically incoherent, and that the role of investment banks in the financial crisis discussed at the outset gives a prima facie case that it is wrong empirically.[7] The liquidity defense is based on definitions of liquidity that are fuzzy, at best, and on narratives about the roles of liquidity that largely contradict the core assumptions of the models used by these analysts and lobbyists.

This liquidity defense is set within, *and only makes sense within*, the framework of neoclassical financial market theory because it assumes that more liquidity *always* leads to greater market efficiency, a proposition that is, in fact, wrong. By contrast, the core propositions of mainstream theory relied on to defend proprietary trading do not hold in the more realistic financial market theories associated with John Maynard Keynes and Hyman Minsky. In Keynes–Minsky (hereafter referred to as KM) theory, the relation between trading liquidity and market efficiency is nonlinear. Clearly, a market with little liquidity cannot create an adequate demand for long-term risky securities, and therefore cannot adequately finance capital investment. On the other hand, a market in which investors believe they can buy and sell cheaply and unload their risky securities instantaneously at the first hint of trouble will encourage excessive speculation and market volatility. Moreover, in the KM world, financial actors like investment banks do not aid "price discovery," they contribute to asset "price creation"; and if the financial actions they engage in, such as proprietary trading, are focused on short-term speculation and manipulation, then the asset prices they help create are unlikely to efficiently further social goals such as employment creation and long-term productive investment.

While for the mainstream, the more market liquidity the better, for Keynes the issue of liquidity presents a genuine "dilemma" (his term). In Chapter 12 of the *General Theory* (*GT*) Keynes called attention to the stark change in the liquidity properties of ownership claims on capital goods that took place between the 19th century and the 1930s when he was writing *GT*:

> In former times, when enterprises were mainly owned by those who undertook them or by their friends and associates, investment depended upon a sufficient supply of individuals of sanguine temperament and constructive impulses who embarked on business as a way of life, not relying on a precise calculation of prospective profit. (Keynes, 1936, p. 150)

He noted that: "Decisions to invest in private business of the old-fashioned type were, however, decisions that were irrevocable, not only for the community as a whole, but also for the individual." That is, capital goods were an illiquid asset not only for the community or the national economy, but also for the individual. Neither could avoid the high risk associated with illiquid capital goods. But the rise of publicly owned corporations whose stock was traded on the market as the dominant form of enterprise ownership created a stark difference between the liquidity properties of capital goods' ownership between the individual and the community. "With the separation between ownership and management that prevails today and with the development of organised investment markets, a new factor of great importance has entered in, which sometimes facilitates investment but *sometimes adds greatly to the instability of the system*" (Keynes, 1936, pp. 150–51; italics added). Market liquidity, Keynes argued, made investors willing to invest in long-term capital that is supportive of capital accumulation, employment, and productivity growth. But liquidity can also lead to excessive speculation, instability, and stagnation.

Thus Keynes identifies a dilemma: he argues that liquidity is a dangerous illusion for society as a whole. Yet, it appears to be required to induce investors to make investments in otherwise long-term, relatively illiquid, socially useful capital. Still, Keynes argued, in actually existing financialized capitalism, there are many processes that undermine liquidity's usefulness. In developing this dilemma, we focus in this chapter on Keynes' views in Chapter 12 of the *GT*. As we show in more detail in Crotty and Epstein (2013):

1. In chapter 12 of the *General Theory*, (*GT*) Keynes stresses the short-termism and speculative aspects that liquidity induces with respect to investment decisions tied to the stock market, leading to capital misallocation.
2. In chapters 13–15, of the *General Theory* Keynes notes the excessive demand for safe assets (money) in crisis that can undermine the accumulation of risky, long-term capital.
3. In chapter 22 of the *GT* these aspects of liquidity contribute to liquidity cycles and real economic cycles, that exacerbate the business cycle in capitalism, and thereby induce significant costs to society without necessarily contributing to the accumulation of long-term capital.

In short, whereas Keynes argues that in some circumstances we might need to accept the necessary evil of liquidity in order to facilitate capital accumulation, in the end, the benefits might not be worth the cost. It might be that effective financial regulation could reduce these liquidity pathologies sufficiently to help facilitate the appropriate accumulation of long-term socially productive investment. But in the absence of effective regulation, the greater the need, according to Keynes, for a much more socialized control over investment processes.

Keynes is not alone in his concern over this dimension of excessive liquidity. James Tobin proposed his financial transactions tax precisely in order to remove excessive liquidity and therefore excessive volatility from the market. Paul Volcker recently said: "There should not be a presumption that evermore market liquidity brings a public benefit. At some point, great liquidity, or the perception of it, may itself encourage more speculative trading."[8] Former chief International Monetary Fund (IMF) economist Simon Johnson asked: "Is maximum liquidity the right goal?" and answered: "Not necessarily, because a high degree of liquidity in good times can lull investors into a false sense of safety and reduce their incentive to do a careful credit analysis."[9] But none of these other economists has developed a coherent framework that can explain why these liquidity problems are endemic to capitalism. We must turn to the KM approach to get the necessary insight.

In what follows, we first explore various definitions of the term "liquidity" and show that this concept is often ill defined and even defined in contradictory ways by mainstream financial economists. We then turn to a general discussion of the KM analysis of the role of liquidity in financial cycles, starting off with some key general methodological points about Keynes' theory that are critical to an understanding of the KM discussions of the role of liquidity in capitalism. In the third section, we focus on Keynes' views in Chapter 12 of the *GT*, where he develops in detail the "liquidity dilemma," both with respect to financial instability and the longer term impact on capital misallocation. In the final section, we discuss Keynes' solutions to the problems of liquidity, and highlight the stark contrast between Keynes' solutions to the "liquidity dilemma" and mainstream finance's "liquidity defense."

WHAT IS LIQUIDITY? THE THEORETICAL INCOHERENCE OF THE MAINSTREAM PERSPECTIVE

Before the treatment of liquidity in mainstream theory and KM theory can be compared, we have to ask: What is liquidity? This is a more difficult question to answer than it might appear because the word is used to represent various dimensions or aspects of financial markets, but it is usually not defined, requiring the reader to intuit its meaning from the particular context or contexts in which the word appears in an article or book. To exaggerate only slightly, it seems as if in the mainstream literature any characteristic of financial markets that is claimed to be "efficient" is said to add to "liquidity." This makes it extremely difficult to critically evaluate theories that incorporate the concept of liquidity in such broad and elastic ways. In a book contrasting the use of models and theories in physics and financial economics, Emanuel Derman, a physicist who became a financial "quant" at Goldman Sachs and later a professor at Columbia University and director of Columbia's program in financial engineering, made the following correct observation:

> The difficulties one encounters in modeling economic abstractions are illustrated by attempts to deal with the notion of market liquidity. Liquidity is the metaphorical quality that makes trading possible: it connotes the easy availability of counterparties to buy something you want to sell or sell something you want to buy, and its disappearance in states of fear causes the great damage that characterized the recent global financial crisis. *Everyone thinks he knows what liquidity means, yet no one has adequately defined and qualified it*. (Derman, 2011, p. 48; italics added)

When they do try to define liquidity, mainstream financial economists often make a distinction between funding liquidity and market liquidity. Funding liquidity refers to the ability of financial actors to fund their positions in financial assets; it plays an important role in the creation of financial cycles and relates to the role of central bank policy and lender of last resort activities as well as the behavior of private financial institutions (for example, BIS, 2011). As for market liquidity, in theoretical discussion neoclassical theory usually defines market liquidity rather narrowly as trading liquidity: the more quickly and cheaply securities can be bought and sold and the lower the cost of transactions, the more liquid the market is with respect to trading liquidity.[10] However, in policy debates and discussions, they often refer to a broader definition of market liquidity: they add the idea that a liquid market is one that allows securities to be sold at an "appropriate" price. We refer to this as "appropriate price liquidity." As we discuss below, using this broader definition of market liquidity which includes both trading and price liquidity creates serious problems for the coherence and meaningfulness of mainstream discussions: under this definition, almost any requirement for financial market efficiency can appear in the implicit definition of liquidity.[11]

In some discussions, the concept of liquidity is defined even more broadly to include in the concept funding liquidity, trading liquidity, and appropriate price liquidity, as well as a fourth concept: safe haven liquidity.[12] For Keynes, this concept plays a key role in defining what money is: A safe asset that can be bought and sold easily with no loss of value or risk. As shown in Crotty and Epstein (2013), according to Keynes money plays a key role in underpinning all other forms of liquidity in the financial system. In recent concerns over the lack of so-called riskless assets in the global economy, this issue has come to the fore in mainstream discussions as well (IMF, 2012, Ch. 3).

The difficulty in interpreting claims about "liquidity" is that the mainstream economists slip back and forth seamlessly using various combinations of these concepts, even though they do not coherently work with their underlying theory and have very different meanings and implications. In what follows, we will be discussing mostly the issue of market liquidity, which often entails only the concept of trading liquidity in mainstream theoretical discussions, but often slide into appropriate price liquidity as well when mainstream economists discuss narratives about actual events or make claims about policy issues. But be prepared for some reference to even broader notions of liquidity (funding liquidity and safe haven liquidity) when connecting these concepts to liquidity cycles and macroeconomic instability.

Market Liquidity: Trading Liquidity and Appropriate Price Liquidity

As discussed above, much of the mainstream discussion of the dangers of financial regulation focuses on the issue of market liquidity. But as we discuss below, this definition of market liquidity is fuzzy and even incoherent. This is especially true when the idea of the "appropriate price" for a security is slipped into the broader definition of market liquidity.

What is the "appropriate price" of a security? The answer depends crucially on the assumption used in the theory about the character of agent expectations of future states of the economy. In their formal mathematical models of financial markets, mainstream economists usually assume "rational expectations" in which the stochastic distributions of future cash flows associated with all securities are predetermined and known by agents prior to their decisions to buy or sell securities. Thus, future cash flows cannot be affected by the agent portfolio selection decisions that co-determine the equilibrium prices of securities. Rather, equilibrium security prices are determined by pre-given agent preferences over risk and return in conjunction with predetermined expected future cash flows. Of course, the only way agents could know the probability distributions that describe future states of the economy is if the future was already determined prior to current agent choice. This logically implies that current decisions cannot affect future outcomes, a peculiar feature of a theory that claims to be micro-founded. Mainstream theory asserts that market prices set in competitive financial markets are the equilibrium price. Thus, in this theory, by assumption, markets are never wrong.

In KM theory, the processes that determine prices are more complex. No claim is made that actual market prices are either optimal or equilibrium prices. They simply are what the forces of supply and demand at any moment force them to be. Moreover, prices move endogenously, they are not predetermined by exogenous expectations and preference functions. Rather, the processes that determine prices are path dependent. As discussed in more detail in the third section, the entry point for this theory is the assumption of fundamental uncertainty. In contrast to neoclassical theory, KM theory insists that because the future does not yet exist and is not yet determined, it cannot be known in the present. The assumption of "rational expectations" is itself considered to be irrational because there is no possible way agents can achieve knowledge of the future. Deprived of certain knowledge of the future, KM agents have to rely on guesses or hunches about future states of the economy based on heuristics and social conventions. Their expectations are normally strongly influenced by the extrapolation of price movements from the relevant past. Agents know that expectations thus formed are not the "truth" about the future, and their confidence in the reliability of their expectations changes over time. These fallible expectations, along with endogenously changing attitudes toward risk, strongly influence the level of current security prices.

When markets are booming, agents tend to extrapolate the rate of growth of security prices, reinforcing the boom's forward motion. However, boom-era expectations eventually outrun the economy's ability to generate cash flows. As Keynes argued in Chapter 22 of the *GT*, booms must eventually end, and they often end in panics and crashes, but post-crisis depressed financial markets eventually recover and at some point begin to boom again. The result is recurring financial cycles around a variable trend, a pattern that can be discerned in the historical record of financial markets. Thus, in theoretical discussions (as opposed to when they bring up narratives or talk about policy issues) neoclassical financial theory can focus solely on the narrow dimension of market liquidity (that is, trading liquidity) because the appropriate price is assumed to be the predetermined optimal price and markets are always assumed to be in equilibrium.

Keynes–Minsky theory, by contrast, must address the broader dimension of liquid markets – what determines the price at which a security can be sold? The short answer is that the demand for securities depends on endogenously determined expectations and risk preferences as well as the confidence investors have in their expectations.[13] The explanation from KM theory for the "appropriate price" is that at any moment in time the current price is determined by the relative strength of bull and bear forces in an ever-evolving market process. This price has no optimality property whatsoever.

A key implication of this viewpoint for our discussion of liquidity is that the mainstream economists claim that investment bank regulations such as the Volcker Rule reduce liquidity and this creates inefficiency, because they simply assume that security prices are at their fundamental (optimal) levels. In this world, regulations over liquidity cannot improve the pricing of securities by definition. So there is absolutely no room to argue that restrictions on investment banks' speculative liquidity creation through proprietary trading, for example, can actually improve the quality of security pricing, say, by lengthening the horizons of effective investor expectations.

With self-contradiction, however, although mainstream theory insists that markets always get prices right, when mainstream economists engage in policy debates in the business and financial press or on television during periods of financial stress, their concept of liquidity is broadened to include the appropriate demand for and price of securities – although no one tells the reader that the definition of market liquidity used in canonical theory has been augmented to include appropriate price liquidity. Equilibrium theory fades from the scene. Mainstream economists now fret about the chaos of market disequilibrium processes, while Keynesians understand that the current turmoil is simply a normal phase of markets that have no stable equilibrium in any case. Apparently, we are all Keynesians in a financial crisis because everyone acknowledges that security prices are driven by a sense of uncertainty and unpredictability, and by a "fear" of capital loss that is the product of emotion as much as analysis. When financial markets are in distress, securities can usually be sold quickly at low transaction cost, but only at a price that is well below recent levels and falling. Even when trading liquidity is perfect, economists inevitably say that liquidity is inadequate, or has "frozen" or "evaporated" because the current price is widely believed to be low relative to something – to some vague notion of market "fundamentals." In these times, market liquidity depends both on trading liquidity and appropriate price liquidity. Mainstream economists cannot explain what the "appropriate" equilibrium price is at any point in a crisis; they only know it should be much higher than it is, and high enough to erase much of the capital loss caused by the market downturn.

When markets crash, many mainstream financial economists demand that the Federal Reserve (Fed) takes aggressive policy actions to raise liquidity levels, by which they mean increasing the demand for and the price of securities (lender-of-last-resort actions). These economists clearly believe that in a crash, markets have gotten prices seriously wrong and they cannot self-correct, an idea that has no place in the canonical mainstream models of financial markets. Note the asymmetry here. When security prices are rising rapidly, few financial economists demand that the Fed reduce liquidity in order to lower prices or at least slow their growth, because they believe that markets know best. But when prices go into free fall, there is a veritable chorus of demands by economists that the Federal Reserve sharply increase the level of liquidity, defined now as the demand for securities, in order to raise prices substantially above current market levels because markets have gotten prices wrong. Apparently, neoclassical economists really believe that markets make mistakes, but only in one direction.[14]

Thus, when economists discuss real-world financial markets, their definition of liquidity almost always includes its effect on the demand for securities and thus on the price of securities. However, there is a serious problem with the usefulness of mainstream financial market theory in policy discussions. Mainstream models define the appropriate price as their model's equilibrium price, but key elements in those models, such as investor expectations and utility functions, have no observable empirical counterpart. It is therefore not possible in principle to tell whether market prices are or are not appropriate prices as defined by theory. In policy discussions, then, mainstream economists in effect assert that markets get prices right except when they don't. Thus, when prices are either stable or acceptable to the average investor, or when they are rising, markets are presumed to get prices right. But when they are stable but disappointing to investors or are falling rapidly, prices are wrong.

The switch from the theory of policy to real-world policy debate reveals a schizophrenia that infects mainstream financial economists. They insist that because neoclassical models of optimal equilibrium financial markets are the whole truth and nothing but the truth, serious government regulation and intervention will destroy market efficiency. Yet when financial crises appear, as they inevitably do from time to time, they insist that markets must be rescued by the government from their self-destructive behavior. This schizophrenia is not surprising. Neoclassical financial market theory is an unrealistic, ideologically based theory whose flaws can be hidden from regulators and the public during market booms but are exposed for all to see when markets fail, as they did so catastrophically after 2007.[15] No one should accept arguments made against the Volcker Rule or any other proposal to strengthen market regulation that are grounded in canonical neoclassical theory. On the other hand, KM theory is based on realistic assumptions and can explain both boom and bust as inherent phases of endogenous financial market processes. It is the theory that should be used to evaluate proposals to strengthen financial market regulation. This becomes even clearer when we consider the second part of the "liquidity defense": the issue of "price discovery."

What about price discovery? In the informal narrative in which efficient financial market theory is embedded, though rarely in the formal models used in the theory, there are discussions of the process through which these optimal equilibrium prices are "discovered" by the market. In these fairy tales, professional arbitrageurs, such as hedge funds and investment banks, "find" the predetermined equilibrium price when markets are temporarily out of equilibrium or when the equilibrium position changes.[16] If irrational or ill-informed investors push prices away from equilibrium, or if unexpected news leads to a different equilibrium, savvy professional investors who are, in the theory, rational and fully informed about future security cash flows, have a profit incentive to push them back toward equilibrium. The process of disequilibrium arbitrage in such narratives does not affect equilibrium prices; it just uncovers or discovers them.

Keynes–Minsky theory takes a polar opposite position on this issue. It argues that market activity cannot "discover" predetermined security prices because *they do not exist*. There is no knowable future out there in the present that can fix prices. Rather, the ever-changing relative strength of bulls and bears operating in an environment of fundamental uncertainty *determines or creates security prices* with no optimality properties at all. Buying and selling in the market that is driven by endogenously changing expectations and an endogenously changing level of agent risk aversion alters the "appropriate" market price of securities. Prices are what they are because they balance the supply and demand for securities at the current instant. In other words, investment banks and other large financial actors are potent *creators*, not discoverers of asset prices.

Two important conclusions related to the debate over financial regulation and reform can be drawn from this discussion. First, in realistic theory, the buying and selling of securities by investment banks, hedge funds, and other institutional agents in pursuit of proprietary capital gains and various forms of fee income not only creates and sustains market liquidity, it simultaneously creates and sustains market bubbles while building the preconditions for market crashes. As noted, these institutions also facilitate gambling by others and create the innovative products and service around which speculation often takes place. They facilitate excessive speculation and volatility creation, not equilibrium price discovery. Such behavior helps to provide the rationale for regulations such as the Volcker Rule.

Second, Keynes convincingly argued that a high degree of trading liquidity is a necessary though not sufficient condition for speculative booms and busts to become inherent endogenous characteristics of financial markets. If agents had to pay large transaction costs and wait for a substantial period of time before they could sell financial assets, and if they had no assurance they could sell without suffering a substantial capital loss, speculation and financial market volatility would be much lower than the historical record shows it to have been.[17]

In the rest of this chapter we consider the KM approach to understanding the nature and impact of liquidity in financialized capitalism. After an important methodological discussion, we consider first the KM approach to understanding the role of liquidity in generating financial cycles; we then discuss the views of Keynes on the issue of financial market liquidity and its effect on financial market efficiency and capital accumulation, focusing on Chapter 12 of the *GT*. Whereas mainstream financial economists and the representatives of giant bank conglomerates argue that maximum market liquidity leads to maximum financial market and real-sector efficiency, Keynes believed that maximum liquidity leads to maximum financial market instability and an unstable real sector with chronically high unemployment rates. Furthermore, Keynes considered the "liquidity dilemma:" in the end, he argued that the "fetish of liquidity" was so dangerous that most capital investment should be disconnected from financial markets and placed under the direct control of government institutions. This is what Keynes meant when he argued in the last chapter of the *GT* that economic efficiency would be best served by the "socialization of investment." These policy implications Keynes drew from his evaluation of market liquidity are contained in the final section of the chapter.

KEYNES AND MINSKY ON ENDOGENOUS INSTABILITY IN FINANCIAL MARKETS AND THE ROLE OF INVESTMENT BANKS IN LIQUIDITY CYCLES

Methodological Concepts of Keynes and their Implications for Understanding Liquidity

To understand Keynes' views on liquidity and what is wrong with the mainstream views, it is important to understand some key aspects of Keynes' methodology in the *GT*. The revolution in macro theory presented in the *GT* is built on two major innovations. The first, familiar even to undergraduate students, is that Keynes rejected the dominant classical theory that free-market forces keep the economy tethered to full capacity supply, while aggregate demand adjusts to aggregate supply automatically. The second innovation is somewhat less well known and is rarely emphasized in either graduate or undergraduate courses. Keynes built his macro theory on the assumption that the future is fundamentally uncertain and therefore unknowable in the present. Mainstream theories, to the contrary, assume that agents either know the true probability distributions that will generate future states of the economy ("rational expectations"), or at least believe they know them (as "subjective" probability distributions), even though such knowledge cannot possibly be available to them in the real world.[18]

This perspective on fundamental uncertainty plays a key role in Keynes' discussion of the nature and impact of liquidity in various parts of the *GT*, including in Chapter 12. Chapter 12 analyzes the factors that determine the demand for long-term capital goods. This is, thus, a key terrain of Keynes' dilemma. To decide whether to invest in a particular capital good, a firm must form expectations about the profit that will be generated by the investment over its expected life. Keynes explained why, in an environment of uncertainty, firms are forced to rely on social and behavioral conventions to formulate expectations of the future states of the economy that will determine the profit rate on investment projects. He used a rather simple assumption about expectation formation as the basis for an analysis of the effects of uncertainty on investment spending.[19] Keynes said (1936, p. 152): "In practice we have tacitly agreed, as a rule, to fall back on what is, in truth, a *convention*. The essence of this convention [. . .] lies in assuming that the existing state of affairs will continue indefinitely, except in so far as we have specific reason to expect a change." Earlier in Chapter 12 (p. 148) Keynes makes the same point: our usual practice is "to take the existing situation and to project it into the future, modified only to the extent that we have more or less definitive reasons for expecting a change."

Since agents are aware that they do not know the future, they can never have complete *confidence* that their expectations will be correct. This means that their decisions will be affected both by their best forecasts and by the degree of confidence they have in the usefulness or validity or reliability or truth content of these forecasts – "on how highly we rate the likelihood of our best forecast turning out quite wrong" (Keynes, 1973, p. 148). "The state of confidence is relevant," Keynes said, "because it is one of the major factors determining [. . .] the investment demand schedule" (1936, p. 149). It would be reasonable to assume that the longer that conventionally formed expectations served investors well, the more confidence they would place in these expectations, and conversely. Note that for Keynes, optimism and confidence are not used as synonyms, which is often the case in the literature. One can have a great deal of confidence in a very pessimistic forecast, as would be common in the depths of a long depression.

Keynes's assumption about the construction of expectations and confidence over time in an uncertain environment is the foundation of Keynes and Minsky's theories of endogenous financial cycles. Agents are assumed to believe that "the existing state of affairs will continue indefinitely" or "will take the existing situation and [. . .] project it into the future" except if there are concrete reasons not to do this. This assumption generates endogenous change in expectations and confidence, and therefore in the demand for and price of securities.

This interacts with liquidity generation to help generate cycles. It also implies an endogenous dynamic in the demand for capital goods by firms. Keep in mind that the "existing state of affairs" does not necessarily imply that agents expect a steady state. The existing state of affairs may be a situation in which stock prices have been rapidly rising for some time. In such conditions, Keynes argues, investors are likely to assume this trend will continue, unless there are specific reasons not to do so. The longer it continues, the more confident they become that the future will see a continuation if not acceleration of this trend. Increasing optimism held with increasing confidence will help this trend continue. In the stock market booms of the late 1920s and late 1990s in the US, an almost universally held expectation developed that the rapid capital gains of the recent past would continue in the future. Similarly, if the achieved profit rate on capital investment has been rising rapidly for several years, firms are likely to assume it will continue to do so – except if there are concrete reasons to expect a change in performance. Since upswings in capital gains and the profit rate can never be sustained forever, booms are eventually self-destructing. As we show next, Keynes believed that excessive or inappropriate liquidity feeds these cycles, and this helps to explains why more liquidity is not always better.

Keynes–Minsky Theory on Liquidity and Endogenous Liquidity Cycles

As just described, the entry point for KM financial market theory is fundamental or Keynesian uncertainty. Minsky improved Keynes' treatment of the implications of agent choice under uncertainty in two ways. First, he stressed the dependence of businesses on borrowing to finance capital investment in the expansion, and thus on the danger posed by increasing leverage as the expansion loses steam. Investment booms leave in their wake an increasingly tight web of interest payment and principal repayment commitments on the part of the investing firm. If profits do not meet the optimistic expectations formed in the upbeat environment of the mid-expansion, investing firms may find themselves in financial distress. Both Minsky and Marx emphasized the importance of the effect of heavy borrowing in a boom or in a longer-term era of financial buoyancy on the balance sheets of borrowers. This is reflected in Minsky's emphasis on "financial fragility" – a condition in which balance-sheet financial commitments become so large relative to current cash flows that any substantial fall in profits or in household incomes can create financial distress, forced deleveraging and even waves of insolvency.

Second, Minsky put equal stress on the effects of uncertainty on decision-making by financial institutions and real-sector firms.[20] When business firms want to increase borrowing to fund investment in the optimism of the boom, banks are likely to believe it is safe to make large corporate loans because they share their conventionally determined optimistic outlook. Given optimistic expectations of future prices, buying securities previously seen as risky will seem like a reasonable decision. As the boom proceeds and optimistic expectations are shown as justified, buying and creating securities with borrowed money will also seem reasonable.

In addition to optimistic expectations in an expansion, investment-bank top executives, traders and salesmen have bonus-driven incentives to maximize firm revenue by maximizing bank risk and leverage.[21] Rising investment-bank proprietary investment as well as increased loans to other institutional and individual investors helped drive the recent financial boom forward, raising overall leverage while raining capital gains on investors. The heaviest rain falls on the most aggressive investors, which leads most agents to believe either that risk is objectively low or that risk-taking brings much higher rewards than it used to. Risk assessment and risk preference are endogenous. When risky behavior is being highly rewarded, fear of risk declines and conversely.

Liquidity, broadly defined to include trading liquidity plus appropriate price liquidity (as the demand for securities), rises endogenously in a boom; funding liquidity also typically expands. Eventually, almost anyone can sell securities for more than they paid for them. In the terms of our earlier discussion, the "appropriate price" increases as the boom proceeds. Neoclassical economists assure investors that each new price is the optimal equilibrium price. Leverage rises as well because borrowers, lenders and financial market regulators come to believe that leverage is not as risky as it used to be in today's efficient financial markets. Interest rates remain low through much of the boom, and credit is available even to agents previously considered to be bad credit risks.

There is a crucial feedback loop joining the real and financial sectors that is missing in efficient financial market theories. Rising security prices in the boom increase the value of individual and institutional agents' assets and net worth. This increases the amount of debt they and their lenders believe they can "safely" hold, and thus increases their borrowing power just as conventional definitions of adequate safety margins become less stringent. Investment banks experience this cyclical change. As Taylor shows (this volume, Chapter 13), rising security prices raise investment banks' net worth and lower their leverage ratio (also see Adrian and Shin, 2010). This allows these banks to increase their own borrowing and use the additional funds to either lend to others to purchase more securities, or to purchase securities themselves as proprietary investments or as added input into their securitization business.

Since every long-term financial boom is accompanied by the widespread belief that we have entered a "new era" in which the forces that ended all previous booms are no longer operative, the current boom, if it lasts long enough, eventually comes to be seen as permanent. A near-universal belief develops that high yields previously achievable only by accepting high risk can now be gained safely.

As both Keynes and Minsky stressed, market ebullience cannot go on forever. As a boom matures, the economy becomes "financially fragile" due to the buildup of balance-sheet commitments. At some point, the economy becomes unable to generate the cash flows needed to sustain euphoria-inflated financial asset prices.

As financial institutions retrench in the face of rising risk, interest rates rise and defaults jump. Fear of higher default rates will cause interest rates to rise further, and credit for riskier agents to be eliminated.

As the market for suspect securities collapses, borrowers will be forced to sell "sound" securities, which will spread the crisis across markets. Mainstream models of efficient financial markets assume both that trading liquidity is perfect and that securities can always be sold at their market-clearing equilibrium price (price liquidity is also perfect). But in a financial downturn, few agents want to buy suspect financial assets, so they can only be sold at fire-sale prices as liquidity, broadly defined, evaporates.

Watching their own asset values and their capital shrink, financial institutions will be less willing to lend to corporations, households or each other.

Both the causes of the recent financial boom and the destructive downward dynamics of the subsequent collapse can be explained by KM theory because its assumption set adequately reflects the endogenous forces that bring instability to financial markets. On the other hand, the assumption set used to construct canonical, neoclassical financial and macro models makes such endogenous instability impossible. Neoclassical theory cannot explain the instability we have observed recently or the role of endogenous liquidity creation that facilitated it: it is a theory in which market dysfunction is impossible, and markets and liquidity provision are *always* efficient.

Investment banks are a major force in the creation of instability because they are crucial to the provision of trading liquidity that, as Keynes argued, magnifies instability tendencies, and also because they are crucial to the creation and subsequent destruction of liquidity broadly defined in financial cycles. In short, in KM theory, financial markets endogenously produce cycles of liquidity. Liquidity, or the demand for securities, is excessive in the boom because it generates prices too high to be sustained, and "evaporates" in the downturn, which aggravates the severity of the crash. Keynes–Minsky theory, then, comprehends theoretically the empirically obvious pro-cyclical role played by liquidity creation in financial cycles of the economy (see the paper by Borio et al. [2012] which fails to even mention Keynes, and has almost no mention of Minsky).

In the next section, we show how Keynes, in Chapter 12 of the *GT*, shows the longer-term dangers of private liquidity creation, showing how it can lead to excessive "speculation" and undermine the efficiency of the capital accumulation process. This is where Keynes poses his "liquidity dilemma," and raises the question of whether the social benefits of private liquidity provision outweigh the social costs.

CHAPTER 12 OF THE *GENERAL THEORY*: "THE FETISH OF LIQUIDITY" – HIGH MARKET LIQUIDITY CREATES HIGH INVESTMENT INSTABILITY

In Chapter 12 of the *GT*, devoted to the "inducement to invest" in capital goods, Keynes analyzes the effect of market liquidity on the behavior of stock prices and, therefore, on the behavior of capital investment spending. His concern, first, is strictly with trading liquidity, the ability to buy and sell securities quickly at low transaction costs. Keynes' main conclusion here is that the high degree of such liquidity in modern financial markets, celebrated by economists and market practitioners, in fact causes capital investment spending to be excessively volatile, so volatile that the state should take *direct* control over the lion's share of investment spending.[22]

As discussed in the introduction, Keynes called attention to the liquidity dilemma: necessary long-term productive capital is highly illiquid both for society, and, in the 19th century, for the investor. With the separation of ownership and control in the 20th century, such capital is still illiquid for society as a whole, but the typical modern investor requires liquidity in order to lure him or her to invest in long-term, illiquid capital. This creates a dilemma because the social costs of generating this liquidity, given the structure of modern financial markets, may outweigh the social benefits of generating the long-term capital investment.

To explore this dilemma, Keynes introduced his innovative concept of the "marginal efficiency of capital" or MEC, an index of the expected profit rate on new capital goods that emphasized the uncertainty of future profits or cash flows. Minsky and other post-Keynesians refer to Keynes' two-price model of the cycle. In Minsky's version of Keynes' model, the price of consumer goods is assumed to be set at unit cost plus a markup that covers profit plus administrative expense.[23] But the price that firms will be willing to pay for capital goods depends on the present discounted value of the future cash flows the firm *expects* to earn on its investment over the *expected* life of the capital good. What Minsky called the demand price of capital goods is thus based on expectations and confidence in a world of fundamental uncertainty, as is Keynes' marginal efficiency of capital. Thus, the price firms are willing to pay for capital goods may be much higher or lower than the cost of production or supply price of capital goods, and will, at times, be quite volatile. This difference drives the business cycle.

In Chapter 12 of the *GT*, Keynes focuses on the stock market as the site of determination of real investment demand. He argues that fluctuations in the stock market inevitably create changes in the same direction in the demand for real investment goods. In Keynes' words (1936, p. 151): "Daily revaluations of the Stock Exchange, though they are primarily made to facilitate transfers of old investments, inevitably exert a decisive influence of the rate of current investment." Much of Chapter 12 is devoted to explaining why the modern stock market, and therefore the level of capital investment spending, is subject to periods of substantial instability. Keynes argues that much of this volatility is caused by the interaction of fundamental uncertainty, liquidity, and speculation.

Keynes investigated the "liquidity dilemma" by raising an important question: Why are financial investors willing to buy and hold risky equity securities whose price behavior over time is so volatile and unpredictable?

There are two parts to Keynes' answer. The first is implicit in his theory of conventional expectations and confidence formation, a behavioral theory that implies that agents' perception of market risk will be low in periods of stable prices and even lower during market bubbles when a confident expectation of rising prices becomes widespread. In ebullient markets, agents come to believe that stocks are not risky investments. The second part of Keynes' answer is that the high trading liquidity of the stock market enables investors to believe that in the event that stock prices begin to fall, they can exit the market before prices decline significantly. This makes potentially high-risk investment in stocks *appear* to be a relatively safe investment. Keynes concluded that the liquidity properties of modern stock markets make them dangerously volatile. We examine these two answers in turn.

Keynes proposed a joint hypothesis to explain why investors are willing to take risky market positions even if they believe that long-term conventional expectations are not reliable. If investors can count on the fact that stocks can be sold quickly and with a low transaction cost, and if most investors rely on conventional expectations and confidence formation over the short-run, they will normally be happy to buy and hold stocks until a serious downturn begins to develop.

> An investor can legitimately encourage himself with the idea that the only risk he runs is that of a genuine change in the news *over the near future*, as to the likelihood of which he can attempt to form his own judgment, and which is unlikely to be very large. For assuming the convention holds good, it is only these changes which can affect the value of his investment, and he need not lose any sleep merely because he has not any notion what his investment will be worth ten years hence. (Keynes, 1936, pp. 152–3; italics in original)

That is, investors believe that outcomes beyond a relatively short-run future are not relevant to their portfolio investment decision as long as markets remain highly liquid in the narrow sense. If, as Keynes claimed, significant unexpected events that will substantially affect stock prices in the short-run are legitimately considered to be "unlikely to be very large," and investors can sell their stock in an instant at little cost, they may come to believe that aggressive investment strategies that would be very risky if the securities had to be held in the long run are in fact relatively safe.

> Investment becomes reasonably "safe" for the individual over short-periods, and hence over a succession of short periods *however many*, if he can fairly rely on there being no breakdown of the convention and on his therefore having an opportunity *to revise his judgment and change his investment position before there has been time for much to happen*. (Keynes, 1936, p. 153; italics added)

Even if investors believe that stock prices can be volatile and unpredictable in the longer run, so that not much confidence can be placed in conventional expectations of future stock prices past the short-run, Keynes argued that they would still be willing to hold stocks if they are convinced that they can quickly exit before stock prices can fall very far in a market downturn.

It is the very high trading liquidity of the market that permits investors to take comfort in the belief that they can exit quickly, at little cost, and with only a modest capital loss if the market starts to fall. Of course, if all investors actually did try to exit the market simultaneously, all but the quickest would suffer large capital losses, so that what may be sensible for the individual investor can be disastrous for the investing class.[24] Keynes thus makes the implicit assumption that agents are not conscious of the collective illogic in their position.

As a result of high liquidity, Keynes argued, stock market investment

> based on genuine long-term expectations is so difficult today as to be scarcely practicable. He who attempts it must surely [. . .] run greater risks than he who tries to guess better than the crowd how the crowd will behave; and, given equal intelligence, he may make more disastrous mistakes. There is no clear evidence from experience that investment policy which is socially advantageous coincides with that which is more profitable. (Keynes, 1936, p. 157)

The problem Keynes is concerned with here is that if most investors are willing to take the high risk associated with stock holdings only because they believe they can exit before the market turns down, long-term capital investment is being guided by stock market investors with very short-term horizons. "Investments which are "fixed" for the community are thus made "liquid" for the individual" (p. 153). This is clearly not a good way to determine the long-run capital investment decision, and with it the future trajectory of the economy.

Keynes's view is thus clear: The stock market would not be so volatile and capital investment would not be so unstable if the stock market was not extremely liquid.

Financial markets are thus potentially very unstable because the future is unknowable, which makes investors *inevitably* "ignorant" of the future and dependent upon psychological mechanisms to guide their decisions. Volatile expectations are "unreasoning" yet "legitimate" because the information needed to make assuredly optimal decisions *does not exist*. There are no knowable future fundamentals to guide investor choice. We are outside the realm of "rational expectations" or of the standard neoclassical assumption that economic agents form subjective probability distributions over all future economic states that they believe – irrationally – are the absolute truths about the future.

Keynes then added an early version of noise-trader theory to argue that professional investors, the heroic arbitrageurs of mainstream theory who force prices to their equilibrium values even in the midst of a sea of incompetent investors, cannot set markets right. If short-term speculators are in the process of driving a price above its sustainable level, it makes sense for the pros to buy the security in anticipation of expected capital gains, which only adds to the forces creating disequilibrium. The pros are concerned not with what "an investment is really worth to a man who buys it 'for keeps,' but with what the market will value it at, under the influence of mass psychology, three months or a year hence." This "is an inevitable result of an investment market organized along the lines described. For it is not sensible to pay 25 for an investment of which you believe the prospective yield to justify 30, if you also believe that the market will value it at 20 three months from now" (Keynes, 1936, p. 155). Moreover, arbitrageurs don't have enough capital to conduct an ongoing battle with the ignorant herds: "An investor who proposes to ignore near-term market fluctuations needs greater resources for safety and must [if risk averse] not operate on so large a scale, if at all, with borrowed money" (ibid., 157).

As a result of high liquidity, Keynes argues, stock market investment based on

> genuine long-term expectations is so difficult today as to be scarcely practicable. He who attempts it must surely [. . .] run greater risks than he who tries to guess better than the crowd how the crowd will behave; and, given equal intelligence, he may make more disastrous mistakes. There is no clear evidence from experience that investment policy which is socially advantageous coincides with that which is more profitable. (Keynes, 1936, p. 157)

Thus, stock market and capital investment volatility is:

> the inevitable result of investment markets organized with a view to so-called "liquidity." *Of the maxims of orthodox finance none, surely, is more anti-social than the fetish of liquidity, the doctrine that it is a positive virtue on the part of investment institutions to concentrate their resources upon the holding of "liquid" securities. It forgets that there is no such thing as liquidity of investment for the community as a whole.* (Keynes, 1936, p. 155; italics added)

This conclusion is as applicable today as it was in 1936.

In Chapter 12 of the *GT*, Keynes furthermore showed that another cost of this fetish of liquidity is excessive and destructive speculation. He defined speculation as "the activity of forecasting the [short-term] psychology of the market" and enterprise as "the activity of forecasting the prospective yield of [real] assets over their whole life" (p. 158). For markets to be economically efficient, the capital investment decision must be guided by enterprise, not speculation. But as market liquidity increases, "*the risk of the predominance of speculation [also] increases*" (p. 159; italics added). The higher the market liquidity, the greater the proportion of speculators in the market.

> Speculators may do no harm as bubbles on a steady stream of enterprise. But the position is serious when enterprise becomes the bubble on a whirlpool of speculation. When the capital development of a country becomes a by-product of the activities of a casino, the job is likely to be ill-done. The measure of success attained by Wall Street, regarded as an institution of which the proper social purpose is to direct new investment into the most profitable channels in terms of future yield, cannot be claimed as one of the outstanding triumphs of laissez-faire capitalism – which is not surprising, if I am right in thinking that the best brains of Wall Street have been in fact otherwise engaged. (Keynes, 1936, p. 159)

Keynes concluded that the disastrous consequences of speculation "*are a scarcely avoidable outcome of our having successfully organized 'liquid' [financial] investment markets*" (ibid., p. 159; italics added).

Hence, Keynes' liquidity dilemma: liquidity is necessary given the modern organization of private investment in capitalism to facilitate capital accumulation; but the modern, unregulated organization of liquidity undermines and distorts the capital accumulation process.

KEYNES' RADICAL POLICY REMEDIES FOR THE PROBLEMS CREATED BY EXCESS LIQUIDITY

What is the solution to the "liquidity dilemma"? Keynes rarely focused on issues of theory that did not have important policy implications. Such is the case with his disquisition on the dangers of excessive financial market liquidity. Chapter 12 of the *GT* discusses three possible ways to reduce or eliminate the deleterious impact of excessive liquidity on the capital investment decision.

First, Keynes believed that the threat posed by excessive liquidity was so serious that he considered a truly radical solution (p. 160): "The spectacle of modern investment markets has sometimes moved me towards the conclusion that to make the purchase of an investment permanent and indissoluble, like marriage, except by reason of death or other grave causes, might be a useful remedy for contemporary evils" caused by excessive liquidity. "For this would force the investor to direct his mind to the long-term prospects and to these only." The fact that this proposal would entail serious costs as long as investment spending depended on stock prices that would have to be weighed against its substantial benefits would, he says, constitute a "dilemma," a word he uses twice in the same paragraph.

> The liquidity of investment markets often facilitates, though it sometimes impedes the course of new investments. For the fact that each individual investor flatters himself that his commitment is 'liquid' (though this cannot be true of all investors collectively) calms his nerves and makes him much more willing to run a risk. If individual purchases of investments were rendered illiquid, this might seriously impede new investment, so long as *alternative ways* in which to hold his savings are available to the individual. This is the dilemma. (Keynes, 1936, p. 160; italics in original)

Keynes argues that as long as investors have the option of holding their wealth in the form of safe financial assets like money or Treasury bills or short-term savings accounts, "the alternative of purchasing risky capital assets cannot be rendered sufficiently attractive [. . .] except by organizing markets wherein these assets can be easily realised for money" (ibid., pp. 161–2).

In Chapters 13 to 15 of the *GT*, Keynes focuses on the dangers of excessive demand for liquidity in a depression or crisis. This "safe haven" demand for liquidity when confidence evaporates, creates a barrier to restored capital accumulation and economic growth. Says Keynes (ibid., p. 161; italics added):

> The only radical cure for the crises of confidence which afflict the economic life of the modern world would be to *allow the individual no choice* between consuming his income and ordering the production of the specific capital asset which, even though it be on precarious evidence, impresses him as the most promising investment available to him.

This would at least "avoid the disastrous, cumulative and far-reaching repercussions of its being open to him, when thus assailed by doubts, to spend his income on neither one nor the other" by hoarding his income in the form of money or other safe short term asset like Treasury bills, thereby lowering aggregate demand, income and employment (ibid., p. 161). The fact that Keynes considered such a radical policy prescription reflects the depth of his concern with excessive financial market liquidity.

Second, Keynes proposes the imposition of a substantial financial transactions tax, now often called a Keynes tax or Tobin tax, that would respond to the dilemma described above by substantially reducing but not totally eliminating the liquidity of financial markets. Keynes observed that the instability of prices on the London Stock Exchange was of a lesser magnitude than on Wall Street. This was because speculation in London was, in comparison with speculation on Wall Street, "inaccessible and very expensive" due to the "high brokerage charges and the heavy transfer tax [. . .] The introduction of a substantial Government transfer tax on all transactions might prove the most serviceable reform available with a view to mitigating the present predominance of speculation over enterprise in the United States" (ibid., p. 160). Since Keynes believed that, given fundamental uncertainty, excessive liquidity made modern capitalist economies dangerously unstable, the transfer tax would have to be very large indeed to be effective. For recent versions of the financial transactions tax, see the work of Robert Pollin (2012).

Third, in the last paragraph of Chapter 12, Keynes presents his preferred policy solution to the twin problems of excessive investment instability and a trend level of investment chronically too low to generate sustained full employment, problems he believed were created in substantial part by the combination of uncertainty and excessive liquidity. It is a radical solution that reflects his belief that this problem is so deeply rooted in modern capitalism that no normal set of market regulations is capable of resolving it. Keynes proposes that the government take responsibility for directly controlling the bulk of capital spending: "I expect to see the State, which is in a position to calculate the marginal efficiency of capital goods on long views and on the basis of the general social advantage, taking an ever greater responsibility for *directly* controlling investment" (ibid., p. 164; italics added). This conclusion at the end of Chapter 12 is missing from virtually all mainstream literature on Keynes and the *GT*. Many economists are familiar with his statement in the final chapter of the book – "I conceive therefore of a somewhat comprehensive socialization of investment will prove the only means of securing an approximation to full employment" – but they tend to dismiss it as an *obiter dictum*, a marginal note with no foundation in the body of analysis (even though it is the main policy conclusion of the crucial Chapter 12 [p. 378] and similar statements appear on pages 219, 220, 247, 320, 325 and 327 of the book). However, as demonstrated by Crotty (1999), government control over the lion's share of capital investment had been Keynes' central proposed policy tool from 1924 until his death in 1946, conventional wisdom to the contrary notwithstanding. He argued that once the state achieved control over the bulk of capital spending through a "Board of National Investment," the counter-cyclical macro policy that is widely believed to be Keynes' *only* policy conclusion would be dysfunctional and should be avoided.

In Volume II of his 1930 *Treatise on Money* Keynes offered the following observation on investment instability (p. 145):

> Perhaps the ultimate solution lies in the rate of capital development becoming more largely an affair of state, determined by collective wisdom and long views. If the task of accumulation comes to depend somewhat less on individual caprice, so as to be no longer at the mercy of calculations partly based on the expectation of life of the particular mortal men who are alive today, the

> dilemma between thrift and profit as the means of securing the most desirable rate of growth of the community's aggregate wealth will cease to present itself.

In 1942 he wrote: "If two-thirds or three-quarters of total investment is carried out or can be influenced by public or semi-public bodies, a long-term programme of a stable character should be capable of reducing the range of fluctuations to much narrower limits than formerly." In 1943 he said: "If the bulk of investment is under public or semi-public control and we go in for a stable long-term programme, serious fluctuations are enormously less likely to occur."

It is astonishing that the central policy conclusion drawn by Keynes that he stated over and over again, including throughout the *GT*, disappeared in expositions of and debates about Keynes's theory of economic policy after his death. In any case, it presents a clear and stark contrast to the "liquidity defense" proffered by bankers and their economist friends, and one which heterodox economists working in the tradition of Jane D'Arista should, we believe, take seriously.

NOTES

1. This chapter has been prepared for a Festschrift in honor of Jane D'Arista. The authors thank Iren Levina for excellent research assistance and the Institute for New Economic Thinking (INET) for financial support
2. See, for example: FCIC, 2011; Crotty et al., 2010.
3. The second and third of these criticisms are discussed later.
4. See Wall Street Watch, 2009, on the history of financial deregulation. See Kuttner, 2011.
5. We refer to this as "trading liquidity." This is a part of what economists call "market liquidity."
6. We call this "appropriate price liquidity" or "price liquidity." Mainstream economists often implicitly slip this meaning into their definition of market liquidity, usually without even knowing it.
7. It is also lacks empirical support, given the role of liquidity in helping to create the financial crisis. But we do not deal with the empirical issues in depth here.
8. See http://www.bloomberg.com/news/2012–02–13/volcker-says-more-market-liquidity-doesn-t-bring-public-benefit.html.
9. See http://mobile.bloomberg.com/news/2012–02–20/liquidity-versus-capital-debate-divides-stanford-simon-johnson. Note the presumption that if everyone did careful credit analyses, there might be no instability, a claim with little credence in a world of uncertainty.
10. In Chapters 13 to 15 of the *General Theory*, Keynes broadens the concept of liquidity to apply not just to markets but to financial assets themselves. In his discussion of "liquidity preference" Keynes defines money and other short-term financial assets such as Treasury bills to be liquid because they can be sold quickly *without a significant capital loss*. We refer to this as "safe haven liquidity." Long-term assets such as bonds and stocks are inherently illiquid under this definition because they can suffer a substantial capital loss at sale. See the Appendix for more detail.
11. See the Appendix for more detailed discussion of liquidity definitions and for a comparison of mainstream and KM notions of liquidity.

12. See, for example, the following. In an article on the relation of liquidity and leverage, two New York Fed economists make the following statement:

> Our findings also shed light on the concept of "liquidity" as used in common discourse about financial market conditions. In the financial press and other market commentary, asset price booms are sometimes attributed to "excess liquidity" in the financial system. Financial commentators are fond of using the associated metaphors, such as financial markets being "awash with liquidity," or liquidity "sloshing around." However, the precise sense in which "liquidity" is being used in such contexts is often left unspecified. (Adrian and Shin, 2010, p. 3)

The concept of liquidity used in the article is virtually synonymous with the demand for securities itself.

13. Since the volatility of the demand for securities is typically much greater than that of the supply of securities, it is not unreasonable to argue that, to a first approximation, changes in demand determine security price movements.
14. Consider this example of the phenomenon. In a *Wall Street Journal* article ("Traders Warn of Market Cracks") written at a time of financial market distress in late 2011, the authors rely on a broad definition of liquidity that includes trading liquidity and price liquidity. "The problem is a lack of liquidity – a term that refers to the ease of getting a trade done *at an acceptable price*" (*WSJ*, 2011; emphasis added).
15. For a discussion of methodological flaws in neoclassical financial market theory, see Crotty (2013b).
16. Some of the reasons why these stories are fairy tales and not realistic descriptions of market processes are contained in noise-trader theory (which is prefigured by arguments made in Chapter 12 of the *GT*) and rational-bubble theory. The main reason is contained in Keynes' theory of decision making under uncertainty.
17. Of course, illiquid markets might also have lowered the average rate of capital accumulation over long periods since they can substantially raise the cost of capital. This is the "dilemma" – Keynes' word – presented in the Introduction.
18. Keynes thus raises key questions about the very meaning of "rationality" in the theory of agent choice. In mainstream theory agents have probabilistic knowledge of future states of the economy that is in fact complete and correct (as in "rational expectations" models of new classical theory) or is believed by the agent to be complete and correct (as in the subjective probability models used in most neoclassical theory) whether it is in fact correct or not. Agents are thus assumed to have a known objective function (at least implicitly assumed not to change in the time that elapses from when a choice is made until the outcome is determined) and complete knowledge of the relation between choice and outcome. An agent is rational if they perform the optimization math correctly and irrational if not. If we replace the obviously unrealistic perfect-knowledge assumption used in these theories with Keynes' obviously correct assumption of fundamental uncertainty, mainstream theories have absolutely nothing to say about rationality in agent choice; they have assumed the problem away. For an extensive analysis of Keynes' approach to decision-making under fundamental uncertainty, see Crotty (1994). For a discussion of the issue of agent rationality in the *GT*, see O'Donnell (1988).
19. In his 1937 article in the *Quarterly Journal of Economics* defending the *GT* against several critics and in other writings, Keynes presented a more complex view of conventional expectation formation.
20. As noted above, Keynes argued that financial market booms require optimism on the part of both market investors and the brokers who lend them money to speculate with.
21. For a detailed analysis of the role of perverse incentives in the ongoing financial crisis, see Crotty (2009) at http://www.umass.edu/economics/publications/2009–13.pdf.
22. Keynes was concerned not just about the dangerous level of volatility of investment

spending, but about the long-term stagnation of investment spending as well. The average growth rate of investment spending in the UK had been too low to generate full employment for several decades. Long-term stagnation is discussed in many places in the *GT*. Keynes ties this problem, in part, to excessive demand for liquidity (safe haven liquidity).

23. See Minsky (1988).
24. *Financial Times* columnist John Kay (2010) made a similar observation about investor strategies in a boom. Each is "riding an unsustainable trend in the hope that [they] will be clever enough to get out just ahead of the crash." He refers to such dangerous behavior as "tailgating."

REFERENCES

Adrian, Tobia and Hyun Song Shin, 2010. "Liquidity and Leverage." FRBNY Staff Report No. 328, December.

BIS, 2011. "Global Liquidity – Concept, Measurement and Policy Implications." Report submitted by an ad-hoc group established by the Committee on the Global Financial System, November.

Borio, Claudio, Mathias Drehmann, and Kostas Tsatsaronis, 2012. "Characterising the financial cycle: don't lose sight of the medium term!," BIS Working Papers No. 380, June.

Crotty, James, 1990. "Keynes on the Stages of Development of the Capitalist Economy: An Essay on Methodology," *Journal of Economic Issues*, September, pp. 761–80.

Crotty, James, 1994. "Are Keynesian Uncertainty and Macrotheory Incompatible? Conventional Decision-Making, Institutional Structure and Conditional Stability in Keynesian Macromodels." In G. Dymski and R. Pollin (eds), *New Perspectives in Monetary Macroeconomics*. Ann Arbor, MI: University of Michigan Press, pp. 105–47.

Crotty, James, 1999. "Was Keynes a Corporatist: Keynes's Radical Views on Industrial Policy and Macropolicy in the 1920s," *Journal of Economic Issues*, September, pp. 1–23.

Crotty, James, 2009. "Structural causes of the global financial crisis: a critical assessment of the 'new financial architecture,'" *Cambridge Journal of Economics*, July, pp. 563–80.

Crotty, James, 2013a. "How Bonus-Driven 'Rainmaker' Financial Firms Enrich Top Employees, Destroy Shareholder Value, and Create Systemic Financial Instability." In B.Z. Cynamon, S. Fazzari and M. Setterfield (eds), *After the Great Recession: The Struggle for Economic Recovery and Growth*, New York: Cambridge University Press, pp. 104 26.

Crotty, James, 2013b. "The Realism of Assumptions Does Matter: Why Keynes–Minsky Theory Must Replace Efficient Market Theory as the Guide to Financial Regulation Policy." In M.H. Wolfson and G.A. Epstein (eds), *The Handbook of the Political Economy of Financial Crises*, New York: Oxford University Press, Chapter 7.

Crotty, James and Gerald Epstein, 2013. "Keynesian vs. Mainstream Perspectives on the Role of Liquidity in Capitalist Economies," Political Economy Research Institute Working Paper.

Crotty, James, Gerald Epstein and Iren Levina, 2010. "Proprietary Trading is a Bigger Deal than Many Bankers and Pundits Claim," SAFER Policy Brief #20, http://www.peri.umass.edu/fileadmin/pdf/other_publication_types/SAFERbriefs/SAFER_issue_brief20.pdf.

D'Arista, Jane, 1994. *The Evolution of US Finance: Restructuring Institutions and Markets. Volume II.* Armonk, NY: M.E. Sharpe.

Derman, Emmanuel, 2011. *Models Behaving Badly: Why Conflating Illusion with Reality Can Lead to Disaster, on Wall Street and in Life.* New York: Free Press.

Duffie, Darrell, 2012. "Market Making Under the Proposed Volcker Rule," Rock Center for Corporate Governance at Stanford University Working Paper No. 106, January.

International Monetary Fund, 2012. "Global Financial Stability Report." April.

Kay, John. 2010. "Tailgating blights markets and motorways," *Financial Times*, January 19.

Keynes, John Maynard. 1930. A Treatise on Money. New York: Harcourt, Brace and Company.

Keynes, John Maynard, 1930. *A Treatise on Money*. New York: Harcourt, Brace and Company.

Keynes, John Maynard, 1936. *The General Theory of Employment, Interest and Money*. London: Macmillan and Co.

Kuttner, Robert, 2011. *A Presidency in Peril.* White River Junction, VT: Chelsea Green Publishing.

The Financial Crisis Inquiry Commission (FCIC), 2011. *The Financial Crisis Inquiry Report*. Washington, DC: Government Printing Office.

Minsky, Hyman, 2008. *Stabilizing an Unstable Economy*. New York: McGraw-Hill.

O'Donnell, Rod. 1989. *Keynes: Philosophy, Economics and Politics*. London: Macmillan.

Oliver Wyman, 2012. "The Volcker Rule Restrictions on Proprietary Trading: Implications for Liquidity," http://www.oliverwyman.com/the-volcker-rule-restrictions-on-proprietary-trading.htm#.UM4gNXewWHs.

Pollin, Robert, 2012. "A U.S. Financial Transactions Tax," *The New Labor Forum*, **21** (2), 96–9.

Wall Street Journal, (2011). "Traders Warn of Market Cracks," October 18.

Wall Street Watch, 2009. "Sold Out: How Wall Street and Washington Betrayed America," http://www.wallstreetwatch.org/reports/sold_out.pdf.

APPENDIX: DEFINITIONS OF LIQUIDITY

The meaning and implications of "liquidity" depend strongly on the theoretical framework that is utilizing the concept. Mainstream economists distinguish between "market liquidity" and "funding liquidity." We call these "M-liquidity" and "F-liquidity." As the discussion above indicates, market liquidity as used by the mainstream entails two concepts: trading liquidity (T-liquidity) and appropriate price liquidity (P-liquidity).

"Funding liquidity" (F-liquidity), on the other hand, refers to the funding needed for financial investors, brokers and market makers, to hold assets and manage financial inventories, thereby facilitating an "appropriate" demand for securities.

In addition to this, a fourth concept of liquidity that is crucial to Keynes' analysis is the idea of "safe haven liquidity" (S-liquidity). This refers to Keynes' argument about demand and needed supply for safe assets to easily buy and hold. This is essential to Keynes' argument about the nature of money.

Table 16A.1 below summarizes the meaning and implications of these different concepts of liquidity as developed by the mainstream and within Keynes' thought.

Table 16A.1 Mainstream vs. Keynesian views on liquidity

Liquidity Type	Specific Type	Mainstream Assumptions and Perspective	Policy Implication	Keynes' Assumption and Perspective	Policy Implications
Market Liquidity	(M-liquidity)	More is better	Financial liberalization	Can be destructive after a point	Financial regulation
Trading Liquidity	(T-liquidity)	Immediacy; sell on short notice, small transactions cost, little loss of value	Financial liberalization	Can lead to excessive short-termism, mis-allocation of capital	Financial regulation, taxes, and so on.
	Price Discovery	More liquidity facilitates "price discovery" of pre-determined "fundamental value" of security	Financial liberalization	This does not exist: prices are created by market forces, not discovered: key role of fundamental uncertainty	Asset prices can be driven into bubbles and crashes or be stable, but they are NOT determined by "fundamentals"
Appropriate Price Liquidity	(P-liquidity)	Mainstream policy perspectives implicitly assume that for a market process to be liquid the asset must be sold easily at an "appropriate price" – in practice this means so as not to take a big capital loss. But this is contradictory to assumption that assets	Undertake policies, such as lender of last resort, to maintain demand for securities and prevent "fire sales"	Keynes agrees that some asset prices are more disruptive than others, but, unlike the mainstream view that is contradictory on this, the idea that assets might not sell for non-disruptive prices is consistent with Keynes views	Lenders of last resort might be necessary at a macroeconomic level, but not necessarily to keep an asset price at a "fundamental value"

		sell at their fundamental, pre-determined values		on asset price determination processes	Financial Transaction Taxes
				With respect to equities, prices are driven by short-termism and conventions to over-come fundamental uncertainty	Financial regulation Socialize investment decisions
	Note on Market Making and Market Makers	Market makers contribute to T-liquidity, which facilitates AP-liquidity and price discovery. They do this by holding inventories and taking risks to act as buyers and sellers to provide "immediacy," that is, T-liquidity	Financial liberalization, for example, no Volcker Rule; or any restriction on market makers	Market "makers" are speculators just like other market participants. Proprietary trading can add to and withdrawl liquidity, and generate price swings, since prices are not predetermined; market makers contribute to price creation, not price discovery	Regulate market makers, Volcker Rule and other provisions
Funding Liquidity	F-liquidity	In normal times, seem happy with free market provision. In crisis times, ambivalent and incoherent on this. Concerns raised about	Liquidity cushions, deposit insurance, LOLR activities,	Liquidity provision based on social conventions that are subject to abrupt change. So can lead to panics and bubbles.	As above

Table 16A.1 (continued)

Liquidity Type	Specific Type	Mainstream Assumptions and Perspective	Policy Implication	Keynes' Assumption and Perspective	Policy Implications
		maturity mis-match, and panics, but no coherent explanation of why this should be a problem. But the theory is incoherent about why this should be a problem apart from Diamond–Dybvig games	possible regulation of funders	Excessive funding liquidity can lead to excessive speculation and short-termism	
Safe Haven Liquidity	S-liquidity	All of a sudden, a great concern about whether there are enough safe haven assets. Not clear where this comes from		Safe haven assets, "money" crucial to analysis of demand for risky assets: need safe asset to switch into; facilitates willingness of investors to hold risky capital, but also facilitates short-term orientation of investors because these investments are seen as highly liquid leads to "anti-social" nature of liquidity	These all add up to an argument for more socialized investment to facilitate socially useful capital accumulation

17. A note on growth and distribution dynamics in an economy with population aging

Codrina Rada[1]

INTRODUCTION

The unprecedented demographic changes that are set to unfold in most of the industrialized world are consequential not only because of the decline in the share of working-age population but also because of the rise of an economic class, the retirees, who are expected to behave differently. Specifically, their consumption and saving patterns can be significantly distinct from those of wage earners or capitalists. Overall, retirees tend to consume all of their income. In this chapter I argue that population aging will affect distribution and growth dynamics through its effects on aggregate demand. Second, the success of fiscal policies implemented in response to higher old-age dependency rates will depend on the distribution and demand regimes in place.

After this short introduction, the present chapter begins with a section on demographic indicators and a counterfactual analysis of population aging effects on growth and distribution for a few selected countries. The third section introduces demographic changes in a Keynesian model of growth and distribution. Next, the focus is on policies that address the rise in old-age dependency rates with Japan and the US as case studies.

A few words about the motivation behind this chapter are finding their place here. In 2007 I contributed to the *World Economic and Social Survey* report published by the United Nations (UN 2007). The report examines development in an aging world and, unlike most of the literature, it departs from the usual assumption of a saving-driven economy and inter-temporal optimization setup. While surveying the literature it became evident that the economic profession has often failed to ask the right questions. Unfortunately, this is nothing new in our dismal science where preoccupation with mathematical sophistication replaces intuition and common sense. Instead, practical knowledge and experience with the workings of an actual economy are essential in building the intuition and asking the right questions. Jane D'Arista is someone who does have the correct intuition. This chapter follows Jane's approach to economic issues by first finding what questions one should ask when thinking about the economics of aging.

ECONOMIC CONSEQUENCES OF POPULATION AGING: WHAT ARE THE QUESTIONS WE SHOULD ASK?

Lower fertility rates and increased life expectancy are the main reasons behind population aging in many countries across the world. Aging creates opportunities for our societies but it also presents us with challenges (UN 2007). Economists are mainly concerned with the decline in the number of working-age individuals relative to the old-age population. Will existing workers be able to produce the output necessary to sustain a growing share of non-working population? The discussion often starts with trends in the old-age dependency rate defined as a ratio between non-working elderly and the working-age population.

Table 17.1 presents forecasts of this ratio as well as total dependency rates for selected countries. Japan is expected to experience the most dramatic aging of its population – by 2050 there will be two individuals aged 65 and over for every three working-age individuals. A slow decline in young-age dependency rates (also computed as a ratio, this time between population of 0–14 years of age and working-age population) will result in total dependency rates close to one. Among selected developed countries the US will benefit from higher rates of immigration and fertility and therefore it will be least affected by population aging.

Taking account of these broad demographic trends two questions come to mind. The first concerns the impact of population aging on economic growth. The second is about the distribution of income, or output, between the working and non-working population. These two questions are nevertheless connected: a change in the distribution of income has an effect on aggregate demand and therefore on the growth rate of the economy. Although important, these linkages between population aging, aggregate demand, growth and distribution have been ignored by most of the economic literature. Instead, the research on population aging assumes that economies are labor constrained and investment is saving-driven. Consequently, proposed policies target savings as a mean to stimulate capital accumulation and economic growth.

A closer look at economic conditions in selected countries suggests that

Table 17.1 Forecasts of old-age and total dependency rates (%) for selected countries and years

	Germany		Italy		Japan		USA		India	
	Old age	Total	Old age	Total	Old age	Total	Old age	Total	Old age	Total
2000	0.24	0.47	0.27	0.48	0.25	0.47	0.19	0.51	0.08	0.64
2025	0.38	0.60	0.43	0.62	0.50	0.71	0.28	0.57	0.12	0.48
2040	0.51	0.76	0.66	0.90	0.64	0.88	0.32	0.61	0.18	0.46
2050	0.50	0.76	0.69	0.95	0.71	0.97	0.33	0.61	0.22	0.50

Source: UN World Population Prospects 2007.

the real challenge posed by rising old-age dependency rates is how to distribute output; and whether the distribution scheme in place is conducive to accumulation, economic and job growth necessary to sustain the retired population. In the words of the former Federal Reserve's Chairman, Alan Greenspan (2003), "The real resources available to fund pension benefits depend on the economy's long-term growth rate, which in its simplest terms is determined by the growth rate of labor employed plus the growth rate of the productivity of that labor." The predicted decline in the growth rate of labor force will have a negative effect on economic growth unless there is a compensatory increase in labor productivity. A rise in productivity translates into an increase in the number of *effective workers* (Palley 1998). In simple terms let real output, X, be given by:

$$X = \varepsilon_L L \tag{17.1}$$

Where L is the amount of labor, and ε_L is labor productivity or output per worker. In growth rates, relation (17.1) becomes:

$$\hat{X} = (\hat{\varepsilon}_L + \hat{L}) \tag{17.2}$$

Subtracting the rate of growth of population from both sides of equation (17.2) we obtain:

$$\hat{X} - \hat{P} = (\hat{\varepsilon}_L + \hat{L}) - \hat{P} \tag{17.3}$$

We can simulate the required productivity growth necessary to sustain a rate of GDP growth of 2 percent per year using equation (17.3). Results are presented in Table 17.2.

Table 17.2 Required labor productivity growth such that GDP per capita grows at 2.5% annually

Labor Productivity	Germany (%)	Italy (%)	US (%)	India (%)	Japan (%)
Fold Increase 1960–2000	2.6	3.3	1.9	2.6	4.8
Annual growth 1960–2000	2.6	3.1	1.7	2.4	4.0
Fold Increase 2000–50	2.9	2.7	2.9	2.5	3.6
Annual growth 2000–50	2.2	2.0	2.2	1.8	2.6

Notes:

a) Unemployment rates are kept at 4% for India, Japan and US for the entire period. Germany and Italy reach a 4% unemployment rate by 2030 and 2035, respectively.

b) GDP per capita for India increases at 4% annually instead of 2% as for the rest.

Sources: World Development Indicators 2006 database for GDP per capita and employment; UN World Population Prospects 2007 database for statistics on demographic changes; International Labour Office, "LABORSTA: economic active population estimates and projections."

From a historical perspective a labor productivity growth in the range of 2–2.5 percent in developed economies is certainly attainable. However, maintaining such growth on an annual basis over several decades is not a trivial task (UN 2007). The numbers in Table 17.2 also point out that labor supply constraints may be less significant than generally believed. This is certainly the case for the US where immigration and higher fertility rates have so far prevented significant labor supply shortages. Arguments that the economy is below its full capacity can be brought forward also for Germany and Italy. Their higher rates of unemployment and low participation rates especially among those 50 and older suggest no labor supply constraints for now. The situation is different for Japan where pronounced population aging is already being felt in the labor markets.

Next, I turn to distributive issues for an economy with a pay-as-you-go scheme where pensions come directly from contributions made by the working population.[2] Wages earned at time t finance consumption of both workers, C_w and retirees, C_R according to:

$$C_W + C_R = \psi X \qquad (17.4)$$

where $\psi = 1 - \pi$ is the wage share and π stands for the profit share. If retirees do not save, their total consumption is $C_R = R_q$ where R is the number of retirees and q is the level of pension. Differentiating (17.4) with respect to time and using relation (17.2) we get:

$$\lambda(\hat{L} + \hat{c}_w) + (1 - \lambda)(\hat{R} + \hat{q}) = (\hat{L} + \hat{\varepsilon}_L) + \hat{\psi} \tag{17.5}$$

where λ is the share of total consumption of wage-earners and a hat over a variable implies a growth rate. Several policy scenarios are available in the event that the number of retirees increases relative to the working-age population:

a. Growth rate of consumption by the working-age population decreases or in fiscal terms the social security tax goes up.
b. Labor force $\hat{L}$ grows faster.
c. Labor productivity $\hat{\varepsilon}_L$ increases.
d. Redistribution towards wages or $\hat{\psi} > 0$.

Option (a) is unsustainable if population aging is significant and taking place over several decades. Option (d) depends on institutional factors and, as we will see in the next section, it can discourage growth if economic activity is profit led. Options (b) and (c) are preferred and macroeconomic policy should focus on boosting labor force and/or labor productivity.

A more detailed analysis provides further insights into policy alternatives. We can use (17.5) and several simplifying assumptions to calculate the gap between the wage bill surplus after deducting consumption by workers and the amount necessary to finance elderly consumption. The exercise is conducted only for the United States for the period 2000–2050. The wage share is constant and set to 60 percent of GDP throughout the entire period. Consumption per capita, which is assumed to increase at 2 percent per year, includes both private and public consumption. Estimates of per capita consumption for the base year 2000 come from the *National Income and Product Accounts* database and from Lee and Mason (2007).

The last row in Table 17.3 indicates that beginning with 2015 the wage bill surplus will be insufficient to sponsor consumption by non-working population that is 65 years or older. Of course we are assuming that retirees' income comes entirely from wages. In reality, retirees in the US receive both social security benefits as well as annuities from their fully funded accounts. Further calculations suggest that a 35 percent tax on corporate profits would help cover the needs of the entire dependent population (young and old) until 2030. It is clear that, even based on these rough estimates, the consumption by the non-working population will be expanding dramatically in the near future. Interestingly, estimates of consumption per capita provided by the *National Income and Product Accounts* and Lee and Mason (2007) show that those 65 and over consume on average 36 percent more than the working-age population. The reason is that public health

Table 17.3 Simulations of the distribution of output between wage-earners and retirees for the US economy

United States	2000	2015	2030	2050
Total consumption 15–64	5,614,864,922	8,677,109,903	12,242,598,194	19,733,224,659
Total consumption 65+	1,430,831,369	2,521,079,012	5,132,155,579	8,953,033,424
Total consumption by workers	4,314,722,600	6,520,922,801	9,193,808,215	14,817,912,592
Wage bill (as 60% of total GDP, where GDP/cap at 2%)	5,816,103,657	8,972,860,071	13,380,227,690	21,760,069,971
Savings by workers (wage bill – total consumption by workers only)	1,501,381,057	2,451,937,270	4,186,419,476	6,942,157,379
Difference between registered from wages surplus and consumption by 65+	70,549,688	(69,141,742)	(945,736,103)	(2,010,876,044)

Source: National Transfer Accounts Database, http://www.schemearts.com/proj/nta/web/nta/show for consumption per capita. Also see Lee and Mason (2007). GDP and wage share from National Income and Product Accounts database.

care expenditures under the Medicare program increase dramatically for individuals over 65 years of age. This suggests that the US should focus on policies that promote cost-efficient health care rather than on reforming the social security system.

INTRODUCING DEMOGRAPHIC CHANGES IN A KALDOR–KEYNESIAN MODEL OF GROWTH

Several preceding conclusions are relevant for the analysis in this section. First, old-age dependency ratios are increasing across the industrialized world. Still, labor supply constraints appear less binding than what has been assumed by most of the literature. Second, economic sustainability of an aging population requires robust labor productivity growth. Third, redistributive measures may be necessary even if economic growth is significant. In other words, it is not only output growth that matters but also how we allocate the *increase* in output.

I use a standard Keynesian model of growth and distribution to trace the effects of population aging and of policies associated with it on economic activity. The model builds on three main core mechanisms. These mechanisms, illustrated in Figure 17.1, describe how economic activity or output, labor productivity growth and changes in income distribution interact with each other.

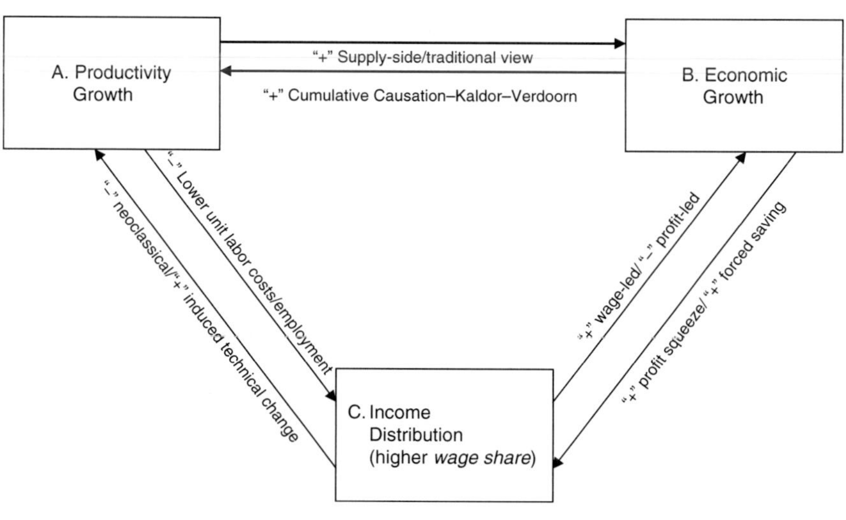

Figure 17.1 Linkages among productivity growth, output growth and income distribution in the Barbosa–Taylor model

The output–productivity relationship is captured by the arrows between box A and box B. All other things equal, higher labor productivity stimulates economic activity. In an economy with excess capacity output responds positively to demand coming from more investment, consumption or government expenditures. Given their higher propensities to consume, an increase in the share of retirees relative to the working-age population is expected to stimulate economic activity through the demand channel. On the other hand, a rise in demand translates into higher prices if the economy is operating at its full capacity. Turning our attention to the reversed linkage, a rise in economic activity induces higher labor productivity growth in the presence of economies of scale through the Kaldor–Verdoorn channel.

Output–distribution dynamics are analyzed next. The wage share acts as the distributive variable. The relation between distribution and output growth is well established in the literature (Taylor 2004; Bhaduri and Marglin 1990). Higher profitability, as measured by the markup or the profit share, stimulates investment while a lower wage share cuts into household consumption. The impact of income redistribution on economic activity depends on which of the two effects dominates. If the rise in investment demand following increased profitability is larger than the decline in household consumption we say that economic activity is "profit-led" or "exhilarationist" (Bhaduri and Marglin 1990; Taylor 2004). If a higher wage share stimulates output growth the economy is said to be "wage-led" or "stagnationist".

How about the effects of economic activity on income distribution? Kaldor (1966) points out that income shares in mature economies tend to stay roughly constant over very long periods of time. Although Kaldor's stylized fact has been under scrutiny recently following the downward trend in the wage share in many OECD countries, the question of what happens with income distribution over cycles (or the medium run) is equally important. Barbosa and Taylor (2006) find out that the US wage share ($\psi = \omega/\varepsilon_L$) responds positively to economic activity. Alternatively, a negative response of the wage share to an expansion in economic activity is known as forced saving (Taylor 2004).

The relationship between productivity growth and changes in income distribution, described by the connections between A and C, is more nuanced. Enhanced labor productivity leads to lower labor costs and possibly to a loss of jobs especially in a wage-led economy. The wage share is expected to decline if gains in labor productivity are not passed on to real wages. The same result applies when productivity growth leads to labor shedding. For economies with a strong profit-led regime higher labor productivity could stimulate economic activity, and therefore employment, enough to minimize the negative effects on the wage share.

The impact of income distribution on productivity growth is also debatable. In neoclassical economics a higher profit share stimulates entrepreneurs to re-invest the additional cash flow into capital and technology. Hence, labor productivity increases. On the other hand, the theory of induced technical change asserts that a decline in the profit share pushes entrepreneurs to search for more labor-saving methods of production thus raising labor productivity (Naastepad 2006).

The mechanisms described above can be formalized by a two-dimensional system in capacity utilization and income distribution as discussed by Taylor (2004). The model can be visually described by the slopes for the distributive curve, $\dot{\psi} = 0$, and the effective demand curve, $\dot{u} = 0$, in the (u, ψ) plane. When growth is profit-led the effective demand is downward sloping – a rise in the wage share results in a contraction of economic activity. An effective demand schedule with a positive slope on the other hand describes the wage-led case.

The response of income distribution to changes in effective demand depends on whether there is a profit squeeze, described by a positive slope of the distributive curve, or a forced saving regime captured by a downward-sloping curve.[3] A multitude of factors – among them the strength of supply constraints, the nature of institutions and bargaining power held by different economic classes – determine which of the two regimes applies. A profit squeeze is usually associated with a low rate of unemployment and significant bargaining power held by workers (Palley 2007). Economic activity is stimulated by more demand, but wages rise fast due to tightening of labor markets, thus creating a squeeze on the profit share. Forced saving originates in capacity constraints when prices tend to rise faster than nominal wages. In a sense, forced saving can be thought of as a situation where moderate price increases are permitted by policy-makers such that expenditures switch from consumption to capital goods (Thirlwall 2004). Finally, forced saving can also result from a situation of fast labor productivity growth and modest real-wage growth.

ECONOMIC IMPLICATIONS OF POPULATION AGING AND MACRO POLICIES

In the light of the Keynesian growth-distribution model two questions become relevant for an economy with an aging population. First, to what extent population aging and the pension system in place will affect the demand-distribution dynamics? And second, how will rising old-age dependency rates impact the effectiveness of macroeconomic policies given different demand-distribution regimes? I focus on the US and Japan as case studies.

Aging and the Demand-distribution Dynamics

How population aging will affect growth-distribution dynamics depends first and foremost on the source of retirees' income. The defined-benefit public and private pension systems provide about three-quarters of old-age income in Japan (Cabinet Office, Government of Japan).[4] Within this category the Employee's Pension Insurance Plan, a pay-as-you-go system, covers most of the retirement income. But Japan has been experimenting with defined-contribution private pension accounts which were established in 2001. These types of accounts, also known as fully funded, appeal to firms because they reduce their responsibilities towards their retired workers. Retirees are paid an annuity that is usually calculated based on the rate of return on capital. Nonetheless, employees' participation in private accounts remains limited. The US, on the other hand, has been moving rapidly towards defined-contribution pension accounts (Poterba et al. 2007). If this trend continues, income of future US retirees is expected to be more evenly distributed between private and public sources of income.

With population aging unfolding an economy with mostly defined-contribution pension accounts will likely turn profit-led. The US falls in this category more so as previous studies suggest that the economic activity is already profit-led (Barbosa and Taylor 2006). Studies by Bowles and Boyer (1995) and Naastepad and Storm (2007) find out that growth in Japan is also profit-led. However, Hein and Vogel (2007) point out that "the identification of an accumulation regime in a certain country in a certain period of time becomes a question of concrete historical and empirical analysis." Following the above reasoning, the Japanese economy may become wage-led if public pensions remain predominant and retirees draw most of their pensions from current wages.

How about the distributive curve in the two economies? Barbosa and Taylor (2006) find that a rise in economic activity in the US causes a decline in the profit share. In other words, there is a profit squeeze.

The wage share appears to vary counter-cyclically to business cycles in Japan – see Figure 17.2. This conclusion is confirmed by a recent econometric study by Wakita (2006). Aside of forced savings associated with business cycles, Japan is also known for its high saving rates. Some would argue that population aging will reduce saving rates in Japan. This predicament remains to be confirmed by reality but ultimately it may depend on the policy stance in place. First of all, forced saving induced by policy is

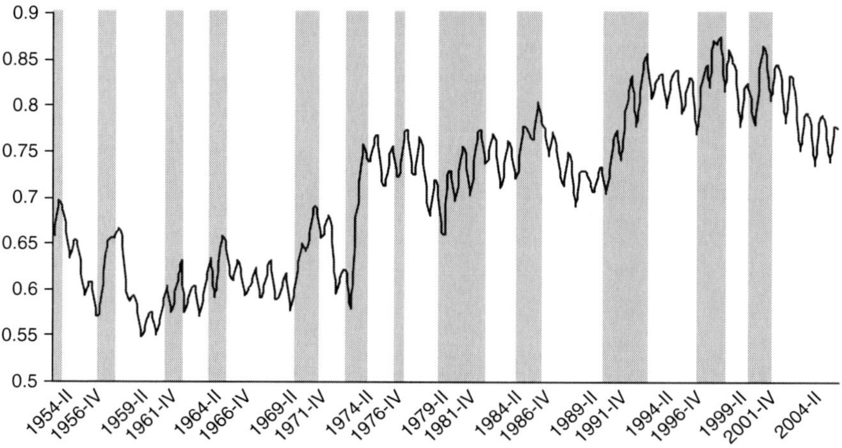

Source: Financial Statements Statistics of Corporations by Industry, Ministry of Finance, Japan, http://www.mof.go.jp/english/ssc/historical.htm.

Figure 17.2 Wage share and business cycles in Japan

possible especially if entrepreneurs respond to a higher profit share by increasing investment in capital and technology and thus enhancing labor productivity growth. Second, accommodating successfully rapid population aging requires robust labor productivity growth. A trade-off ensues between incentives (such as a forced saving regime) to firms to boost productivity and a certain level of real income for wage earners and retirees. This trade-off is expected to be more evident when a pay-as-you-go system provides most of the old-age income, as is the case for Japan. To counteract the negative effect on wages and pensions the government can step in by increasing expenditures for vulnerable groups such as retirees, or by subsidizing some essential services such as health and long-term care.

Aging and Macroeconomic Policies

It was suggested above that with population aging underway the US economy is likely to remain profit led/profit squeezed, while Japan may become a wage-led/forced-saving economy. Over the cycles the two cases are described by Figures 17.3a and 17.3b, respectively.

Demographic changes have a direct impact on growth-distribution dynamics through the effective demand, and an indirect effect through changes in fiscal policies. In an attempt to stimulate economic activity expansionary policies may not always benefit retirees and their pensions.

An expansionary policy in the US works through a shift rightwards of

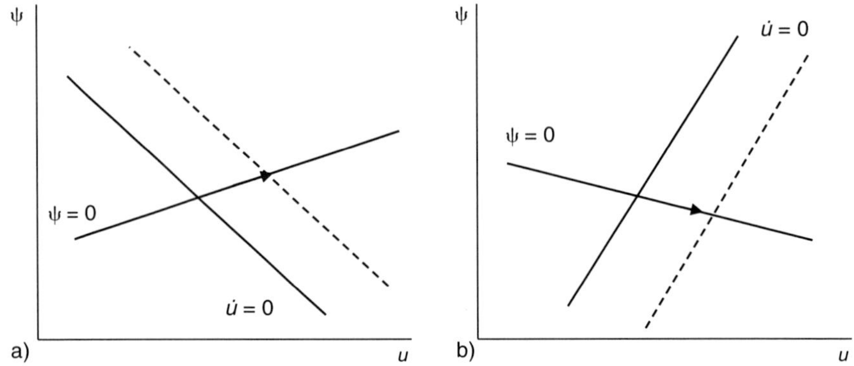

Figure 17.3 a) Profit-led and profit-squeeze economy; b) wage-led and forced-saving economy

the effective demand curve – see Figure 17.3a. In the short run, economic activity picks up the pace and through the Kaldor–Verdoorn channel it causes positive responses from both productivity growth and employment. As a result wages also increase. Eventually, wages end up growing faster than productivity thus raising the wage share. As the profit squeeze kicks in, investment in our profit-led economy declines bringing down output expansion. The impact on retirement income depends on how much of it comes from profits and how much as transfers from wages.

Let retirement income be $Y_R = qR + \alpha_R \pi X$, where $\alpha_R \pi X$ is the share of profits distributed to retirees based on their stock of wealth α_R; and qR are the pensions received from the pay-as-you-go system. Assuming that q is a proportion e of the prevailing wage we can rewrite the income received by retirees as $Y_R = (e^* \omega) R + \alpha_R \pi X$. Dividing this relation by the level of output and multiplying the first term on the right-hand side by L/L one gets:

$$Y_R/X = e^*(1 - \pi)^* d + \alpha_R \pi \tag{17.6}$$

where d is the old-age dependency rate. It can be easily observed that a squeeze on profits depresses income received from private pension accounts while it raises the wage share and therefore transfers from current wages. Thus, retirees face a trade-off between private and public retirement income. In a profit-led economy where fully funded pension accounts predominate taxing wages, or in other words raising e, is a more effective way to sustain a growing share of retirees. A redistributive policy towards wages, on the other hand, would cause a reduction in output in the medium run. An expansionary policy such as a rise in public investment works better in this case. It would shift the demand schedule to the right towards a higher wage share but also a higher output.

In a wage-led/forced saving regime a redistribution from profits to wages may not work either as it will only set off an inflationary reaction as higher taxes on profits are passed into a higher markup, τ, and therefore higher prices. The distributive schedule in the end will not shift unless the inflationary reaction overshoots. In this case higher prices will cut into the real income of both wage earners and retirees.

The effect on retirement income can be established using the definition that $\pi = \tau/(1 + \tau)$ and rewriting (17.6) as $Y_R/X = e^*[1/(1 + \tau)]^* d + \alpha_R \tau/(1 + \tau)$. As τ increases transfers from wages are expected to decline. However, the decline in public pensions is being compensated by an increase in private pensions due to a higher profit rate.

How about the effects of higher productivity growth? In a profit-led economy a rise in labor productivity growth shifts the distributive curve down. The equilibrium wage share drops and capacity utilization rises.[5] In a wage-led economy a downward shift in the distributive curve causes a decline in both capacity utilization and the wage share. Changes in retired households' income follow from the same relation (17.6). The policy question is how to redistribute more equitably the benefits of higher productivity especially when pensions come from current wages. If the economy features a profit-led/profit-squeeze regime the easiest way to do this is through higher government spending which would shift the demand curve upwards towards a higher wage share and higher capacity utilization. Such policy would not work by itself in the forced saving case due to inflationary pressures, which would cut into the real wages. But what could work in this latter case is a reallocation of government expenditures towards retirees in order to compensate for the decline in their real income combined with an overall expansionary policy to restore output growth.

FINAL REMARKS

The focus in this chapter has been on understanding how a rising share of old-age population, which behaves differently in economic terms, may affect an economy over the business cycles. More work has to be done in order to extend the analysis to several decades. Nonetheless, one important conclusion is that regardless of the time span we are looking at, demographic changes are becoming an important determinant of macro policies that target income distribution. Redistributing income, on the other hand, has an impact on economic activity and growth and therefore trade-offs as the ones discussed above will surely surface. However, the chances that the economy will adapt successfully to demographic transitions are higher if policy makers recognize ahead of time which policy choices are right for the existing economic environment.

NOTES

1. I am especially grateful to Lance Taylor and Rudiger von Arnim for their valuable comments as well as to the participants of *Political Economy of Monetary Policy and Financial Regulation: A Conference in Honor of Jane D'Arista.*
2. It can be shown that a fully funded or a combination of fully funded and pay-as-you-go produce similar results.
3. A negative slope of the distributive curve can also occur in the case of an unstable profit squeeze. However, we rule out this case and focus on the stable dynamics.
4. The mean share of overall income provided by defined-benefit pensions is smaller for those in the 65–70-years-old bracket who continue to supplement their old-age income through earnings from work.
5. The wage share is lower following a labor productivity growth because the growth in output per worker exceeds the increase in real wages, or in other words not all productivity gains are passed through into wages.

REFERENCES

Barbosa-Filho, N.H. and L. Taylor (2006). "Distributive and Demand Cycles in the US Economy – A Structuralist Goodwin Model," *Metroeconomica*, **57** (3), 389–411.

Bhaduri, A. and S.A. Marglin (1990). "Unemployment and the Real Wage: The Economic Basis for Contesting Political Ideologies," *Cambridge Journal of Economics*, **14**, 375–93.

Bowles, S. and R. Boyer (1995). "Wages, Aggregate Demand, and Employment in an Open Economy: An Empirical Investigation," in G.A. Epstein and H.M. Gintis (eds), *Macroeconomic Policy after the Conservative Era*, Cambridge: Cambridge University Press, pp. 143–71.

Cabinet Office, Government of Japan (various years). *Annual Report on the Ageing Society*, http://www8.cao.go.jp/kourei/english/annualreport/index-wh.html.

Greenspan, A. (2003). "Aging Global Population," Testimony before the Special Committee on Aging, US Senate, February 27.

Hein, E. and L. Vogel (2008). "Distribution and Growth Reconsidered: Empirical Results for Six OECD Countries," *Cambridge Journal of Economics*, **32**, 479–511.

Kaldor, N. (1966). *Causes of the Slow Rate of Economic Growth in the United Kingdom*, Cambridge: Cambridge University Press.

Lee, R. and A. Mason (2007). "Population Aging, Wealth, and Economic Growth: Demographic Dividends and Public Policy," Background paper prepared for the UN World Economic and Social Survey 2007.

Naastepad, C.W.M. (2006). "Technology, Demand and Distribution: A Cumulative Growth Model with an Application to the Dutch Productivity Growth Slowdown," *Cambridge Journal of Economics*, **30** (3), 403–34.

Naastepad, C.W.M. and S. Storm (2007). "OECD Demand Regimes (1960–2000)," *Journal of Post Keynesian Economics*, **29**, 211–46.

Palley, T.I. (1998). "The Economics of Social Security: An Old Keynesian Perspective," *Journal of Post Keynesian Economics*, **21** (Fall), 95–112.

Palley, T.I. (2007). "Macroeconomics and Monetary Policy: Competing Theoretical Frameworks," *Journal of Post Keynesian Economics*, **30** (1), 61–78.

Poterba, J., J. Rauh, S. Venti and D. Wise (2007). "Defined Contribution Plans, Defined Benefit Plans, and the Accumulation of Retirement Wealth," *Journal of Public Economics*, **91** (10), 2062–86.

Taylor, L. (2004). *Reconstructing Macroeconomics: Structuralist Proposals and Critiques of the Mainstream*. Cambridge, MA: Harvard University Press.

Thirlwall, A.P. (2004). "The Mobilisation of Savings for Growth and Development in Developing Countries," mimeo, University of Kent at Canterbury.

Wakita, S. (2006). "The Lost Decade in the Japanese Labor Market: Labor's Share and Okun's Law," *Public Policy Review*, **2** (1), 77–96.

United Nations (2007). *World Economic and Social Survey: Development in an Ageing World*. New York: United Nations Publishing Section.

Index